# COOKS
# MARKETPLACE

## SAN FRANCISCO
## BAY AREA SOURCEBOOK

## BY SHERRY VIRBILA

**101 PRODUCTIONS • SAN FRANCISCO**

COVER DESIGN AND BOOK DESIGN: Patricia Glover.

Much of the material on Middle Eastern food stores, Italian bakeries, and food stores in the Mission area of San Francisco was written with Angela Zawadski and first appeared in *New West*, now *California* magazine. Some of the material on other ethnic bakeries and stores was also written with Angela Zawadzki and was published in *San Francisco* magazine. Many of the take-out entries first appeared in an article in *Focus* magazine, while some of the section on wine tastings and classes was published in *California Living*, and information on growing truffles in California appeared in *Food and Wine* magazine.

Printed and bound in the United States of America.
Distributed to the book trade in the United States
by Charles Scribner's Sons, New York.
Published by 101 Productions
834 Mission Street
San Francisco, California 94103

*Library of Congress Cataloging in Publication Data*

Virbila, Sherry.
    Cook's marketplace.

    Includes index.
    1. marketing (Home economics)--California--San
Francisco Region--Directories.    2. Grocery trade--
California--San Francisco Region--Directories.
3. Kitchen utensils--California--San Francisco Region--
Directories.    4. Booksellers and bookselling--California
--San Francisco Region--Directories.    I. Title.
TX356.V57          382'.45641'0979461          82-7839
ISBN 0-89286-198-3                                AACR2

# Contents

# Introduction

I first had the idea for this book while working as a cook. Everyone I knew was involved in some aspect of food or wine, and we spent a lot of time trading information among ourselves: where to get Spanish saffron in large quantities; where to find a hot sausage just right for jambalaya, or the *crema fresca* that is so good with fried plantain slices. I was cooking all the time then, at work and at home, and reading my way through every cookbook I could find, the more exotic the better. On my days off I'd make expeditions to the city in search of ingredients I needed for special dishes, and I soon developed an instinct for finding the hard-to-find. I'd come back from these foraging trips with bags of tempting loot and show it off with great delight to my fellow cooks—who immediately wanted to know where I'd found everything.

My list of good suppliers grew and grew. It increased even more when I taught classes in ethnic cuisines, and again when I began to work as a restaurant consultant. But I was really inspired to collect this information into a book when I was later living in Paris, studying wine and wandering the city.

I walked all over Paris and somehow always found myself in the markets. After all, they were always on the way to somewhere else. I haunted the weekly outdoor markets in the various *quartiers*, where I loved finding pale cheeses set out on straw mats in the milky early morning light, heaps of wizened sausages from Auvergne, stiff lengths of *baccalà* stacked like boards, or bright *clementines* piled high in all their orange splendor.

Farther out, in the largely Arab neighborhoods, herb vendors sat behind small tables piled high with fresh coriander, parsley, lemons, and garlic. Other merchants sold nuts, rice, and gorgeous olives slick with oil, in every hue of green and black and purple. Butchers called out from stalls hung with lamb and kid, while a few streets away I found stores selling tropical foodstuffs from the West Indies: fresh coconuts, mangoes, pineapples, avocados, dates, sugar cane, and other exotica in the midst of the damp and gray city.

I remember most the fall and winter, shopping in my own *quartier*, when from where I stood in the dark street, each store, open across its entire front, was as brightly lit as a stage setting. I would stand a while watching everyone else make their purchases, accept their newspaper-wrapped packets, and secret them away deep in their mesh shopping bags before I made my own purchases.

I loved being out in the streets at twilight, scurrying from store to store as the night closed around us, reciting the shopworn, but often genuine, *politesses* as I bought *crème fraîche* and *brie de meau* or a mold-encrusted *crottin* at the *fromagerie*; a half kilo of pale endive and some *frisée* next door; then a fat chicken for a *coq au vin*, a dab of goose *rillettes*, a slice of smoky *lardon*, and a liter of black country wine. It was all there at the bottom of my street, in every neighborhood where I lived in Paris. It didn't take planning and expeditions to put together a wonderful repast.

When I came home to San Francisco, I kept up my Paris habits, exploring San Francisco and its environs for information for this book. Looking at the city with the eye of a detective trained to uncover *les bonnes choses*, I revisited my favorite haunts and prowled all the neighborhoods, alert to new sources for both basic and hard-to-find ingredients.

I wasn't at all surprised to find coming home to San Francisco such a cook's pleasure. While Paris does have its considerable charms, San Francisco is a great town for food. There's no other city in the world that has ingredients

Oops!—OH'S doors are not really closed as mentioned in the Introduction—only their telephone is no longer there. In our diligence to double-check every entry by phone just prior to publication, we found no phone and no current listing for the venerable Mission Street store. It seems when Merritt Anderson took over the business from his uncle, he decided to do without the convenience or the distraction of a telephone. The store's many long-time customers know OH'S is still there—we thought you should know about this excellent source for all kinds of bulk grains, flours and legumes, too. OH'S FINE FOODS is located at 2651 Mission Street between 22nd and 23rd streets in San Francisco. And we'll certainly include a detailed listing when we revise and update *Cook's Marketplace.*

SHERRY VIRBILA

for so many different kinds of cuisines in such abundance. Once you begin to cook here, it becomes clear just how cosmopolitan San Francisco really is. With the city's diverse ethnic population and its exposure to a wide range of culinary influences, San Franciscans are among the world's most sophisticated cooks.

And it's getting better all the time. When I began my research for this book I had a list of things I wished I could find here—fresh ricotta and mozzarella, *poussins* (baby chickens), Belon oysters, Italian regional breads, fresh local goat cheeses—but I didn't think I had a chance of locating them. Yet during the course of researching this book, they've all become available from new suppliers and stores.

At the same time, sadly, some old and venerable stores have closed their doors in the last few years, taking with them some old skills and their share of San Francisco history: a Greek store that stretched *filo* dough by hand and made its own yogurt; the best source for grains, legumes, and other staples in town, Ohs Fine Foods; and some of my favorite butcher shops, bakeries, and greengrocers.

The quality of your ingredients is just as important as your skill as a cook. Even in France where there is such exceptional quality and variety in even the most basic ingredients—but-

*fine Oranges fine Lemons* Mar-

ters classified by area of origin, each with its unique flavor; grain-fed, free-run chickens from different regions; several kinds of duck, each used for a type of cooking that exploits its particular qualities—chefs do their own shopping in the early hours of the morning to ensure getting the best of that day's produce, fish, meat, and poultry.

Supermarkets may be wonderful for convenience, but you shouldn't shop in only one place if you want the best of everything. Besides, it's much more entertaining and instructive to spend a few minutes talking poultry with a poultry man, produce with a greengrocer, and cheese with a cheese merchant than just grabbing a standard item off the shelf. Shopping in small ethnic stores also satisfies at least some of my unrelenting wanderlust and often inspires me to bursts of creativity in my cooking.

*Cook's Marketplace* will tell you where to find *crème fraîche*, quail eggs, fresh truffles, green coffee beans, *brioches*, handmade *filo* dough, chestnut flour, semolina or *couscous*, whole anchovies under salt, Egyptian *ful medames*, Central American cheeses, fine Tuscan olive oils, the *dendê* oil used in Brazil and the Caribbean, edible gold and silver leaf, house-cured prosciutto and *jambon de bayonne*, savory goat meat, fresh suckling pig, caul fat, *pancetta*, tiny *poussins*, fresh game birds, live crayfish from the Sacramento Delta, California-cultured oysters, soft-shell crabs, live sea urchins, *couverture* chocolate, and California caviar.

In keeping with its European inspiration, *Cook's Marketplace* has expanded the idea of alimentation to include not just basic, raw ingredients, but some prepared foods that you can use to put together a complete meal. You'll find bakeries, cheese shops, ice cream and chocolate stores, as well as *traiteurs*, or shops that make fine food to take out.

When the French set out to make a meal, it often means stopping in at a *charcuterie* for a pâté or two for the first course, then picking up a fruit tart or some petits fours at the local *pâtisserie*, along with a selection of cheeses from the neighborhood *fromagerie*, a baguette at the *boulangerie*, and a packet of freshly roasted coffee beans from the *brûlerie*. The French shop this way because they are a nation of fine cooks. And in the San Francisco area, cooks can shop in the same way now in any number of neighborhoods. It may mean some driving and a little planning ahead, but there are superb possibilities in the many stores prepared to sell you the makings of a fine meal in any number of ethnic traditions.

This book is organized by types of foods, services, and cook's aids: meat, poultry, *charcuterie*, cookware, cook's books, cooking classes, etc. Many sections are divided into subsections, with stores listed alphabetically within each subsection. You'll find ethnic markets listed at the end of the book, but many of the listings in other sections are arranged ethnically as well; for example, Italian pastry will be found under "Italian" in the Pastry section.

Since San Francisco's food stores are much more eclectic in content than stores in Europe, you should check for cross-references at the beginning of each section. For example, flours and grains will be found in the Natural Foods section and the Ethnic Markets sections as well as in Staples.

I've included some local wholesalers who do not sell directly to the public, because I wanted to catalog the kinds of food products made in San Francisco. These include Eduardo's egg pasta, fresh ricotta and mozzarella from Ferrante Cheese Company in Walnut Creek, fresh Sonoma County goat cheeses from Laura Chenel in Santa Rosa, local Pigeon Point oysters, California Sunshine's marvelous sturgeon and golden whitefish caviar, and Saag's large repertoire of German and Swiss-style sausages. Though you may not always be able to buy these products directly from their maker, they are available at many of the retail stores listed in the book. Some wholesalers will sell to the public in certain quantities and this is noted.

Also included here are some specialized sources that are used mostly by the restaurant trade but that will, on occasion, sell to the public. These include cheese dealers, meat wholesalers, restaurant supply houses, butcher suppliers, and the early-morning produce markets.

Mail-order sources for some unusual or hard-to-find items, such as culinary seeds, are also included.

We have noted hours for all the stores, but these do change, and many small stores have variable hours. Call first to check hours before visiting stores, and remember that many are closed on holidays. I would greatly appreciate any information on changes, corrections, or new stores and sources; please send to Sherry Virbila, care of 101 Productions.

I would like to acknowledge my special thanks to Angela Zawadzki, and my thanks to so many people in the food and wine community who were generous with ideas and information, including Antonia Baranov, Ron Batori, Bruce Cost, Marion Cunningham, Bonita Hughes, Paul Johnson, Janice Lo Lowry, Michael McClernon, Michael Schaefer, Judith Stronach, and Alice Waters. For easing the hardship of this long project, I want to thank Jules Backus, Chico Bandarin, Nick Bertoni, Susan Chamberlin, Robin Cowan, Susan Dintenfass, Elena Fontanari, Joanna Gard, Doug Hollis, Peter Honigsberg, Marcia Kemp, Mireille Merx, Luis Ospina, Susan Roether, Millie Rosner, Ray Saunders, Kay Virbila, La Vonne and John Virbila. And to a very patient editor, Carolyn Miller.

# Bread

The first breads were unleavened flat breads cooked over coals or on top of hot stones. It was the Egyptians who first discovered leavened bread, made with yeasts from their beer making. They were also the first to make "sourdough" bread. Each night a piece of dough left over from the previous morning's baking was used to leaven the new batch of bread.

The Greeks and the Romans both improved breadmaking techniques, developing many kinds of loaves and flat breads, but it was the rich Romans who first started the demand for white bread. And the desire for the wondrous white rather than the rough peasant breads has continued into our own times.

My mother grew up in the thirties on a farm in Nebraska. To her and her brothers, "boughten" bread—white, cottony, and ultra-refined—was preferred over even homemade white bread. To them, it was as much a treat as cake. Most of us grew up on white store-bought bread, and unless our families had kept strong ethnic ties, we rarely tasted real bread.

Fortunately, in recent years there has been some reversal of this trend. It began with a revival of home bread-making. Then small neighborhood bakeries began opening and making a business selling quality breads. Except for the strictly French or Italian bakeries, most are quite eclectic, baking breads from a variety of traditions. You'll see sourdough, French bread, *challah*, and rye breads all from the same bakery.

In San Francisco's many small bakeries you can find ring-shaped *buccellato* scented with anise; skinny hand-rolled *grissini*; huge wheels of rustic *pan pugliese*; flour-dusted rounds of hearty Bavarian rye; attractive *baguettes d'épine* cut to resemble stalks of wheat; braided wreaths of *vasilopita* (Greek Easter bread); tall domed *kulich* (Ukrainian Easter bread);

giant discs of Armenian flatbread called *lavash*; Boston brown bread; and Swedish *knäckebröd*, a crisp bread with a hole in its middle.

But San Francisco is most famous for its sourdough. Gold miners first brought their starter to the tent town bundled in their knapsacks, and they sustained themselves in the remote gold country with a simple bread. San Franciscans fell in love with the tangy sourdough produced by the combination of well-bred "mothers" and the city's unique climate.

These days, not all of the city's sourdough is as good as it used to be. Some bread companies have tried to speed up the lengthy process, adding yeast and less "mother." But sourdough is an entrenched tradition in this town, and most of the new small bakeries are making it, too, along with lots of other breads.

If you include the city's restaurants as sources, you can enjoy an even wider range of ethnic breads: delicious Indian flat breads, some cooked in earthenware *tandoori* ovens; Hungarian *langos*, individual deep-fried breads rubbed with garlic while still hot; *injera*, a tender Ethiopian flat bread made from a fermented millet batter; Hunan-style fried onion cakes; Salvadoran *pupusas*, thick patties of *masa* dough stuffed with cheese; and wonderful spoon breads and cornbreads from our own southern cooking tradition.

Some of the bakeries listed here are strictly bread bakeries, but most make some pastries as well. And since many pastry shops make some bread (or, at the very least, croissants), check the Pastry section as well as Cheese and Ethnic Markets listings for more breads.

# BAGELS

### San Francisco
## BAGEL PASTRY BAKERY

*5625 Geary Boulevard, San Francisco 94118. Telephone (415) 387-5464. Hours: SUN–TH 8-7, Friday 8 am to one hour or one-half hour before sunset.*

Opened as a bakery in 1978, this *glatt* kosher restaurant, bakery, and deli serves home-style cooked dishes like cheese or potato knishes, blintzes, and potato-filled *pirogen*, plus home-smoked lox and other fish.

The bakery produces over fifty kinds of bagels, dinner rolls, breads, *challah*, sweet rolls, and strudels. The bagels are chewy and flavorful, the onion rolls pillowy and fragrant with their topping of sweet onions, but the sweet yeast baking is the real delight: cinnamon-raisin crescents; dark glazed pecan horseshoes; almond rolls; and sweet cheese Danish, rich with eggs and sour cream.

### San Francisco
## THE BAGELRY

*2134 Polk Street, San Francisco 94109. Telephone (415) 441-3003. Hours: M–T, T–SAT 7-7; SUN 7-4.*

The Bagelry on Polk Street turns out almost five thousand bagels a day in eighteen varieties, from traditional bagels with poppy seeds and onions to the more unusual *bialys*, made from the same dough, but omitting the initial water boil.

Breads include rye, pumpernickel, corn rye, and caraway stick. Weekends they make a *streusel* with bagel dough, brown sugar, fresh apples, and sweet butter.

### East Bay
## BROTHERS' BAGEL FACTORY

*1281 Gilman Street, Berkeley 94706. Telephone (415) 524-3104. Hours: M–SAT 8-6, SUN 8-3.*

In the East Bay, Brothers' Bagel Factory on Gilman Street in Berkeley fills the bagel demand. And, of course, in health-conscious Berkeley, you might expect a few new twists: their salted plain bagels have no eggs, and they also make a tasty whole-wheat bagel, with or without raisins, from Deaf Smith County stone-ground flour, without eggs.

And to top your bagels they sell butter, natural cream cheese, lox, and Westbrae fruit butters.

### Sonoma County
## HOMEGROWN BAGELS

*122 West Napa Street, Sonoma 95476. Telephone (707) 996-0166. Hours: M–F 7 am–2:30 pm, SAT–SUN 8-2 (weekend closing hours variable).*

This concern makes six kinds of regular bagels, plus whole wheat, pumpernickel, and *bialys*.

### San Francisco
## HOUSE OF BAGELS

*5030 Geary Boulevard, San Francisco 94118. Telephone (415) 752-6000. Hours: 7-5:30 daily.*
*2427 Noriega Street, San Francisco 94112. Telephone (415) 661-2865. Hours: M–W 8-5, TH 8:30-6, F 8-6, SAT–SUN 8-5.*

Owner Sid Chassy is from Brooklyn and has been making bagels for thirty years. His House of Bagels supplies San Francisco with eight kinds of the shiny, chewy rounds. He bakes breads, too: whole wheat, water twist, egg twist, rye corn, rye onion, and pumpernickel.

# CRUMPETS

**San Francisco**
## THE ENGLISH TEA SHOPPE: A CRUMPET BAKERY

*511 Irving Street, San Francisco 94122. Telephone(415) 564-2255. Hours: T-F 8-5:30, SAT 9-5.*

After jogging or a tennis game in the park, stop by the English Tea Shoppe on a quiet stretch of Irving Street for a spot of well-brewed English tea and some fresh crumpets. They should properly be eaten heaped with sweet butter, jam, or cream cheese or ricotta.

Crumpets are similar to what are known as English muffins in this country but are very much better. Owners Bill and Jim Uhlman bought the recipe that supplies Seattle and Victoria, B.C. And just so you won't have to waste time trying to imagine just how a crumpet is made, they make them right in the window for all the world to

see. The thick batter is poured into steel crumpet rings that sit right on the griddle. Honeycombed with holes for all the sweet butter to settle in, crumpets are a sumptuous morning or teatime treat.

And if you'd like to take some home for breakfast, the English Tea Shoppe carries renowned English jams and tins of Twining's teas. Toast the crumpets over a fire with a fork, or, less authentically and certainly less romantically, use your common toaster.

Crumpets are baked every day except Monday, when the shop is closed.

# EUROPEAN INTERNATIONAL

**Contra Costa**
## ALANO'S PASTRIES

*1237 Boulevard Way, Walnut Creek 94595. Telephone(415) 938-7277. Hours: T-SAT 8:30-4:30.*

Alano's Pastries is the kind of bakery that every neighborhood needs: the kind of bakery where the warm-bread and cinnamon smell creeps out onto the street and draws you right through the doors. The kind of place where there's a neighborhood bulletin board; where it's homey inside, and intimate; where you want to buy two of everything and leave the store munching.

The real heart of Alano's is a simple, long glass counter filled with an abundance of fresh-baked goods. Some things are made daily—like the very good croissants, marzipan croissants, scones, and Danish pastries. And every day there's a different kind of bread, from brioche or *challah* to oat rye.

Owner Alan Oswald has been making some breads without any refined sugar and has experimented with breads without any wheat for hypoglycemics and people with allergies.

At Christmastime he makes long loaves of German *stollen,* lively with wine-soaked raisins and bright with cranberries and citrus peel he candies himself.

**East Bay**
## THE BERKELEY BAKERY AND CAFE

*1881 Solano Avenue, Berkeley 94707. Telephone (415) 527-9616. Hours: M–SAT 7–6, SUN 8:30–6.*

Berkeley Bakery croissants are made with sweet butter, the *pain au chocolat* with a substantial buttery dough and dark chocolate. The good homemade breads include whole wheat, rye, and pumpernickel, and on Fridays, braided loaves of *challah.*

**Marin County**
## BREAD AND CHOCOLATE BAKERY

*1139 Magnolia Avenue, Larkspur 94939. Telephone (415) 461-9154. Hours: T–SAT 8–6, SUN 8–3.*

Exuding smells of good things baking, just like grandma's kitchen, this unpretentious neighborhood bakery run by Fred Heitman, Mary Taurek, and Nan Weiser produces Danish pastries, comforting chocolate cakes, and fresh-baked breads. Their 100 percent whole-wheat bread, made from freshly ground flour from Vital Vittles, is high and light, its flavor full and sweet.

Bread and Chocolate's namesake *chocolatina* has a center of straight bittersweet chocolate wrapped with fine layers of Danish dough, their version of the French schoolchild's afternoon *pain au chocolat.* Enthusiastic customers, tempted by the heaps of good old-fashioned cookies, stop in to have a coffee and chat throughout the afternoon.

**East Bay**
## THE CHEESE BOARD

*1504 Shattuck Avenue, Berkeley 94709. Telephone (415) 549-3183. Hours: T–SAT 10–6.*

A cheese store is not such an unlikely place to find some of the best bread in the Bay Area. After all, cheese tastes better if the bread is better. It should accent and complement the taste and texture of the cheese. Strong cheeses need bread with a full-bodied taste.

The Cheese Board Collective bakes a baguette with both texture and flavor. Indisputedly the best baguettes in the Bay Area, these are sourdough, made from a lively starter kept in big old-fashioned earthenware crocks in the kitchen in back. The bread is made entirely from flour, starter, and water, no yeast. Baguettes are skinny and long so there's more crust than doughy center to them—a revelation spread with some ripe goat's milk Camembert.

At the front of the store, big baskets are filled with plump rounds of sourdough beer rye made with white and rye flours, oats, cracked rye, and dark beer. There is a bread cheesy with cheddar and onions, and a welcoming loaf of buttermilk corn cheddar made with corn meal and corn kernels.

Another day's baking brings a whole-wheat rye, a poppy seed raisin with whole wheat and rolled oats, or a crusty multi-grain sesame buckwheat with rolled oats, steel-cut oats, triticale, barley, millet, and wheat berries.

On Friday mornings, they make tender, braided loaves of eggy *challah*. On Saturday, stop in for a loaf of Sunday bread, a honeyed, yeasty round stuffed with walnuts and raisins, irresistible toasted and spread with some of the Cheese Board's sweet country butter.

Don't leave without buying some of the store's excellent cheeses at good prices. They have an especially good selection of Italian and French cheeses, plus Laura Chenel's French-style goat cheeses.

*Discounts for senior citizens.*

## Contra Costa
## NARSAI'S MARKET

*389 Colusa Avenue, Kensington 94707. Telephone (415) 527-3737. Hours: M–SAT 10–7, SUN 10–4.*

Breads baked here every day include plain croissants, almond croissants, classic sweet baguettes, sourdough baguettes, and lovely *baguettes d'épine*: spiny baguettes reseembling sheaves wheat.

But the best time to buy bread at Narsai's is Monday afternoon, when the special bread baked for Monday night's international menu is sold in the market. The store's newsletter tells you what will be available: delicious and unusual breads like Strauss rye, a light rye bread with cracked wheat, orange, and fennel; *elepsomo*, olive bread with onions and mint; monkey bread, composed of small balls of dough dipped in butter; *pain de seigle*, light

rye bread with hazelnuts; *pane all' olio*, a bread with olive oil; *focaccia con la salvia*, a Ligurian pizza bread flavored with sage; or a Burgundian walnut bread fragrant with walnut oil and whole nuts.

## Monterey Area
## SAN JUAN BAKERY

*319 Third Street, downtown San Juan Bautista 95045. Telephone (408) 623-4570. Hours: M–F 7–7, SAT 8–7, SUN 9:30–6.*

A wide variety of breads, including sourdough French.

## Napa Valley
## THE SUGARHOUSE BAKERY

*1357 Main Street, St. Helena 94574. Telephone (707) 963-3424. Hours: T–SAT 6:15–6.*

Rudy and Therese Frey came here from Aigle in French-speaking Switzerland ten years ago and established a small bakery in the center of St. Helena.

Baskets in the windows of their Sugarhouse Bakery show off round cross-hatched loaves of their Swiss farm bread, made with both rye and white flours and baked to a dark brown on the floor of their fifty-year old brick oven. The big, light kitchen is dominated by a huge wooden table for kneading and rolling the dough. Flours are kept in old wooden wine barrels fitted with lids, and, just as in a traditional *boulangerie*, Monsieur Frey leaves his sweet baguettes to rise on lengths of coarse woven linen, pleating the cloth up between the loaves to prevent their sticking to each other.

The Freys make lovely sweet cinnamon rings, fruit rings, and pecan rings, and a tall glazed rum raisin *kugelhopf*, too. For children, they have Swiss *Leckerli* and lots of cookies.

# —FRENCH BREADS—

### San Francisco
## BAKERS OF PARIS

*1605 Haight Street, San Francisco 94117. Telephone (415) 626-4076. Hours: M, W–SUN 8:30–6:30.*

Parisians Gilles Wicker and Lionel Robbe-Jedeau, together with San Francican Joy Powers, are the triumvirate behind Bakers of Paris. The bakery itself, staffed by master French bakers and located in South San Francisco, began last year baking quality French-style breads for the city's restaurants.

Their single retail store, or rather "bread depot," on Haight Street is the first of a series of neighborhood stores planned all over the Bay Area. Inside, the breads for sale that day are arranged neatly on wooden shelves. Their French bread is made in *boules*, or rounds, and *batards*, or medium-long loaves wider than baguettes. There is also the more substantial *pain parisien*, a longer version of the *batard*. Baguettes come in three graduated sizes: *parisien*, *petite*, and *mini*; they also make *pain d'épis*, the

baguette-sized loaf slashed to resemble a stalk of wheat, and *couronne*, the same slashed loaf shaped in a ring.

The rye is the most beautiful loaf in town, shaped like a dark leaf and bearing the imprint of the cloth on which it proofed before going into the oven. Sometimes there is whole wheat or a big loaf of traditional Normandy bread made with butter.

A glass counter shows off the *Viennoiserie*: individual morning loaves of tender *pain au lait*, sugared on the outside; miniature top-knotted brioches; splendid buttery *palmiers* made from puff pastry; and glazed whorls of *pain au raisin* studded with dark raisins. They also make croissants and *pain au chocolat.*

### San Francisco
## BEACH STREET BAKING COMPANY

*Ghirardelli Square, 900 North Point, San Francisco 94109. Telephone (415) 771-6400. Hours: M–TH 8–8, F–SAT 9–9, SUN 9–8.*

This new small bakery on Beach Street, owned by Errol Melnick and opened in March of 1981, is headed by bakers trained at Fantasia Confections, the California Culinary Academy, and Narsai's Bakery. For such a small operation, they make an appealing variety of interesting baked goods.

French bread is sold as baguettes, *baguettes d'épine*, round loaves, and dinner rolls. The round balls of dark pumpernickel loaded with raisins are a delicious variation on classic pumpernickel. The rotating line-up of breads includes a light cinnamon raisin, a whole wheat, a satisfying Jewish rye, and a pecan bread. On weekends, they make *challah.*

Croissants come four ways here: regular, with almonds, as *pain au chocolat*, or stuffed with sharp Cheddar. For your *petit déjeuner* they also bake individual brioches and different varieties of buttery Danish sweet rolls.

A pastry case is stocked with rich tortes and cakes, available whole or by the slice.

## Marin County
### BORDENAVE

*1553 Fourth Street, San Rafael 94901. Telephone (415) 453-2957. Hours: M–T, TH–SAT 8–5.*

San Rafael's Bordenave bakery is the only sourdough French bakery in Marin County. Established in 1918 by Frank Bordenave, a Frenchman from Pau in southern France, it is still a family-owned business, now run by Monsieur Bordenave's granddaughter Joanne and her husband, Paul Henderson. The head bakers have all had lots of experience working with the temperamental sourdough: most of them have worked at Bordenave for over twenty-five years.

Eighty percent of the bread and rolls made here is sourdough; the rest is sweet. Bordenave's thick, chewy crust is crisped on the floor of their big hearth brick ovens. The bread, baked in one-pound loaves, baguettes, and rolls, is unloaded from the ovens all morning long, hot and crackling. For parties, you can special order loaves five feet long. On Valentine's Day they bake sourdough hearts, and for St. Patrick's Day, bread shamrocks.

Look for Bordenave bread in supermarkets in Marin, too.

## San Francisco
### BOUDIN BAKERY

*156 Jefferson Street, San Francisco 94133. Telephone (415) 928-1849. Hours: M–F 8–6, SAT–SUN 8–7.*

At Boudin Bakery in the heart of Fisherman's Wharf, bread is baked the slower old-fashioned way, made only from sourdough starter with no yeast and no preservatives. This makes for a well-flavored sour baguette, baked fresh every day, including Sundays. But get there early. The production at this bakery is limited and the demand is high.

And just so you'll understand how the bread gets that way, the bakery has installed a giant picture window to show off the whole baking process—it goes on every day from 8 to 2, and if you're there by 8:30 you can see the bakers mix the mother with the flour and water.

Boudin will ship one-pound loaves of fresh-baked bread out of state, once a week, on Tuesdays. Come in and fill out a shipping form (minimum order six loaves).

## East Bay
### THE BREAD GARDEN

*2912 Domingo Avenue, Berkeley 94705. Telephone (415) 548-3122. Hours: W–F 7–7, SAT–SUN 8–6.*

In November of '73, the Bread Garden opened on a quiet block in Berkeley across from the Claremont Hotel. Owner David Morris wanted a bakery that would be a real neighborhood institution, with lots of customers stopping in every day for their morning croissant and dinner loaf or rolls. Now the Bread Garden is the center of a cluster of food-oriented stores: Peet's Coffee, a produce store, and Jackson's well-provided liquor store.

A home baker with no professional experience, David Morris is best known for his crusty baguettes. He'll state outright that he has never been to France. In fact, the only real French bread he's ever seen was a suitcase-full of baguettes his cousin brought back to London from Paris during a London bread strike. He explains, "I don't claim to make an authentic French bread. I'm trying to make the best bread I can."

The front of the bakery displays appealing crooked baguettes, fatter French loaves, smooth ovals of dark rye, and plump satin-glazed braids of *challah*. The salt-rising bread made from sour corn starter has a wonderful cheesy flavor and fine texture. The flour used in his popular whole-wheat bread is at most a few days old, ground in Oakland by Vital Vittles from wheat from Arrowhead Mills in Texas. (The fresher the flour, the higher the loaf rises.) You can pick up a schedule of the breads baked daily at the store.

Mr. Morris's affection for rolls shows in the baskets filled with onion rolls, dinner rolls, whole-wheat rolls, French hard rolls, and lovely torpedo-shaped French sandwich rolls. Then there are muffins and homey pound cakes, hefty *Linzertortes*, and plenty of cookies—try the snickerdoodles.

## Sonoma County
## COSTEAUX FRENCH BAKERY

*421 Healdsburg Avenue, Healdsburg 95448. Telephone (707) 433-1913. Hours: W–SAT 7–5, SUN 7–12:30.*

Healdsburg's Costeaux French Bakery is justly famous for its sourdough French bread. In 1981, Costeaux's sourdough took the gold medal and the sweepstakes in the Sonoma County Harvest Fair.

Why is it so good? The bread is made slowly and carefully. The dough is mixed at 10 pm and spends the night maturing and developing its distinctive sourdough flavor. Starting at 4 am the next morning, the shaped and risen loaves are loaded into the brick oven, which dates from the turn of the century. All morning long, baguettes, medium French loaves, rounds, and classic rolls—250 to 600 one-pound loaves of French sourdough a day—

emerge crackling and fragrant from the oven.

The bread is sold only from the bakery itself, so out-of-towners on their way to wine tasting should be sure to stop at Costeaux for a loaf. They also bake an excellent croissant, as well as Danish pastries.

## San Francisco
## DELICES DE FRANCE

*320 Mason Street, San Francisco 94102. Telephone (415) 433-7560. Hours: M–SAT 10–9:30.*

This downtown *charcuterie* has its own bakery where they make excellent long skinny Parisian baguettes, slightly sour, as well as loaves of farmer's bread, whole wheat, and a light rye.

A bevy of pastry chefs turns out scrumptious individual desserts: shiny glazed fruit tartlets, napoleons, raspberry-filled chocolate baskets, éclairs, etc.

## Peninsula
## LA BAGUETTE

*170 Stanford Shopping Center, Palo Alto 94305. Telephone (415) 321-0535. Hours: M–F 10–9, SAT 10–6:30, SUN 10–5:30.*

The head baker here is from France, and he knows his bread. Everything is made fresh every day in traditional French-style ovens where the bread cooks right on the oven floor.

Wooden shelves behind the counter are stacked with long plaited breads, spiny *baguettes d'épine*, large half-kilo baguettes, narrow *ficelles*, crusty rounds, and small country loaves.

The 40-percent whole-wheat breads come in baguettes, rounds, and long braids. There are tender brioches and, of course, croissants: plain, almond, or cheese-filled, fresh every morning.

### San Jose Area
## LA BOULANGERIE

*683 East Brokaw Road, San Jose 95112. Telephone (408) 294-6531. Hours: M–F 9–4, SAT 9–3.*

La Boulangerie is in business making sweet baguettes, supplying many East Bay and San Francisco restaurants. On weekends seven bakers are kept busy making up to five thousand of the crusty French loaves a night. In between batches, they mix up a whole-wheat bread with honey, rich *brioches a tête*, and plain croissants or croissants with ham or chocolate inside, plus an array of tarts, tortes, napoleons, cream puffs, and cookies.

La Boulangerie's baguettes are sold all over the Bay Area in cheese stores and delicatessens.

### East Bay
## LA FARINE

*6323 College Avenue, Oakland 94618. Telephone (415) 654-0338. Hours: W–SAT 10–6, SUN 10–2.*

Lili Le Coq is a master of sweet yeast doughs. Witness her splendid morning buns, spirals of sweet, light dough freckled with cinnamon and glazed with a brittle burnt caramel. Her *chocolatine* doesn't look like much, a round plop of a bun, but how it tastes! A tender yet substantial dough, and inside, a wedge of melting chocolate so dark it's black, its bittersweetness a wonderful contrast with coffee. Or try the twinky, an elongated twist of flaky pastry filled with a mealy almond paste rubbed with cinnamon. In the weeks before Easter Lili makes traditional hot-cross buns.

And every day the flat baskets above her pastry case are heaped with French country bread, egg bread, light rye, and fresh-baked baguettes.

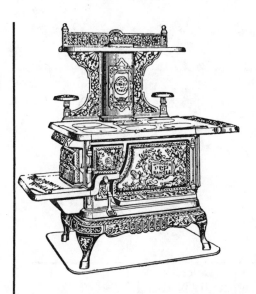

Maybe you'll see Lili in the back, resplendent in Mexican silver folk jewelry, an embroidered blouse, and a white cut-work apron, her hair tucked in a blue gingham kerchief. She always has a small pot of her homemade jam going on the back burner of the stove, bubbling away in a round-bottomed copper pot. You can sit at the huge lace-covered round table at the front with a cup of coffee and a pastry.

### Contra Costa
## LE MOULIN FRENCH BAKERY

*1250 Newell Hill Place, Walnut Creek 94596. Telephone (415) 932-0222. Hours: M–SAT 10–6.*

The two owners of Le Moulin come from the south of France near the Côte d'Azur and, like bakers in any small French *boulangerie*, make croissants, baguettes, *pains au chocolate*, brioches, and classic fresh-fruit tarts with a custard base. They accommodate this country's sweet tooth with all kinds of cookies, apple turnovers, and individual custard cakes.

Le Moulin baguettes and pastries are also sold at A la Carte in Walnut Creek.

Parisian's fresh sourdough is sold all over the city in familiar red, blue, and white packages. The day-old bread returned from stores unsold is available at big price reductions at the bakery itself. Warm it in your oven to freshen it up or make into a royal supply of buttered croûtons and coarse bread crumbs.

## Sonoma County
## SONOMA FRENCH BAKERY

*470 First Street East, Sonoma 95476. Telephone (707) 996-2691. Hours: W–SAT 8–6, SUN 7:30–12.*

Lili and Gratein Guerra moved to Sonoma from France almost thirty years ago to open a bakery. Their years of French-bread expertise are evident in their unique and delicious sourdough French bread, sold from their cozy gingham-curtained store on Sonoma's Spanish-style town square. They make sour French in baguettes or small torpedoes, as well as a whole-wheat sour French in round loaves, and a sourdough caraway. Mornings bring croissants and *chocolatine* with dark-chocolate centers.

Italian *panettone* is made all year round in one-pound loaves.

## San Francisco
## PARISIAN BAKERY

*1995 Evans Avenue, San Francisco 94124. Telephone (415) 641-1000. Hours: M–SAT 9–5:30.*

Parisian Bakery has the oldest sourdough mother in the city. Every day for over 125 years, a chunk of starter for the day's batch of bread is taken from the mother, and, at the end of the day, she is replenished with some of that day's bread dough. The mother has to be "fed" every day to stay strong and vigorous.

Parisian's mother is reputed to be the issue of two different sourdough strains that met in San Francisco: one, from Mongolia by way of the Klondike, carried in a gold miner's knapsack; the other, a strong Basque sourdough stock brought over by a Basque adventurer.

At Parisian the bread is still made with only flour, water and salt, no yeast—the mother does all the work. And in her own good time, too. Whereas most commercial white breads take less than four hours to make, Parisian's French bread takes a full twenty-two hours from start to finish. The slower bread takes to rise, the more the flavor "ripens" in the bread.

## East Bay
## THE SWALLOW CAFE

*The University Art Museum, 2625 Durant Avenue, Berkeley 94704. Telephone (415) 841-2409. Hours: 11–9:30 daily.*

In between ovenfuls of quiches, cakes, brownies, and extravagant desserts, the Swallow Collective bakes batches of satisfying, slightly sour baguettes. Have one there with a homemade pâté or galantine, or eat one as a *tartine*, warmed and spread with fresh butter. They'll also sell you baguettes to take home.

# —GERMAN BREAD—

## San Francisco
## HEIDI'S SUNSET PASTRY SHOP

*742 Irving Street, San Francisco 94122. Telephone (415) 664-9056. Hours: T–F 7–6, SAT 7–5.*

Martha and Hans Graeb recently took over Heidi's Sunset Pastry. Though originally from the Rhineland, Hans had worked for twenty-two years at the Sugar Bowl in Petrini Plaza.

His special German-style breads are rye, heavy rye, and a whole-grain bread similar to pumpernickel—all sourdough. At Christmas time he makes Dresdner *stollen* in four sizes with citron, raisins, nuts, and marzipan inside. On Fridays and Saturdays, they have Jewish butter twists with raisins and, on Saturdays only, German beer pretzels.

## East Bay
## MÜNCHNER KINDL BAKERY

*745 Buena Vista, Alameda 94501. Telephone (415) 769-9154. Hours: M–T, TH–SAT 6 am–11 am.*

The mustachioed baker here, recently arrived from Munich, works with old recipes from Bavaria, a region renowned for its breads—almost two hundred kinds of bread are made in Bavaria alone.

All the breads baked in this Alameda bakeshop are sourdough: home bread in big rounds with coriander seeds on top; rye baguettes; Swiss bread, also rye, but a lighter mix; and twin bread, two dark whorls of bread joined together and dusted with flour. On the weekends the baker makes seed bread with cracked rye and sesame and flax seeds; bread sticks; and fat Bavarian pretzels.

The bakery in Alameda is not really a retail shop—in fact, it's very hard to find, but walk-in customers can buy a loaf or two. Most German delicatessens carry Münchner bread, however, including Hans Speckmann in San Francisco, Saag's in Oakland, Petrini's in San Francisco, and the Sonoma Sausage Company in Sonoma.

## San Francisco
## HANS SPECKMANN

*1550 Church Street, San Francisco 94131. Telephone (415) 282-6850. Hours: M–TH 11–6:30, F–SAT 11–7, SUN 12–6.*

This complete German delicatessen, overflowing with tasty *Wurstwaren,* has German-style breads on hand: they'll cut you a generous slab of rye bread from a huge loaf or sell you flat square packages of moist pumpernickels.

# —INDIAN BREAD—

## San Francisco/East Bay
## BOMBAY BAZAR

*548 Valencia Street, San Francisco 94110. Telephone (415) 621-1717. Hours: M–F 10:30–6, SUN 12–5.*
*1034 University Avenue, Berkeley 94710. Telephone (415) 848-1671. Hours: T–SAT 10–6:30, SUN 11–6.*

This supplier of Indian foodstuffs, spices, curries, and *dal* has *pappadams* (South Indian *dal* wafers)—both the smaller four-inch-diameter southern style and the more usual six-inch size— in plain, garlic, curry, green chili, and *moong* flavors.

You can deep-fry these flat wafers for just a few seconds in very hot oil, toast them over the gas flame with a fork, or even broil them. They will puff up high, turn a rich gold, and fill your kitchen with their pungent, toasty aroma. Use them to accompany drinks, or as a bread for an Indian meal.

Bombay Bazar also sells specially ground *roti* flour for Indian breads.

**San Francisco**
## HAIG'S DELICACIES

*642 Clement Street, San Francisco 94118. Telephone (415) 752-6283. Hours: M–SAT 10-6.*

Haig's has tiny shell-shaped *pappadams* for cocktail snacks, and green *pappadam* strips flavored with vegetables.

# ——IRISH BREAD——

**East Bay**
## BIT OF IRELAND

*1252 Davis, San Leandro 94577. Telephone (415) 568-4767. Hours: M–SAT 6-6.*

San Leandro's Bit of Ireland makes Irish soda bread as well as breakfast scones and what they call Irish coffee cake, made with cinnamon and butter.

# ——ITALIAN BREAD——

**San Francisco**
## CUNEO ITALIAN FRENCH BAKERY

*1501 Grant Avenue, San Francisco 94133. Telephone (415) 421-3796. Hours: M–SAT 7-6, SUN 7-1.*

The actual selling area is rustic and tiny, but the bakery behind, built in the twenties around two enormous brick ovens, turns out between three and five thousand loaves daily made almost entirely by hand. The ovens are the old type called "Dutch peel" because the bread is "peeled off" the floor of the oven with the long-handled paddles called "Dutch peelers." The big ovens are heated continuously. If they ever were allowed to cool down, it would take a week to bring them back up to temperature. The bread is European style: just faintly sour from the "mother" saved from the previous day's dough, and made with hard winter wheat, water, salt, and a small amount of yeast. Ask for your loaves *ben cotto,* with a darker, crisp crust rather than the paler doughy bake Americans favor.

They also bake northern-style *grissini* (bread sticks); *panettone;* and ringshaped *buccellato,* a semisweet bread from Lucca, flavored with raisins and anise and of ancient origin: *buccellatum* was the military bread toasted for the Roman legions.

**San Francisco**
## IL FORNAIO

*2298 Union Street, San Francisco 94123. Telephone (415) 563-3400. Hours: T–SAT 8-7, SUN 8-5.*

Il Fornaio is the most beautiful bakery in San Francisco. Built entirely of wheat-colored wood both inside and outside, its enormous windows are filled with an ever-changing, beautifully arranged display of Italian regional breads in rustic country baskets. This living museum of bread is sister to similar bakeries all over Italy; it was designed and conceived by Signor Carlo Veggetti, a third-generation *arredatore,* or bakery furnishings designer, with attention to every detail. Signor Veggetti traveled all over Italy searching out old recipes and finding bakers in small villages who still made their region's traditional breads. Bakers and pastry makers came from Italy to train the San Francisco store's staff.

You'll find long knobbled loaves of *pane con uvete* (raisin bread); big wheels of *pan pugliese;* loaves of *pane siciliano* coated with sesame seeds; long sticks of *parigini,* or baguettes; *pane con patate* (potato bread); *pane al peperoni* (with peppers); *pane con pomodori* (with tomatoes) in the form of huge bread hands striated with orangy red and white; high-crowned breads with dates; and even southern Italian breads shaped like alligators curled around hard-cooked eggs.

There are fat *grissini*, or bread sticks, and familiar *panini*, the smooth oval rolls used for sandwiches in bars and *rosticcerie* all over Italy. Try the beautiful darker *panini al caffè*, colored with coffee.

All breads are sold, some of them at a hefty price, by the kilo. Because they make so many things, many with which the public is unfamiliar, you can occasionally get a stale bread at Il Fornaio.

And just as in any *panificio* in Italy, they also make and sell trays of *pizza al taglio* (pizza by the slice), *pizzette* (small round snack pizzas), *biscotti*, and regional cakes and pastries.

Six more Il Fornaios are planned for the Bay Area, including one in the Embarcadero Center.

---

San Francisco
## LIGURIA BAKERY

*1700 Stockton Street, San Francisco 94133. Telephone (415) 421-3786. Hours: M–SAT 8–5:30, SUN 7–12.*

You'd think that one of the most successful bakeries in North Beach would have enticing windows and counters overflowing with goodies, but Liguria's are practically bare. They don't go in for display here. They make very few things, but they make them very well. Balls of *panettone* are shelved behind the counter, and below are rings of *buccellato*. A hand-lettered sign lists the prices of *focaccia* (the thick pizza bread of northern Italy). The door's bell keeps ringing as the sunny store fills with shoppers from the neighborhood. Old Italian women settle in the chairs against the wall to wait their turn. One corner is commanded by *genovesi* laughing and gossiping in dialect, waving new arrivals into their circle with handshakes all around.

When the mustachioed *genovese*, Signor Asti, takes an order for *focaccia*, he tears white paper off a roll and lays it down on the counter in front of him. Then he disappears into the back where he lifts an entire slab of just-baked *focaccia* from its pan, carries it to a wooden table and cuts it in big squares. Slapping them together face to face Roman-style, he stacks them high—green and white and red, the colors of the Italian flag—folds the paper around them to make a package, and ties it with string.

Signor Soracco, also a *genovese* whose family has had an interest in the bakery for over thirty years, is out delivering to bars and coffee shops all over the city. The third partner, Augusto Azzolino from Vittorio, Veneto, is in the back preparing the trays of *focaccia* that cover the surface of so many work tables they form a whole terrain. Over a hundred trays of it are baked here every day. They make just a little of the *bianco*, sweet and spongy, garnished only with olive oil. It's a favorite in Italy in the early mornings, when workers get it hot from the oven and make a hearty breakfast by stuffing fresh ricotta and mozzarella inside. Here the Chinese in the neighborhood order it most. The *focaccia con le uve* has dark raisins

imbedded in the dough, and the *focaccia con le cipolline* has scallions scattered over the top. Liguria's concession to American taste is the *focaccia* with tomato sauce, which is, in fact, similar to the Roman *pizza rossa*, glazed with a simple tomato sauce and dribbled with olive oil.

Smooth, dark-brown loaves of the faintly sweet anise bread baked in the very early morning are lined flank to flank on shelves all over the kitchen. When the bakers are done with the day's *focaccia* baking, these will be sliced an inch thick and toasted in the oven to make the *biscotti* sold by weight out front. They're delicious dunked in your morning *cappuccino.*

# LATINO BREAD
# TORTILLAS

### San Francisco
### CASA SANCHEZ

*2778 Twenty-fourth Street, San Francisco 94132. Telephone (415) 282-2400. Hours: 9–6:30 daily.*

Casa Sanchez is an old, family-run operation on Twenty-fourth Street making the best corn tortillas in the area. The back of the store is dominated by a vast tortilla-making factory, where huge dough-rolling machines turn out the enormous number of tortillas needed for the large Latino community of the Mission.

### San Francisco
### DOMINGUEZ BAKERY

*2953 Twenty-fourth Street, San Francisco 94132. Telephone (415) 824-6849. Hours: 9 am–10 pm daily.*

With so many Central Americans moving into the Mission, Domínguez now makes broad, braided loaves of a Central American bread called *pan picon*, with

cheese mixed into the dough, and another small, round loaf of egg bread, also from Central America.

Though there are dozens of sweets and breads displayed in the cases at the front of the store, you should follow the rest of the crowd to the back where you can find even more kinds just fresh from the oven (see Pastry).

### San Francisco
### LA MORENA FACTORY TORTILLERIA

*3391 Mission Street, San Francisco 94110. Telephone (415) 648-0114. Hours: M-SAT 8-6.*

Aurelio Villereal presides over the long counter stacked with packages of his La Morena–brand tortillas. The hand-made ones are the most delicious around.

### San Francisco
### LA PALMA MEXICATESSEN

*2884 Twenty-fourth Street, San Francisco 94110. Telephone (415) 648-5500. Hours: 8–6 daily.*

La Palma Mexicatessen is especially renowned as a *tortillería*. Freshly made tortillas are tender, delicate, and delicious, a completely different experience from the sad leathery rounds sold in most supermarkets. Tortillas here are baked on big griddles in the back of the store several times a day. Tall stacks of still-steaming corn and flour tortillas cover the counter, but the real delicacies are the thicker hand-patted tortillas made by some of the skilled women in the back.

East Bay
## MJ RANCHO MEXICAN STORE

*464 Seventh Street, Oakland 94607. Telephone (415) 451-2393. Hours: M-SAT 8-6.*

In back of this well-stocked Mexican delicatessen is a small tortilla factory that makes corn and flour tortillas as well as hand-patted corn tortillas.

# MIDDLE EASTERN BREAD

San Francisco
## ACROPOLIS BAKERY AND DELICATESSEN

*5217 Geary Boulevard, San Francisco 94118. Telephone (415) 751-9661. Hours: T-SAT 9-7, SUN 8-4.*

Gregory Triantafillidis custom bakes Greek breads. Try his homemade white bread, and a domed bread cross-hatched on top. Although he's Greek, he was born in Russia and at Easter he makes *kulich*, the buttery, high-domed Ukrainian Easter sweet bread rich with eggs, raisins, almonds, and candied fruits.

San Francisco
## HAIG'S DELICACIES

*642 Clement Street, San Francisco 94118. Telephone (415) 752-6283. Hours: M-SAT 10-6.*

Haig's always has a tall stack of packaged *lavash*, Armenian cracker bread, made in big rounds. It is baked daily in Fresno, plain or whole wheat with sesame. Break the *lavash* into small pieces and use like crackers, or sprinkle a whole round with water, spread with layers of roast beef, cream cheese, lettuce, and tomato, then roll it up and slice into rounds for hors d'oeuvres. *Lavash* is also sold at most Middle Eastern groceries and cheese stores.

Central Valley
## HYE QUALITY BAKERY

*537 L Street, Fresno 93721. Telephone (209) 445-1511. Hours: T-F 8:30-5:30, SAT 9-4.*

The Ganimian family bake *lavash*, or Armenian cracker bread, daily. The large crisp rounds are white, or light, medium, or dark whole wheat.

Hye's Armenian cracker bread is available at Middle Eastern groceries and at cheese stores all over the Bay Area.

San Francisco
## OLYMPIC GREEK AMERICAN PASTRIES

*3719 Mission Street, San Francisco 94110. Telephone (415) 647-6363. Hours: 8:30-7:30, SUN flexible but usually 8:30-3.*

Every Friday Teta Panagiotides bakes huge crunchy loaves of homemade bread covered with sesame seeds. Her loving kneading brings out the shine in the gluten of the bread. It's crystallized and shiny inside like stalactites.

At Easter she makes the traditional large braided rings of bread decorated with hard-cooked eggs dyed red for the blood of Christ. She also makes smaller versions of the same bread.

At Christmas and New Year's, Teta and her husband Pete stay up for three days straight baking all the *krystopsomo* bread they'll need for their Greek and American customers. The round loaves are slightly sweet with anise, and skinny ropes of dough decorate the tops with the numerals of the new year. The custom is for the head of the family to serve *krystopsomo* after both Christmas and New Year's Day dinners. Whoever finds the coin hidden in his or her piece of bread will be prosperous in the coming year.

# NATURAL FOODS

## East Bay
## NABALOM BAKERY

*2708 Russell Street, Berkeley 94705. Telephone (415) 845-BAKE. Hours: T–SAT 8:30–6, SUN 9–1.*

The eight-member Nabalom Bakery Collective has been producing good bread and baked goods from a quiet storefront off College Avenue for over five years. The park bench in front is always crowded with customers taking a little sun, drinking coffee, and munching on fresh-made pastries.

Every morning you can pick up rich crumbly scones, walnut croissants, honey-sweetened raisin bran muffins, blueberry muffins, sour cream coffee cakes, and pastries.

Breads baked every day are a braided egg bread, a healthy multi-grain bread, and a cheese bread. Breads baked just one day a week (pick up a schedule at the bakery) include Cornell (a high-protein white bread with soy, gluten, bran, and poppy seeds), light rye, unsweetened whole wheat, oat sesame, oatmeal walnut, and sourdough French. Seasonally, there are hot-cross buns, *stollen* rings, and fruitcakes.

## Contra Costa
## THE RISING LOAFER

*160 North Hartz Avenue, Danville 95426. Telephone (415) 838-8800. Hours: T–SAT 9–5.*

Baker Endy Stark learned her trade at Odiyan, the Nyingma Institute Country Center in Sonoma County, where good natural foods and fine home-baked breads are served to the institute's students.

When she returned to the Bay Area, Ms. Stark opened the Rising Loafer, where she bakes the same kinds of high-quality breads, made with stone-ground flours and sweetened only with honey and molasses: honey wheat, cinnamon raisin, garden herb, molasses oatmeal, and French baguettes, plus pumpkin-banana or zucchini sweet breads and berry or bran muffins.

## San Francisco
## TASSAJARA BREAD BAKERY

*1000 Cole Street, San Francisco 94117. Telephone (415) 664-8947. Hours: M–F 7:30–6:30, SAT 8–6.*
*Green's, Building A, Fort Mason Center, San Francisco 94109. Telephone (415) 771-6330. Hours: T–SAT 10:30–4.*

When the Zen Center first decided to open a small bakery in San Francisco, they found Nino Cerruti, a former North Beach baker, to advise them. The bread served to Zen students and guests at the center's Tassajara retreat first came to a wider public notice when Ed Brown published *The Tassajara Bread Book.* This classic text of home bread-baking techniques is filled with recipes Mr. Brown developed when he was chef at the Zen Mountain Center. Some of the same breads are made by the San Francisco bakery.

Since breads were needed to create interest in the Zen students' simple diet of grains, beans, vegetables, and fruits, he worked to make their flavor full, the texture varied. Each dough is handled differently, worked gently. As one baker explained, "We do all right for a bunch of Zen students."

At Tassajara Bakery, fresh breads, at least five delicious kinds, all made with fresh sweet butter and eggs from hormone-free chickens, start coming out of the oven at nine in the morning: whole wheat, dark Heidelberg rye, braided *challah,* millet bread, country French, and sourdough corn rye. The delicious potato bread, moist with fresh grated potato, is irresistible spread with good country butter, and the hand-shaped baguettes are some of the tastiest around.

At Christmas, they make _panettone_ and _stollen_, both rich with glacéed fruits and nuts. And year round they make perilously tempting brownies, chocolate cake, and an opulent poppy seed cake.

Not all of the breads are baked every day. Pick up a bread schedule at either store so you'll know when to expect your favorite bread.

Tassajara bread is also sold at the center's Green Gulch Greengrocer, 297 Page Street, San Francisco (431-7250).

### East Bay
### VITAL VITTLES
### PREMIUM NATURAL FOODS

_1011 Heinz, Berkeley 94710. Telephone (415) 845-3186. Wholesale to the trade only._

Joe Schwinn knows you can't make good bread without good flour, so, committed baker and resourceful American that he is, he decided to stone grind his own. Carloads of organically grown hard winter wheat and other whole grains arrive regularly at Vital Vittles from Texas's famed Arrowhead Mills in Deaf Smith County.

A whole-wheat loaf made from freshly ground flour will rise higher and taste sweeter than a loaf made from the same flour weeks older. Joe Schwinn mills all the flour for his breads, fifteen hundred loaves of it baked twice weekly using fresh oils and freshly ground spices. They're distributed all over the Bay Area to markets and health food stores under the Vital Vittles label.

His original idea was to distribute small packages of dated fresh-ground flours to health food stores for home bakers, but the demand was never consistent enough for his efforts.

Vital Vittles bakes seven kinds of breads, each loaf shaped by hand. The best seller is hearty sesame millet with whole wheat. The Real Bread, a whole-wheat loaf that's sweet and high, comes in rolls too.

And he is the only maker of kosher parve whole-grain breads in the Bay Area.

## ——PORTUGUESE——

### San Jose Area
### SOUZA'S BAKERY

_2079 El Camino Real, Santa Clara 95051. Telephone (408) 243-5443. Hours: M–F 7–7, SAT 7–6._

Souza's Bakery makes breads for the local Portuguese community: Portuguese sweet bread in rounds with a hole in the middle; Portuguese dinner bread, similar to French bread; and _mulsaldes_, raised doughnuts covered with either granulated sugar or chocolate.

## ——RUSSIAN——

### San Francisco
### TIP-TOE INN DELICATESSEN

_5423 Geary Boulevard, San Francisco 94118. Telephone (415) 221-6422. Hours: M–SAT 9–7._

This Russian delicatessen makes _kulich_ at Easter. They also sell wooden forms in the shape of a truncated pyramid to make _pahska_, the creamy cheesecake traditionally served with _kulich_ on Easter morning. Iced and decorated with flowers, the _kulich_ is brought to the church to be blessed. The long procession of women, each carrying her splendid flower-bedecked _kulich_, is a nostalgic memory for many Russians.

# *Charcuterie*

*Charcuterie* literally means "purveyor of cooked flesh" in French. These stores traditionally make and sell fresh sausages, pâtés, and galantines; cured, smoked, and dried sausages; and all sorts of cooked meats. *Charcuteries* are the perfect places for harassed cooks to pick up the makings for impromptu picnics or easy-to-prepare suppers. They range from the simple, with just a few sausages, one or two pâtés, a baked *jambon d'os* (bone-in ham), and several salads, to the fabulous Parisian gourmet shrines where crowds gather to stare at elegantly arranged displays behind huge plate-glass windows.

In San Francisco, we have a wide range of *charcuterie*-like shops where cured meat and sausage makers from many traditions make their ethnic specialties: Italian blood sausage studded with raisins and pine nuts, creamy French *boudin blanc* and its fiery Creole version, dozens of kinds of German *Wurstwaren*, smoky Portuguese *linguiça*, Swiss *cervelat*, Filipino *langoniza*, sweet Chinese *lop cheong*, spicy Mexican chorizo—even Hungarian, Czechoslovakian, and Lithuanian sausages.

In Paris, charcuteries are almost always *traiteurs* as well, selling prepared dishes such as quiche, *saucisson en brioche*, *cassoulet*, and *choucroute garni*. San Francisco has always had its share of Italian, German, and Chinese stores of this type, selling ravoli, sausages, rock salt chicken, and roast duck. But it is only recently that *charcuteries* in the strict French tradition have become part of the city's food scene. (Berkeley's Pig by the Tail, opened ten years ago, was the first *charcuterie* in the country.) Most of them are listed here, but for more *traiteurs*, see the Take-Out section.

## GLOSSARY

### FRESH SAUSAGES
#### FRENCH

**Boudin blanc** A traditional French Christmas sausage made with pork and cream. Sometimes chicken breast or veal is added.

**Boudin noir** French blood sausage. The best are made with pork blood, but in California most often with beef blood.

**Crépinette** A flat sausage patty of pork, lamb, or other meat, often with spinach or truffles, wrapped in lacy caul fat.

**Toulouse** The simplest French sausage, pure pork with salt and pepper, no herbs, no wine. The classic sausage for *cassoulet*.

#### GERMAN

**Blutwurst** The German version of blood sausage.

**Bockwurst** A delicate German sausage made with finely ground pork, veal, eggs, milk, and chives.

**Bratwurst** Pale Nürnberg sausage made of pork and/or veal flavored with cooked onions.

**Frankfurter** The German ancestor of our hot dog, made with finely ground lean pork, then smoked.

**Weisswurst** A mild veal and pork sausage.

#### ITALIAN

**Calabrese** Hot Italian pork sausage seasoned with red pepper and fennel.
**Sicilian** Milder Italian pork sausage.
**Toscana** Mild sausage seasoned with nutmeg, cinnamon, and other spices.

#### SPANISH

**Chorizo** Mexican or Spanish sausage, all pork, red with pimiento and spicy with chili, cumin, and garlic.

**Longaniza** The Portuguese version of chorizo.

**Morcilla** The Spanish version of blood sausage.

## SCANDINAVIAN

**Medisterpolse** A mild Danish pork sausage.

**Potatis korv** A Swedish sausage made with pork and beef mixed with cold boiled potatoes and sweet onions.

## DRIED SAUSAGES AND COOKED SAUSAGES

**Andouille** A marbled pork tripe sausage from the Loire Valley.

**Cervelat** Mild German and Swiss smoked sausage made from finely ground beef or pork.

**Kielbasa** A Polish-style smoked sausage of pork and beef spiced with garlic and cayenne.

**Lop cheong** A dried Chinese pork or beef sausage flavored with soy sauce.

**Linguiça** A Portuguese pork sausage, coarsely ground and spicy. Good grilled over charcoal.

**Pepperoni** A dried Italian sausage made of coarse chopped pork and beef flavored with spices and red pepper.

## HAMS AND OTHER MEATS

**Black Forest** A German-style ham, traditionally made from pigs fed on the acorns of the huge forests of Westphalia.

**Bündnerfleisch** A Swiss-style air-dried beef similar to your childhood's chipped beef, but this one is marvelous.

**Jambon de Bayonne** The southern French version of raw ham, or *jambon cru*, soaked in a brine with red wine and rosemary, then smoked.

**Prosciutto crudo** Raw cured ham in the style of Parma, Italy.

**Virginia or Smithfield** Delicious hickory smoked hams made from peanut-fed pigs.

## SUPPLIES

**Sausage casings** Both hog and sheep intestines. Hog is the standard size, and the sheep comes both smaller (for baby links) and larger (for salami-sized). Some are packed in brine and have to be soaked overnight before use. Those for industrial use are water packed and can be used right away, but they are only sold in rather large quantities.

Artificial and collagen casings are also available. Natural casings are more expensive, but they're thinner and don't toughen in cooking, and nothing else gives the plump, handmade look to your sausage.

**Caul fat** Lacy white fat used to wrap *crépinette* patties and also used in some braised dishes such as rabbit with mustard and cream. Very hard to find because it's not used much in this country, and bakers, who make a leaf lard from it for layered doughs, have first chance at it from the slaughterhouses.

**Fatback** The most common fat used in sausage making.

## MEAT SUPPLIERS

Sausages and pâtés are often made from parts of the pig that Americans rarely eat. While local butcher stores may have liver and tripe, they're often not very fresh since the turnover isn't very fast. To find the best ingredients for sausage making, you should go to stores that sell a lot of pork. These are generally found in the ethnic communities where the cheaper more uncommon parts of the animal are commonly cooked. Check Chinatown for the freshest pork liver, and black neighborhoods for good-looking tripe and pigs' feet.

# ——CHINESE——

San Francisco
## KWONG JOW SAUSAGE MANUFACTURING COMPANY

*1157 Grant Avenue, San Francisco 94133. Telephone (415) 397-2562. Hours: M–F 9–5, SAT 9–4:30, SUN 8:30–4:30.*

Great bunches of chewy dried Chinese sausage called *lop cheong,* made with sweet Cantonese-style pork, duck liver, or beef, are hung across the back of this tiny store. To one side, you'll see garlands of mahogany *cha siew* (barbecued pork), barbecued pork snouts, and curly twists of bacon rind for seasoning Chinese dishes. Cut sausages into rounds and serve steamed with rice or use in stir-fry dishes.

San Francisco
## SUN SANG

*1205 Stockton Street, San Francisco 94133. Telephone (415) 989-3060. Hours: 8:30–5:30 daily.*

Sun Sang Market is one of the best places to buy roast pig, one of the oldest in Chinatown. Be sure you specify roast pig; it's not the same as roast pork (roast pig is the entire pig roasted whole; roast pork is the butt or loin treated with curing salts, then roasted). Whole sides of it are hung from big iron hooks overhead. The butchers quarter and chop it with swift strokes of a heavy cleaver. They'll cut it any way you like, but the meat closest to the bone is sweetest.

In addition to roast pig, you can buy boiled chicken, soy sauce chicken, roast squab, chitlings, and hog maw. They'll slice the fat pork sausage into rice for you. Buy the roast chicken or duck either whole or by halves.

# ——EUROPEAN——

San Francisco
## ACROPOLIS BAKERY AND DELICATESSEN

*5217 Geary Boulevard, San Francisco 94118. Telephone (415) 751-9661. Hours: T–SAT 8–7, SUN 8–4.*

The Acropolis Bakery and Delicatessen has moist, delicate, European-style ham perfectly cooked by owner Gregory Triantafillidis in his large, comfortable kitchen. He doesn't always keep it out front, so if you don't see it, ask for it.

East Bay
## HASENKAMP'S MEAT AND DELICATESSEN

*3418 Village Drive, Castro Valley 94546. Telephone (415) 581-2361. Hours: M–SAT 8–6.*

Hasenkamp's makes homemade sausages, too: a spicy *linguiça,* a garlicky Polish sausage, and a beef-and pork-based German sausage that they smoke themselves. And for hot dog fanciers, they make an old-fashioned veal frankfurter.

Marin County
## JERRY'S MEATS AND DELICATESSEN

*414 Miller Avenue, Mill Valley 94941. Telephone (415) 383-3423. Hours: M–SAT 9–6:30, SUN 10–5:30.*

Jerry Cook, the butcher at Jerry's Meats and Delicatessen in Mill Valley, makes sausages with a sure and inspired hand: his Italian sausages are veal, salt free, and flavored with Sauternes and sweet basil. He adds fennel to some of them and, for a hot version, anise and cracked chili pepper. The Lithuanian sausage is made with pork, ham, and onions sautéed in butter with garlic and allspice. His Portuguese sausage made with pork, hot pepper, wine, garlic, and paprika is a little sweeter than the better-known *linguiça*, and it's not smoked. Anglophiles will love his bangers, a tasty all-pork version of this English classic.

He also makes a wonderful veal bacon, cured in salt and sherry and then custom-smoked over light fruit woods.

### San Francisco
## JURGENSEN'S GROCERY

*2190 Union Street, San Francisco 94123. Telephone (415) 931-0100. Hours: M–SAT 9–6.*

A section of Jurgensen's meat counter is devoted to *charcuterie*. The pâtés include a smooth *pâté maison* made with pork and pork liver laced with Madeira, a rich duck liver pâté perfumed with truffles, and a chicken liver pâté. At the holidays they present a rich truffled goose liver pâté.

Jurgensen's makes both sweet and hot Italian sausages as well as a mild French sausage, all pork, seasoned with aromatic herbs and often with wine.

### Amador County
## LASICH MEAT PROCESSING

*Empire Street (P.O. Box 121), Plymouth 95669. Telephone (209) 245-6675. Hours: M–SAT 8–5, SUN 9–5.*

Since 1961, John Lasich has been selling his special smoked meats from a small shop in Amador County. His country smokehouse produces delicious hams and bacons, but he also makes sausages: breakfast patties, Italian sausages, and an unusual *kobasica* sausage. The recipe for this spicy, lightly smoked sausage,

made from coarsely ground beef and pork lavished with garlic and rosemary, comes from Mr. Lasich's Yugoslavian father, a gold miner who arrived in California in 1910. One of the owners at Lake Merritt Wine & Cheese Revival likes *kobasica* so much, she sells it in her Oakland store.

*Mail order by UPS.*

### East Bay
## MADE TO ORDER

*1576 Hopkins Street, Berkeley 94707. Telephone (415) 524-7552. Hours: M–SAT 10–6.*

Sylvana La Rocca cures her own prosciutto just like her grandmother did in the Italian region of Abruzzi-Molise. A dark, bruised color, she sells it by the pound, and, for the pleasure of her customer-cooks, sells the prosciutto ends at two-thirds the price. The robust Italian country pâté is pork based, with prosciutto and Italian herbs. As a service to the many older people who live in the neighborhood and who must restrict their salt intake, the store began making a chicken galantine with no salt—it is now the most popular item in the *charcuterie* counter. For kosher customers, they make a chicken liver pâté entirely of chicken products.

The lovely roast beef *maison* is larded and blessed with a rosy center. The Florentine roll is a spiral of top round, dark-green spinach, and cream cheese surrounding a carrot flower center. They also make a boned leg of lamb marinated in herbs and then roasted. And in the tradition of European *charcuteries*, Sylvana often has marinated chickens or shish-kebobs ready for the grill, or thick, tender stuffed lamb chops for a quick dinner at home.

The salads sold by the pound are made fresh every day and might include coleslaw, German potato salad, *rata-*

*touille,* or French vegetable salad. There's a bowl of the store's homemade pickles and a tin of *mostarda di Dondi,* a type of Italian fruit chutney, on top of the counter.

The store's pasta, made with eggs and both semolina and golden durum wheat, can be cut to your specifications. The delicious *maltagliati,* or scrap ends, are sold for soup. The refrigerator case stocks fresh basil *pesto; salsa casalinga,* a heavy meat and tomato sauce; and *salsa bolognese,* light on the tomato, with veal, chicken, pork, and prosciutto.

All the basic stocks and mother sauces are made and sold unsalted. There's beef stock both regular and concentrated, chicken stock, mushroom *duxelles,* and *glace de viande.* Every month there's a featured "mother" sauce such as *sauce espagnol.*

Once a week, Sylvana churns a big batch of unsalted butter just as her grandmother did. Some of it she leaves plain and some she flavors: *pesto,* mint, strawberry, pear, orgeat, lemon with lemon zest, orange with orange zest. And there's always fresh whole egg mayonnaise.

The cheeses, of course, include Italian cheese, along with the store's own *formaggio fresco,* similar to a fresh ricotta, and fresh cheese imported from Italy, such as seductive *mascarpone* and *mozzarella di bufala.*

## Contra Costa
## NARSAI'S MARKET

*389 Colusa Avenue, Kensington 94707. Telephone (415) 527-3737. Hours: M-SAT 10-7, SUN 10-4.*

Narsai's Market follows Narsai David's restaurant next door in being basically French with some leanings toward the Middle East. The duck liver pâté with port aspic and the *galantine de*

*canard* are exquisite examples of the best of the French *charcutier's* art. But on the eastern side, he's developed a Moroccan lamb sausage (finely ground lamb with currants, curry powder, and spices) and an Assyrian lamb sausage with pomegranate juice, red wine, and basil. These are quite lean and can be cooked faster than a pork sausage.

High quality take-out entrées such as medallions of veal are available and change weekly. You can also buy mayonnaises, a *bordelaise* sauce, a *glace de viande,* and various stocks for your own cooking.

A selection of Narsai's *charcuterie* products is also sold at Edibles, I. Magnin's gourmet department.

## San Jose Area
## NETO SAUSAGE COMPANY

*3499 The Alameda, Santa Clara 95050. Telephone (408) 296-0818. Hours: M-TH 7-5, F 7-6, SAT 8-5.*

The Santa Clara Valley has a large Portuguese population, descendants of farmers who came in the nineteenth century to work the rich land. Arthur Goncalves started in the forties with a modest shop making Portuguese-style sausages. Neto Sausage Company, with three generations of Goncalves's family working, now makes over five thousand pounds of sausages a day: an all-pork

Portuguese *linguiça*, a piquant *chouriço* (hot *linguiça*), a *morcels* (beef-blood sausage), and a robust Mexican-style chorizo stained with pimiento and hot with cayenne. After they've been stuffed into their casings and hung to dry a bit, the sausages are smoked over alderwood.

The factory has a small deli in front that sells imported Portuguese and Brazilian foodstuffs: *carne seca* for the Brazilian national dish, *feijoida*, black beans cooked with meats and sausage; dried *lupini* beans, black beans, and garbanzos; guava paste; hearts of palm; manioc; Portuguese cheeses; frozen *congrel*, *espada*, and *pescadina*; and *bacalao*, or dried cod; plus Brazilian soft drinks and beers, and Portuguese wines.

For sweets, they have Brazilian and Portuguese candies and cookies, and round loaves of eggy Portuguese sweet bread and *pain de miel*, a type of cornbread.

## San Jose Area
## THE ROMAN SAUSAGE COMPANY

*1810 Richard Avenue, Santa Clara 95050. Telephone (408) 988-1222. Hours: 6–5 daily.*

Santa Clara's Roman Sausage Company produces several kinds of Mediterranean sausages: fresh Italian pork sausages, both hot and mild; smoked Portuguese *linguiça*, Portuguese-style *morcels*, or blood sausage; Spanish chorizo as well as regular pork links.

The meat counter will sell you choice meat, but in wholesale quantities: thirty pounds of spareribs, whole pork loins, New York strips, fresh ground beef. Call the day before.

The little deli in front is not Italian, but Portuguese, stocking imported foodstuffs such as olive oils, dried codfish, tins of sardines and octopus, Portuguese cookies and cheeses. They also sell a Portuguese sweet bread made exclusively for them.

## East Bay
## SAAG'S

*1799 Factor Avenue, San Leandro 94597. Wholesalers only to the trade.*

Saag's supplies delicatessens and restaurants all over the city with German-style sausages, frankfurters, liverwursts, hams, and other cured meats.

The business started in 1933 as a retail pork store in the old Payless Market in downtown Oakland. When Walter Mosle, a sausage maker trained in Switzerland, and his wife Kathi bought the business in the fifties, they moved it to a small storefront on Williams Street in Oakland, where Walter developed an extensive repertoire of sausages and other meats.

Now the small factory, based in San Leandro, produces dozens of products, including real German frankfurters made with veal and pork, all kinds of bratwurst and *Weisswurst*, *cervelat* (a beef salami), garlic-laced Polish sausages, bolognas, and a rich pistachio-studded liverwurst. The blood sausage is a dark wine-colored mosaic, imbedded with chunks of savory tongue. Try the Westphalian-style ham, the Black Forest ham, and the Swiss *Bündnerfleisch* (beef soaked in a wine and spice brine, then air-dried). Recently, in response to the growing public concern over nitrites, Saag's began processing hams every week in order to use the minimum amount of nitrite.

Walter has now retired, and his wife Kathi Mosle carries on in the same fine tradition. The company does a tremendous wholesale business (sixty thousand pounds of sausage a week), and until recently maintained their retail store on William Street in Oakland. It is now owned by Werk and

Sons, who sell Saag's products as well as their own in-house sausages.

Check your local delicatessen for Saag's products. Send a self-addressed stamped envelope for a copy of Saag's sausage selector, with a description of their products, or for their *Twenty-four Ways Cookbook.*

### San Jose Area
## SILVA SAUSAGE COMPANY

*1266 East Julian Street, San Jose 95116. Telephone (408) 293-5437. Hours: M–SAT 9–5.*

Silva Sausage Company makes smoked Portuguese *linguiça*, Italian sweet and hot sausages, Portuguese-style *morcels* (blood sausage), and regular pork links.

The small store in front has imported Portuguese products: dried codfish, tins of sardines and octopus, beans and other dried foods, plus a Portuguese sweet bread made with lots of butter and eggs.

### East Bay
## TAYLOR'S SAUSAGE COMPANY

*818 Jefferson at Clay (Housewives' Market), Oakland 94607. Telephone (415) 832-6448. Hours: M–SAT 9–6.*

You won't find any fancy French pâtés at Taylor's Sausage Company, but you will find fancy French chefs buying sausages, which is the only thing Taylor's makes. And if you stop in at the right time of day, you'll be able to see the sausages being made in this tiny stall at the back of Oakland's Housewives' Market.

The Taylor family were originally from Canada, of English origin, and they naturally began with English recipes; the English banger was their specialty for years. Then, to satisfy the demands of customers, they began making more and more types of sau-

sages until their repertoire became truly international. Mr. Taylor retired to Oregon a few years ago and sold the business to his neighbors Eddie and Sylvia Chow, but he still makes and ships hickory-smoked sausages down to the store. His Portuguese *linguiça* is good grilled over charcoal. There's a chewy pepperoni and a garlicky Polish pork sausage, too. The smoked pork sausages sold here are mild, medium hot, and extra hot—the last kind is best for gumbo.

Before Mr. Taylor left for the wilds, he left all his recipes. Taylor's fresh sausages include a fine breakfast pork sausage flavored with sage; sausage for gumbos and barbecue; Louisiana-style barbecue links (a mix of pork and beef, hot or mild); extra-lean sweet Italian sausages; Swedish potato sausage (beef, pork, potatoes). They make a French *boudin blanc*, all pork and delicately seasoned, but their spectacular Louisiana "Bull-Dang" is the Creole version of *boudin blanc*, made with pork, rice, butter, celery, chicken stock. The mouth-searing hot variety is spectacular, but you can get mild as well.

If you want to try your hand at making a sausage you can't find here, Taylor's sells salt-packed sausage casings in fifteen-yard lengths; these need to be soaked in water one hour before using. More convenient is the professional water-packed casing sold in bags of one hundred yards. They'll keep, sitting in water in your refrigerator, for up to six months.

The small meat counter is packed with absolutely fresh pork hocks, country-style ribs, pork loin, and various chops. And for blood puddings and blood sausages, you can buy pork blood by the pint.

The shop's small crew clearly love their sausages and are generous with advice on how best to cook them. Tell them what you want to make and they'll gladly advise you.

## Napa County
## THE WURST PLACE

*Vintage 1870, Washington Street, Yountville 94599. Telephone (707) 944-2224. Hours: T–SUN 10–5:30.*

The Wurst Place looks like it's been in Yountville for fifty years. It hasn't. Four and a half years ago Tom Catterson was a management person at Lockheed when he and his wife Nancy decided to give up the big city life and make sausage for a living. They've got French sausages such as a *boudin noir* and *boudin blanc* (Normandy style with apples); both sweet and hot Italian sausages; Spanish *linguiça;* and a spicy Armenian lamb sausage; but the specialty, of course, is German *Wurstwaren:* fresh kielbasa, bratwurst, Swiss-style bratwurst, Polish sausages, Polish rings, and all the smoked varieties of wurst. Tom Catterson doesn't leave it at that. He's constantly experimenting. He'll bone duck legs, then stuff them with a dried fruit- and walnut-studded forcemeat for one week's special, and do something equally imaginative the next week.

For your *choucroute garni* (braised sauerkraut garnished with several kinds of wurst), they'll sell you bulk sauerkraut by the half gallon and a packet of their special seasoning, enough for a pint. Every Wednesday during the season, there are live crayfish from the Sacramento Delta, but call on Tuesday to reserve your share. Customers can buy sheep and hog casings in twenty-five-foot packages, caul fat in five-pound increments (it can be frozen), and, for rendering your own lard, they'll order extra fatback.

At Christmas, Nancy Catterson's Italian background emerges in the festive *salsiccie di natale* (northern Italian Christmas sausage): long skinny links of pure pork mixed with Parmesan and creamy pine nuts. They're best braised in white wine, in the style of the Veneto region, and served with their own juice and sautéed peppers and onions over a bright golden mound of polenta.

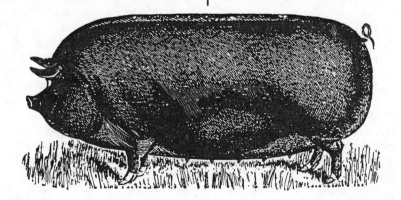

# FRENCH

## San Francisco
## DELICES DE FRANCE

*320 Mason Street, San Francisco 94102. Telephone (415) 433-7560. Hours: M–SAT 10–9:30.*

Delices de France, an uptown *charcuterie* and an informal bistro-type restaurant, is one of the fanciest shops of its kind in the city.

The long *charcuterie* counter is filled with lavish pâtés, elegant *terrines*, and fresh country sausages made by the French *charcutier* and his staff. The exceptional *jambon de bayonne*, a French raw-cured ham similar to a fine *prosciutto crudo*, is house cured and a marvel of delicacy and finesse. A row of sculpted, beautifully crafted *pâtés en croûte* embellished with aspic are succeeded by an extravagant salmon *terrine* or a rich pheasant *terrine*. There are both pork and a duck *rillettes* molded in loaves and a savory *fromage de tête* (head cheese). Among the sausages, the *andouille* is the most unusual; it cuts into beautiful cream and pale-gray marbled slices.

Though all the *charcuterie* here is well made, the array of salads is generally unimaginative. There's a small selection of imported cheeses to accompany their skinny Parisian baguettes.

Plump, flaky croissants, delicious *pain au chocolate*, and mouthwatering individual French pastries stuff a long counter at the back.

## San Francisco
## MARCEL ET HENRI

*2000 Hyde Street, San Francisco 94109. Telephone (415) 885-6044. Hours: M–SAT 9–6.*

From the outside Marcel et Henri looks like a straightforward neighborhood butcher shop. You'd never suspect that the simple awning shades the site of the city's most sophisticated line of pâtés. The *charcuterie* began in 1962, when Henri Lapuyade, a native of Béarn in the Pyrenees, went into business using his mother's trusted recipes. Today Henri still directs the kitchen with a sure Gallic hand.

All the pâtés are pork based, including a chunky country-style *pâté maison*, a *pâté de lapin*, and a *pâté de canard*. In late December, they make a special holiday pâté of rabbit, pork, and veal marinated in red wine and herbs; and a classic *boudin blanc*, a blend of chicken breast and heavy cream sweetened with onions.

A few basic French-style sausages are made year round: *saucisson à l'ail*, or fresh garlic; *boudin noir*, or blood sausage; a pork sausage with wine; and a pure-pork *béarnaise* sausage. And for San Francisco's large Basque comunity, they make a robust Basque sausage.

Though Marcel et Henri pâtés are sold at delicatessens, cheese stores, and restaurants all over the city (including Maison Gourmet delis inside Petrini's markets), the prices are lower here at their own store.

---

## East Bay
## PIG BY THE TAIL

*1512 Shattuck Avenue, Berkeley 94709. Telephone (415) 843-4004. Hours: M 11:30-5:30, T–F 10-6, SAT 10-5:30.*

When Victoria Wise opened Pig by the Tail in 1973, it was the first *charcuterie* in the country. The original chef at Berkeley's famed Chez Panisse restaurant, Victoria found early on she didn't like working nights and so decided to open a daytime food store. Familiar with French *charcuterie* from the years she had lived in Europe and travelled all over the French countryside, she began by opening a French country-style *charcuterie* with just a few basic sausages, pâtés, and cooked meats, but over the years the store has evolved into a city-style *charcuterie* with more salads and prepared dishes.

Victoria has worked hard to develop excellent suppliers for pork and lamb, for caul fat and the blood for her thick *boudin noir*. She uses fresh herbs and has many of the vegetables, such as *haricots verts* (delicate French beans) and the baby cabbages for her stuffed cabbages, specially grown for her in Hayward. The first-rate quality of her ingredients is reflected in the quality of the foods she sells.

Pig by the Tail retains the look and feel of a country *charcuterie* with its wide screen door, gingham curtains, and a simple counter with baguettes stacked in baskets and a tin of home-made *madeleines* near the cash register, but the food sold here is so sophisticated it can only be Parisian. The sausages are all pork based, with natural casings: the classic Toulouse sausage; a winey garlic sausage with red pepper; a delicate *saucisse au champagne*, champagne sausage; and juicy Italian sausages peppery with fennel. Her savory *crépinettes*, wrapped in caul fat, are green with spinach and fresh herbs, and the *boudin blanc* are tender and creamy.

The ready-to-eat sausages include sausages, ready to be eaten cold, are *saucisse á l'ail* (fresh garlic sausage) and an extravagant *poulet en saucisse* (whole boned chicken lined with spinach leaves, stuffed with a ham mousse around a center of asparagus, then rolled up like a sausage and poached in Chinese *loo* sauce. The pâtés include *maison, campagne,* and *poulet;* and there are *galantines de canard* or *de dinde* and velvety mousses (chicken or duck liver puréed with cream, butter, and herbs.).

In addition, Pig by the Tail makes *rillettes*, a rich, pure pork version delicious spread on the fresh-baked baguettes from the Cheese Board next door. And from other producers, there is salami, both *genovese* and *toscana; prosciutto crudo;* and *Bündnerfleisch.* From the sunny kitchen in back comes a rosy prime roast beef, a moist *jambon maison* (baked ham), and a *gigot Provençal* (tender leg of lamb from Victoria's secret source, roasted with garlic and Provençal herbs). You can try any of the meats and pâtés in a sandwich on sweet or sour baguettes.

Salads change seasonally and according to Victoria's whims. They are made using fresh herbs and fresh mayonnaise, and each is sauced differently. You might find broccoli *remoulade;* pickled pigs' feet; a squid, roast beef, or lamb salad; or a familiar Provençal *ratatouille,* a crunchy, celery root *remoulade,* or a salad of tiny French lentils.

Small restaurants in Paris always offer an hors d'oeuvre plate from the *charcuterie* across the street, and French housewives often buy half-pints of several salads and a selection of pâtés to serve as the first course of a formal meal. These are also excellent picnic foods.

Victoria sells Emmaraude red wine vinegar from a big barrel and mustard in large tins from Dijon. At Christmastime, she used to get fresh foie gras from France, but since FDA regulations now require that it be cooked so much it ruins the delicate goose liver, she no longer carries it. But she does sell precious Perigord truffles during their season (November through January). And in the fall and spring, she has locally gathered chanterelles. To replace imported dried *cèpes* and morels, now prohibitively expensive, she sells dried Oriental *shiitake* mushrooms.

For those who like to do their own cooking, Victoria has many hard-to-find supplies. Bakers can buy the same buttery pastry doughs (frozen, in one-pound balls) used to make the quiche and tarts sold on top of the counter: *pâte brisée* (enough for an eleven-inch quiche) and *pâte feuilletée* (puff paste, enough for a cookie sheet–sized tart). The home sausage and pâté maker can buy fatback, caul fat, water-packed sheep or hog sausage casings, and *saindoux* (freshly rendered pork lard). And those ambitious enough to try their hands at *cassoulet* (slowly cooked *flageolet* beans, pork, duck, and sausage) can buy goose fat rendered from the fat of the fresh geese she sells at Christmastime. You can also buy her rich chicken stock or concentrated *demi-glace* (meat glaze)—it's expensive, but two ounces is enough to make a sauce for steak for two.

The prices here are even more Parisian than the food, enough to shock a visiting French gourmand—especially for the pâtés and *terrines*.

# GERMAN

**Sonoma County**
## SONOMA SAUSAGE COMPANY

*411 First Street West, Sonoma 95476. Telephone (707) 938-8200. Hours: M-SAT 9:30–5:30, SUN 1–5:30.*

Herb Hoeser, Jr., had been in the butcher business all his life when he decided two years ago to close down his meat-packing business and go into sausage making. With that in mind, he went to Boëblingen, Germany, to observe and learn sausage-making techniques. He visited master sausage makers and small sausage plants. While there, he met a young German sausage maker and brought him back to Sonoma. When he returned, he designed his efficient sausage-making kitchen after the best he had seen in Germany. The big walk-in refrigerator, filled with hanging pieces of meat and enormous hams, opens onto an immaculate stainless steel work area equipped with big meat saws and grinders.

Now, after just two years, the Sonoma Sausage Company is already making over sixty kinds of sausages—their goal is one hundred. In Germany it's not uncommon for small sausage-makers to have over a hundred sausages in their repertoire.

Almost all the fresh sausages are nitrite free, including the *Weisswurst*, a pale creamy frankfurter like they make in Frankfurt using veal, parsley, and leeks; small baby *Nurnberger* bratwurst rolled in marjoram; the local favorite, North Country sausage lightly smoked with olive wood; *Fleischkase; Schinkenwurst; Kalbsleberwurst*, a velvety calf liverwurst made of veal liver with onions and cream; and a whole belly of bacon stuffed with pork and beef sausage, studded with pistachios.

Their international repertoire includes a British banger with the traditional ground rusk in it, and there is a paprika-stained *linguiça*. There is even a Hawaiian-Portuguese sausage with red hot pepper and white wine, and garlicky hot beer sausages. Backpackers should try the skinny red-and-white pebbled dried blood sausage.

Herb has luscious huge hams with bone in that he gives a maple sugar cure and smokes with alderwood, or with hickory in the winter. And he plans soon to make his own Black Forest- and Westphalian-style hams. At holiday time, he has boned-out turkeys stuffed with sausage meat, and special German Christmas sausages.

### East Bay
### WERK AND SONS

*550 William Street, Oakland 94612. Telephone (415) 832-6562. Hours: M–SAT 9–5:30.*

Located at the William Street storefront that once housed Saag's, Werk and Sons sells some Saag's products, mostly the cured meats, plus their own German-Swiss sausages: *Weisswurst, Nürnberger,* smoked bratwursts, German veal frankfurters, and smoked Polish sausages, plus their own blood sausage, liver paste, and braunschweiger. Their small meat counter sells fresh pork, veal, lamb, and beef. They also carry imported German and Swiss mustards, horseradish, and other foodstuffs, plus authentic dark sourdough rye and fat pretzels from Alameda's Münchner Kindl bakery.

# ITALIAN

### San Francisco
### GLORIA SAUSAGE FACTORY AND DELICATESSEN

*635 Vallejo, San Francisco 94133. Telephone (415) 421-5283. Hours: M–SAT 9–5.*

Started by F. Maggiore, now run by his daughter Alda and her cousin Cy Miravell, Gloria Sausage Factory makes sausages just as it did sixty years ago when F. Maggiore first opened his doors: fresh garlic sausage, a French *boudin noir,* an Italian-style blood sausage dotted with pine nuts and raisins, a hot Italian pork sausage and another sweet with fennel seed, as well as a homemade spicy pepperoni. Their prosciutto and other cold cuts come from the East Coast.

The small but good selection of cheeses includes a wonderful slightly sour and fresh-tasting Teleme, Monterey Jack, and a dry Jack popular with Italians as eating cheese; Italian Fontina, fresh *pecorino romano, reggiano* with some age on it, and a sweet creamy Gorgonzola.

You can buy sweet butter from a big hunk on the counter, three brands of Italian espresso, quart jars of capers, *tonno di Genova* (tuna packed in olive oil), imported *panforte di Siena,* and gallon tins of virgin olive oil. There are some necessary staples like chestnut flour, *cannellini* beans, imported pasta, and Arborio rice.

At the holidays, Gloria's sausage makers used to make Modena's famous specialty, *zampone:* boned pigs' trotters stuffed with pork, pork rind, and traditional spices all ground to a fine paste. There isn't much call for it anymore. It's a great deal of labor and the health department doesn't like it on principle. But Gloria continues to make *zampone's* close cousin *cotechino*. It's the same stuffing as the beloved *zampone* but packed in an ordinary casing. *Cotechino* simmered with golden lentils is the traditional Italian New Year's Eve dish. The round slices of sausage and countless tiny lentils represent coins and will attract wealth in the new year. *Che conta le lenticchie il primo dell'anno, conta soldi tutto l'anno:* "He who counts lentils at the first of the year will count money all year round."

Throughout the season, Gloria prepares special galantines; a boned suckling pig stuffed with their own rosy pork and veal *mortadella*, and a boned-out turkey filled with a spicy pork-and-veal forcemeat punctuated with pistachios.

## San Francisco
## R. IACOPI

*1460 Grant Avenue, San Francisco 94133. Telephone (415) 421-0757. Hours: M–T, TH–SAT 8–6.*

The big windows of R. Iacopi on Grant Avenue in North Beach are strung with knobbly sausages red with pimiento and pepper. Inside, the store is just like a *salumeria* in a small town in northern Italy, complete with green plants on top of the meat counter. Fragrant bundles of fresh rosemary Mr. Iacopi has collected at his mother's farm in Sonoma are hung all over the store. The Iacopi family is from Lucca, and Bruno represents the third generation to run the store. Dating from 1896, Iacopi may be the oldest butcher store in San Francisco. According to Bruno, they make everything exactly as they did years ago, but these days they just don't make as many things.

Two or three mornings a week, they make sausages: the *calabrese* is hot with red pepper and fennel, while the Sicilian sausage tastes sweeter, because it's not *piccante*. The *toscana* sausages

are garlic links seasoned with cloves, nutmeg, and cinnamon. All the sausages are 35 percent beef and veal in the same proportions; the remainder is pork. Only the spicing and grinding differentiates the sausages. The *calabrese* and Sicilian sausages are sold in dried versions, too.

Though there are no more rolls of home-cured *pancetta* (unsmoked bacon), this is the only place in North Beach that cures its own *prosciutto crudo*, the wonderful raw-cured Italian ham. Unfortunately, Mr. Iacopi will only sell it whole, and a prosciutto weighs about fifteen pounds. But wrapped in a cloth and kept in the cool dark, it will keep for months. Sliced paper thin, it's served as an antipasto alone or with ripe melon or fresh figs. Prosciutto is also an important ingredient in pasta sauces and in fillings for plump *tortellini bolognese*. And if you have a whole prosciutto tucked away in the back of your pantry, you'll never again have to agonize over what to bring to a dinner party.

## San Francisco
## ITO CARIANI

*2424 Oakdale Avenue, San Francisco 94124. Telephone (415) 647-0586. Hours: M–F 7–12, 12:30–3:30.*

Ito Cariani is primarily a manufacturer and wholesaler of salami. His spicy pork and beef mixtures are either Genovese style, the most common in this country, or what is known here as *toscana*, a larger, coarse-textured salami. His tiny *salametti* are just right for a solitary picnic.

But Mr. Cariani also sells other delicatessen meats; frankfurters, Polish sausage, *zampone*, head cheese, turkey rolls, roast beef, and bologna. The prices are low, and you needn't buy in bulk.

## JEWISH

**San Francisco**
### GILBERT'S KOSHER STYLE DELI

*2445 Noriega Street, San Francisco 94122. Telephone (415) 566-3032. Hours: M-TH 8-6, F 8-5, SAT 8-6, SUN 8-5.*

This popular Jewish grocery and delicatessen in the Richmond district has a wealth of bagels, bagel twists and breads, and *mandelbreit*, plus cream cheese, belly and nova lox, several kinds of herring, kippered cod, pastrami, corned beef and kosher salami, bologna and liverwurst.

Hot take-out entrées include beef brisket and kasha, stuffed cabbage, and blintzes filled with farmer's cheese.

**San Francisco**
### SHENSON'S DELI

*5045 Geary Boulevard, San Francisco 94188. Telephone (415) 751-4699. Hours: T-SUN 8-5:30.*

Shenson's is another good Jewish delicatessen with a full line of kosher salami, corned beef, pastrami, hot dogs, and other meats, plus Nova Scotia salmon, cream cheese, and delicious herring.

## LATINO

**San Francisco**
### SIMON'S SPANISH MEAT MARKET

*1305 Castro Street, San Francisco 94114. Telephone (415) 647-4170. Hours: 10-8 daily.*

Simon's Spanish Market, on Castro near Twenty-fourth Street, is one of the few neighborhood butcher shops that still make their own sausage. Here, it's a Mexican-style chorizo, sold loose rather than in links, a delicious fatty pork mixture spiked with vinegar, chili, cumin, and lots of garlic. In general, his customers like it spiced mild, but if you want it hot, Simon will make a small batch on request.

## SCANDINAVIAN

**East Bay**
### THE NORDIC HOUSE

*3421 Telegraph Avenue, Oakland 94609. Telephone (415) 653-3882. Hours: M-SAT 9-5.*

There is nothing better to take away winter's chill than Peter Carde's Swedish *potatis korv*, a sausage made of boiled potatoes and pork with lots of sweet onions and seasoned with sage. He also makes *medisterpolse*, a delicate, fresh-tasting Danish pork sausage with a fine texture; a hearty blood pudding; and the Danish-Norwegian *rullepolse*, a sausage roll rich with pork and lamb. Try his homemade liver paste, sold frozen and uncooked: just bake 45 minutes in a 350-degree oven. He also has frankfurters and *falukorv*, a smoked Swedish sausage made of beef and pork.

At Christmas, you will find *uleskinka*, a flavorful Swedish Christmas ham; Danish *flaeskestege*, pork roast with the rind intact; or *fenalaar*, smoked and cured leg of lamb from Norway. Pop them in the oven for a hearty Christmas dinner.

*Note:* For more Scandinavian *charcuterie*, see Affolter Brothers Meats, the Deli Factory, and Scandinavian Deli in the Scandinavian section under Ethnic Markets.

# Cheese

There are hundreds of different kinds of cheese, each with its own taste, but they are all made from one thing: milk—mostly cow's milk, but also sheep, goat, and even water buffalo milk. When rennet, a substance present in the lining of calves' stomachs, is added to fresh milk, it causes the milk solids to clot, separating into curds and watery whey.

Some of the curds are barely pressed and left to drain in loose-woven baskets; others are cooked and poured into molds; some are innoculated with mold and ripened in damp caves.

Many of the cheeses gracing the shelves of your local cheese vendor were made in big factories. Others are still made by shepherds in lonely huts high in the mountains as they have been for centuries.

Cheese is one of the oldest foods known to man. Sheep and goats were being domesticated for their milk over ten thousand years ago, and prehistoric earthenware vases made with holes for draining the curds have been discovered in Switzerland. The ancient Athenian army lived on a diet of honey and milk and cheese. The Romans made all kinds of cheeses: creamed cheeses; fresh cheeses; hard cheeses; cheeses flavored with nuts, garlic, or pepper; and salted cheeses. Their monumental Luna cheeses, bearing a stamp of the moon, were made in wheels of one thousand pounds.

Many of the cheeses we enjoy today have old pedigrees: the Romans found Roquefort when they invaded what is now southern France, and Cheshire when they reached Britain. Gorgonzola, Italy's creamy blue cheese, dates from the ninth century. English farmhouse Cheddars have been made since the Middle Ages. Parmesan has been made since the thirteenth century, and *feta*, the salted sheep's milk cheese from Greece, is probably older than all of them.

The forms, textures, and colors of cheeses are a continual delight: miniature ash-covered pyramids; small piglets and horses shaped from *provolone*; rounds of *tomme au raisin* covered with a skin of grape pulp and pips; Corsican *brin d'Amour* shaggy with its coating of wild aromatic herbs; giant wheels of Swiss Emmentaler riddled with holes; the blue-veined magnificence of English Stilton mimicking Renaissance marble; flat rounds of ripe oozing Bries and Camemberts; dried-up little *crottins* (strong French goat cheeses); buttery yellow Cheddars; crumbly white slabs of Bulgarian *feta* in brine; and *treccie*, braids of *mozzarella di bufala* swimming in milk.

To learn about cheese, find a good shop and become a regular customer. Taste everything you're going to buy and a few things you might want to buy the next time you visit the store. All that cheese experience will soon accumulate. After a while you'll notice the differences in cheeses from different suppliers, the taste of each cheese at various stages of ripeness, and even the differences in cheeses through the seasons as the milk grows richer in spring and thins out in winter.

A cheese book is a good investment, too. There are several very good recently published pocket guides to cheese. Some cheese stores also hold periodic classes in cheese or the art of matching cheeses with wines (see Cheese Classes at the end of this chapter).

Some of the sources listed here are wholesale. They will sell to the public (usually with a minimum order) and, in general, you must buy the cheese uncut, just as it comes from its maker. Most wholesalers have a printed list of the weights and sizes of the cheeses they sell.

Note: For other cheese sources, see Gourmet Markets and the ethnic sections.

# —RETAIL CHEESE—

## San Francisco
## RAUL BARRAZA
## "B" PRODUCTOS MEXICANOS

*2840 Mission Street, San Francisco 94110. Telephone (415) 824-4474. Hours: M-SAT 8:30–5.*

Raul Barraza sells Latino foods, including a wide selection of chilies. But his chief glory is an assortment of cheeses: *chontaleño*, used for *quesadillas* and beans; *capulín*, which is somewhat like *feta* and delicious inside *pupusas* (fried Salvadoran *masa* rounds); *patacón*, a cousin of *capulín*, named after *patacónes* or Spanish gold coins.

## East Bay
## THE CHEESE BOARD

*1504 Shattuck Avenue, Berkeley 94709. Telephone (415) 549-3183. Hours: T-SAT 10–6.*

The Cheese Board is a worker-owned collective in the East Bay. Open almost fifteen years now, the store on Shattuck Avenue near Walnut Square is always busy. Take a number right away, and then you can read the notices on new cheeses, articles on cheeses, and community information on the wall. Sometimes the service is not as "efficient" as it could be; it does take time to give tastes, advice, and information about cheese. But the Cheese Board members behind the counter really know their business. Each of them has worked in all its aspects: ordering, storing, cutting, baking, accounting. And they can describe the cheeses as if they were friends of the family.

The store sells over three hundred kinds of domestic and imported cheeses, and they keep them all with the care of any generations-old *fromagerie* in France. If you ask for Brie or Camembert,

you'll get it *à point* if you're serving it right away, a little less ripe if you'll be keeping it some days before serving it. (Try the wonderful small goat cheese Camemberts.)

Watch one of the cheese workers evaluate the cheeses: they have great patience in offering tastes—even comparisons of two different kinds or wheels of the same cheese—sometimes to the impatience of people waiting in line. Many of the Cheese Board members have logged in fifteen years of working with cheese, and they still love it.

The Cheese Board has a special love for Italian cheeses: rich and subtle Fontina Val d'Aosta, pungent blue-veined Gorgonzolas, sharp *pecorino romano*, and peppery Sicilian *pepato*. When the shipment comes in, they have *mozzarella di bufala, mascarpone,* and sometimes *stracchino*. Their locally made fresh ricotta is superior to commercial brands, closest to *ricotta romana*. They also have several kinds of *torta*; one of the best is *torta con basilico*, Gorgonzola layered with fresh basil and creamy pine nuts.

Another favorite is the Corsican *brin d'amour*, a handmade sheep's milk cheese coated with wild herbs and juniper berries.

The Cheese Board is also one of the few cheese stores to have Laura Chenel's French-style fresh goat cheeses, made in the Napa Valley.

Every day the Cheese Board bakes marvelous breads, robust enough to match their full-flavored cheeses (see Bread section).

**San Francisco**
## THE CHEESE COMPANY

*3893 Twenty-fourth Street, San Francisco 94132. Telephone (415) 285-2254. Hours: M–F 10–7, SAT 10–6, SUN 12–5.*

Noe Valley's source for good cheese is the Cheese Company on Twenty-fourth Street. This straightforward store has all the classic cheeses you'd expect to find in a discriminating store, plus wonderful delicacies such as French *lou peralou*, a creamy sheep's milk Brie, or *fourgerou*, a small raw-milk Brie. Italian cheesemakers tempt you with the small *bourino*, a mozzarella with a center of butter; and fresh *mozzarella di bufala*, *mascarpone*, and raw-milk Taleggio.

The store also has huge twelve-pound loaves of Jewish-style rye bread flown in from Chicago; imported *grissini torinese*, breadsticks from Turin; and small rounds of imported Scotch shortbread, tied with a plaid ribbon.

Try the Anderson Valley vinegar, made by Edmeades vineyard. Produced by a *solera* system, the vinegar is made in sixty-gallon French barrels.

Announcements of the store's weekly formal wine tastings are posted.

**San Francisco**
## THE CHEESE SHOP

*1526 California Street, San Francisco 94109. Telephone (415) 771-5311. Hours: M–F 10:30–6:30, SAT 10–6, SUN 12–6.*

Betsy Carter and her brother Kendall Brautigan are the fifth generation of their family to work as cheese merchants. The family also has cheese stores on the East Coast.

Ask Betsy about any of the many domestic and imported cheeses. She'll recount the history of English Derby (try it in the wine and sage versions, too), Welsh Caerphilly, double Gloucester, blue Cheshire, and Stilton.

Sometimes you can find raw-milk Monterey Jack or a raw mild Cheddar from Vermont.

Choose your *assiette de fromage* from their many French cheeses. And for Italian cooking, they have *reggiano*, aged *asiago*, sheep's milk *romano*, *grana padano*, *fontina*, and Gorgonzola.

For your baking, there is fresh pot cheese, sweet butter, and fresh cream cheese.

At holidays, there is an even bigger selection of French cheeses, especially the rich double and triple *crèmes*.

**San Francisco**
## CRANE AND KELLEY
## FINE WINE AND CHEESE

*2111 Union Street, San Francisco 94123. Telephone (415) 563-3606. Hours: M–F 10–6:30, SAT 10–6, SUN 11–6.*

This small Union Street shop has a large selection of French cheeses including blues and Saingorlon, the French Gorgonzola. The *chèvres* include a Provençal with herbs, pungent *crottins*, and lovely fresh goat cheeses. French Comté and Swiss Gruyère are purchased whole and then aged by the proprietors.

Cheeses from all the Italian regions are represented, including *reggiano*, *ricotto pecorino*, Fontina Val d'Aosta, provolone, domestic *asiago*, and, occasionally, fresh *mascarpone* and Taleggio from Lombardy.

The Mid-East provides *feta*, *kasseri*, and Kalamata olives.

Someone has gone crazy ordering mustards, dozens and dozens of them, including a "military" mustard made

in Wales. You can also find special items like sweet butter, varietal grape jellies, pâtés from Marcel et Henri, and chocolate truffles.

Watch for special tastings. They've done a mustard tasting with pretzels, and an olive tasting. Wines can be sampled at the small wine bar, where such eclectic tastings as Stilton with walnuts and port, or oysters and Dom Perignon, sometimes take place.

### East Bay
## CURDS AND WHEY

*6311 College Avenue, Oakland 94618. Telephone (415) 652-6311. Hours: M–SAT 10–6:30.*

Once isolated in the middle of a block of College Avenue, near Alcatraz Avenue in north Oakland, Curds and Whey is now the center of a remarkable food shopping area that includes a French bakery, a good butcher, a poultry man, and a produce market. Originally a cheese store, over the years the cheese seems to have taken second place to a stock of gourmet groceries, an adjoining wine section, and a *charcuterie* and catering business. It's still the best source in the neighborhood for good eating cheeses. In fact, sometimes it's a pleasure to shop there because the selection isn't overwhelming. You can look right in the case and see for yourself: *crème fraîche*, baker's cheese, pot cheese.

Then shop for fine mustards, vinegars, and olive oils; Eduardo's local dried egg pasta; Parisian baguettes, both sweet and sour; fresh Malossol caviar; Armenian cracker bread; and a splendid array of local and imported jams and preserves.

They have California-grown olives direct from the grower. A policy of buying some items in bulk, then repacking and selling them, means good buys for such items as Guittard bittersweet chocolate, Dutch-process cocoa, nuts, semolina flour, wild rice, dried mushrooms from Chile and California, and fruity green California olive oil. They make their own flavored vinegars: blueberry, raspberry, cherry, and spice, plus basil and rosemary.

### San Francisco
## DOMINGUEZ BAKERY

*2953 Twenty-fourth Street, San Francisco 94132. Telephone (415) 824-6849. Hours: 9 am–11 pm daily.*

In the Mission, Domínguez: Flor de Jalisco has a good selection of slightly salty fresh cheeses made from curds at various stages of aging; there are also Central American and Mexican cheeses as well as a luscious *crema fresca*, a delicious accompaniment to golden-fried slices of plantain.

### Contra Costa
## FERRANTE CHEESE COMPANY

*1607 Palos Verde Mall, Walnut Creek 94596. Telephone (415) 945-1583. Hours: M–F 10–4; may also open on weekends.*

Vicenzo Ferrante, a native of Sicily, used to make his own fresh ricotta and fresh whole-milk mozzarella-type cheese for use at Mondello's, the family's Italian restaurant in Moraga. When he had extra, he would sell it to his customers to take home for their own cooking. The cheese was such a success that now Vicenzo and his son Roberto are starting their own cheese factory in Walnut Creek. Their excellent mozzarella, made from whole raw cow's milk, as is most mozzarella-type cheese made and sold in Italy under the name *fior di latte*, is also available at the Cheese Board in Berkeley.

**East Bay**
## THE LAKE MERRITT WINE AND CHEESE REVIVAL

*552 Grand Avenue, Oakland 94610. Telephone (415) 836-3306. Hours: M–F 10:30–8:30, SAT 10:30–6.*

This Oakland store has a shrewd selection of domestic and imported cheeses, crackers, olives, and condiments. The wine section features wines from small California wineries, and a tasting bar. The restaurant-café at the front serves hot entrées, salads, and cheese boards.

**East Bay**
## MADE TO ORDER

*1576 Hopkins Street, Berkeley 94707. Telephone (415) 524-7552. Hours: M–SAT 10–6.*

Sylvana La Rocca and Linda Briganti, owners of Made to Order, a delicatessen with an Italian emphasis, make a light fresh cheese they call *formaggio fresco*, as well as their own *crème fraîche* and fresh-churned butters. They stock a selection of interesting imported Italian cheeses, too.

**San Jose Area**
## THE MILK PAIL

*2585 California Street, Mountain View 94040. Telephone (415) 941-2505. Hours: M–F 10–8, SAT 10–7, SUN 11–6.*

The Milk Pail has close to one hundred domestic cheeses on hand, including fresh cheeses from raw milk, plus grains and legumes, dried fruits, and nuts. Cheese bought in bulk gets a 10 to 15 percent discount, and almost any cheese can be special ordered.

**Napa Valley**
## ST. HELENA CHEESE FACTORY

*V. Sattui Winery, White Lane, St. Helena 94574. Telephone (707) 963-7774. Hours: 9:30–5:30 daily.*

Built in 1885, V. Sattui Winery houses a cheese shop on the ground floor where you can purchase a selection of cheeses from all over the world. Prices are by the pound. Sample some of your purchases with any of the eight different wines made by the winery and available for tasting here.

**San Francisco**
## SAY CHEESE

*856 Cole Street, San Francisco 94117. Telephone (415) 665-5020. Hours: M–F 10–7, SAT 10–6.*

Owners Bob Wiskotzil and George Kovatch opened their cheese store extraordinaire, Say Cheese, in 1976, where if you say it, they can weigh out an astonishing variety of cheeses. What they haven't got, no matter how esoteric, they can get for you if it's available at all in this country.

They'll cut you a taste of handmade English farm Cheddar from a sixty-pound wheel, or some Cheshire cheese, a type that's been made in England since Roman times. They've got creamy Wesleydale, Leicester for Welsh rabbit, and royal Stilton, England's superb blue cheese. From Switzerland, try the *vacherin mont d'or*, a winter cheese made with extra-rich milk and cured in pine bark.

The French cheese selection is fat with rich *triple crèmes*, fresh and aged *chèvres*, nutty French Gruyères, and prized Roqueforts. The *gratte paille*, a faintly salty *triple crème* from the Ile de France, and the *lou peralou*, a melting rich ewe's milk Brie from the southwest, are cheeses you might have only tasted in France until recently.

The partners are both avid fans of Italian cheeses and receive a shipment every few weeks of specialty cheeses like Lombardy's *stracchino*, fragile ivory *mascarpone*, or *toma di Carmagnola*. Their provolone is made by Auricchio, a Cremonese firm now making it in Wisconsin, and the *reggiano* here is aged at least two years. The *scamorze*, a kind of dried mozzarella, is delicious grilled as they do it in Rome.

As for *chèvres*, the selection is exceptional, including a goat cream cheese from Israel. Don't tmiss your chance to try some of Laura Chenel's local goat cheese—here they have even the hard-to-get heart-shaped ones.

Say Cheese also has all the makings for a hearty Swiss *raclette* meal: the cheese itself, tiny boiled onions, boiled potatoes, French gherkins, and sliced ham. They'll even rent you a *raclette* machine for a small fee.

But Say Cheese has a lot more than cheese: unsalted goat butter from Deux Sevres, slightly salty Danish butter, sweet Normandy butter, their own *crème fraîche*, and crusty baguettes, plus a gourmand's stash of luxurious items like imported mustards, *extra-vergine* olive oil, aged vinegars, fresh green peppercorns, pink peppercorns, Madagascar vanilla beans, exquisite paprikas, baking chocolates, candied violets and angelica, crystallized stem ginger. In the fall there are fresh imported truffles, smoked pheasant, and fresh sauerkraut; year round there are dried French *cèpes* and Italian *porcini* mushrooms. Lavish your table with American sturgeon caviar, fruits in alcohol from Provence, and truffle pastes. Bring a big shopping basket. Besides all that, they have pâtés and galantines

from local and East Coast suppliers, slab bacons including a double-smoked Irish-style bacon, sausages from local *charcutiers*, and George Kovatch's home-made chopped chicken liver made with his own rendered chicken fat *(schmaltz)*.

The store's newsletter keeps customers abreast of new cheeses and gourmet items.

## Sonoma County
## SONOMA CHEESE FACTORY

*2 West Spain Street, Sonoma 95476. Telephone (707) 938-5225. Hours: 9-6 daily.*

Established in 1931 by Celso Viviani and now situated on Sonoma's historic plaza, the Sonoma Cheese Factory is still making Sonoma Jack with the same recipe the Viviani family used to make the first wheels of it over fifty years ago. A natural cheese, it is made from the milk of the dairy herds that graze in the Sonoma Valley.

At the back of the large, rather touristy cheese store carrying over one hundred varieties of cheese, you can look through a big window and watch the cheese being made in huge stainless steel troughs. You can also taste the delicious Sonoma Jack made here, in all its variations. Try the version with hot green chili or with caraway.

*Mail order catalog. Tours available.*

## Sonoma County
## VELLA CHEESE COMPANY

*315 Second Street East, Sonoma 95476. Telephone (707) 938-3232. Hours: 9-6, SUN 10-5.*

When Joe Vella arrived in San Francisco from Italy in 1916, he sold butter, eggs, and cheese. After he learned the business and accumulated some capital, he opened his own business in Sonoma in 1931. Since that time, Vella Cheese Company has been making and selling excellent Monterey Jack cheese to wine country residents.

The store is very plain, just a business-like counter with colorful children's drawings of Vella Cheese tacked to the walls. Any day visitors can come and watch the whole cheesemaking process. The curds are generally ready from noon on throughout the day. In addition to the Monterey Jack, sold both fresh and in a nuttier dry version popular with local Italians, they produce a sharper Cheddar-type cheese and sell a blue, a *feta*, and a Swiss-type cheese. The Jack also comes in blocks flavored with *jalapeño* or caraway.

Though Vella Cheese Company is happy to sell you cheese by the pound, uncut wheels or blocks are sold at lower prices.

*Mail order: P.O. Box 191, Sonoma 95476.*

## Peninsula
## VILLAGE CHEESE HOUSE

*157 Town and Country Village, Palo Alto 94303. Telephone (415) 326-9251. Hours: M–SAT 9–5:30.*

Village Cheese House has domestic and imported cheeses, plus gourmet groceries such as fresh *filo* dough, Greek olives, green peppercorns, and imported olive and walnut oils, as well as a selection of cold cuts, prosciutto, and Marcel et Henri pâtés.

## Contra Costa
## WALNUT CREEK WINE AND CHEESE COMPANY

*1522 North Main Street, Walnut Creek 94596. Telephone (415) 935-7780. Hours: M–SAT 10–7.*

The Walnut Creek Wine and Cheese Company tries to obtain the best cheeses imported to this country. Every year there are new types imported for the first time and available in limited quantities. We've recently seen the introduction of English farmhouse cheeses still made by old-fashioned methods. WCWCC has English farmhouse Cheddar, Cheshire, rare blue-veined Cheshire, and crumbly Lancashire, plus an excellent Stilton.

From Italy, they have authentic Fontina Val d'Aosta with its characteristic rich nutty taste, delicate satiny *stracchino*, seductively rich *mascarpone*, and a raw milk Taleggio. Splurge on the wonderful *torta*, *mascarpone* layered with creamy blue Gorgonzola.

They also carry French Brie, Camembert, Roquefort, *chèvres*, soft-ripening cheeses, and *double* and *triple crèmes*; domestic Jack, *asiago*, Cheddar, blue, and classic cheeses from the rest of the world.

Lunches are served daily in the store's indoor-outdoor café. There is a wine and cheese hour every day from 4 to 7, when you can taste wine by the glass with either a cheese or a pâté board.

## San Francisco
## THE WINE AND CHEESE CENTER

*205 Jackson Street, San Francisco 94111. Telephone (415) 956-2518. Hours: M–F 9:30–6:30, SAT 11–6.*

The Wine and Cheese Center is strategically located between the financial district and North Beach. One of the best-stocked cheese stores in the city, it is owned by Helen and Dick Allen, who learned their cheeses by touring *fromageries* in Camembert, Pont l'Eveque, and Normandy, working with Brie *affineurs* in Paris and with Emmentaler makers in Switzerland. Almost ten years in the cheese business has taught them quite a bit more.

Everything in the recently remodeled store is well labeled and accessible, and the clerks are informed and interested. Business people on their lunch hour can buy a small piece of *pre clos* or the exquisite *brin d'amour*, a Corsican sheep's milk cheese cured in wild aromatic herbs, along with a few crackers and retire to the back room called the Wine Mine. Here you can taste wines with your cheese.

Helen Allen has a special interest in French raw-milk cheeses, *triple crèmes*, and other fragile French cheeses. When she can get them, she has true *Normand* Camemberts and both fresh and aged *chèvres*.

The store has arranged to ship a special Gruyère from the Swiss Canton de Vaud, and a wonderful Emmentaler made by Herr Karl Gerbe in the town of Lutzelfluh. He makes only one of these cheeses a day throughout ten months of the year, using unpasteurized milk. Pasta makers should try the *sbrinz*, a Swiss cow's milk grating cheese similar to *grana padano*.

And from Italy they have *parmigiano reggiano* from a consortium of producers in the delimited zone, Taleggio di Monte, and very good Gorgonzola. Fresh *mozzarella di bufala*, *mascarpone*, and *tortas* made of layered cheeses are flown in from Milano.

In addition to cheeses, they have a selection of coffees roasted at Starbucks in Seattle, including Ethiopian Mocha Harrar, Mexico Pluma Oaxaca, espresso, and a decaffeinated dark roast. Special groceries include premium olive oils from selected Italian estates as well as oils from Spain, France, and California; fresh Beluga caviar; golden whitefish roe packed locally by the Engstroms at California Sunshine in Sacramento; a selection of *charcuterie* and cured meats including Black Forest ham, prosciutto, *coppa*, and spicy Calabrian-style *soppressata;* plus a selection of fresh-made salads.

Seasonally the store has fresh black truffles and fresh foie gras.

**San Francisco/Marin County**
## THE WINE AND FOOD SHOP

*254 West Portal Avenue, San Francisco 94127. Telephone (415) 731-3062. Hours: M-F 10-6:30, SAT 10-6.*
*1807 Larkspur Landing Circle, Larkspur 94939. Telephone (415) 461-5800. Hours: M-TH and SAT 10-6, F 10-9, SUN 12-5.*

The Wine and Food Shop has domestic and imported cheeses and a selection of gourmet groceries and fine wines.

# WHOLESALE CHEESE

Some of the following stores will sell wholesale to the trade only; others will sell to retail customers who buy a certain miminum amount of cheese. See individual listings.

**Sonoma County**
## CALIFORNIA CHEVRE

*Laura Chenel, 1550 Ridley, Santa Rosa 95401. Telephone (707) 575-8888. Wholesale to the trade only.*

When she moved to the Napa Valley, part of Laura Chenel's idea of living in the country was to keep a few goats. She had always liked their affectionate, sensitive natures. She'd been living in the country and raising goats for around seven years when someone introduced her to French goat cheese. She loved it and immediately set to work researching methods of making goat cheeses, or *chèvres*, with her own goat's milk. There wasn't much information available. She wrote to the author of the one book she could find on making French goat cheeses (in French) and told him she'd like to come to France to learn cheesemaking. He arranged for her to live with several families who made *chèvres* in different regions of France.

After a wonderful four-month apprenticeship with these generous families, she returned home armed with enough practical knowledge to make her dream work.

From the very beginning, Laura has had more buyers than she has had cheese. Her marvelous goat cheeses are served at Chez Panisse restaurant in Berkeley and sold in the city's best cheese stores in limited quantities. Her recent move into a small cheese factory in Santa Rosa will soon make the cheese more widely available, though there are no retail sales at the factory.

She makes six different *chèvres*: the ash-covered *pyramide*; Chabichou; a small *crottin*, and three flat disc-shaped cheeses, one rolled in herbs, another in crushed peppercorns, and a third in bright paprika; as well as a snowy, perfectly plain disc of fresh *chèvre*.

Though she loves aged goat cheese she sends all of these out fresh, because she doesn't have the space to age them herself. But they can be kept unwrapped in a basement or cellar or wrapped in plastic wrap and stored in the refrigerator for some weeks. Check them from time to time and eat them at the stage of ripeness you prefer.

Just as the taste of goat cheese changes as it ages, the fresh cheese has a different flavor in different seasons. Laura explains that in spring the goat's milk is fresh and very creamy, and as summer progresses, the milk becomes more watery. Then in the fall, the milk becomes creamier again, with a pronounced strong flavor.

Her cheeses are available at several cheese stores and gourmet groceries, including the Oakville Grocery, the Wine and Cheese Center, Narsai's Market, the Cheese Board, Curds and Whey, Truffles, and Let's Eat.

---

### East Bay
## THE DISCERNING MOUSE

*P.O. Box 641, Berkeley 94701. Telephone (415) 658-6920.*

The Discerning Mouse distributes both domestic and imported cheeses, but you must buy them in full wheels or bricks. Domestic cheeses include regular and white New York sharp Cheddar; Oregon and Treasure Cave blue cheeses; Monterey Jack and dry Jack; five kinds of raw milk cheeses; *kasseri*; aged *asiago*; ricotta and farmer's cheese. Imported cheeses include Danish Havarti and *feta*, Finnish Lappi, aged Canadian white Cheddar, Austrian Gruyère, French Roquefort, Swiss *raclette* and Gruyère plus Dutch Edam and Gouda.

Any domestic or imported cheeses not listed in the catalog are usually available on request.

---

### East Bay
## IMPERIAL PACKERS

*214 Madison Street, Oakland 94607. Telephone (415) 835-2364. Hours: M–F 9–5.*

To take advantage of Imperial Packers' wholesale prices, you must order a day in advance and order a minimum of $50 worth of cheeses. But these days $50 isn't all that much cheese. And grating cheeses improve with aging; others do just fine properly wrapped and stored in the refrigerator for a month or two. Be clear about what you want. Mr. Imperial services both restaurant and cheese shops with local Jack, New York Cheddars, Greek *kasseri*, Danish *feta*, Italian *fontina*, French Brie, Finnish Lappi, and a host of other cheeses from around the world.

## Marin County
## MARIN FRENCH CHEESE COMPANY

*7500 Red Hill Road, Petaluma 94952. Telephone (707) 762-6001. Hours: 9–5 daily.*

The Marin French Cheese Company has a long history: the same family has owned it since its modest beginnings in 1865. The company now produces over 500,000 pounds of French-style cheeses a year under their Red and Black label: a "Camembert," a "Brie," and a breakfast cheese made from a firm bland curd.

Tours of the cheese factory are given every half hour daily.

Special buys on odd-weight rounds of soft cheese are available at the factory. A small lake surrounded by a picnic area makes this a good spot for a warm-weather outing.

# — CHEESE CLASSES —

## San Francisco
## SAY CHEESE

*856 Cole Street, San Francisco 94117. Telephone (415) 665-5020. When: Sporadically, usually on Wednesday evenings.*

Bob Wiskotzil and George Kovatch, owners of Say Cheese and authors of the *Chronicle's* cheese column, periodically offer cheese classes explaining the classifications of cheeses, how they are made, how to recognize them, and how to buy them.

Watch for their "Wine and Cheese Comparison" evenings, too. Which wines should be served with which cheeses is not at all self-evident. Even seasoned chefs are hard put to suggest a wine for a specific cheese or vice versa. The only combination that seems to be relatively undisputed is that of port with Stilton. This class gives you a chance to taste and compare for yourself.

## San Francisco
## THE WINE AND CHEESE CENTER

*205 Jackson Street, San Francisco 94111. Telephone (415) 956-2518. When: Evenings; call store for schedule.*

San Francisco's Wine and Cheese Center offers an evening cheese class. The four consecutive lecture tastings introduce the great families of cheese and discuss methods of manufacture and ripening, standards of excellence, and the use and care of cheeses. Learn about Swiss, Danish, Norwegian, Dutch, Italian, and French cheeses, as well as blue cheeses, English farmhouse cheeses, fresh cheeses, goat cheeses, and grating cheeses.

The class is taught by Helen Allen, who, with her husband Dick, owns the store and has been importing and marketing cheese for over ten years.

## San Francisco
## THE WINE AND FOOD SHOP

*254 West Portal Avenue, San Francisco 94127. Telephone (415) 731-3062. When: Evenings; call for schedule.*

The Wine and Food Shop gives a cheese class taught by the store's staff.

# Chocolate & Sweets

Good health

When Cortez arrived in Mexico in 1519, Montezuma presented him with his first taste of chocolate from a bowl of pure gold. *Chocolatl,* as prepared at the Aztec court from a paste of pounded cocoa bean, was a dark bitter beverage, and for the Spanish explorer, something of an acquired taste.

Naturally, the Spanish sent this exotic discovery back to Spain, where it quickly gained a reputation as an aphrodisiac. But no one much liked its flavor until one inventive Spaniard mixed the bitter paste with sugar and milk. The hot drink immediately appealed to the gentry's sweet tooth, and hundreds of fashionable chocolate-drinking establishments sprang up all over the country. For well over a century the Spanish managed to keep the secret of making chocolate to themselves before the rest of Europe discovered it. Then the French began making velvety dark-chocolate bars. Adding their rich milk to the bar, the Swiss created the milk chocolate for which they are still famous.

In America, it was James Baker who opened our first chocolate factory on the East Coast, but it wasn't until around 1800 that chocolate was generally used in baking. Today cooks can choose from several kinds of chocolates made for specific purposes.

*Note:* This chapter also contains sources for some ethnic sweets.

## CHOCOLATE

**Bitter chocolate** Also referred to as unsweetened or baking chocolate; made without sugar.

**Bittersweet** Has some sugar, but much less than semisweet chocolate.

**Semisweet** Has added sugar and cocoa butter and is sold both as bars and as drops or bits. It is both an eating chocolate and a baking ingredient.

**Milk chocolate** The most common form of eating chocolate. It is also sometimes used in baking.

**Cocoa powder** What remains when most of the cocoa butter is removed from the chocolate liquor. Used to make chocolate drinks and in baking.

**Dutch process** Cocoa powder that has been treated with alkali to neutralize the natural acids.

**White chocolate** Actually not chocolate at all. Though it is usually made from vegetable fats, coloring, and flavorings, it is sometimes made with cocoa butter.

**Couverture** Fine coating chocolate with a higher cocoa butter content than most cooking chocolates. Professional bakers use it for chocolate glazes because it flows easily and dries to a glossy finish. It can also be used in baking.

## San Francisco
# THE CANDY JAR

*210 Grant Avenue, San Francisco 94108. Telephone (415) 391-5508. Hours: M–SAT 9:30–5:30.*

The Candy Jar on Grant Avenue is a charming miniscule shop filled with handmade chocolates from European *chocolatiers,* fine glacéed fruits, bright hard candies, and freshly made chocolate truffles displayed in shiny silver bowls.

Maria Stacho spent one whole year experimenting with and perfecting her basic truffle recipe, and is still adding new truffles to her already considerable repertoire. She makes them dark, with light and dark fillings; others are striped with white chocolate or dipped half and half. Some are filled with haunting fruit-flavored creams, others with nuts and liqueurs. Try the Grand Marnier truffle with its unctuous chocolate center steeped in orange and enclosed in a dark-chocolate shell, or the dark coffee truffle, or the hazelnut truffle...

At the holidays, she makes the Hungarian Christmas cake she ate as a child in Budapest. Her *ludlab* ("goose leg") cake is a low, dark-chocolate cake filled with her own cherries soaked three months in rum, and a rich chocolate cream, and covered with a silt of dark cocoa. For Christmas stockings, there are chocolate bears and soldiers and little disks of assorted fresh chocolates sold by the pound.

*Mail order.*

## San Francisco/East Bay
# COCOLAT

*3324 Steiner Street, San Francisco 94123. Telephone (415) 567-9957. Hours: T–SAT 10:30–6:30, SUN 12–5.*
*1481 Shattuck Avenue, Berkeley 94709. Telephone (415) 843-3265. Hours: M–SAT 10–6, SUN 11–5.*
*3945 Piedmont Avenue, Oakland 94611. Telephone (415) 653-3676. Hours: T–SAT 10–6.*

When Alice Medrich's Paris landlady, Madame Lastelle, gave her a recipe for home-style chocolate truffles, she couldn't have envisioned the prospering three-store truffle empire that would grow from such a modest beginning. Back home in Berkeley Alice experimented with American ingredients until she got the recipe right, then she approached the then newly opened *charcuterie* Pig by the Tail to see if they'd like to sell her truffles. They ordered thirty-six dozen right away, then more and more. The rest is truffle history. Now there are three of Alice's Cocolat stores, a thriving mail order business, and a veritable truffle-making factory.

The home-style truffles are a mix of chocolate, sweet butter, nuts, and a liqueur such as cognac or rum. Shaped by hand, they are then rolled in unsweetened dark cocoa. Their irregular shape is meant to imitate that of the famous black truffles of Perigord. Other types are dipped in dark or white chocolates. Her best sellers are the large rum-drenched truffle and a smaller bittersweet truffle *maison* available every day along with a rotating selection of a half dozen other truffles from her full repertoire of almost thirty: blanc de blanc, dark on dark, brandy, mint, hazelnut, Grand Marnier, chestnut, Kahlúa, Brazil nut, framboise, pistachio.

## San Francisco
# FINDLEY'S FABULOUS FUDGE

*1035 Geary Street, San Francisco 94109. Telephone (415) 673-6655. Hours: M–F 10–6, SAT 11–5.*

Since 1963, Lorraine Findley of Findley's Fabulous Fudge has been luring passers-by off the street and out of the matinee movie lines with the irresistible smell of deep, dark, chocolaty fudge cooking.

The fudge here truly is fabulous, made in small twenty-five-pound batches. Each batch is watched carefully throughout its long slow cooking until Lorraine and the fudge cook, Eddy, declare it done. Then they pour the hot fudge out onto a table and work it by hand until it's cool enough to be formed into large slabs. When completely cool, the freshly made fudge is then sold at a brisk pace by the pound up front.

If it's your first visit to Findley's, the thing to do is to buy one of the bags with a piece of each of the twelve fudges made here.

The Walnut Harvest is the classic: deep, dark, and creamy, and loaded with big walnut pieces; Chicago Cream Supreme has no walnuts to interrupt its velvety texture. Almond Offering replaces the walnuts with almonds, and the peppermint chip is riddled with delicious mint candies. Don't miss the Rum du Café, spiked with rum and dark coffee, or the Royal Family, a milk-chocolate fudge with a slight mocha edge.

Then there are the non-chocolate fudges: County Fair, a divinity fudge flavored with walnuts and orange peel; the green Irish Isle, studded with walnuts and pistachios; the Strawberry Rose, a strawberry fudge; and the Grand Penuche, a buttered-sugar fudge.

*Mail order. Send a self-addressed stamped envelope for brochure.*

## San Francisco
# KRÖN CHOCOLATIER

*349 Geary Street, San Francisco 94102. Telephone (415) 421-5766. Hours: M–SAT 9–5:30.*

The San Francisco store of New York's Krön chocolates is just two years old. The Krön family emigrated to this country from Hungary in 1956, where they had been in the fine chocolate and confectionery business for several generations.

Krön chocolates are made by hand from traditional European recipes. They include chocolate-covered Hungarian-style prunes and apricots or imported brandied dark cherries; wonderful chocolate-coated logs of pure almond paste or a mixture of ground apricot, prunes, and raisins with almonds; and macadamia nuts dipped in chocolate. Truffles are made right at the San Francisco store where they also hand dip seasonal fruit—oranges, strawberries, pineapple, green grapes—in chocolate.

Krön carries the hundreds-of-years-old European tradition of molded chocolates into the last quarter of the twentieth century with such *csokoládé formak,* or "shapes in chocolate," as golf balls, tennis rackets, a magnum-sized champagne bottle, a life-sized female leg with a ribbon garter—even a ruler of chocolate presented in an old-fashioned sliding-top box and a chocolate long-playing record. Buy your milk chocolate as letters of the alphabet and spell out words with them.

For those who like their chocolate straight, they have one-pound bricks of plain milk, dark, or white chocolate, or either milk or dark chocolate studded with cashews or macadamia nuts.

*Mail order. Ask for rate schedule.*

## San Francisco
## LA CABAÑA

*2929 Sixteenth Street, near Mission, San Francisco 94103. Telephone (415) 861-0434. Hours: M–SAT 8–7:30.*

An unexpected pleasure, this small store has the best selection of home-made Latin American candy in the Mission. Handmade *melcocha* (taffy), *alfajores* (coconut candy), *rosquillas* (a milk candy with coconut), *jamoncillo* (fried milk), and *calabaza enmelada* (honeyed pumpkin). Very sweet, very satisfying, these candies are a traditional Latino way to end a meal.

## San Francisco
## MEE ON COMPANY

*812 Washington Street, San Francisco 94111. Telephone (415) 982-4456. Hours: 10:30–10 daily.*

Mee On Company is both a liquor store and a candy store. In its center, the display of all kinds of dried and candied fruit covers two tables: melon, ginger, pineapple, wheels of candied lotus fruit, and mouth-puckering dried plum, as well as shriveled dried olives.

## Marin County
## MOREAU CHOCOLATS

*Sarky's Square, 1207 Bridgeway, Sausalito 94956. Telephone (415) 332-4621. Hours: M–F 9–5, SAT 11–5.*

Swiss chocolates, famous the world over, are made today by mostly industrial methods with few exceptions. Moreau Chocolats are made by hand in the village of La Chaux-de-Fonds, where the small family-owned factory has a hundred years of experience in making fine chocolates. Made from a mixture of Venezuelan, Guatemalan, and Brazilian cocoa beans; cocoa butter; pure Swiss cream; imported hazelnuts and California's own almonds, the Moreau chocolate "collection" is composed of eighty-four different flavors of molded and filled chocolates.

Now they are available in San Francisco through Moreau Chocolats in Sausalito. The freshly made chocolates are put on a night flight from Geneva to Frankfurt to San Francisco, so that they arrive here at most a few days old.

Also available at Jurgensen's Grocery, Narsai's Market, the Oakville Grocery, and the Wine and Cheese Center.

*Mail order.*

## Marin County
## VALENTINE'S

*1112 Fourth Street, San Rafael 94901. Telephone (415) 456-3262. Hours: M–SAT 10–5:30.*

Daria Baranoff grew up with European chocolates in Japan, where her Russian grandfather Fedor Morozoff had a thriving confectionery shop. At her store in

San Rafael, Valentine's, she dips fresh and dried fruit in the velvety chocolate that her father, Valentine Morozoff, still refines in Japan. The rest of her chocolates—exquisite fruit-sweetened Russian caramels, satiny pralines in tiny pleated foil cups—come from the family's Cosmopolitan Confections in Kobe, Japan.

"Drunken prunes," moist fat prunes soaked in liqueurs, are covered with barely sweet dark chocolate. Her subtle homemade truffles seem to carry the essence of chocolate. The dark Odile truffle is named for Tchaikovsky's black swan, and Daria called the first truffle she made in California "Marinco." They seem very elegant and ladylike when compared with most California-bred truffles, which are huge, tremendously rich, and very often overly sweet. Daria's are barely sweet, complex tasting, delicate, and *small*. They are lovely taken after dinner with a tiny cup of properly made espresso.

On summer weekends, she dips fresh raspberries and strawberries in white or dark chocolate. And all year she has delicious homemade fudge: chocolate, no-nut fudge, and penuche (or buttered sugar). The luscious pastries—*Linzertorte*, chocolate-almond torte, Thalhof torte, and more—are from La Viennoise in Oakland.

# BAKING CHOCOLATE

Some pastry shops will sell you some of their store of baking chocolates. It is well worth buying full ten-pound bricks or bars or at least a big chunk, rather than small half-pound or one-pound packages of baking chocolates. Stored away from heat and damp, dark chocolate will keep indefinitely, while white and milk chocolates will keep at least one year.

### San Francisco/East Bay
## COCOLAT

*3324 Steiner Street, San Francisco 94123. Telephone (415) 567-9957. Hours: T-SAT 10:30-6:30, SUN 12-5.*
*3945 Piedmont Avenue, Oakland 94611. Telephone (415) 653-3676. Hours: T-SAT 10-6.*
*1481 Shattuck Avenue, Berkeley 94709. Telephone (415) 843-3265. Hours: M-SAT 10-6, SUN 11-5.*

Cocolat has Ghirardelli's wonderful bittersweet chocolate, a type and quality sold only to bakeries. To encourage chocolate experimentation, they sell it in ten-pound blocks, or by the pound in half-pound chunks.

### East Bay
## GHIRARDELLI CHOCOLATE

*1111 139th Avenue, San Leandro 94578. Telephone (415) 483-6970. Wholesale to the trade only.*

Domingo Ghirardelli, founder of San Francisco's own chocolate manufactory, arrived in San Francisco from his birthplace of Rapallo, Italy, via Lima, Peru, where he worked as a chocolate and coffee merchant. He disembarked in San Francisco in 1849, just as the first boatloads of forty-niners were arriving and promptly opened a store in a tent in Stockton where he supplied the golddiggers with dry goods and general goods. He parleyed that money into a hotel in San Francisco and a food importing business. When both businesses were destroyed by fire, he reappeared in the coffee business and, a year later, started a confectionary company that he soon renamed Ghirardelli's California Chocolate Manufactory.

When the enterprising Domingo retired in 1892, his sons bought the Pioneer Woolen mill and started the expansion and construction that became the complex of buildings now known as Ghirardelli Square. Though the factory itself long ago relocated to San Leandro, the square still has a chocolate store selling Ghirardelli products, with the old chocolate factory machines in the back.

### San Francisco
### GHIRARDELLI
### CHOCOLATE MANUFACTORY

*900 North Point, San Francisco 94109. Telephone (415) 771-4903. Hours: SUN–TH 11:30 am–10 pm, F–SAT 11:30 am–midnight.*

The Ghirardelli chocolate store in Ghirardelli Square, site of San Francisco's own chocolate manufactory established in 1892, sells five-pound bars of semisweet chocolate, milk chocolate, and their new unsweetened baking chocolate, plus real chocolate chips and a large assortment of small bars and candies made from Ghirardelli chocolate. Ten-pound bars of chocolate, usually sold only to bakeries, are available by special order.
*Mail order. Write for price list.*

### Peninsula
### GUITTARD
### CHOCOLATE COMPANY

*10 Guittard Road, Burlingame 94010. Telephone (415) 697-4427. Wholesale only.*

Burlingame's Guittard Chocolate Company is the oldest independent chocolate factory in the United States, founded over one hundred years ago by Etienne Guittard, a Frenchman who came to California to make his fortune in the Gold Rush. To barter for his grubstake, he brought fine French chocolate from his uncle's Paris factory where he had worked. After three hard years in the goldfields, he decided he might make his fortune faster by making chocolate nuggets than by digging gold nuggets out of the hills.

Persuaded by local merchants that a chocolate business really would be successful, Etienne headed back to Paris for the special equipment he needed. In 1868, he returned to San Francisco and opened a small factory on Commercial Street. Today, Guittard Chocolate Company is headed by Horace A. Guittard, grandson of Etienne.

To buy chocolate direct from Guittard, you must buy in four-hundred-pound quantities. Two of Guittard's distributors, however, will sell ten-pound blocks of the company's various chocolates on a will-call basis. Call first, then come in to pick up your order:

Pacific Coast Products, 1050 Twenty-sixth Street, San Francisco, telephone (415) 647-2700

Buchwald and Sons, 1320 Marshall Street, Redwood City, telephone (415) 364-3131

Guittard makes bittersweet and semisweet chips, maxi-chips, and ten-pound solid bars of French vanilla dark chocolate or old Dutch milk chocolate, as well as four grades of cocoa powders.

## San Francisco
## KRÖN CHOCOLATIER

*349 Geary Street, San Francisco 94102. Telephone (415) 421-5766. Hours: M–SAT 9–5:30.*

This fine European *chocolatier* has one-pound bricks of bittersweet, milk chocolate, and white chocolate, as well as nine-ounce tubs of bitter, unsweetened chocolate; semisweet chocolate chips; and pure cocoa powder for baking or hot chocolate.
*Mail order.*

## East Bay
## MADE TO ORDER

*1576 Hopkins Street, Berkeley 94707. Telephone (415) 524-7552. Hours: M–SAT 10–6.*

Made to Order will sell you a pound or two of the unsweetened baking chocolate and dark coating chocolate they use in their own kitchen, depending on their supplies. Call first.

## Marin County
## MOREAU CHOCOLATS

*Sarky's Square, 1207 Bridgeway, Sausalito 94956. Telephone (415) 332-4621. Hours: M–F 9–5, SAT 11–5.*

Moreau Chocolats sells their bittersweet baking chocolate in ten-pound blocks only (you can buy it in smaller pieces from Narsai's and the Oakville Grocery). The satiny white chocolate is sold in pieces or by the pound.

## San Francisco
## THE OAKVILLE GROCERY

*1555 Pacific Avenue, San Francisco 94109. Telephone (415) 885-4111. Hours: M–F 10:30–6:30, SAT 10–6, SUN 12–6.*

The Oakville Grocery has an impressive array of baking chocolates from Wilbur, Lanvin, Ghirardelli, Guittard, Moreau, and Callebaut in bars and big chunks.

## San Francisco
## TARTS, INC.

*509 Laguna Street, San Francisco 94102. Telephone (415) 863-5572. Hours: T–F 11–6, SAT 11–5.*

Tarts, Inc., has ten-pound bars of Ghirardelli bittersweet chocolate or Guittard French vanilla chocolate at very good prices.

## Marin County
## VALENTINE'S

*1112 Fourth Street, San Rafael 94901. Telephone (415) 456-3262. Hours: M–SAT 10–5:30.*

Daria Baranoff sells her father's velvety unsweetened baking chocolate in big bars. The bittersweet is refined for a very long time to achieve its unparalleled silken texture.

## San Francisco
## WILLIAMS-SONOMA

*576 Sutter Street, San Francisco 94102. Telephone (415) 982-0295.*

Williams-Sonoma stocks three kinds of Callebaut chocolate from Belgium, suitable for baking. This fine-textured chocolate melts to a silky consistency and dries to a high gloss. It comes in bittersweet, milk, and white chocolate.
*Mail order.*

*Coffee arabica* was first discovered growing wild in Ethiopia. Though it has been cultivated since the sixth century, it wasn't until the fourteenth century that coffee brewed from the plant's roasted berries became a popular beverage throughout the Middle East. Men crowded into cafés to drink cup after cup of it, sticky and sweet with a fine silt of powdered coffee at the bottom. This manner of preparing coffee is called Turkish style today.

In Europe, the Italians were the first to enjoy coffee, in the sixteenth century. At first the church viewed it with suspicion, as a stimulant and drink originating from the land of the infidels, until one pope tried it and was converted. Today's Italians are still among the world's foremost coffee drinkers, imbibing countless tiny cups of perfectly brewed espresso every day.

It wasn't until a century later that the French and the English adopted the custom, but they took to it with a passion. Paris soon had a café on every corner; eighteenth-century England had almost two thousand coffee houses within the city of London alone.

In America, after the Boston Tea Party spoiled the colonists' pleasure in tea, coffee became the preferred beverage. Despite its popularity here, much of the coffee drunk in America has been and continues to be remarkably bad. But with the advent of specialty coffee stores and quality roasters in the last fifteen years, Americans have learned to appreciate and brew an excellent cup of coffee.

San Francisco boasts several good roasting companies and a number of small coffee stores that roast coffee on the premises. The coffees sold are classed by their country of origin (Colombia, Sumatra, Ethiopia). Each roasting establishment has its own blends of coffees as well. The many varieties of coffee may then be roasted to several degrees of darkness. The mildest is standard roast, followed by "Viennese," then "Italian roast" and the nearly black dark-French roast.

You can buy the coffee as whole beans or you can have it ground to suit your particular method of making coffee. Some stores will also pulverize coffee to the fine powder required to make Turkish-style coffee. If you do buy it ground, buy it often in small quantities, as it loses its intensity and flavor quickly. And if you'd like to try roasting each day's coffee yourself, you can sometimes buy green unroasted beans from your local coffee roaster.

## San Francisco
## CAFFE MALVINA

*512 Union Street, San Francisco 94133. Telephone (415) 392-4736. Hours: M-SAT 8-6, Sun 9:30-5:30.*

At street level, Malvina's is a caffè serving all kinds of coffee drinks and one of the best *cappuccinos* in North Beach. It's wonderful early in the morning to sit at a sunny table with all the locals, indulging in a rich *cappuccino* with one of Victoria Pastry's plump *brioschi.* Best of all, the warm smell of fresh-roasted coffee wafts up from the basement to make your cup of coffee taste even better.

Coffee is roasted seven days a week: eight of the basics, including of course, Italian and espresso. Malvina's dark French roast is superb. Also downstairs, they sell espresso machines and old-fashioned Neapolitan coffee makers still used in Naples, the kind you flip over when the water boils.

Unfortunately, Malvina lost some of its former charm when it was recently remodeled.

### San Francisco
## CAFFE TRIESTE

*609 Vallejo Street, San Francisco 94133. Telephone (415) 392-6739. Hours: M-SAT 10-6.*

The endless cups of *cappuccino, caffè latte,* and espresso served up at Caffé Trieste are all made from beans the Giotta family roasts themselves in their adjoining coffee store. You can buy coffee in the bean or ground, as well as all kinds of coffee paraphernalia.

The best time to stop in is on Saturday afternoon between 12:30 and 2, when you can idle a little in the caffè to enjoy the weekly opera singing by the Giotta family.

### San Francisco
## CAMEO COFFEE

*3913 Twenty-fourth Street at Sanchez, San Francisco 94132. Telephone (415) 824-7879. Hours: M-SAT 9:30-6:30, SUN 9:30-6.*

Cameo Coffee sells house blend, dark French, light French, Americana, Brazil, Guatemala, Mexican, Costa Rican, and espresso coffees roasted on the premises. (Try the homemade butter-cream fudge cooling in waxed paper-lined pans: vanilla nut, peanut butter, maple nut, vanilla peanut, chocolate rocky road, and more.)

### San Francisco
## CAPRICORN COFFEES

*353 Tenth Street, San Francisco 94103. Telephone (415) 621-8500. Hours: M-F 8:30-5:30, SAT 10-2.*

Capricorn Coffees has a long and complicated history of mergers, new names and new locations. The predecessor of Capricorn Coffees was a retail store called Hardcastle's. Established in 1963 by James Hardcastle, at a time when gourmet coffee was hardly known in this country, Hardcastle's boasted its own small roaster. In the late sixties, Mr. Hardcastle sold his successful retail business and reappeared at the head of Capricorn Coffees, a new wholesale coffee-roasting company on Fillmore Street. In 1974 the business moved to Tenth Street, its present location.

The company has a policy of using only top-quality coffee. If they can't buy top-quality beans of a certain variety, then they discontinue roasting them until a better-quality bean appears on the market. Coffees are fresh roasted. This means that small quantities of different coffees are roasted almost every day to ensure freshness.

They have twenty coffees from various countries, including Arabian Mocha from Yemen, Mandheling from Sumatra, Mocha Harrar from Ethiopia, Oaxaca Pluma from Mexico, and Bourbon Santos from Brazil, plus six blended coffees

including a New Orleans blend with French chicory. The Turkish-style coffee, blended and pulverized to order, is as fine ground as possible short of using a mortar and pestle. Capricorn Coffees is one of two U.S. coffee roasters who obtain the rare Wallensford Estate Blue Mountain directly. All decaffeinated coffee is 100 percent Colombian made in four roasts; the French-roast Colombian is water-process decaffeinated.

All the coffees are available in the retail store at the Tenth Street location and at specialty coffee stores from Millbrae to Santa Rosa.

## San Francisco
## COFFEE TEA AND SPICE

*1630 Haight Street, San Francisco 94117. Telephone (415) 861-3953. Hours: M–SAT 10–6, SUN 12–5.*

Coffee Tea and Spice has over twenty varieties of coffee—including various degrees of dark roasts—roasted daily right in the store, plus dozens of black, smoked, green, and herb teas sold in bulk, and a profusion of culinary herbs and spices, also sold in bulk.

## San Francisco/Marin County
## GRAFFEO COFFEE ROASTING COMPANY

*733 Columbus Avenue, San Francisco 94133. Telephone (415) 986-2420.*
*1314 Fourth Street, San Rafael 94901. Telephone (415) 457-5131. Hours: M–F 9–6, SAT 9–5 (both stores).*

When the wind is blowing just right, the rich bitter smell of coffee roasting at Graffeo's can tug at you all the way across Washington Square Park. Follow the scent to Columbus Avenue between Filbert and Greenwich, where Graffeo's Coffee House has been in the coffee roasting business, Italian style, since 1935, through three generations of the Repetto family. The small shop is filled with rough open sacks of the green coffee beans (Costa Rican, Tarrazu, A-grade New Guinea, Java, and Colombian) that are blended to make the coffee. Italian-style coffee is always a blend, to ensure a consistent flavor and taste. The blend may vary slightly depending on the kinds of beans and the quality of beans available.

At Graffeo's the beans are roasted to a dark "Italian" roast (which they say takes out all the bitterness) or a lighter regular roast. When roasted, the beans are shiny, dark, and oily. Making just two roasts means the beans are always fresh. They don't sit around waiting for the customer with esoteric tastes to buy one of a couple of dozen varieties. In addition to their dark and light roasts, Graffeo's has recently introduced a dark-roasted 100 percent pure Colombian decaf, water-processed without chemicals.

There is a second store in San Rafael, and Graffeo beans are sold in Oakland at Ratto's, Le Picnique, and Curds and Whey, and on the Peninsula at Tea and Spice in Los Altos and Sweet Surprises in Palo Alto.

## San Francisco
## HAS BEANS

*2411 California Street, San Francisco 94115. Telephone (415) 563-2004. Hours: M–SAT 10–6.*
*4117 Nineteenth Street, San Francisco 94114. Telephone (415) 626-5573. Hours: M–SAT 10–6.*
*683 Market Street, San Francisco 94105. Telephone (415) 957-1255. Hours: M–F 10–6.*

J. B. Loucks, proprietor of Has Beans, roasts fourteen kinds of beans for his three stores, among them French roast, Royal Kona, Mocha Java, Arabian Mocha, and J.B.'s blends.

The flavored coffees—Viennese cinnamon, Swiss chocolate almond and Bavarian chocolate—are roasted elsewhere. The Bavarian chocolate is comforting in the morning. It's made by roasting coffee beans with cocoa beans. Then, while the freshly roasted cofee beans are still warm, ground cocoa beans are lightly dusted over them so that they absorb the faint sweetish taste of the cocoa.

## San Francisco
## HOUSE OF COFFEE

*1618 Noriega Street, San Francisco 94122. Telephone (415) 681-9363. Hours: T–SAT 9:30–6:30.*

Andy Devletian comes from Rumania, part of an Armenian family experienced in all aspects of the coffee business.

He had his own coffee store in Bucharest until just after the war. In 1954, he and his wife Silvia left their life in Rumania behind them and emigrated to America, eventually settling in San Francisco where over fifteen years ago they opened a premium coffee store in the Sunset District. The House of Coffee introduced many San Franciscans to the full range of coffees from around the world.

Andy loves to explain the differences between his custom-roasted and -ground coffees. You can sample perfectly brewed cups of it right in the store, and Andy will advise you how to make it correctly yourself. Most of his customers started their coffee education with Andy's well-balanced house blend, a mix of four different beans. Lovers of strong coffee should try his Italian roast or French roast.

Andy also sells Middle Eastern staples such as *lavash*, olives, grape leaves, and pistachios (see Middle Eastern section).

## East Bay
## PEERLESS COFFEE

*260 Oak Street, Oakland 94607. Telephone (415) 763-1763. Hours: M–F 8:30–5:30, SAT 9–5.*

Until just a few years ago, Peerless Coffee was based in a wonderful old wooden building with a roll-up front. Now, they've moved to a larger, concrete hunk of a warehouse in Oakland's warehouse district. Right at the front, though, there is still a small area to serve retail customers, complete with all manner of coffee makers, grinders, filters, cups, and gadgets. The coffee is the same as that sold to restaurants and coffee specialty stores all over the Bay Area.

They carry over twenty varieties of coffees, all roasted at the Oakland warehouse. These include French, Italian, and Viennese roasts; Mocha, Brazil, and Colombian blends; plus varieties like Ethiopia, Java, Maragogipes, New Guinea, and Sumatra. French roast and Colombian come decaffeinated, too. Prices are among the lowest in town.

Six teas—black China, Darjeeling, Earl Grey, English breakfast, jasmine, orange spice—are sold by the half pound.

*Mail order. Orders over twenty-five pounds get a 10 percent discount.*

### East Bay/Peninsula
## PEET'S COFFEE

*2124 Vine Street, Berkeley 94709. Telephone (415) 841-0564.*
*2916 Domingo Avenue, Berkeley 94705. Telephone (415) 843-1434.*
*899 Santa Cruz Avenue, Menlo Park 94025. Telephone (415) 325-8989. Hours: M–SAT 9–6 (all stores).*

Peet's Coffee and Teas is famous for the consistently high quality of its custom-roasted coffees and choice teas. Though there are now three stores, the first Peet's opened in 1966 in Berkeley's Walnut Square. Peet's success is no accident. Alfred Peet, the founder, has spent a lifetime in the coffee and tea business. He began learning it at age seventeen in Holland under the tutelage of his father. Peet's is now incorporated, but Mr. Peet still acts as a consultant to the stores, choosing the beans from his network of reliable suppliers and supervising the blending and roasting. He also has undertaken the training of a new generation of roasters working for Peet's.

Alfred Peet is a master coffee blender—the superb house blend and Major Dickason's blends are consistently major sellers—along with the dark French roast, Mocha Java, and Sulawesi-Kalossie. In all, Peet's roasts over thirty kinds of coffee, with the selection weighted toward the full-bodied coffees, plus four kinds of decaffeinated coffees, including water-treated French roast.

In addition, the stores stock almost thirty teas: black teas from India, Sri Lanka and China, green teas, fermented teas and special blends, plus peppermint sticks, fine chocolate bars, and irresistible chocolate-covered espresso beans.

To brew your coffee, choose from the best in coffee paraphernalia: porcelain Melitta drip coffee makers and filters, French *café filtre* makers, coffee thermoses; Italian-style cast-aluminum Moka Express pots for making from one to eighteen cups of espresso; copper Neapolitan flip-drip pots; and narrow-waisted Middle Eastern *ibrik* for making Turkish coffee—even electric "travel" coffee makers. Then there is an impressive line of espresso makers, from the Vesuvius stovetop models to the ornate self-contained brass and copper models. You'll also find hand coffee mills from England and all manner of electric coffee grinders, plus reusable cotton filters, and coffee and espresso cups.

For tea fanciers, they have teapots, tea cups, tea balls, and strainers.

Peet's makes it convenient to mail order with a printed order form. Check for grind and kind of coffee; the minimum order is two pounds. Your coffee will be sent by UPS or by air.

Once you really start to cook, you are bound to leave your first cookbooks behind and move into unexplored territory. Amuse yourself making dishes you've never tasted. Teach yourself complex techniques. Become an armchair traveler and a culinary explorer by reading about the cuisines of the world. You can get to know Mexico through the food of the Yucatán, or Russian Georgia through a native son's memoir of childhood banquets and picnics. One week you can feast on the spicy dishes of Bahia, the next on fiery Thai dishes.

As you delve deeper into gastronomical scholarship, you may go through a period of researching different versions of a recipe, say, for *cassoulet*, the Languedoc's marvelous white bean dish, or you might trace the origins of a special dish such as North Africa's *couscous*, which becomes *cuscussu* in Trapani, Sicily; cornmeal *coo coo* in the West Indies; and *cuzcuz* in Brazil. Or you may move back in history, investigating old cookbooks to recreate a Dickensian Christmas or a Renaissance banquet.

These days, with San Franciscans' high interest in food and wine, most bookstores stock a good selection of cookbooks. But you'll have to look a little farther afield to satisfy more esoteric interests. This chapter tells you where: specialty bookstores, mail-order sources, libraries, newsletters, and food societies.

*Note:* For wine books, libraries, and societies, see Wine section.

## COOKBOOKS

### San Francisco
### COOKBOOK CORNER

*620 Sutter Street, San Francisco 94102. Telephone (415) 673-6281. Hours: M-SAT 11–5:30.*

Just up Sutter Street from Williams-Sonoma cookware store and across from wine merchants Draper and Equin, *inside* the YWCA at 620 Sutter Street, is Cookbook Corner, a bookstore entirely devoted to cookbooks. It's a real pleasure to spend the afternoon browsing in this sunny, quaint store where the shelves are filled with just about every English-language cookbook currently in print—and some that are out of print. You can check the latest battalion of books, re-find old favorites, and indulge your esoteric side in ethnic cookbooks from all over the world. A footnote in *The Anthropologists' Cookbook* edited by Jessica Kuper mentions Alan Davidson's first book, *Fish and Fish Dishes of Laos*, written when he was British ambassador to Laos. Cookbook Corner has it and lots of other specialized cookbooks, including artists' cookbooks and a big collection of cookbooks published by museums or women's societies from all over the country.

The wine section is not extensive, but there are unexpected finds—a German wine atlas, a guide to the wine roads of Italy—studded among the old and new standards.

*Search service provided. Mail orders welcome.*

*Radishes or lettis tow bunches a peny*

## San Francisco
# GOURMET GUIDES

*1767 Stockton Street, San Francisco 94133. Telephone (415) 391-5903. Hours: M-F 12-5, F-SAT 12-3.*

Gourmet Guides has floor-to-high-ceiling shelves stacked with cookbooks, maps, and travel books. The books are mostly English language, with many imported from Britain—so many books that owner Jean Bullock has room to stock only one or two of each.

There are books for scholars and professional cooks, too, in inspired juxtapositions: Claude Levi Strauss's *The Origins of Table Manners* shelved next to Calvin Trillins's wry books on eating in America; histories of food; and *Lost Country Life* by Dorothy Hartley, with all the details and lore of old English country life. Hering's *Dictionary of Classical Cuisine*, a basic in any working chef's library, sits next to Pellaprat, a text on buffets and receptions, and other books for the professional cook.

The hundreds of cookbooks are classed in sections: ice cream, *charcuterie*, pastry, etc. Of special interest is owner Jean Bullock's collection of American regional cookbooks. She boasts fifteen books on Creole and Cajun cooking alone. "Charity books" from museums and Junior Leagues collect regional recipes from all over the country. Every part of the world is represented in the ethnic cookbooks. The Asian section includes unusual Malay, Siamese, and Thai cookbooks published in Singapore.

Overwhelmed? There's a beginner's section—and diet books. Gourmet Guides has maps, too, so you can follow Waverly Root's rambles in *The Food of Italy* or Michael and Sybil Brown's in *The Food of Southwest France*.

# —ETHNIC BOOKS—

## San Francisco/East Bay * Indian
# BOMBAY BAZAR

*548 Valencia Street, San Francisco 94110. Telephone (415) 621-1717. Hours: M-F 10:30-6, SUN 12-5.*
*1034 University Avenue, Berkeley 94710. Telephone (415) 848-1671. Hours: T-SAT 10-6:30, SUN 11-6.*

Paperback cookbooks from India not seen elsewhere.

## San Francisco * Italian
# A. CAVALLI
# ITALIAN BOOKSTORE

*1441 Stockton Street, San Francisco 94133. Telephone (415) 421-4219. Hours: M-SAT 9-5:30.*

Founded in 1880 and one of North Beach's oldest landmarks, A. Cavalli has cookbooks in Italian. Buy Ada Boni's huge volume *Le Recette d'Oro* that was too big to carry back from Italy.

In English, they have volumes of the handsomely designed series on regional cuisine you might have coveted in Italy—*Milano in bocca, Sardegna in bocca*, etc.—with traditional recipes from each region printed in dialect, Italian, and English. Plus the best of the recent books by Marcella Hazan, and Giuliano Bugialli's wonderful *The Fine Art of Italian Cooking*.

## Paris * French
# EDGAR SOETE

*5, quai Voltaire, Paris. Telephone 260-72-41.*

Of course, when you're in Paris, there is the famous, but grumpy and high-priced dealer in rare old culinary books on the quai Voltaire: Edgar Sôete.

**San Francisco ✳ European**
## THE EUROPEAN BOOK COMPANY

*925 Larkin Street, San Francisco 94109. Telephone (415) 474-0626. Hours: M–F 9:30–6, SAT 9:30–5.*

The European Book Company and its sister store, the International Corner, stocks classic cookbooks in French as well as books on nouvelle cuisine hot off the French presses. You can read Bocuse's *La Nouvelle Cuisine,* Roger Verge's *La Cuisine du Soleil,* or the Troisgros brothers' latest tome in the original (with the original ingredients, too). Actually, your French doesn't have to be *coulant.* With the help of a simple dictionary and a metric scale, you can decipher the recipe and hone your culinary French at the same time.

The classics include Fernand Point's *Ma Gastronomie,* Le Nôtre's *Patisserie,* the re-publication of Alexandre Dumas's impressive *Le Grand Dictionnaire de Cuisine,* and Brillat Savarin's *La Physiologie du Gout.* There are books on regional cuisine in both hardcover and paperback, too.

Books on wine cover a wide range, from general-information pocket books and guides to France's wine country to specialized texts on specific wine regions.

**San Francisco ✳ Middle Eastern**
## HAIG'S DELICACIES

*642 Clement Street, San Francisco 94118. Telephone (415) 752-6283. Hours: M–SAT 10–6.*

Arabic cookbooks and books on Lebanese, Greek, and Turkish cooking.

**San Francisco ✳ Greek**
## HELLENIC AMERICAN IMPORTS

*2365 Mission Street, San Francisco 94110. Telephone (415) 282-2237. Hours: M–SAT 10–6.*

Books on Hellenic cuisine from Saints Constantine and Helena Book Fund, plus five or six cookbooks in Greek.

**San Francisco ✳ European**
## THE INTERNATIONAL CORNER

*500 Sutter Street (at Powell), San Francisco 94102. Telephone (415) 981-1666. Hours: M–F 9:30–10, SAT 9:30–5, SUN 11–5.*

Foreign-language cookbooks. See European Book Company, above.

**San Francisco ✳ Middle Eastern**
## ISTANBUL PASTRIES AND IMPORTED FOODS

*Ghirardelli Square, 900 North Point, San Francisco 94109. Telephone (415) 441-7740. Hours: SUN–TH 10–6, F–SAT 10–9.*

Greek, Armenian, Lebanese, Turkish, and Arabic cookbooks.

**San Francisco ✳ Oriental**
## KINOKUNIYA BOOKS

*Japan Center, 1581 Webster Street, San Francisco 94115. Telephone (415) 567-7625. Hours: 10–7 daily, except first Tuesday of each month.*

This immense bookstore has books about the Far East from Japan and all over the world. The small Oriental cookbook section has titles not often seen in regular bookstores: *Homestyle Japanese Cooking in Pictures* by Sadako Kohno; *The Encyclopedia of Asian Cooking* (in paperback) edited by Jeni Wright; and the series of books on *tofu, miso,* and *tempeh* production and cooking by William Shurtleff and Aikido Aoyagi. In the art section, a series of books on the beauty of everyday Japanese objects includes books on Japanese spoons and ladles and one on Japanese knives.

## Contra Costa ∗ Thai
### MAHANAKORN MARKET

*10557 San Pablo Avenue, El Cerrito 94530. Telephone (415) 525-2777. Hours: 12–5 daily.*

Thai cookbooks.

## San Francisco ∗ Middle Eastern
### SAMIRAMIS IMPORTS

*2990 Mission Street, San Francisco, 94110. Telephone (415) 824-6555. Hours: M–SAT 10–6.*

Cookbooks from the Arab world, like *Sahtein: Middle Eastern Cookbook*, with recipes from Lebanon, Palestine, Syria. And a book by the Arab Women's Union in Detroit.

## San Francisco ∗ Chinese
### THE WOK SHOP

*804 Grant Avenue, San Francisco 94108. Telephone (415) 989-3797. Hours: 10–10 daily.*

A great Chinese cookbook selection, including some from Hong Kong and mainland China.

# USED RARE BOOKS

Check used-book stores for cookbooks. Some, such as Moe's in Berkeley, have as big a section of food and wine books as the best new bookstores. Browsing well-stocked shelves may reward you with Waverly Root's *The Food of France*, Madelaine Kamman's *The Making of a Cook*, or a real find such as Beverly Pepper's *See Rome and Eat* or John Phillip Crowell's *The Hellfire Cookbook*, for adherents of hot cuisine.

With persistent visits, you'll be able to collect a whole series of Time-Life Books' *Foods of the World* (usually minus the small recipe booklet, but most recipes are in the bigger text, too) and occasional volumes of the excellent *The Good Cook* series. Trade in cookbooks you've outgrown for books to stretch your cooking ability now.

Most used-book stores have a search service.

## San Francisco
### THE BOOKSTALL

*708 Sutter Street, San Francisco 94109. Telephone (415) 673-5446. Hours: M–SAT 12–5:30.*

The Bookstall is a rare-book store specializing in cookbooks, children's books, and books on mountain climbing and physics.

Louise Moises publishes *Bon Appetit*, a newsletter listing books on cooking, food, and beverages, from the shelves of the Bookstall.

A few minutes' browsing recently located *Venus in the Kitchen*, or *Love's Cookery Book* by Pilaff Bey, a compilation of "recipes aphrodisiac in nature"; *Love and Dishes* by Niccolo de Quattrociocchi (who would be more qualified than an Italian to write about food and seduction?) and, in French, *La Cuisine*

*Exotique Insolite Erotique* by I. C. Izzo, five hundred recipes from around the world.

Recipe books from exotic locales include *Food and Drink in Ancient Bengal* by T. Chakravarty, *The Kenya Settlers Cookery Book and Household Guide*, and Mrs. Stade's South African cookbook, as well as a two-volume edition of Escoffier's French classic in Swedish!

And from America, there are regional and historical titles such as *Pueblo and Navajo Cookery*, by Marcia Keegan, with color photos; *The Alaskan Cookbook*; *The Missouri Traveler's Cookbook*, by Mary Hosford; *The Mennonite Community Cookbook*, by Showaller; and the mysterious Lafcadio Hearn's *La Cuisine Creole: A Collection of Culinary Recipes.* And there are some very old books with irresistible titles: *The Bachelor and the Chafing Dish*, by Dessler Welch; Hans Hinrich's *The Glutton's Paradise*, and *Reminiscences and Ravioli*, by Nika Standen.

## San Francisco
## COLUMBUS AVENUE BOOKS

*245 Columbus Avenue, San Francisco 94133. Telephone (415) 986-3872. Hours: M-TH 10 am-11 pm, F 10 am-midnight, SAT 11 am-midnight, SUN noon-10 pm.*

Used and out-of-print cookbooks.

## San Francisco/East Bay
## THE HOLMES BOOK COMPANY

*22 Third Street, corner of Market, San Francisco 94103. Telephone (415) 362-3283. Hours: M-SAT 9-5:15.*
*274 14th Street, Oakland 94612. Telephone (415) 893-6860. Hours: M and F, 9:30-9; T-TH 9:30-5:30, SAT 9:30-5:30, SUN 11-5.*

Used cookbooks.

## East Bay
## MOE'S BOOKS

*2476 Telegraph Avenue, Berkeley 94704. Telephone (415) 849-2087. Hours: 10 am-11 pm daily.*

Used cookbooks and wine books.

# MAIL-ORDER BOOKS

## COOKSBOOKS

*T. A. McKirdy, 34 Marine Drive, Rottingham, Sussex, BN2 7HQ, England. Telephone (0273) 32707 (cables: Cooksbooks, Brighton).*

Cooksbooks specializes in books on food, wine, cookery, and virtually all related subjects. The five thousand volumes include rare books, out-of-print books, facsimiles of earlier works. Catalogs are issued every second month and are available (world wide) free of charge.

## HOUSEHOLD WORDS

*Kay Caughran, P.O. Box 7231, Berkeley, CA 94707. Telephone (415) 524-8859.*

When Kay Caughran retired after twenty years at the Berkeley Library, she still wanted to do something with books. As she had always been interested in cookbooks, she had decided to deal in books associated with cooking, eating, drinking, and kindred subjects—books that were one of a kind, out of print, and hard to find, like Roy Andries de Groot's *Auberge of the Flowering Hearth.* Her catalog *Household Words* lists the books she's collected in her wide-ranging searches, often buying whole collections.

Who could resist Patricia Bronte's *Vittles and Vice: Recipes and Legends*

from a Brawling Part of Chicago or Audrey Gertens's In Defense of British Cooking ("200 wonderful recipes prove the English can cook"). There's an Irish cookbook, Rosalind Cole's Of Soda Bread and Guinness; Klassic Korean Kuisine by the Women's Association of the United Presbyterian Church, Kangneung, Korea; and F. W. Waugh's 1916 Iroquois Foods and Food Preparation. Caughran does have some foreign titles, many of them German. In French, there is a 1927 Les Boissons: Vin, Biere, Alcools, Liqueurs, by Monsieur A. L. Girard.

Recently she's begun to accumulate books about servants and the history of manners, such as The Unnatural History of the Nanny or A Butler's Recipe Book from 1719, or a memoir by Madame Allaret, the housekeeper in Proust's well-regulated household on Boulevard Haussman.

Ms. Caughren offers a search service, too. Her catalog is $2.

## NEW WORLD BOOKS

_2 Cains Road, Suffern, NY 10901. Telephone (914) 354-2600._

If you are very patient and know exactly what you want, you can order any hardcover book over $10 currently in print and published in the United States at a 30 percent discount from New World Books. Send them the author, title, publisher, and price. Take your 30 percent discount, add $1.35 for postage, and enclose a check or an international money order for the total. Allow at least two to three weeks for delivery.

## THE WINE AND FOOD LIBRARY

_Ms. Jan Longone, 1207 West Madison, Ann Arbor, MI 48103. Telephone (313) 663-4894._

The Wine and Food Library is a mail-order bookshop described by its catalog as "devoted to the old, rare, interesting, unusual and out of print in the following fields: cookery; wine and other beverages; food history; hotels and restaurants; herbs and spices; decorative arts relating to the table; the social history of eating and drinking—in other words, that broad range of topics that can be included in the word 'gastronomy.' "

The bookshop was started by Jan Longone, an Ann Arbor food scholar, to supply research material for students in her history of gastronomy courses for the University Extension Service. Nine years later, the shelves of the Wine and Food Library are stocked with over ten thousand volumes, ranging from select current titles to the scarce to the rare, including the earliest printed works on wine and food from the sixteenth century.

Every year she sends an annotated catalog to her customers. Catalog No. 7 (1981), The Pleasures of Cellar and Table, listed more than six hundred books, including special sections on American regional food (Hawaii, Texas, Appalachia, the Ozarks) and foods from the rest of the world (an Irish cookbook; a Hebridian cookbook; books from Jamaica, Panama, Brazil, and Trinidad; from Indonesia, Syria, Ghana, and Israel; and the first Burmese cookbook in English).

Her extensive collection of wine books is listed by wine regions. The French section includes Raymond Brunet's Le Marriage des Vins et des Mets, which matches classic culinary dishes with the appropriate wines; a history of the wines of the Clos de Vougeot; Robin and Judith Yopps's *Vineyards and Vignerons* of the Loire and Rhône valleys; and Nicolas Faith's engrossing history of the Bordeaux wine trade.

She has a facsimile collector's edition of Andre Simon's *Biblioteca Vinaria*, a bibliography of books on wine and wine making compiled in 1913; as well as nineteenth-century works on viniculture from France and Italy.

And there are books on the wines of America, ports, sherries, wines of the Douro, Chiantis, Moselles, and books on beer and beer making.

About six times yearly, Ms. Longone issues a special list with all books referenced by subject: she has published lists on mushrooms, truffles, and edible wild plants; tea, with books on its history, the tea ceremony, and the tea trade; decorative arts including silverware, table setting, and flower arrangement; and books on bread, baking, desserts, ice cream, cake decorating, candy and chocolate, wine and the arts, etc.

She has back issues of culinary magazines, including the English edition of *Revue du Vin de France*, Canada's *Epicure*, and the limited-edition *Petits Propos Culinaires*.

Ms. Longone will undertake searches for specific books or help build collections. Catalogs are $2 postpaid to new customers, with catalogs and six special lists yearly free to regular customers.

# ———— LIBRARIES ————

**East Bay**
## NATURAL RESOURCES LIBRARY

*Giannini Hall, University of California at Berkeley, Berkeley 94720. Telephone (415) 642-4493. Hours: M–TH 9–9, F 9–5, SAT–SUN 1–5.*

This library has reference material related to the history of food, food processing, agribusiness, the history of agriculture, and international cuisines.

**Contra Costa**
## NEW AGE FOODS STUDY CENTER

*P.O. Box 234, Lafayette 94549. Telephone (415) 283-2991.*

An extensive research library collected by William Shurtleff and Aikido Aoyagi, authors of *The Book of Tofu, The Book of Tempeh,* and *The Book of Miso.* The collection emphasizes Oriental cuisines, the use of vegetable proteins, diet and nutrition, etc.

**East Bay**
## SAN FRANCISCO PROFESSIONAL FOOD SOCIETY

*Mireille Isler, Librarian, 2323 Rose Street, Berkeley 94708. Telephone (415) 841-2175.*

The fledgling San Francisco Professional Food Society is accumulating a research library intended to be wide ranging and eclectic. The library will be a much needed resource for food writers, consultants, cooks, and everyone involved in food professions in the Bay Area.

# —FOOD SOCIETIES—

## Santa Cruz
## FRIENDS OF THE CALAMARI

*Tom Brezsny, India Joe's Restaurant, Santa Cruz Art Center, 1000 Center Street, Santa Cruz 95060. Telephone (408) 427-3554.*

Friends of the Calamari is a society dedicated to the promotion of the scientific, artistic, and gastronomic exploration of squid. The society organizes the annual International Calamari Festival held each September since 1980 in Santa Cruz, where squidophiles can taste dozens of dishes featuring squid and buy squid cookbooks, potholders, T-shirts, and even a squid calendar and other *calamari* memorabilia. There are movies and slide shows about squid, poems and songs, skits, a squid punk rock band, and even a parade.

In the planning: a *calamari* newsletter.

## Contra Costa
## THE GALVANIZED GULLET

*Geraldine Duncann, 3440 Mountain Spring Road, Lafayette 94549. Telephone (415) 937-5360.*

Galvanized Gullet, a society for lovers of hot food, is an informal group that meets irregularly for a "hot fix." Meetings are potluck: cook-members each bring the hottest dish they can concoct. Noncooks who love hot food bring great quantities of good beer. Contact Geraldine Duncann for news.

## Boston
## THE HERB SOCIETY
## OF AMERICA

*300 Massachusetts Avenue, Boston, MA 02115. Telephone (617) 536-7136.*

Organized in 1933, the Herb Society of America's purpose is "to bring together people interested in the knowledge and use of herbs." There are fourteen units in the national society; northern California is one of them. Members receive the society's annual publication, *The Herbarist,* and can join committees on bibliography, botanical or library research, and other topics of interest.

Requests for membership information should be addressed to Chairman, Membership Committee.

## East Bay
## LOVERS OF THE
## STINKING ROSE

*526 Santa Barbara, Berkeley 94707. Telephone (415) 527-1958.*

Lovers of the Stinking Rose is a society formed by Lloyd J. Harris, author of *The Book of Garlic,* for garlic lovers, scholars, and addicts all over the world. Membership in LSR is $14, and includes a copy of *The Book of Garlic* and a two-issue subscription to the society's newsletter, *The Garlic Times* (see entry under Newsletters). A lifetime membership of $30 includes a lifetime subscription to *The Garlic Times.*

## San Francisco
## MYCOLOGICAL SOCIETY
## OF SAN FRANCISCO

*P.O. Box 11321, San Francisco 94101. Telephone (415) 566-7363.*

Since 1950, the Mycological Society of San Francisco has promoted the study and exchange of information about mushrooms. Cooks can learn under the guidance of experts how to identify the many types of edible mushrooms to be found in local areas, such as the chanterelle and the boletus.

In addition to monthly meetings, which include lectures and slide shows, members can join field trips led by experienced members and professional mycologists, participate in the yearly fungus fair with its marvelous specimen displays, and have the use of a specialized mycological library.

Cook's note: Within the society there is a small group that meets monthly to prepare and eat a splendid dinner that includes wild-mushroom dishes. Another group concentrates on the cultivation of mushrooms, others on taxonomy and toxicology.

## San Francisco
## THE SAN FRANCISCO PROFESSIONAL FOOD SOCIETY

*P.O. Box 77105, San Francisco 94107.*

The San Francisco Professional Food Society was founded in 1979 and now counts as members over two hundred chefs, cooking teachers, caterers, food and wine writers, restaurateurs, wine merchants, graphic designers, food stylists, food photographers, and others involved in working with food. Julia Child, James Beard, Barbara Kafka, M.F.K. Fisher, Pat Brown, Marcella Hazan, Diana Kennedy, Rita Leinward, Jacques Pepin, and William Rice are all honorary members.

Meetings are held once a month with guest speakers and, always, wonderful food and wine. A resource guide and directory of members is revised and published every year. Dues are $50 yearly.

Prospective members should contact Sandra Griswold, 963 North Point Street, San Francisco 94109, telephone (415) 775-4272, or the Society at the address above.

## East Bay
## WEST COAST NUTRITIONAL ANTHROPOLOGISTS

*Dr. Angela Little, Department of Nutritional Sciences, University of California, Berkeley 94720. Telephone (415) 642-0646.*

Membership in the active West Coast Nutritional Anthropologists is open to those interested in the cultural, social, and nutritional aspects of food. There are two regional groups, one meeting on the UC Berkeley campus and another in Vancouver, B.C.; people outside these areas can participate through the quarterly newsletter.

Membership is $5 per year. Make checks payable to West Coast Nutritional Anthropologists.

# —NEWSLETTERS—

## CHOCOLATE NEWS

*P.O. Box 1745, FDR Station, New York, NY 10151. Telephone (212) 750-9289.*

*Chocolate News* is a monthly newsletter for chocolate lovers, with notes on chocolate history, recipes, and the latest in "accouterments." A year's subscription is $9.95.

## THE DEPARTMENT OF FISH AND GAME

*1416 Ninth Street, Sacramento, CA 95814. Telephone (916) 445-3531.*

The California Department of Fish and Game publishes some excellent small books useful for identifying fish that you might catch or that you might encounter in some of the ethnic markets, especially in Chinatowns.

*Write for free publications price list.*

## GARLIC TIMES

*Lovers of the Stinking Rose, 526 Santa Barbara, Berkeley, CA 94707. Telephone (415) 527-1958.*

*Garlic Times* is the digest of the Lovers of the Stinking Rose, a society founded by Lloyd J. Harris, author of *The Garlic Cookbook*, to promote the use and understanding of the edible bulb. The newsletter is packed with the latest garlic news: new medical evidence, folklore, fantastic recipes (LJH gets Chez Panisse, Fourth Street Grill, Cajun cooks to give away their garlic secrets), testimonials to garlic, garlic philosophy, growing tips, accounts of anti-garlic prejudice. The society also collects and sells such garlic paraphernalia as garlic presses, garlic amulets, T-shirts, bumper stickers, buttons, and books about garlic, all available by mail through *Garlic Times*.

A $14 membership to LSR includes a copy of *The Book of Garlic* and a two-issue subscription to *Garlic Times*. Re-subscription rate $4.50 for two issues. Back issues, all six for $5, or $2 each.

## PETITS PROPOS CULINAIRES

*Prospect Books, 45 Lamont Road, London SW10 0HU. U.S. Agent: Ms. Matt Lewis, 335 Greenwich Street, Apt. 12B, New York, NY 10013. Telephone (212) 254-7774.*

*Petits Propos Culinaires*, essays and notes to do with food, cookery, and cookery books, is published three times a year by Prospect Books, a publishing partnership whose members include Elizabeth David, Alan Davidson, and Richard Olney. This small magazine is beautifully printed, a cooks' scholarly journal with eight to ten articles per issue, illustrated with drawings and old prints.

There are eclectic regional recipes such as Georgina Masson's Paschal Pizza from the Abruzzi (given to the author twenty-five years ago in a remote Italian village), and a nineteenth-century recipe for trifle, as well as modern recipes for dishes such as Moussaka Minceur and Jane Davidson's autumn preserves.

The magazine provides a forum in which writers like Alan Davidson and Elizabeth David can indulge in scholarly erudition. You'll find articles on the history and origin of the samovar, the use of blood in cooking, and ice cream and water ices in seventeenth- and eighteenth-century England. When Elizabeth Lambert Ortiz writes an article discussing *mole poblano*, she traces legends and folklore about the dish, which may be older than the Aztecs; the origins of chocolate and how turkey got its name; and gives a delicious recipe for *mole poblano de guajalote*.

Articles include book reviews and queries from cooks and food scholars.

Subscriptions are $17.50 for three issues. Back issues are available for $5.50.

## WOK TALK

*The Chinese Grocer, 209 Post Street, San Francisco, CA 94108. Telephone (415) 982-0125.*

*Wok Talk* is a bimonthly newsletter, six to eight pages, "for the interest and edification of Chinese food lovers," and consists of a series of articles on the regional cuisines of China—Cantonese, Shanghai, Northern, Szechwan, Fukien, etc.—travelers' notes from China, recipes, cooking techniques, notes on new equipment available, book reviews.

*Wok Talk* also organizes culinary tours to different regions of China.

Subscription: one year $9.50, two years $15.00.

# Cooking Instruction

## COOKING CLASSES

### San Francisco
## CALIFORNIA CULINARY ACADEMY

*215 Fremont Street, San Francisco 94105. Telephone (415) 543-2765.*

The California Culinary Academy is San Francisco's school for professional chefs. Unfortunately, they offer only a full-time program, four 4-month semesters, with a new cycle beginning every four months. Students clock in 2,240 hours of classes and professional instruction in basic and advanced professional cooking techniques, basic and advanced pastry baking, restaurant theory and service, *garde-manger*, wines, and restaurant management. The program is flexible enough to provide credit for work and study abroad or apprenticeships with master chefs. The Academy is a wonderful mix of students: young people just out of high school as well as older people making a career change. Graduates are in high demand; you'll find them manning the stoves in restaurants all over the city.

To get a glimpse of the workings of the school, you can have lunch or dinner at the school's formal dining room. Through a glass wall you can watch a legion of fledgling chefs at work in the kitchen preparing the elegant multicourse meal you'll be served.

### San Francisco
## THE CHARCUTERIE COOKING SCHOOL

*25 Buena Vista Terrace, San Francisco 94117. Telephone (415) 431-0211.*

San Francisco's Charcuterie Cooking School, directed by Scottie McKinney and Gayle DeKellis, offers classes taught by working professionals in food and wine. The day-long classes cover, of course, *charcuterie*, including a class in pâtés, *terrines*, and galantines, and another in *saucisses françaises*; as well as classes in such subjects as sauces, *boulangerie*, or *pâtisserie*.

Inexpensive evening classes instruct students in aspics, French culinary terminology, wild mushrooms, cheese and wine, or Spanish *paella*. There is also a four-session series in the basics of French cooking.

In the past, the school's wine evenings were special events with local experts instructing in their expertise—Darrell Corti on sherry, Andrew Quady on port, Sergio Treviso on champagne—but Ms. McKinney has recently launched the Wine Education Center at the Vintners Club in San Francisco, where all wine events and classes will now be held (see Wine section).

**Peninsula**
## CHARLOTTE COMBE COOKING SCHOOL

*959 Woodside Road, Redwood City 94061. Telephone (415) 365-0548.*

From her remodeled house in Redwood City fully outfitted with a professional teaching kitchen, Charlotte Combe teaches a remarkable series of cooking classes. The orientation here is French, with an emphasis on solid technique and knowledge of ingredients. Ms. Combe did a rigorous five-year training with master French chef Jacques Pepin and is the only person in this country to hold a certificate of apprenticeship from him.

She schedules her classes for a two-year program, giving five-week sessions at a time, but students may take just one series if they wish. Classes in each five-week series are held once a week, and students can enroll for either morning or evening sessions. Because Ms. Combe wants students to be able to see every step of every dish, classes here are always demonstration. She feels that participation classes are distracting because nothing gets undivided attention.

Write for a schedule of classes with their menus. Closed during August and September.

**Napa Valley**
## CUISINE RENAISSANCE

*3415 Solano Avenue, Napa 94558. Telephone (707) 252-9400.*

Cuisine Renaissance offers individual classes in subjects such as *paella, sorbet,* the food processor, etc., in the store's big demonstration kitchen. Watch for guest teachers like Diana Kennedy, author of several authoritative cookbooks on the cuisines of Mexico; or Sacramento's Biba Caggiano, who teaches classes in her native northern Italian cuisine.

Write for schedule.

**San Jose Area**
## FLOCKS AND MELENDY COOKING SCHOOL

*19720 Stevens Creek Boulevard, Cupertino 95014. Telephone (408) 996-0556.*

In Cupertino, the Classic Kitchen cookware store is associated with Flocks and Melendy Cooking School. Individual morning and evening classes include soups, hot and cold; a salad seminar; Italian seafood; barbecuing; and a French dinner series.

**Napa Valley**
## THE GREAT CHEFS OF FRANCE

*Robert Mondavi Winery, 7801 St. Helena Highway (P.O. Box 106), Oakville 94562. Telephone (707) 963-9611.*

Three or four times a year, the Great Chefs of France arranges a week-long class with a visiting French chef in the kitchen of the Robert Mondavi winery in Napa Valley. Classes are taught by such culinary luminaries as Gaston Le Nôtre, Jean and Pierre Troisgros, Michel Guerard, Simone Beck, and our own Julia Child. Students spend a sybaritic week in the Napa Valley working hard, but also enjoying lavish lunches and dinners prepared by chef Michael James and his staff, as well as tastings of rare California wines.

**San Francisco**
## JUDITH ETS-HOKIN CULINARY INSTITUTE

*3525 California Street, San Francisco 94118. Telephone (415) 668-3191.*

In 1972 Judith Ets-Hokin founded her culinary institute after studying at Le Cordon Bleu in London. She explains that the school's goal is "to give the aspiring home cook an opportunity to learn the concepts and basic skills necessary to create exciting and interesting meals."

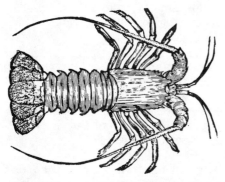

The "Basic Cooking" series (eighteen classes) takes an inexperienced cook through basic cooking methods, concepts, and techniques including stocks, glazes, mother sauces, poaching, sautéing, grilling, pastry, cake, bread, and pâtés. The class is offered both mornings and evenings.

The school also schedules individual classes in specific techniques such as boning poultry and fish, pastry making, pasta making, or food processor cooking.

After students have mastered the basic skills, they are ready for intermediate-level classes in Chinese family cooking, northern Italian menus, or Viennese pastry.

The school has a student assistant program in which participants help prepare for classes and do practical food work in exchange for classes.
*Write or call for schedule.*

**East Bay**
## THE KEN HOM COOKING SCHOOL

*P.O. Box 4303, Berkeley 94704. Telephone (415) 843-5579.*

Ken Hom started his cooking apprenticeship early. As an 11 year old, he started working in the kitchen of his uncle's Chinese restaurant in Chicago. Since his uncle would bring in chefs from Hong Kong from regions all over China, Ken learned about all the cuisines of China. Later, as a film student in Europe, he lived with French families and was introduced to the best of the *cuisine bourgeoise.*

He's been teaching cooking classes in the Bay Area for eight years, is on the faculty of the California Culinary Academy, and is the author of the recently published book, *Chinese Technique.* Several times a year Mr. Hom holds private cooking seminars at his large, well-equipped kitchen in Berkeley. These intensive three-day classes are intended primarily for professional cooks and advanced students. Classes are small, just six to eight students. He likes to combine Chinese techniques with French cuisine in these master classes, demonstrating both with grace and skill.

In 1982, Mr. Hom will be opening a cooking school in Hong Kong to teach Chinese cuisine to classes of mostly western students. For information about this program, contact Ms. Susan Maurer, Director, Ken Hom in Hong Kong, 1057 Cragmont Avenue, Berkeley 94708, telephone (415) 524-4899 or 254-8433.

San Francisco
## LA CUISINE COOKING SCHOOL

*1555 Pacific Avenue, San Francisco 94109. Telephone (415) 441-3548.*

Associated with La Cuisine cookware store next door to the Oakville Grocery on Pacific, this cooking school offers Saturday afternoon and evening workshops and classes taught by guest chefs: dinner classes with Jean-Luc Chassereau from the California Culinary Academy; "Sunday supper" menus with Peter Brown, head chef of the Cypress Point Club at Pebble Beach; breads and pastries with Bo Inge Friberg, pastry chef; fresh pasta and regional pizza classes with David Pellerito, a student of Giuliano Bugialli in Florence. Most classes are demonstration, limited to twenty; participation classes are limited to eight.

Marin County
## LE CORDON ROUGE

*1020 C Street, San Rafael 94901. Telephone (415) 459-2026.*

Le Cordon Rouge offers classes in an enormous range of skill levels and formats, from individual two- or three-hour classes (basic, basic, *basic* cooking; classes for men only; a French sauce workshop) to full-time and part-time professional courses (basic, intermediate, advanced, and master levels) and a course for would-be cooking teachers.

Most of the individual classes are held in the evening, with an occasional morning class, and cover a tremendous amount of culinary ground, including Donna Nordin's all-day croissant workshop; a quiche workshop; classes in charlottes, Viennese pastry, and pasta; a class in the art of *confit,* or preserved duck, goose, and pork, as practiced in southwestern France.

Those with professional cooking ambitions should investigate the school's professional courses at four levels. Each course involves approximately 350 hours of work. Day students attend classes all day Monday through Friday for ten weeks, whereas evening and weekend students may take up to five months to complete each level. The classes are small, limited to twelve students, and taught by classically trained French chefs.

For further information on the program, contact Jay Perkins, director.

The school also offers a six-session professional catering course.

A new kitchen will soon provide space for private cooking classes for one to four people.

San Francisco
## THE JACK LIRIO COOKING SCHOOL

*747 Monterey Boulevard, San Francisco 94111. Telephone (415) 587-8908.*

After a sojourn in France where he studied French cooking at Le Cordon Bleu in Paris, and pastry making at Gaston Le Nôtre's famous school and at the Richemont pastry school, Jack Lirio came home to open his own cooking school. These days he spends much of the year giving demonstrations and classes as a guest teacher at other cooking schools in cities all over the country. Between stints he has written a cookbook, *Cooking with Jack Lirio,* which was published this spring by William Morrow. Because of his impossible schedule, his San Francisco-based cooking school is open only in summer, when he gives participation classes for small groups of students.

An intensive one-week course is custom-tailored to the needs of the student-participants for the week. Before the class is planned, students choose the dishes they'd like to learn from a long list of possibilities. One week is a pastry week, other weeks are for advanced students only, and another is for intermediate and advanced cooks. Students work from 10 to 2, then break for a lunch that includes a tasting of fine California wines matched with the day's menu. And on Thursday night of the week's class, guests are invited to a gala champagne buffet with hors d'oeuvres, hot dishes, and elegant pastries, all made by students in the class.

## San Francisco
## LONI KUHN'S COOK'S TOUR

*91 Commonwealth Avenue, San Francisco 94118. Telephone (415) 752-5265.*

At San Francisco's Cook's Tour Cooking School, Loni Kuhn, a generous, energetic woman with an earthy sense of humor, shares her considerable knowledge of the cuisines of the Mediterranean and Mexico with her students. Her two- to four-week series of classes are given once a week, both mornings and evenings.

Northern Italian cooking is her specialty. (When noted Italian cooking teacher Marcella Hazan comes to town, she holds her classes at Loni's school.) Come to cook and eat dishes from a series of well-researched regional menus. Students can and are encouraged to repeat the class. She's taught over fifteen different series of Italian classes.

Though she specializes in Mediterranean food, Ms. Kuhn has an unabated interest in exploring other ethnic cuisines. She'll give classes in Moroccan cooking, regional Mexican food, and ocasionally, Oriental cuisine. She also gives small groups of students walking and shopping tours of the Mission, Chinatown, or North Beach.

In the sausage-making class, you can learn to make a sausage from a different

country each week: Italian pork sausage, Armenian lamb, New Orleans seafood, French *boudin blanc.* The appealing country French series emphasizes shrewd peasant dishes like braised pork, lentil and goat cheese salads, fresh fruit *sorbets.*

Loni knows the city backwards and forward, and she believes in searching for the best ingredients for her fresh cuisine. She shops early Saturday mornings at the Farmers' Market and grows leeks, chard, lettuce, and herbs in her San Francisco backyard.

Loni Kuhn also teaches at Le Cordon Rouge in San Rafael and at Tante Marie's Cooking School in the city.

Single classes at Cook's Tour are available as space permits. Write for a listing of upcoming classes.

## East Bay
## NEIGHBORLY KITCHENS

*2932 Harper, Berkeley 94703. Telephone (415) 540-5916.*

Neighborly Kitchens was started three years ago by a Berkeley-based community group to inform the public about the political and physical aspects of nutrition. The group offers small workshops in food-preserving methods such as canning, drying, freezing, sourdough baking, pickling, and fermenting (*tempeh, yogurt*).

Write or call Fiona Herron at Neighborly Kitchens for information. The three-hour workshops are limited to ten to twelve people. The cost is nominal.

Eventually the group hopes to have a big well-equipped central kitchen where neighbors can get together regularly to make their own high-quality preserved food products.

**Peninsula**
## PECKS COOKING SCHOOL

*275 Primrose Road, Burlingame 94010. Telephone (415) 348-5344.*

Pecks Cooking School (associated with Pecks Gourmet Cookware) initiated its cooking class program in 1981. A wide range of one-session classes is offered almost every day. Most are morning classes, but evening classes are also scheduled.

There are menu classes for students who want to increase their repertoire of dishes, and classes in techniques such as honing and boning, basic and intermediate pastry, *filo* dough or puff pastry, and, of course, food processor cooking—even microwave oven–food processor cooking.

Expert guest instructors also offer classes in their area of expertise: Donna Nordin teaching pâtés and *terrines,* advanced pastries, or entertaining in the French manner; and Loni Kuhn giving a special Italian food class.
*Quarterly schedule of classes.*

**Contra Costa**
## THE QUESTING FEAST

*Geraldine Duncann, 3440 Mountain Spring Road, Lafayette 94549. Telephone (415) 939-6369.*

The Questing Feast is a small cooking school where students learn to cook dishes from the world's cuisines, accompanied with the "history, legends, and traditions behind the development of the foods and culture that produced them."

Logging over twenty-one thousand miles of travel this past year, Geraldine Duncann has researched the cuisines of Mexico, the Cajun and Creole country, the American Southwest, England, Scotland, Wales, Normandy, Brittany, Languedoc, Provence, Burgundy, Pied-

mont, and Sicily. Though she spends much of the year traveling and researching, Ms. Duncann is at home every winter to teach classes in her Lafayette home and to write her syndicated food and travel column, which appears in the *Examiner.* Her list of one-day classes changes constantly with her impulse and inspiration: "Foods of Catalonia," "Victorian English Breakfast," The Cornish Kitchen," "Pub Grub," "The Foods of Brittany," "Foods from the Irish Countryside," or "Regency Baking of Bath" (the teatime delights described in Jane Austin's novels). Evening tastings might include a Tom Jones dinner or a feast of Russian *bliny* piled high with sour cream, caviar, and smoked fish, washed down with flavored vodkas.

At Christmas she offers courses in plum puddings and Christmas cakes (using recipes dating as early as the fifteenth century), pâtés, Christmas candies, and Christmas breads.
*Write for brochure.*

**East Bay**
## RICHARDSON RESEARCHES

*26046 Eden Landing Road No. 1, Hayward 94545. Telephone (415) 785-1350.*

Terry Richardson has worked in the confectionary and chocolate industry for almost thirty years, including a stint with a company in London that supplied chocolates to the royal family. His company, Richardson Researches, a confectionary-industry research company, periodically offers intensive weeklong courses in commercial chocolate and confectionary techniques. In the "Continental Chocolates" course, students first learn chocolate handling and tempering and then learn to make chocolates using a variety of commercial techniques. "Confectionary Technology" explores the properties of ingredients used in confectionary. During the "Chocolate Technology" course, students learn chocolate manufacturing and processing from the cocoa bean to the tempering of chocolate and the molding and enrobing of candies, as well as the operation of standard chocolate-making machinery. If you adored *Willie Wonka and the Chocolate Factory*, this is the course for you.

*Very expensive.*

**San Francisco**
## TANTE MARIE'S COOKING SCHOOL

*271 Francisco Street, San Francisco 94133. Telephone (415) 771-8667 or 397-5522.*

Mary Risley, director of Tante Marie's Cooking School, studied at fine cooking schools both here and in Europe, including Le Cordon Bleu in London and La Varenne in Paris. The school's all-day year-round classes are intended for people who are serious about fine cooking, whether professionally or nonprofessionally. A variety of programs are offered, with courses ranging in length from one week to nine months. You can attend all day every day or once a week, or you can sign up for individual demonstration classes.

For the very serious, the nine-month certificate course, divided into beginning, intermediate, and advanced terms, is a "thorough in-depth examination of fine cooking, from stocks and sauces to aspic and sugar work." The three-month certificate course is a condensed version of the nine-month course.

Tante Marie's also offers intensive one-week courses all through the year. Mornings are spent in participation classes preparing menus from fine classical cuisine. After lunch each day, there is an afternoon demonstration with a guest chef. These are open to other students as space allows. Periodically, pastry chef Diane Dexter gives a pastry week. Twelve students in these "hands on," all-day classes learn

to make French *gâteaux*, Viennese tortes, handmade strudel, yeast pastries, and candies.

The less-intensive evening classes meet once a week for six weeks. Students prepare both simple and elaborate menus, then sit down and eat together.

But for those without a lot of time to commit, afternoon demonstrations, which are part of the curriculum for full-time students, are ideal. These are open to the public as space allows. You might find Carlo Middione teaching the Italian way with veal or with fish, Annie May de Bresson demonstrating ice creams and *sorbets*, or Donna Nordin making pâtés, *terrines*, and galantines. Guest chefs present classes in this format, too: Mark Miller of the Fourth Street Grill, Sally Schmidt of the French Laundry in Yountville, or Alice Medrich of Cocolat. And once a week, British wine expert Peter Wilkins holds a class in wine tasting. Each week is an investigation and tasting of a different varietal or combination of wine and food.

Ask to receive *Tante Marie's Newsletter* for best bets, recipes, news of graduates, and upcoming courses, workshops, and demonstrations.

**San Francisco**
## THE UNIVERSITY OF CALIFORNIA EXTENSION

*55 Laguna Street, San Francisco 94102. Telephone (415) 642-1061.*

The University of California Extension has classes grouped under "Food and Wine Studies." The classes vary throughout the year, but you might find courses such as a class in pasta and sauces or "Cooking Without Recipes," taught by Joyce Esersky Goldstein, founder and former director of the California Street Cooking School and head chef at Café Panisse; classes in French food or California cuisine, taught by Marinette

Georgi; or the history of French food, taught by food scholar Mireille Isler.

If you're interested in learning how to collect or cultivate edible mushrooms, check "Cultivation of Edible Mushrooms," offered under "Natural Environmental Studies." It's intended for amateur gardeners interested in cultivating the common *agaricus* and other species such as *shiitake,* oyster, and paddy straw mushrooms.

# COOKING TEACHERS

Following is a listing of chefs who give cooking classes. This, however, is only a partial listing of the Bay Area's many cooking teachers. If you'd like to find someone to help you with special cooking problems or techniques, contact the San Francisco Professional Food Society, P.O. Box 77105, San Francisco 94107, for a more complete listing of professional cooking teachers.

### San Francisco
## JOSEPHINE ARALDO

*2666 McAllister Street, San Francisco 94118. Telephone (415) 221-1685.*

The *grande dame* of cooking teachers in San Francisco is Madame Josephine Araldo, a tiny French woman who graduated from the Cordon Bleu in the twenties, was at one time Isadora Duncan's chef, and has cooked for many prominent San Francisco families.

Her mentor was Henri-Paul Pellaprat, who was at the Cordon Bleu in her day. "He gave me my first *toque blanche* and said 'I crown you chef.' "

Now well over eighty years old, Josephine continues to teach the popular cooking classes she's given for years in her own kitchen. The classes are all demonstration, with Josephine keeping up a steady stream of advice, stories, songs, and variations on the recipe at hand. Every year she draws dish after dish out of her magician's hat of memories and inventions. Most are from the tradition of French country cooking.

When class is over and everything is cooked, students sit down with Josephine to a congenial family-style meal. Josephine's husband Charles, whom she affectionately calls "my gigolo," sometimes serenades the company on his accordion.

Josephine is the author of two cookbooks: *Cooking with Josephine* and *Sounds from Josephine's Kitchen.*

### Marin County
## LENORE BLEADON

*170 Rancharia Road, Kentfield 94904. Telephone (415) 461-0998.*

Lenore Bleadon teaches classes in northern Italian cuisine both privately and at the College of Marin.

### Peninsula
## FLO BRAKER

*1441 Edgewood Drive, Palo Alto 94301. Telephone (415) 327-0221.*

Cooking teacher Flo Braker specializes in both fine European and traditional American pastries. She'll also consult with individuals or small groups with special pastry or baking problems.

### East Bay
## ANNIE MAY DE BRESSON

*1438 Hawthorne Terrace, Berkeley 94708. Telephone (415) 841-0265.*

Annie May de Bresson, a native of France but educated here, has been teaching French cuisine in the Bay Area for over ten years. Her evening classes are held in her comfortable home and can be taken individually or as a series. They cover a wide range of subjects such as French bread and main-course soups, tarts and quiches, "Cuisinartistry," chocoholics' cakes and pastries, boning, sausage and pâté making, etc.

At holiday time she offers "Christmas Favorites" classes, one with traditional English sweets like plum pudding, mincemeat, and fruitcake, another with French *bûche de Noël* and other seasonal pastries.

She periodically teaches a series of classes on basic techniques, pastry, *nouvelle gastronomie*, country cooking, and summer cooking. She also teaches daytime classes at Tante Marie's Cooking School in San Francisco.

For those who would like to experience the cuisine of France firsthand, each year she takes a group of Americans to France on a gastronomic tour.

## Sacramento
## BIBA CAGGIANO

*1411 Forty-sixth Street, Sacramento 95819. Telephone (916) 453-1466.*

Biba Caggiano teaches classes in her native northern Italian cooking at the William Glen School in Sacramento and occasionally at Cuisine Renaissance in Napa and elsewhere in northern California. Her weekly cooking program appears on a local Sacramento television station, and her cookbook, *Northern Italian Cooking,* was published last year.

## East Bay
## MIREILLE ISLER

*2323 Rose Street, Berkeley 94708. Telephone (415) 841-2175.*

Food historian Mireille Isler, librarian for the San Francisco Professional Food Society and a member of the West Coast Nutritional Anthropologists, the California Archive Association, and many gastronomic clubs, has lectured and written for years both in her native France and here on the intriguing topic of food history.

Each year she gives three series of five-week classes on "How to Talk Cuisine." Students in one class learn how to read menus, how to speak up to an arrogant waiter, and where and how to shop in Paris, all in impeccable French. In her French conversation class, students discuss "the table as center-stage and plot" in readings from French literature from Rabelais to Colette. Ms. Isler discusses the origin and history of culinary terms in a class called "The Story Behind the Table"—this one in English. You can learn the why and how of such familiar terms as *cognac, croissant, champagne, maître d'hotel,* etc.

Not all her classes are for francophiles. She has offered classes in a variety of subjects such as the chronological history of liqueurs, and the food and drink of birth, marriage, and death rituals around the world.

She has also taught at Tante Marie's Cooking School in San Francisco and through the University of California Extension.

## San Francisco
## JOYCE JUE

*262 Corbett Avenue, San Francisco 94114. Telephone (415) 863-7881.*

Joyce Jue is a free-lance cooking instructor specializing in Chinese cuisine. She will also lead small groups on Chinatown culinary tours.

## San Francisco
## MARLENE LEVINSON

*55 Raycliff Terrace, San Francisco 94115. Telephone (415) 921-4060.*

Marlene Levinson teaches classes in French cooking, and food processor workshops.

**East Bay**
# SHEILA LINDERMAN

*765 Rand Avenue, No. 104, Oakland 94610. Telephone (415) 451-8750.*

Sheila Linderman, pastry chef at Cocolat, offers lessons in pastry making to those interested in European pastry.

**San Francisco**
# CARLO MIDDIONE

*131 Delmar Street, San Francisco 94117. Telephone (415) 431-9513.*

Carlo Middione, the familiar chef on "AM San Francisco" and one of the proprietors of Vivande, Fillmore Street's elegant deli, teaches classes in fine Italian cuisine at both the California Culinary Academy and at Tante Marie's Cooking School. At Tante Marie's he teaches a wonderful Italian dinner series as well as classes in pasta and the Italian way with veal or with fish.

Though his schedule is quite crowded, he will occasionally teach small classes in his own home for individuals and private small groups.

**Napa Valley**
# BELLE RHODES

*Bella Oaks Vineyard, P.O. Box 409, Rutherford 94573. Telephone (707) 963-3520.*

Belle Rhodes teaches cooking, demonstrates equipment, and coordinates and presents chefs' classes, primarily at Napa Valley wineries.

**East Bay**
# DANIEL STRONGIN

*Augusta's Restaurant, 2955 Telegraph Avenue, Berkeley 94704. Telephone (415) 548-3140.*

Daniel Strongin, chef at Augusta's Restaurant in Berkeley, teaches a four-week, four-class, intensive cooking seminar in French cuisine. Recently arrived in the Bay Area from Boston, where he cooked at the Ritz-Carlton, Chef Strongin has also taught in Boston and New York. Ask him to see a copy of the wonderful review of his all-night French cooking class that appeared in the *New Yorker.* Daniel Strongin is a rare find: a classically trained chef and a good teacher with a lively spirit of fun.

**San Francisco**
# BARBARA TROPP

*176 Pixley, San Francisco 94123. Telephone (415) 922-4789.*

Barbara Tropp—Chinese scholar, freelance cooking teacher, food writer, and caterer—offers classes in Chinese food and culture.

**Contra Costa**
# KEN WOLFE

*P.O. Box 456, Lafayette 94549. Telephone (415) 939-1629.*

Chef Ken Wolfe has been an inspiring teacher in the Bay Area for many years. His former students are running fine restaurants and food stores all over the city. Though he gives professional training courses through Contra Costa College, he also offers a five-week series of classes in his home in Lafayette. And for return students and professionals, he has a series of four-hour master classes in which students learn to prepare elaborate dishes using specialized techniques.

His once-a-month "social seminars" on Saturday mornings include a sit-down lunch of the class dishes. As interest dictates, he plans individual classes in a wide range of subjects.

# Cookware

With a sophisticated cookware store in every neighborhood, some cooks' kitchens are more arsenals of cookware than *batteries de cuisine*. Although all the ingenious kitchen gadgets are fun, and using the perfect pan to make a certain dish is a pleasure, an imaginative cook can do a lot with just a few basics. M.F.K. Fisher tells a wonderful story about an accomplished cook she once knew, who never used any utensil more sophisticated than a fork.

San Francisco chef Josephine Araldo's French cooking classes are all about what you *don't* need in order to execute complicated dishes. Trained at the Cordon Bleu in the twenties under Henri Paul Pellaprat, she can make a fine *paella* in a dented aluminum saucepan rather than the wide shallow traditional pan. She seems content with a few wooden spoons and a whisk to do just about everything. Even when Josephine succumbed to the charms of the Cuisinart, she still cooked in the battered and decidedly not-copper pans she'd used for years.

Some of the city's more unusual or ethnic-oriented sources for cookware are described below, followed by a listing of Bay Area cookware stores.

## BARBECUE & PICNIC SUPPLIES

### East Bay * Grills
### CARTER RENTAL

*1501 Eastshore Highway, Berkeley 94710. Telephone (415) 527-3330. Hours: 7:30–5:30 daily.*

For big outdoor parties, Carter Rental has barbecue grills on rolling legs. Two feet by five feet, they're big enough to grill a side of ribs, a couple of dozen hot links, and five cut-up chickens at one time. Lay in a supply of Lazzari's hot-

burning mesquite-wood charcoal for a superior grilled taste.

Carter's also rents fifteen-quart chafing dishes, fifty-five- to one-hundred-cup coffee makers, punch bowls, champagne glasses, and china and glassware.

### Peninsula * Charcoal
### LAZZARI FUEL COMPANY

*Geneva Avenue and Bayshore Boulevard, South San Francisco 94080. Telephone (415) 467-2970. Hours: M–F 8–4:30, SAT 9–12.*

Recently, it's become quite fashionable to grill meats and fish over mesquite-wood charcoal. But it's more than fashionable, it's delicious. Mesquite-wood charcoal is made by the Yaqui Indians of north central Mexico. The charcoal itself is beautiful—carbonized chunks of wood, all odd sizes—no uniform square chunks here. Its advantage is its superb flavor and the fact that it burns very hot, as high as 1000 degrees. This means the meat or fish is seared quickly to seal in the natural juices and flavor.

Mesquite wood charcoal is certainly more expensive than briquettes; however, it burns a long time and the food cooks quickly. Some people even reuse it once.

Lazzari mesquite-wood charcoal is widely distributed. You can find it at Safeway stores, Alpha Beta stores, and many cookware stores in the smaller bag size. But it's a real savings to make the trip to Lazzari in South San Francisco and buy a twenty- or forty-pound bag direct from them. Split it with a friend if it seems more than you can envision using.

### San Francisco ∗ Picnic Supplies
### TISKIT A TASKET

*Ghirardelli Square, 900 North Point Street, San Francisco 94109. Telephone (415) 775-5263. Hours: 11–6 daily.*

San Francisco's only picnic-supply depot, Tisket a Tasket, has picnic baskets from the very inexpensive (a simple brown bag) up to the Rolls Royce of picnic baskets, the Brexton. Made by the English since the 1800's from un-split full reeds, these splendid baskets will last literally for generations: grown-up great-grandchildren are still using their great-grandmothers' baskets. They have another wonderful picnic basket in infrequent supply, made by only one family in Italy, along with baskets from Vermont and the South, and even a thoroughly modern clear Lucite bas-ket. And to transport delicate pastries to your picnic spot, they have old-fashioned "pie-saver" baskets that hold two pies or pastries.

The full supply of fittings for baskets includes plastic dishes, thermoses, glasses, wine goblets, cutlery, wine caddies, linens, tablecloths, and napkins, plus blankets and spreads for the ground.

Soon to be installed: a mini-deli stocked with fine picnic foods.

# BUTCHER SUPPLY
# SAUSAGE MAKING

### San Jose Area
### CALIFORNIA
### BUTCHER SUPPLY

*451 Los Coches, Milpitas 95035. Telephone (800) 662-6212. Hours: M–F 8–5, SAT 9–1.*

This store has butcher blocks, Forschner knives, sharpening steels, and professional sausage-making supplies such as natural sheep and hog casings (dry or water packed). For a one-hundred-yard hank, you'll need one hundred pounds of sausage meat, but they sell the commonly used hog casing by half-doll, too: 7-1/2 yards for ten pounds of meat, appropriate for the home sausage maker. There are also Chop Rite grinders, blades, stuffing horns, and packaged spices for pork, *linguiça*, chorizo, and Polish sausages. Each packet seasons fifty pounds of sausage meat.

### Peninsula
### CARLSON BUTCHER SUPPLY

*2609 San Bruno Avenue, South San Francisco 94080. Telephone (415) 468-3335. Hours: M–F 9–5.*

Carlson Butcher Supply has everything for sausage making except the meat and the fat: big sausage grinders with their own stuffers, fine or coarse grinding plates, even a special plate for grinding chilies. They have sausage-stuffing attachments for both hog and sheep casings.

Their water-packed sausage casings are hog, sheep, or beef. Teach yourself how to do it all with *Great Sausage Recipes and Meat Curing* by Rytek Kutas. For pumping brine into a ham, they have a hand meat pump. There are Forschner knives for butchers; stainless steel, they say, keeps a better edge.

Basic spices are sold in bulk, and Carlson's sells their own seasoning mixes for sausages—Italian, southern-style pork, or farm-style pork. Sea salts and curing salts are here, too.

**Peninsula**
## URBAN P. DRESDEN

*2259 Spring, Redwood City 94063. Telephone (415) 365-1062. Hours: M–F 8–4.*

Urban P. Dresden deals only in butcher blocks: all new, all maple, and in various sizes. Sometimes he has a used one, but rarely. He also resurfaces old butcher blocks, evening out the inevitable hollows and dents from years of usage.

# CAKE DECORATING
# COOKIE MAKING

**Marin County**
## CAKE ART

*2144 Fourth Street, San Rafael 94901. Telephone (415) 456-7773. Hours: M–SAT 10–4.*

Cake Art is Marin County's center for cake decorating supplies. Owner Maria Klopfer stocks professional sheet pans; graduated sizes of cake pans in rounds, squares, and rectangles; and all kinds of odd-shaped pans—animals and other fancy shapes—plus dozens of cake decorating tips, pastry bags, and sets of colors.

She gives inexpensive six-session cake decorating classes at beginning, intermediate, and advanced levels, as well as one-day classes in candy making where you can learn to make chocolate, filled chocolates, and English toffee. No cake pan rental.

**San Francisco**
## COOKIE QUEEN

*P.O. BOX 15475, Station A, San Francisco 94115. Mail order only.*

Lawrence Maloney once had a wonderful tiny store on Fillmore Street called Cookie Queen. This store was a marvel of design and ingenuity, filled to bursting with every kind of equipment for making cookies from all over the world: hundreds of cookie cutters, cookie molds, cookie presses, cookie stamps, cookie rollers, hand-carved German *Springerle* molds and *Springerle* rolling pins, carved molds for *speculaas,* or honey gingerbread, and *pain d'épice, pizzelle* irons and rosette irons.

Now the irrepressible Mr. Maloney has transformed Cookie Queen into a mail order business. Catalogs are $1.50.

**San Francisco**
## THE FLUTED EDGE

*1469 Church Street, San Francisco 94131. Telephone (415) 282-0577. Hours: T–F 11–5, SAT 11–3.*

At this tiny store on Church Street, owner Janet M. Phillips dispenses advice to local aspiring cake decorators. She's got all the metal pastry tips—for making simple outlines to the most fol-de-rol fluted edges and fantastic flowers—but she herself confesses to using just three to do everything. You can find parchment paper to make your pastry bags, commercial food coloring dyes, and professional cake pans.

She also gives cake decorating lessons. No cake pan rental.

**East Bay**
## OUR PERSONAL TOUCH

*4100 Redwood Road, Oakland 94619. Telephone (415) 530-3828. Hours: T–SAT 10–6.*

Our Personal Touch is another cake decorating supply store where you'll find all the standard-sized pans, even half-circle pans sixteen or eighteen inches across for ovens too small to fit the whole, as well as novelty pans.

Make a Big Bird or Superman and Superwoman cake. Set it up properly on one of the store's doilies and cake boards and deliver your creation in one of their professional-looking pink bakery boxes.

For candymakers, they have candy molds and candy boxes.

## San Francisco
## SUGAR AND SPICE

*3200 Balboa Street, San Francisco 94121. Telephone (415) 387-1722. Hours: M–SAT 10-5.*

Sugar and Spice has "everything you need to put together a cake," including decorative wedding and birthday cake tops. No cake pan rental.

# CUTLERY
# KNIFE SHARPENING

## San Francisco
## COLUMBUS CUTLERY

*358 Columbus Avenue, San Francisco 94111. Telephone (415) 362-1342. Hours: M–TH, SAT 9:30-6; F 9:30-5.*

Pietro Malattia's father was seventy-eight when he opened Columbus Cutlery in 1964. His father had opened up shop as a knife sharpener in Bucharest in 1850. After peregrinations through Rumania, France, Switzerland, and the Veneto worthy of a gypsy band (which they are) the Malattia family landed in North Beach, where their shop has been constantly busy ever since.

Bring in your dull knives. Pietro or his wife Ottilia will look at them and give you an estimate. They'll also give you expert advice on choosing from any of the hundreds of knives for sale in their very tiny shop: imported Henckels, Solingen, R. H. Forschner,

and U.S.-made Chicago and Dexter brands. There are heavy-duty cleavers from Germany, grinding stones and steels, and, for the restaurant trade, meat and bone saws hanging overhead. Any knife they don't have, they'll order for you.

And of course, because they come from northern Italy, there are *mezzalune* (the double-handled half-moon–shaped blade for chopping herbs), meat grinders for sausage making, sausage-stuffing funnels, Atlas pasta machines, and corkscrews. And dozens of culinary utensils like pastry brushes, garlic presses, ravioli cutters, meat larders, oyster knives, and melon ballers.

Pietro also repairs Swiss army knives—he'll replace your lost tweezers or toothpick and fix your scissors.

## East Bay
## THE EDGE OF THE WORLD

*Jack London Square, 55 Alice Street, Oakland 94607. Telephone (415) 763-0523. Hours: M–SAT 10:30-6; F 10:30-9:30; SUN 11:30-6.*

A sheetmetal worker and an amateur knife maker, Al Ernst opened the Edge of the World six years ago. Originally, he planned to make knives in the back while his wife Cyrilla and his daughter sold the knives in the front, but their busy knife repair and sharpening work hasn't given him the time. All the sharpening is done strictly by hand grinding; they have no grinding wheel.

Once he's given a fine edge to your knife, he'll demonstrate the use of either natural Arkansas whetstones or man-made carborundum whetstones to keep that edge.

He carries only the brands of knives he has found to be consistent: Henckel's, Trident, two brands of Sabatier (both imported by Forschner's) and a big selection of Forschner in both plastic and wooden handles, including butcher knives and meat cutters and twenty different boning knifes. Mr. Ernst considers Gerber, made in Portland, Oregon, to be the best American-made cutlery on the market. He has both the wooden-handled professional series and the chrome-handled.

You can find meat saws, aluminum butcher sheaths, knife rolls (a cloth roll with narrow pockets for storing knives), knife blocks, oyster knives, clam shucking knives, egg shears, grape shears, etc.

## San Francisco
## THE EXCLUSIVE CUTLERY SHOP

*170 Geary Boulevard, San Francisco 94108. Telephone (415) 421-2412. Hours: M–SAT 9:30–5:30.*

In 1911 the original Exclusive Cutlery opened at 115 Stockton Street, later moving to its present location on Geary Boulevard near Union Square. The grandfather of the present owner, Herman Bergfried, Jr., had come from Brazil, and at the turn of the century ran the Henckels cutlery office in New York. He later represented Henckels in the West, and in 1911 opened his own cutlery store in San Francisco.

Of course the store still carries the fine-quality J. A. Henckels knives, but the Exclusive Cutlery Shop "specializes in the specialists": a few very small cutlery concerns with limited production. The Bergfrieds have done business with some of them for many years, and they maintain the contacts with frequent trips to Europe.

In addition to Henckels, they carry knives from Friedr. Herder (an old German concern) and a very fine line of French knives, Tichet from Nogent. The two American lines are W. R. Case from Bradford, Pennsylvania, and Russell Harrington from South Bridge, Massachusetts.

They have a complete line of knife blocks, knife rolls, scissors, shears, stones, and steels; and they will do complete sharpening, regrinding, and repair of knives, shears, and cutters.

## East Bay
## WOODLINE: THE JAPAN WOODWORKER

*1731 Clement Avenue, Alameda 94501. Telephone (415) 521-1810. Hours: M–SAT 9:30–5.*

It's hard not to covet everything in the Japan Woodworker: the beautifully designed books, the handsome traditional chisels and saws for woodworking, and the fine Japanese cutlery. Owners Keith Nason and Fred Damson have established and maintained contacts with families of craftsmen in Japan who have been making the same traditional tools for generations.

The professional chef's knives (*hocho*) are hand forged by master toolmakers from a combination of hard and soft carbon steels. The Japanese technique of sandwiching a core of steel between layers of soft iron so that only a thin line of steel is exposed enables the blade to take and hold an edge far sharper than any western knife. The highest-quality *hocho* have magnolia wood handles and buffalo-hide ferrules. The store has a selection of *deba hocho*, an all-purpose knife; *sashimi hocho*, for paper-thin slicing of fish and meat; and *usubu hocho*, a vegetable-slicing knife.

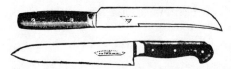

Prices are in the same range as for fine western kitchen knives. Instructions for sharpening are given with each knife, and it's wise to invest in a whetstone when buying knives. The Japan Woodworker has two classes of the Japanese water stones used all over Asia. Made especially for these knives, they work well for western knives too. There are *toishi* (coarse stones) of various grit sizes for initial sharpening, and *shiai toishi* (finish stones), composed of a rare earth polishing-compound for the final honing and polishing of the edge. You'll need one of each. Water stones cut much faster and give much finer edge than the Arkansas stones also carried here.

# ETHNIC
# COOKWARE

### San Francisco * Italian
## BIORDI ARTIGIANATO ITALIANO

*412 Columbus Avenue, San Francisco 94133. Telephone (415) 392-8096. Hours: M-SAT 9-6.*

Since 1946, Biordi Artigianato Italiano has been the local source for imported Italian cookware and pottery. A visit to the Etruscan museum at Pisa inspired Mr. Biordi to introduce the original Etruscan clay cooker in 1964, long before clay pot cookery became a rage. His design is very plain, very beautiful, and comes in three sizes for cooking juicy chicken. Mr. Biordi retired a few years ago, and Giovanni Savio now presides over the store, but Mr. Biordi still comes in on Wednesdays and Fridays to chat with customers.

Mr. Savio goes to Italy two or three times a year to personally select the pottery for the store: peasant ware from Tuscany, enormous serving platters and hand-painted dinnerware and pasta plates, earthenware in fresh, lovely colors and designs, big cream-colored platters from Puglia with a blue design, soup tureens, water pitchers. He has ceramic *aceto-olio* combinations and tiny espresso cups from the very simple to the gaudy Neopolitan style.

You'll find all the traditional Italian cooking utensils, too: hand-cut marble mortars from Carrara in three sizes, ravioli cutters, *cialde* irons, garlic presses, cheese graters, manual and electric pasta machines.

### San Francisco/East Bay * Indian
## BOMBAY BAZAR

*548 Valencia Street, San Francisco 94110. Telephone (415) 621-1717. Hours: M-F 10:30-6, SUN 12-5.*
*1034 University Avenue, Berkeley 94710. Telephone (415) 848-1671. Hours: T-SAT 10-6:30, SUN 11-6.*

Bombay Bazar on Valencia Street has a long wall stacked with cookware and utensils for Indian cuisine. There are *tavas*, the cast-iron griddles used for making Indian flat breads; brass *thali*, the wide, shallow trays used for serving Indian foods in small portions arranged like a painter's palette; *katori*, tiny straight-sided brass bowls used to serve individual portions of *dals*, *raitas*, meats, and vegetables; and *karhai*, India's version of the wok, for deep frying. Brass coconut graters effectively ream out coconuts for the coconut milk necessary for authentic curries. And from Kenya, there are piles of inexpensive stainless steel cookware.

**San Francisco * European**
## THOMAS CARA

_517 Pacific Avenue, San Francisco 94133._
_Telephone (415) 781-0383. Hours: M–F_
_10:30–4:30; SAT 11–3._

Founded in 1947 just after the war, Thomas Cara is the oldest culinary store in the city. (Bazar Français was the oldest, but it's closed now.) Located in a wonderful old brick building on Pacific Street, its windows display serious and professional-looking espresso machines, Melior _café filtre_ makers, copper pans, big whisks, and ladles. The streamlined silver Pavone at the front of the store is the first espresso machine Mr. Cara brought in from Italy after the war. Now much of his business is rebuilding and selling restaurant machines, usually the one- and two-group piston models phased out by the bigger four-piston models preferred in Europe. He replaces gaskets and coils, then cleans the machines and converts them from gas to American electric. His biggest customers are young people opening up bars and cafés all over California.

Thirty years ago, he was the first to sell home espresso machines. He stocks Lacara, Riviera, and Pavone. The more inexpensive Atomic has a steamer and a pressure gauge, but it's not electric— you use the gas flame on your stove to heat it. Mr. Cara will repair and replace parts on home espresso machines, too. And he'll gladly give expert advice on their use and care.

Young Christopher Cara, an enthusiastic cook, will show you the store's collection of kitchenware: pasta rolling pins, meat grinders, sausage stuffers, pizza cutters, decorative pastry tips, St. Nicholas chocolate molds, ice cream molds.

**San Francisco/East Bay ***
**International**
## COST PLUS IMPORTS

_2552 Taylor, San Francisco 94133. Tele-_
_phone (415) 673-8400. Hours: M–F 10–_
_9, SAT 10–7, SUN 11–7._
_101 Clay, Oakland 94607. Telephone_
_(415) 834-4440. Hours: T–F 10–6:30,_
_SAT 12–6:30, SUN 12–5._

There are always good bargains in Cost Plus Imports' extensive cookware section: bamboo ginger graters from India, aluminum _couscousières_ from Morocco, earthenware casseroles from France, shallow _paella_ pans from Spain, inexpensive colorful enamelware from China and Mexico, oversized Chinese bamboo _dim sum_ steamers, etc.

**Paris * French**
## E. DEHILLERN

_18 rue Coquillière, Paris, France. Mail_
_order._

For almost 150 years, the grand chefs and graduates of the Cordon Bleu have furnished their kitchens with a full _batterie de cuisine_ from E. Dehillern. Located just at the edge of Les Halles, the store is stacked from floor to ceiling with hundreds of marvelous pots, pans, soufflé dishes, casseroles, _daubières_, molds, sieves, gadgets, and excellent knives.

_Catalog on request._

**San Francisco * Italian**
## FIGONI HARDWARE

_1351 Grant Avenue, San Francisco 94133._
_Telephone (415) 392-4765. Hours: M–T,_
_TH–SAT 8–5:15._

North Beach's Figoni Hardware dates from _before_ the earthquake! The original sliding wood ladders are still in place so clerks can have access to stock stored high above. One half of the store supplies the city's Italian gardeners, fishermen, and handymen. The other side sells all kinds of homey, familiar Italian cooking utensils: wooden cheese-grating boxes with a toothed metal grater on top and a wooden drawer to hold the grated cheese; another kind of grater that cranks, with a wooden drum studded with nail points; chopping blades to fit shallow wooden bowls; old-fashioned pyramid toasters; authentic extra-long pasta rolling pins to be used with a lot of muscle; wooden scaffolded ravioli pins; *mezzalune* (the curved, two-handled Italian cutting blades); ravioli cutters; and hand-cranked tomato presses. Sort through inexpensive espresso and *cappuccino* cups, pasta bowls, gaily painted peasant-ware platters, big bread bowls, enamel spaghetti cookers with a colander inside, and large aluminum colanders to drain the whole family's pasta.

Of course, they have newfangled pasta machines, meat grinders for sausage making, food mills, heavy mallets to tenderize your *scaloppine*, and heavy copper polenta pots and *zabaglione* pans as well as such treasures as Italian farming tools, bocce balls, corks for wine bottles, spigots for vinegar and wine barrels, and fishing gear and permits.

### San Francisco * Chinese
### GIN WAH COMPANY

*656 Grant Avenue, San Francisco 94108. Telephone (415) 362-4689. Hours: M–SAT 10–10, SUN 10–5:30.*

This emporium of Chinese cookware is a regular stop on Chinese cooking students' expeditions to Chinatown. You can see flocks of them gathered round their teachers, filling shopping bags with woks, bamboo steamers, wire sieves, soup bowls, and wonderful Oriental gadgets for forming dumplings.

There are yard-wide woks, *dim-sum-parlor*-sized steamers, heavy-duty sieves. The latest automatic rice cooker sits next to Ghengis Khan broilers, unglazed clay barbecues, molds for moon cakes, lazy Susans to spin your sauces and condiments. And enamel Camel-brand thermoses from China painted with flowers, from baby up to honorable-great-grandfather sizes. There are also unglazed red earthenware casseroles and teapots from mainland China.

### San Francisco * Middle Eastern
### HAIG'S DELICACIES

*642 Clement Street, San Francisco 94118. Telephone (415) 752-6283. Hours: M–SAT 10–6.*

Haig's has the round, high-sided aluminum pans used in Greece and Turkey to cook and display colorful stuffed vegetables, and narrow-waisted coffee pots for Turkish-style coffee.

### East Bay * Latino
### MI RANCHO MEXICAN STORE

*464 Seventh Street, Oakland 94607. Telephone (415) 451-2393. Hours: M–SAT 8–6.*

This Mexican food store has *comals* (heavy griddles for cooking tortillas), tortilla presses, corn grinders, *metates* (granite mortars), whisks for chocolate, blue-speckled enamelware.

### San Francisco ✳ Middle Eastern
## SAMIRAMIS IMPORTS

*2990 Mission Street, San Francisco 94110. Telephone (415) 824-6555. Hours: M–SAT 10–6.*

Carved wooden molds for making Middle Eastern *mamool,* semolina cookies stuffed with dates and nuts.

### San Francisco ✳ Japanese
## SANKO COOKING SUPPLY

*1758 Buchanan Street, San Francisco 94115. Telephone (415) 922-8331. Hours: M–SAT 10–5:30.*

This cookware store in Japantown carries everything for Oriental cuisines: heavy specialized and all-purpose Japanese knives and grinding stones; *suribachi* and *surikogi* (Japanese mortars and pestles, scribed inside for more efficient grinding and pulverizing); *maki-su* (the fine bamboo mat used for rolling *sushi,* omelets, and vegetables); wooden pickle barrels and lids; graters for giant *daikon* radishes and for very finely grating ginger or *wasabi* horseradish; *tomago-aki nabe* (the rectangular frying pan used to make neatly rolled omelets); *sukiyaki-nabe* (the round, flat-bottomed cast-iron pans for preparing *sukiyaki*); *donabe* (lidded earthenware casseroles that can be used over direct flame or in the oven); *horuku* (unglazed earthenware casseroles used to steam-broil foods over beds of coarse salt); chopstick rests; sake servers; small bowls for dipping sauces; covered noodle bowls; *zaru* (bamboo draining baskets); condiment dishes; savory-custard cups; lacquered soup bowls; bamboo and stainless steel skewers for grilling; long chopsticks for cooking.

### San Francisco ✳ Japanese
## SOKO HARDWARE COMPANY

*1698 Post Street, San Francisco 94115. Telephone (415) 931-5510. Hours: M–F 8–5:30, SAT 9–5:30.*

Soko Hardware has a new two-story location on Post Street across from Japantown. The upstairs is packed with all the usual hardware items, plus traditional Japanese carpenter's and woodworking tools, which are completely different from their western counterparts. Consult *The Care and Use of Japanese Woodworking Tools,* available in the store, for more information about these tools.

For your *batterie de cuisine,* there are cleavers from the People's Republic of China, German-made Henckels knives, and a line of Japanese cutlery including a pocket knife and a small, broad-bladed fish scaler.

Downstairs you'll find a profusion of cookware and gadgets, a mix of East and West. A lovely dovetail-jointed wooden box is a vegetable slicer. The heavy iron pots with dark, rough-grained wooden lids are used for cooking simmered dishes. Of course, there are *suribachi* and *surikogi* (Japanese mortars and pestles); steamers for making *mushimono,* or steamed foods; bright golden metal tea kettles from baby up to great-grandfather size; aluminum *bento* (flat, book-sized Japanese lunch boxes); and *sushi* molds in different shapes.

Soko Hardware also sells seeds for Japanese vegetables. Grow your own clear-tasting Japanese cucumbers; tiny sweet Japanese eggplants; *horenso,* fleshy Japanese spinach; *kabocha,* a pale-green pumpkin with bright-orange flesh; sugary *satsuma-imo,* sweet potato; and *mitsuba,* an Oriental relative of parsley.

**San Francisco * Chinese**
**TI SUN COMPANY**

*1123 Grant Avenue, San Francisco 94133. Telephone (415) 982-1958. Hours: 9:30–6 daily.*

Ti Sun Company is Grant Avenue's Chinese hardware store, with a complete selection of home hardware—nuts, bolts, trash cans, brooms—along with lots of gourmet western cookware. For Chinese cooking, you can get a wok, and big lazy Susans to spin the teapot and condiments round your table.

Ti Sun also has Chinese chopping blocks, thick slabs of resiny pine trees from eleven inches on up to twenty inches in diameter. The larger sizes are for restaurants only; the usual home size, reasonably priced, is twelve to fourteen inches.

**East Bay * International**
**WHOLE EARTH ACCESS COMPANY**

*2990 Seventh Street, Berkeley 94710. Telephone (415) 845-3000. Hours: M–SAT 9–5:30, SUN 11–5.*

Whole Earth Access Company, a big barn of a store on Seventh Street in Berkeley, was originally an outgrowth of *The Whole Earth Catalog.* Then, you could go down and browse through their wholesale catalogs of tools and equipment and order at a considerable discount. Now they continue the policy of carrying simple, well-made, but ver-satile cooking equipment at very low prices. They stock a whole line of spun steel woks, shallow double-handled *paella* pans, heavy griddles, omelet and sauté pans from hermit size up to huge commune dimensions. Chicago Cutlery and Henckels knives are 25 percent off the list price. You'll find just about every model of Chop Rite grinders, flour mills, Atlas pasta machines, even an electric butter churner. But it's not all down on the farm: there are copper polenta pots, copper bowls for beating egg whites, blenders, Kitchen Aid mixers, commercial aluminum Calphalon cookware, and salad spinners, all at good prices. They have cookbooks too, along with books on beekeeping, raising goats, making cheese, and butchering; also wood stoves to warm your kitchen, butcher blocks, and hanging pot racks.

# RESTAURANT SUPPLY

Many restaurant suppliers also sell to the public. Since these stores supply small restaurants as well as giant industrial kitchens, many items are quite useful in the home kitchen.

The products sold here are usually simple and functional. Sturdy and well made, they come in a wide variety of sizes. You'll find well-designed utensils like wire whisks, soup ladles, spatulas, and tongs, as well as big stainless steel bread bowls, sturdy stockpots, and generous colanders. You can buy knives and grinding stones, restaurant tableware and glassware, too. And if you've always dreamed of cooking on a six-burner professional stove, you can get one at these stores, new or used.

Since you're not paying for fancy displays and helpful clerks, sometimes you may find service a bit abrupt. Just browse through the crowded shelves yourself. You may find something you never knew you needed.

## Peninsula
## CHEFS

*926 Broadway, Redwood City 94063. Telephone (415) 364-3604. Hours: W–F 9:30–5, SAT 10–4.*

Chefs introduced Calphalon cookware, now featured in most cookware stores, to the Bay Area. Owner Marie Summers has one of the most extensive lines of heavy-duty pots and pans around, including the coveted copper pans made for heavy use in the finest restaurants. They are a real investment, but one that will give you pleasure for years.

This big warehouse is filled with all the furnishings for restaurant and institutional kitchens: professional stoves, microwave ovens, steam tables, refrigerators, dishwashing machines, stainless steel sinks, convection ovens, and salamander broilers that mount over professional ranges.

## East Bay
## EAST BAY
## RESTAURANT SUPPLY

*49 Fourth Street, Oakland 94607. Telephone (415) 465-4300. Hours: M–F 8–5, SAT 8:30–12.*

East Bay has everything imaginable for fancier restaurants. A sea of tables displays the store's selection of glassware, dishes, and flatware. They have a full line of utensils, pots and pans, stoves, refrigerators, and appliances, both new and used.

## San Francisco
## ECONOMY
## RESTAURANT FIXTURES

*950 Mission Street, San Francisco 94103. Telephone (415) 362-5187. Hours: M–F 8–4:30.*

The basement is filled with bargains, but you've got to have the patience to sift through the piles of used and abandoned restaurant fixtures and equipment. Upstairs, you might find a high-quality Wolf restaurant range, either used or new. A six-burner is only a little bigger than your home range, but you can get six pots on it side by side, the gas burners are powerful, and the oven is quite large.

## San Francisco
## EMPIRE SALES

*1061 Howard Street, San Francisco 94103. Telephone (415) 552-2888 or 552-1441. Hours: M–F 9–5.*

After twenty-five years on Valencia Street, last year Empire Sales moved to Howard Street where they're still doing a brisk business with restaurants, bars, and hotels. Browse through their large inventory until you see something to catch your cook's fancy: commercial aluminum cookware in a huge range of sizes from sauce-for-two pans to restaurant-sized high-sided sauté pans; rolled steel woks; gratin dishes; colanders big enough to rinse six whole ducks in.

You can buy individual soufflé dishes, a fancy duck press, or a yard-long potato masher. Over in the bakery section, investigate the plastic containers, the canvas pastry bags, the professional black-steel loaf pans, and the earthenware bread bowls. The bar section sells spill-stop liquor pourers and milkshake machines.

Empire Sales handles a lovely line of earthenware crocks from very small up to fifteen gallons. Use an appropriate size for making pickles or for curing pieces of meat in a spice-laden brine.

If there is something you want, but don't see, ask. A Wolf stove? They can get it for you.

**East Bay**
## PETERS AND WILSON

*2324 San Pablo Avenue, Oakland 94612. Telephone (415) 832-7760. Hours: M-F 8-5, SAT 9-12.*

This fifty-year-old store is a favorite with owners of small restaurants. It's not large and overwhelming. The service is friendly and the stock good-quality basics: cooking utensils like ladles, tongs, whisks; small appliances like blenders and mixers; glassware; big earthenware bowls for breadmaking; tall crocks for your pickles; heavy-duty pots and pans and tall aluminum stockpots.

**East Bay**
## JOHN SARDELL AND SONS

*258 Eleventh Street, Oakland 94607. Telephone (415) 444-1956. Hours: M-F 8:30-5:30, SAT 9-1.*

Sardell's has new equipment and cookware, but they're worth checking for used refrigerators and restaurant stoves, too. Let them know what you'd like to find.

# SERVICES
See also Cutlery/Knife Sharpening

**San Francisco * Tinning**
## WILLIAM CAMPANA AND SONS

*162 Clara (between Fourth and Fifth near Harrison), San Francisco 94107. Telephone (415) 421-7689. Hours: M-F 7-3.*

Herman Campana at William Campana and Sons will reline any kind of copperware for both individuals and restaurants, except, he stresses, he does not do teakettles. The shop was established in 1899 by his father, William Campana, who learned the craft in Switzerland. Young Herman began his training in triple-dip hot tinning at an early age, assisting his father in the technically exacting work.

Herman always has lots of work—you'll see it stacked all over the workshop—well-used copper pots and pans in every shape and dimension. Expect the job to take one to two weeks. But he'll return your copper pan to you bright and gleaming, ready for years more service in the kitchen.

**East Bay * Kitchen Design Consultant**
## KITCHEN BY DESIGN

*2515 Etna Street, Berkeley 94704. Telephone (415) 843-1074.*

Joyce Esersky Goldstein will put her years of experience as a cooking teacher and kitchen-design consultant to work for you in planning your own kitchen. She considers your personal taste, budget, and needs in designing the space and storage systems, and in choosing equipment, lighting, and other materials.

Joyce has an M.F.A. from the School of Art and Architecture at Yale University and teaches cooking for the

University of California as well as giving classes for architects in kitchen design. She was the founder and director of the California Street Cooking School in San Francisco and is currently the head chef and manager at Chez Panisse Café.

## ——TABLEWARE——

### Marin County * Wineglasses
### MARJORIE LUMM'S
### WINE GLASSES

*112 Pine Street, San Anselmo 94960. Telephone (415) 454-0660. Mail order only.*

It's not easy to find a classic wine-tasting glass—well balanced, crystal clear, slightly elongated, and narrowing toward the top to gather the wine's bouquet. Recognizing the pleasures of drinking wine from a proper glass, Marjorie Lumm had wineglasses hand blown to her specifications at a small glass factory in West Virginia. As well as the wine taster's glass, chimney glasses, and other all-purpose glasses, she has glasses traditionally associated with the service of certain wines: elegant thin-stemmed Burgundy glasses, narrow-bowled Bordeaux glasses, champagne flutes, French-style fox heads, Rhine wine glasses, and the only traditional Spanish *copita* glass (for sherry) made in this country. All the glasses in her illustrated catalog are open stock and available by mail, safe delivery guaranteed.

### San Francisco * Italian Pottery
### SUE FISHER KING

*3075 Sacramento Street, San Francisco 94115. Telephone (415) 922-7276. Hours: M–SAT 10–6.*

Sue Fisher King loves Italian folk pottery and fills much of her Sacramento Street store with dinnerware she selects every year in Italy. One young designer in Tuscany makes big square plates decorated with small naive flowers. From Puglia, in the south, she has the creamy blue-strigged earthenware plates, shallow pasta bowls, and a huge *pasta asciutta* platter for serving *alla famiglia.* From Siena, there are finely painted plates with family crests; and from Orvieto, dishes in blue and white windowpane checks.

Check the supply of fine table linens, too.

# VINEGAR-MAKING SUPPLIES

Once you've tasted and used a good homemade vinegar, most commercial vinegars will seem taut and shrill to your palate. You'll find that a well-made vinegar can taste almost as complex and varied as the wines that go into its making. Vinegar is a living thing that changes constantly with the seasons and its stage of maturation. By steeping some of your vinegar in herbs, you can have a whole palette of vinegars at your disposal. Some *vinaigriers* like to play with varietal vinegars, keeping Cabernets, Zinfandels, or Chenin Blancs separate. But champagne or first-growth Bordeaux vinegars seem excessive—what kind of oenophile has the heart to make vinegar from even the sedimented dregs of fine wines?

Candidates perfect for your vinegar barrel are the partial contents of a bottle accidently left open overnight. Take your revenge on genuinely undrinkable wines by ceremoniously dumping them into the vinegar barrel.

It's not true that simply leaving the wine open to the air will produce a good vinegar. Nor can you just add a dose of any vinegar from your pantry. Since most commercial vinegars are pasteurized, the bacteria in them are dead.You need either a good-quality unpasteurized vinegar or some vinegar mother to start your vinegar. After the initial addition of mother to your wine, the bacteria will stay alive, provided with adequate alcohol and air.

Most wine-making supply businesses stock vinegar mother with accompanying directions. Then you'll need a small wine barrel or a wide-mouthed gallon glass jar covered with cheesecloth. Even better, get two containers, one for white wines and the other for reds.

**Napa Valley**
## BARREL CELLAR

*Vintage 1871, Yountville 94599. Telephone (707) 944-8057. Hours: 10–5:30 daily.*

Small wine barrels.

**East Bay**
## OAK BARREL WINECRAFT

*1201 University Avenue, Berkeley 94702. Telephone (415) 849-0400. Hours: M–SAT 10–6:30.*

Oak Barrel's vinegar culture does not produce the heavy "mother of vinegar" that forms a film on top of the liquid, but instead acts throughout the medium. The culture comes with a printed instruction sheet that gives detailed information about making vinegar as well as methods for flavoring it.

**East Bay**
## WINE AND THE PEOPLE

*907 University Avenue, Berkeley 94710. Telephone (415) 549-1266. Hours: M–SAT 10–6, SUN 11–5.*

Small wine barrels and vinegar mother.

# COOKWARE STORES

## SAN FRANCISCO
AUBERGINE, 3 Embarcadero Center, 397-0182

CARAVANSARY, 2263 Chestnut Street, 921-3466; 310 Sutter Street, 362-4641

CREATIVE COOKWARE, 900 North Point, 475-4999

DANS LA CUISINE, 2800 Leavenworth, 771-7415

THE EPICUREAN UNION, 2191 Union Street, 567-0941

JUDITH ETS-HOKIN CULINARY INSTITUTE, 3525 California Street, 668-3191

FORREST JONES, 3274 Sacramento Street, 567-2483; 151 Jackson Street, 982-1577

FREDERICKSEN HARDWARE, 3029 Fillmore Street, 567-3970

KITCHENS ETC., Pier 39, 781-6860

LA CUISINE, 1555 Pacific Avenue, 441-3548

LE PETIT CHOUX–LES SUNZERI, 633 Clement Street, 668-8484

LIVING LIGHTLY INC., 1326 9th Avenue, 665-0564

RUSHCUTTERS, 2501 Sacramento Street, 922-5100

THE SPICE OF LIFE, 1736 Haight Street, 751-1400

TAYLOR AND NG, 1 Embarcadero Center, 391-7796; 2349 Market Street, 626-5993

WILLIAMS-SONOMA KITCHENWARE, 576 Sutter Street, 982-0295

THE WOK SHOP, 804 Grant Avenue, 982-3797; 14 Stonestown, 665-5591

## PENINSULA/SAN JOSE AREA
ARVEY'S OF CALIFORNIA, 3666 Stevens Creek Boulevard, San Jose, (408) 984-1111

BATTERIE DE CUISINE, Arbor Road and Creek Drive, Menlo Park, 322-8127

CLASSIC KITCHEN, 19720 Stevens Creek Boulevard, Cupertino, (408) 996-0556

DINING ARTS, 170 State Street, Los Altos, 948-6445

EPICURE, 1219 Burlingame Avenue, Burlingame, 342-2555

GOOD COOKS AND COMPANY, 240 Main Street, Palo Alto, 326-4952

LESAND'S ARTICLES DE CUISINE, 1139 Chestnut Street, Menlo Park, 325-1712

MILIEU, 2142 Vallco Fashion Park, Cupertino, (408) 255-0400

PECKS GOURMET COOKWARE, 275 Primrose Road, Burlingame, 348-5344

POTS 'N PANDEMONIUM, Old Mill Specialty Center, Mountain View, 941-3475

TAYLOR AND NG, 149 Stanford Shopping Center, Palo Alto, 321-3245

TIN PAN GALLEY, 110 Pruneyard, Campbell, (408) 371-4011

TSANG AND MA INTERNATIONAL, 1306 Old Country Road, Belmont, 595-2279

WILLIAMS-SONOMA KITCHENWARE, 36 Town and Country Village, Palo Alto, 321-3486

## MARIN COUNTY

M AND S BLOOM COOKWARE, Larkspur Landing, Larkspur, 461-1640

CALIFORNIA COOKWARE, 7050 Northgate Mall, San Rafael, 479-4994

CAPRICORN GOURMET COOKWARE, 100 Throckmorton Avenue, Mill Valley, 388-1720

CARAVANSARY, 230 Strawberry Town and Country Village, Mill Valley, 383-4161

FORREST JONES, 1016 C, San Rafael, 453-9444

LA PLACE, 108 Caledonia Street, Sausalito, 332-0676

THE SCULLERY, 155 South Hartz, Danville, 820-4036

SOMEONE'S IN THE KITCHEN, 609 San Anselmo Avenue, San Anselmo, 459-1488

## EAST BAY/CONTRA COSTA

AUBERGINE, 286 Bayfair Mall, San Leandro, 278-1322; 375 Sun Valley Mall, Concord, 827-1077; 2301 Stoneridge Mall, Pleasanton, 827-6471

JOHN A. BROWN, KITCHENWARE, 5940 College Avenue, Oakland, 654-6462

CARAVANSARY, 2908 College Avenue, Berkeley, 841-1628

COOKWORKS, 1893 Solano Avenue, Berkeley, 525-1611

CREATIVE COOKWARE, 1455 Newell Avenue, Walnut Creek, 934-5410; 1975 Diamond Boulevard, Concord, 687-2274

DUKES, ETC., 1745 Santa Rita Road, Pleasanton, 462-3332

THE KITCHEN, 2213 Shattuck Avenue, Berkeley, 548-2648

LA CUISINE, 2106 Vine Street, Berkeley, 841-1141.

MISSION GOURMET COOKWARE, 165 Anza Street, Fremont, 651-2990

THE SCULLERY MAIDS, 55 Alice Street, Oakland, 465-5352

TWELVE GLEN KITCHENWARE, 12 Glen Avenue, Oakland, 544-4727

ZEBRA, 2110 Vine Street, Berkeley, 848-6887

## NAPA VALLEY

BAH HUMBUG, 1201 Main Street, St. Helena, (707) 963-7423

CUISINE RENAISSANCE, 3415 Solano Avenue, Napa, (707) 252-9400

THE KITCHEN NOOK, 811 Coombs, Napa, (707) 252-4155

THE KITCHEN STORE, Vintage 1870, Yountville, (707) 944-8100

SHACKFORDS, 1350 Main Street, Napa, (707) 226-2132

# Co-ops & Services

## San Francisco
## THE FOOD CONSPIRACY

*439 Cole Street, San Francisco 94117. Telephone (415) 386-9914.*

Organized in 1968, the Food Conspiracy is one of the oldest and best-known programs of the White Panther Party and is still alive and well, with over three thousand members in 1981. Members band together to purchase bulk foods, cheeses, fruits and vegetables, and other foods at wholesale prices. The more members, the greater the buying power and the lower the prices. The Food Conspiracy claims, in some cases, to provide families with 40 percent more food per dollar spent, but though prices are low, they aren't yet that low.

The joining fee is ten dollars, payable with the first order. Each week, there's a printed order form listing the foods available. It must be mailed by Sunday each week to 439 Cole Street in San Francisco. Paid members purchase the food and divide it into individual orders. Members then pick up at a number of locations in both San Francisco and Berkeley on the following Wednesday. A delivery service is also available.

Fruits and vegetables are bought at the produce market on the day you receive them. Canned goods and condiments do not have to be bought in cases to take advantage of low prices. In addition, you can buy juices, pastas and rice, dried beans, flours, grains, teas and coffee (including 100 percent Colombian decaf and Malvina's house blend), dried fruits and nuts, spices, eggs, oils, and ten basic cheeses (including Monterey Jack and provolone) in any quantities you wish—and even personal necessities such as toothpaste and dental floss.

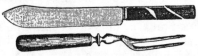

## San Francisco
## THE SAN FRANCISCO GROCERY EXPRESS

*Telephone (415) 641-5400.*

Frazzled? Reclusive? No time? Call this number and John Coghlan and Michael Meagher, founders of the San Francisco Grocery Express, will send you a catalog of the groceries they have stockpiled in their warehouse. Make up a grocery list of well-known canned goods, fresh fruit and vegetables, even meats and poultry, and one of the Grocery Express trucks will deliver it to your door for a small fee. You can pay with cash, check, or MC/VISA. The prices? Somewhat higher than the supermarket. Minimum order $20, delivery charge $2.25.

Discounts are available for the elderly and the handicapped.

## East Bay
## WEST OAKLAND FOOD CO-OP

*925 West Grand Avenue, Oakland 94610. Telephone (415) 834-5854. Hours: M–F 9–9, SAT 9–8, SUN 10–5.*

The West Oakland Food Co-op was begun "to make quality food available in West Oakland at competitive prices." Members of the West Oakland Food Project started a farmers' market in 1981 to enable the neighborhood to buy produce direct from small truck farmers, the first step in establishing a consumer's co-op that will eventually include a pharmacy and a bank.

They now have a regular grocery store selling meats, produce, dairy products, standard canned goods, and other products like toilet tissue or dish detergent at low prices. Community members are encouraged to support the store by buying a membership share in the West Oakland Food Co-op.

*Call for information.*

# Dairy Goods

See the Natural Foods section for additional markets selling raw milk and additive-free cream.

## ACROPOLIS BAKERY AND DELICATESSEN
San Francisco

*5217 Geary Boulevard, San Francisco 94118. Telephone (415) 751-9661. Hours: T–SAT 8–7, SUN 8–4.*

Gregory Triantafillidis will sell you some of the same delicious natural sour cream he makes and serves in big dollops with his homemade borscht and *bliny*.

## MADE TO ORDER
East Bay

*1576 Hopkins Street, Berkeley 94707. Telephone (415) 524-7552. Hours: M–SAT 10–6.*

Made to Order sells their own *crème fraîche*, a light fresh cheese they make called *formaggio fresco*, and fresh churned butter, often flavored with lemon or strawberries or mint or orange. Butters can also be special ordered.

## NARSAI'S MARKET
Contra Costa

*389 Colusa Avenue, Kensington 94707. Telephone (415) 527-3737. Hours: M–SAT 10–7, SUN 10–4.*

Narsai's market has *crème fraîche* and Devonshire, or clotted, cream from England with a walloping 45 percent butterfat, plus the wonderful Glen Oaks heavy cream with flavor like all cream used to have.

## THE OAKVILLE GROCERY
San Francisco

*1555 Pacific Avenue, San Francisco 94109. Telephone (415) 885-4411. Hours: M–F 10:30–6:30, SAT 10–6, SUN 12–6.*

*Crème fraîche*, bottled Devon cream imported from England, and the famous sweet butter, pricey but delicious, made from Normandy cream.

## PENINSULA CREAMERY
Peninsula

*900 High Street, Palo Alto 94301. Telephone (415) 323-3175. Hours: M–SAT 8–6, SAT 8:30–4:30.*

Peninsula Creamery has old-time non-homogenized cream-topped milk, sold in real glass bottles from their store on High Street in Palo Alto.

## SAY CHEESE
San Francisco

*856 Cole Street, San Francisco 94117. Telephone (415) 665-5020. Hours: M–F 10–7, SAT 10–6.*

*Crème fraîche*, Devonshire cream, and Normandy butter.

## SUN VALLEY DAIRY
San Francisco

*300 Alemany Boulevard, San Francisco 94110. Telephone (415) 282-5105. Hours: M–SAT 7:30–7, SUN 9:30–7.*

A life-sized black and white cow and her calf graze over the entrance of the small Sun Valley Dairy store located just on the edge of the San Francisco Produce market. Here shoppers can pick up old-fashioned bottles of cream-topped milk, fresh-churned buttermilk, fresh eggs, sweet butter, and a full line of other dairy products.

# Fish & Shellfish

The best way to ensure getting truly fresh fish is to buy it from a fishmonger who sells it in the round. Its eye should be bright and clear. Check the color of its gills and make sure the flesh is firm. If it has anything other than a bracing briny aroma, don't buy it. Fresh fish should not smell "fishy." Since you may have rarely seen really fresh fish, it may take some time to learn to recognize it.

A knowledgeable fishmonger advises stopping in at fish markets often, even when you don't intend to buy anything. Go in and really look at the fish. Since it's too hard to tell the state of fillets, concentrate on whole fish. Get familiar with several kinds. You'll learn to recognize when the colors are fresh and bright, and when they're faded. Each kind of fish is different. Some are meant to have the pristine hues of rainbows; others are supposed to be slightly slimy. After you've gained enough experience, you'll be able to see when a fish is fresh without having to poke and sniff.

Chinatown is one of the best places to carry out this exercise because they sell a wide variety of fish. Some of it you won't recognize; Chinatown has its own sources for seafood not usually sold commercially. Since business is brisk, fish does not sit around for days waiting for a buyer. But you the consumer have still got to be knowledgeable and on your toes. Most of the fish is very fresh, but there will be some that has been frozen and refrozen. You've got to be able to assess the quality for yourself.

Never buy fillets in Chinatown—the Chinese don't. The fillets of fish you see displayed in windows are intended to draw the tourists in off the streets. The Chinese themselves know how to buy fish and they usually buy it whole, so they can assure themselves of its freshness. They also like to have the bones and the head. If they don't cook a fish whole, they'll steam the skeleton over *tofu* and eat the flesh still clinging to the bone.

Buy your fish whole if you can and have the dealer fillet it. You can take home the head, bones, and scraps for a fish *fumet*. Mussels, clams, and oyster shells should be firmly clamped shut when purchased.

After you've gone to the trouble to find your fresh seafood, don't let it sit on your refrigerator shelf for a few days before cooking it. At the most, buy it one day, use it the next. Any leftover cooked fish can be used in a seafood salad or served cold with a mayonnaise.

## — FISH MARKETS —

### San Francisco
### AMERICAN FISH MARKET

*1790 Sutter Street, San Francisco 94115. Telephone (415) 921-5154. Hours: M-F 8:30-6, SAT 8:30-5:30.*

The blue awnings and the sparkling plate glass windows stacked with produce make the American Fish Market a standout at its corner location in Japantown. A sign reading "Fresh Tuna from Hawaii," the day's special, is posted on the front door. Inside, there's standing room only at the fish counter, where shrewd-eyed customers check the day's catch: coils of spiraled octopus tentacles, clear gray curls of shrimp, milky squid, spiny sea urchins, salmon roe, fresh trout, tuna, and bonito.

The Spanish mackerel, salted and dried, is delicious broiled. And if all that makes you hungry, you can get small packs of assorted *sushi* to take out at the stall in the corner.

The freezer case is stocked with fishy rareties like broiled eel, prepared herring roe, and perfect rose-colored octopus, already cooked and floating whole in a frozen slush. Choose from a myriad of fried fish cakes, fish balls, and all kinds of steamed fish cakes.

### San Francisco
## ANTONELLI AND SONS

*Cal-Mart Market, 3585 California Street, San Francisco 94118. Telephone (415) 752-7413. Hours: M-SAT 8-6:30.*

Antonelli and Sons is a fish and poultry store inside Cal-Mart supermarket on California Street. The twenty-year-old family business is run by Tony Antonelli; his two sons Silio and Don have been helping their dad since they were six or seven years old.

Every morning between 5 and 6, it's down to the wharf to buy the day's catch. Back at the store, the fish is cleaned, scaled, and cut. Fillets of sand dab or red snapper are arranged in overlapping patterns. There are thick halibut, swordfish, and salmon steaks; beautiful whole salmon; whole red snapper; and fresh lake trout from Washington. The shellfish includes scallops, cherrystone clams, prawns,

and East Coast mussels. They'll get you live Maine lobster or the requisite *oursin,* or sea urchin, for your *bouilla-baisse* on request, and they occasionally have sturgeon and shad roe. "Once in a blue moon" Antonelli's has fresh eels: "They're hard to get because everybody at the wharf takes them home for themselves."

Since they do a lot of their own filleting, Antonelli's should be able to supply you with fish bones for your fish *fumet,* too.

### East Bay
## BERKELEY FISH

*1504 Shattuck Avenue, Berkeley 94709. Telephone (415) 845-7166. Hours: M-SAT 9-6:30.*

This fish market shares a space with the Cheese Board in Berkeley. Fresh fish is sold here both in the round or as steaks and fillets, along with scallops and shellfish flown in from the East Coast. The market supplies all the fish for Koetsu Akasawa's *sushi,* made right in the store's front window. His Berkeley Fish Kitchen at the back also prepares Japanese box lunches, rice bowls, and soup to take out. (See Take-out section.)

### East Bay
## CAL EAST FOODS

*505 Cedar Street, Oakland 94607. Telephone (415) 465-0220. Hours: M-F 5 am-4 pm.*

Cal East Foods, a wholesale fish dealer, will sell to the public from their plant in Oakland. Choose from a complete line of fresh and frozen fish plus shellfish, including California-raised Belon oysters and littleneck and cherrystone clams and mussels from the East Coast. Bushels get even more of a discount. *$100 minimum for deliveries.*

**Marin County**
## CARUSO'S

*Foot of Harbor Drive, Sausalito 94965. Telephone (415) 332-1015. Hours: 5 am–5:30 pm daily.*

Since Caruso's fish market in Sausalito is right next to the sportfishing dock, they open early, *early*—at 5 am. The store takes reservations for the sportfishing boats, acts as a complete bait and tackle shop, and outfits prospective fishermen with fortifying sandwiches.

Owner John Wheeler buys mostly from small boats and has the day's catch unloaded on the dock just outside the store. To get an even wider variety of fresh fish for the store, he often gets up a little bit earlier and drives down to San Francisco's Fisherman's Wharf for the official opening of the wholesale market at 4 am.

All the fish sold at Caruso's is cut from the round, or whole fish, daily. The counter is usually stocked with sole, sand dabs, halibut, thresher shark, rock cod, and all the other fish caught locally, plus highly seasonal fish like albacore and salmon.

Special tanks hold live Maine lobster, Dungeness crab in season, and live shellfish (bluepoint oysters, eastern mussels, littleneck clams). Occasionally he'll get in such unusual items as blue Louisiana crab or eel.

**Peninsula**
## CRYSTAL SPRINGS FISH AND POULTRY

*116 Crystal Springs Shopping Center, San Mateo 94402. Telephone (415) 573-0335. Hours: M–F 9–6:30, SAT 9–6.*

This is Mr. Scialanga's second store. (See Mission Market Fish and Poultry.)

**San Francisco**
## DOMENICO'S

*4735 Mission Street, San Francisco 94112. Telephone (415) 585-0730. Hours: M–SAT 9–6:30.*

One of the partners in Domenico's fish market comes from a long line of fishermen. Andy Tardio explains: "All my forefathers were fishermen for generations back in Sicily, in a little town near Palermo. I learned to fish there with my father and later he made a living fishing out of Monterey and San Francisco. But I'm the first in my family to have a fish market."

Andy and his partner Domenico Infantino alternate mornings down at the wharf, where they buy everything in the round and then fillet it themselves. Though their three-year-old fish market sells a big variety of fish—sea bass, sand dabs, thresher shark, swordfish, halibut, rock cod—much of their business includes fillets of English, petrale, rex, and flounder soles. And, of course, bright salmon steaks and whatever else is in season stock their counter, too.

The shellfish includes prawns, scampi, bluepoint oysters, cherrystone clams, and eastern mussels. They also have tanks of live Maine lobster and Dungeness crab in season.

**San Francisco**
## DUPONT MARKET

*1100 Grant Avenue, San Francisco 94133. Telephone (415) 986-3723. Hours: 8–6 daily.*

There is always an impressive hustle-bustle going on inside Dupont Market in Chinatown, as shoppers sort through huge piles of fresh fish, fat shrimp and prawns, and clams of every size and description, including black freshwater clams. The clerks deftly wrapping each order of fish in newspaper seem as numerous as the customers. Specials are posted in the window: fresh ground fish or fresh baby octopus just a few inches long.

The large aquarium below the main window is filled with golden-scaled carp. When the crab season begins, the always-bustling market is even more crowded, if that's possible. The Chinese crowd around a huge wooden crate filled with squirming live crabs. Those close enough rummage through the crate, looking for a princely crab. They give the big pincers a squeeze and hold the creatures up to see how lively they are. Sluggish, feeble crabs are summarily rejected. At the height of the season, the market may sell as many as five thousand crabs a day.

In addition, the Dupont sells quail eggs and fresh Petaluma ducks and poultry, and there's a pork counter provided with every part of the pig including neckbone, spleen, tail, and liver,

Dupont will vacuum pack their rock salt chicken or roast duck so it can be carried on a plane or train. They will also pack crab, fish, or fresh poultry in dry ice.

## San Francisco
## LEE SANG FISH MARKET

*1207 Stockton Street, San Francisco 94133. Telephone (415) 989-4336. Hours: 8–6 daily.*

If you want really fresh fish, Lee Sang Fish Market has a tank of live fish. You'll sometimes even see hardheads, also called steelheads. When you buy a live fish, ask them to club it and then fillet it. But take the carcass home with you. If you steam it on top of some *tofu*, the rich fish flavor will permeate the *tofu* and then you can suck on the fish bones, which will still have a lot of meat on them.

The fish counter itself is well supplied with fresh fish at good prices. If you don't recognize what you see, ask. The variety of fish available in Chinatown fish markets is often overwhelming. For special dishes, sometimes you can get fish stomachs, too. Seasonally, there are live Dungeness crabs as well as blue crabs from the East Coast. The market will also sell you fish bones for your *fumets* or fish stews.

## San Francisco
## MISSION MARKET
## FISH AND POULTRY

*2590 Mission Street, San Francisco 94110. Telephone (415) 282-3331. Hours: M–TH and SAT 8:30–6, F 8:30–6:30.*

Owner Tino Scialanga, an Italian soldier captured by the American army in Africa in World War II, came to the United States in the late forties. With his son Bob he goes down to Fisherman's Wharf every day to hand-pick the catch. The quality of the fish he sells reflects this personal care; the fish here all look fresh, fat, and glossy. The Mission is a good place to buy fish because Latino customers demand the very freshest to make the many national versions of *seviche*, and serious cooks in the Mission all seem to buy their fish here. The store, the last of the open-front shops in the new Mission Mart Mall, sells beautiful golden-scaled whole carp and small, perfect silver pompano for Caribbean cooks. From Louisiana there are buffalo fish and catfish, as well as all the makings for *cioppino*, *paella*, and jambalaya: crabs, prawns, clams, scallops, and squid. They sell rarely seen skate wings, Spanish mackerel, and whatever good-quality fish the boats bring in.

The poultry selection includes stewing hens, fresh Pekin duck, and both frying and stewing rabbit.

**East Bay**
## MONTEREY FISH MARKET

*1582 Hopkins Street, Berkeley 94707. Telephone (415) 525-5600. Hours: M 10-6, T-SAT 11-6.*

Three years ago chef Paul Johnson took off his whites and started going to the fish market for a few small restaurants. Because none of them had the buying power of the big fish restaurants, they had trouble obtaining the best fresh fish the big wholesalers had to offer. Paul quickly educated himself to the business of custom buying seafood for a list of clients that now includes Chez Panisse, the Hayes Street Grill, the Fourth Street Grill, the Santa Fe Grill, and Augusta's. One year ago he opened a retail fish market in Berkeley called Monterey Fish Market, where he sells the same fish he buys for the restaurants.

Paul knows all the local suppliers and now buys from a whole network of sources—you have to if you want good fish.

Not only does it mean buying from a lot of sources, mostly from small one-day boats, (most of San Francisco's fleet is small), it means developing your own sources. For example, a woman who has her own boats in Hawaii supplies him with yellowfin tuna and mahi-mahi, both flown in fresh from the islands.

To get the best of the catch, he has to be at Fisherman's Wharf *early*—this means no later than 3:50 or 4 when the market officially opens (in all of the city, there may be ten buyers who are that conscientious). Paul is known on the wharf for his shrewd buying.

If you visit his store in Berkeley you might be surprised by the modest size of his counter; but he only carries what's fresh, and, sometimes, due to

weather and other factors, it's not a big selection. But everything in his case is as fresh as it's possible to get in this city, and it is handled carefully from the time that he buys it.

You'll find most of the fish caught locally: ling cod with its turquoise-tinged flesh, leopard shark, soup fin shark (the fins are dried and exported to the Orient), seven gill or cow shark with its pure white meat, the small California halibut averaging about four pounds, the various rock cods, petrale sole, rex sole, flounder, sand dabs, and sablefish (or black cod, known as butterfish in the supermarket).

Thresher shark and swordfish are caught farther south. Bonito and mackerel are trucked up the coast along with southern winter squid. Steelhead salmon, big Pacific halibut, and the Manila clams or native littlenecks are trucked down from Washington.

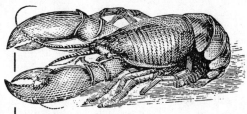

Occasionally he has John Dory from New Zealand or Australia, or delicious farm-raised salmon from Norway. Raised in colder waters, they develop more fat and have a taste distinctive from California salmon. From Louisiana, he'll get Gulf grouper, sweet Gulf oysters, and, occasionally, redfish. From the East Coast he has eastern clams and mussels (better in winter).

He sells Pacific oysters, too—the delicate Pigeon Point and Tomales Bay oysters—from two or three sources. Around the holidays, he'll have locally raised Belons. In season, he has the tender local squid from Monterey Bay and sometimes even local octopus caught near San Francisco or Monterey.

Ouiftre a    l'efcaille.

Ie crie ouiftre en efcaille, efcaille vuue efcaille,
Pour faire defeenfner ceuz ç i ie froot le noui:

**East Bay**
# NEW SANG CHONG MARKET

*377 Eighth Street, Oakland 94607. Telephone (415) 451-2018. Hours: 9–6 daily.*

Half of New Sang Chong Market sells fresh poultry and take-out dishes, while the other half is a small fish counter with a tank for live carp beneath. The golden beauties average three to four pounds. The day's catch of fresh fish—bonito, sea bass, squid, trout, tiny bay shrimp, and abalone—is sold at a good price and handed across the counter wrapped in yesterday's newspaper.

**Peninsula**
# PENINSULA SEAFOOD

*135 El Camino Real, San Bruno 94066. Telephone (415) 589-0532. Hours: M–W 9–6, TH 9–6:30, F 9–7, SAT 9–9, SUN 9:30–6.*

Dan Strazzullo and his sister Sue Lafon have really got themselves a fish market: "We'll try to sell anything that can be fished out of the sea, at least once," says Dan. Their father and grandfather sold fish at the wharf. As kids they sold cooked crab—in those days crab sold

three or four to the dollar, depending on whether you bought it cracked or not.

If you want something a bit esoteric, try Peninsula Seafood: they supply fish for the very diverse ethnic population of the San Bruno–South San Francisco area, which includes Italians, Chinese, Polynesians, Samoans, and Maltese.

Peninsula Seafood is one of the few places to sell sea urchin, either live or out of the shell. On a good day they can sell three to five hundred of the spiny creatures with their desirable musky roe. And until they started selling them, Dan says, he never realized just how many ethnic groups ate the sea urchin—the Italians, of course, but also the Spanish, French, Japanese, Samoans, and Chileans.

He has even sold one of the giant squid caught off the coast of California. One day Dan found a fisherman with one of these giant squid and brought it into the store where it took up the length of one of their cases. A little later, a Samoan customer walked into the store, asked him how much he wanted for the fifty-pound squid and promptly bought it. The next day he brought in some of the quite delicious stew he'd made from it, and put in his reservation for the next giant squid caught.

Though they don't handle eastern eel, Peninsula Seafood does sell the moray and dog eels that occasionally are fished out with the crab pots here. Their tanks hold live Maine lobster, abalone, big white-shelled sea snails (known as conch), octopus from Half Moon Bay, and Dungeness crab in season. Shellfish includes littleneck clams, mussels, bluepoint oysters, shucked Pacific oysters, and three sizes of prawn.

The majority of fish sold here is bought in the round: local rock cod

(Bolinas, yellow tail, black or blue, rosefish, and, occasionally, "snapper"), ling cod, sand dabs, flounder, kingfish, salmon, farm-raised trout from Idaho or Utah. Occasionally, they'll even sell a whole shark. Four kinds of sole are usually available in fillet.

**San Francisco**
## STANDARD FISHERIES CORPORATION

*Fisherman's Wharf, foot of Leavenworth Street, San Francisco 94133. Telephone (415) 673-5858. Hours: SAT 5 am–9 am.*

This San Francisco wholesaler has an open fish market Saturday mornings when they sell what they've overbought from the week before. This means the selection varies from week to week, but may include frozen prawns, crab, shrimp meat, and fresh kingfish, mackerel, rock cod fillets, and other fresh fish. The low prices are the great attraction here.

**San Francisco**
## TOKYO FISH MARKET

*1908 Fillmore Street, San Francisco 94115. Telephone (415) 931-4561. Hours: W–F 9–6:30, SAT 9–6, SUN 10–6.*

Unlike some of the bigger Japantown markets, the pace at the Tokyo Fish Market is comfortable and unhurried. While you choose *nori,* the purple laver seaweed used to wrap *norimaki sushi,* the owners cut fish at the fish counter to the right. Neat rows of Asahi beer are lined up behind. All of the seafood looks absolutely fresh: large octopus, bonito, two cuts of tuna.

# SPECIALTY FISH SOURCES

## OYSTERS

**Belon** *(Ostrea edulis)* This is the delicious flat European oyster indigenous to the Continent from Scandinavia down through the Mediterranean. The Greeks ate them, the Romans ate them in prodigious quantities, and eighteenth-century France just about depleted them. They're now grown in commercial beds up and down the coast from seed oysters raised off Brittany. You may have eaten this intense briny oyster in France as Belon or Marenne, in Normandy as *pied de cheval,* in England as Colchester, or in Belgium as Ostend.

Though in the last few years the Belon has been successfully cultivated on the East Coast, there was greater difficulty with it on the West Coast because of the Pacific's greater salinity. But after several years of experimentation, International Shellfish Enterprises harvested California's first crop of Belons from Moss Landing in 1980.

**Bluepoint** *(Crassostrea virginica) Crassostrea virginica* is the oyster indigenous to the entire East Coast. When Europeans first arrived in America, they were astounded at the quantity of oysters on the New England coast. The Indians ate them with great relish, but only cooked, never raw. In the 1800s oysters were commercially fished from the Chesapeake Bay on such a grand scale that the bay was eventually overfished. These days most of the commercial oysters known as bluepoints come from Long Island, and in America they are the most common oyster eaten on the half shell.

**Gulf Oyster** *(Crassostrea virginica)* For the past year or two we've seen more Gulf oysters arriving in the Bay Area. These are *virginica* as well, the same species as the bluepoint, but raised in the warmer Gulf waters. Oysters acquire different tastes depending on their habitat, and with the bluepoint this is particularly marked.

The Gulf oysters from Florida are sweet, velvety, and mild, but to confirmed oyster lovers, perhaps a bit bland. Those from Louisiana (available from Gulf Coast Oyster Company in Oakland) are slightly more aggressive, with a marvelous flavor.

**Olympia** *(Ostrea lurida)* Besides the European *Ostrea edulis,* the only other *Ostrea* is the miniscule Olympia oyster indigenous to the north Pacific. Concentrated in Washington and British Columbia, these exquisite tiny shellfish are almost impossible to get commercially today. Sensitive to pollution, overfished in the nineteenth century, and routed from their beds by the hardier imported Pacific oyster, they've almost disappeared. Occasionally in San Francisco, you'll find shucked Olympias and, even more rarely, the oysters in the shell, at a price almost three times that for Pacific oysters.

**Pacific Oyster** *(Crassostrea gigas)* The Pacific oyster is not an oyster indigenous to America. It's an Asian oyster, introduced to the Pacific Coast from Japan for commercial cultivation, and it is so hardy it has virtually wiped out the native Olympia oyster.

Though its taste doesn't seem to differ dramatically from Tomales Bay to Humboldt Bay, two of the locales where it is raised, it does vary depending on how the oyster is cultivated. Until 1965 all the oysters were grown using traditional Japanese methods of bottom culture called "cultches." The oysters

produced were fat and somewhat tough, better suited to barbecuing than eating on the half shell. Recently, both Pigeon Point Oysters and International Shellfish Enterprises have been cultivating the Pacific oyster using a "cultchless" method developed by some American hobbyists including William Budge and Charles Black. Grown off the bottom and maturing early, the resulting oysters, tender and sweet, prove that if you grow a Pacific oyster correctly, you can eat it on the half shell and enjoy it. These oysters, however, are more expensive to produce than the oysters cultivated by the Japanese cultch method.

### San Francisco * Smoked Fish
### BAGEL PASTRY BAKERY

*5625 Geary Boulevard, San Francisco 94121. Telephone (415) 387-5464. Hours: S–TH 8–7, F 8 to one hour or one-half hour before sunset.*

Partners Mark Rappaport and Louis Nasra use traditional European methods to cure and smoke their own moist lox as well as other fish including whitefish, tuna, mackerel, and trout. The masterful smoking is done, without preservatives, in the smokehouse at the back of the restaurant's small garden.

### East Bay * Sashimi/General
### BERKELEY BOWL FISH

*2777 Shattuck Avenue, Berkeley 94705. Telephone (415) 841-1458. Hours: M–F 9–7, SAT 9–6.*

In addition to a supply of basic local fish—rock cod, ling cod, butterfish—this fish market inside Berkeley Bowl Market Place specializes in *sushi-ya,* the varieties of fish and shellfish used for *sashimi* and *sushi.* In fact, they supply many *sushi* bars with fresh dark tuna, lighter bonito, golden rich sea urchin roe, halibut or tilefish, and the giant geoduck clam.

They also stock many fish used in ethnic cuisines: garfish, buffalo fish and catfish, from Louisiana (sold whole or pan ready), or whole carp, a favorite with the Chinese and an essential ingredient in gefilte fish.

The shellfish includes littleneck clams, Pacific oysters, and prawns.

---

**Sonoma County ∗ Fish Farm**
## BOB AND SHAUN'S FISH FARM

*5570 Lone Pine Road, Sebastopol 95472. Telephone (707) 823-9483. Hours: W–SUN 8–6.*

Bob and Shaun Funez have operated this Sebastopol fish farm for eight years. The sixteen ponds, one for public fishing, are stocked with catfish and trout. You can fish them out yourself or simply drive in and purchase some of these absolutely fresh fish. Then race home, put the fire on, and melt a big nugget of golden butter in your frying pan.

Bob and Shaun's Fish Farm is open year round.

---

**Sonoma County ∗ Oysters/General**
## BUCHAN'S FISH AND OYSTER COMPANY

*1105 Bodega Avenue, Petaluma 94952. Telephone (707) 763-4161. Hours: T–TH 10–6, F–SAT 10–7, SUN 11–6.*

Buchan's Fish and Oyster Company is a retail fish market selling the local Tomales Bay oysters once grown by Buchan's but now raised by International Shellfish Enterprises. The Pacific oysters are available both in or out of the shell along with East Coast clams, Mexican prawns, live and cooked Dungeness crab in season, scallops flown in from Nova Scotia, and fresh

squid from Monterey Bay, plus locally caught fish and smoked salmon.

You can buy your fish fresh to take home or you can choose from a whole menu of fresh-fried seafood at the seafood bar. Warm up with a bowl of the hearty clam chowder, made here every day.

---

**Sacramento/San Francisco ∗ Caviar/Crayfish**
## CALIFORNIA SUNSHINE

*Plant: 1217 C Street, Sacramento 95814. Telephone (916) 442-9101.*
*Office: 2171 Jackson Street, San Francisco 94115. Telephone (415) 567-8901. Wholesale to the trade only.*

After the proprietors of California Sunshine, Swedish-born Mat and Daphne Engstrom, learned that sturgeons were present in California waters, a fisherman friend presented them with some of the roe. Though Daphne Engstrom's first attempts at making caviar were not a success, with much frustrating, but fascinating, research and experimentation she perfected her technique. Marketed under the label Tsar Nicolai, the superb caviar is made from sturgeon roe air freighted down from Oregon but available only in limited quantities. Since commercial sturgeon fishing is illegal in California and the supply of roe from farther north is sporadic, the Engstroms have decided to develop their own sturgeon supply by aqua culture. They're experimenting with these techniques now with the help of scientists from the University of California at Davis. Though it takes nine to fifteen years for the females of this slow-growing species to develop the roe that is made into caviar, it is possible to take the eggs from the sturgeon without killing the fish so that they can produce for many years. The primitive sturgeon, the largest freshwater fish, may live to the age of one hundred.

California Sunshine's much less expensive "golden caviar" is a delicious caviar made from freshwater whitefish from the Midwest.

Though best known for its caviar, California Sunshine actually does the bulk of its business in crayfish. It was Daphne Engstrom who fell in love with Delta crayfish shortly after the family moved to California. During the season, the company distributes them live, the rest of the year they are available frozen in a sauce made with beer and dill in the Swedish style. In fact, their version is so traditional, they export over half a million pounds of it to Scandinavia each year (where the crayfish population was decimated by disease several years ago).

California Sunshine's products are sold at the Oakville Grocery, San Francisco; Jurgensen's (black caviar, when they have it), San Francisco; Let's Eat, Tiburon; Corti Brothers, Sacramento; Great Atlantic Lobster Company, Oakland (frozen crayfish in dill sauce).

---

Solano County * Crayfish
DELTA CRAYFISH

608 Highway 12, Rio Vista 94571. Telephone (707) 374-6654. Hours: M–SAT 8–5, SUN 10–5.

From the first of May until the beginning of November, it's crayfish season in the Delta. If you're in the area anytime during the season, stop in at Delta Crayfish where Bill Tate and Norm Burkham will sell you enough

of the small blue creatures, live and wriggling, to feed the whole crew at home. Just put on a big pot of water and strew it with savory herbs and spices (bay, thyme, cayenne), a few celery stalks, quartered onions, and some bags of "crab boil." When it all has boiled for a few minutes, add the live crawfish and cook for about ten minutes. Delicious dipped in drawn butter.

But if you'd like to see how it's really done deep in the bayou, don't miss a showing of Berkeley resident Les Blank's film about the Louisiana Cajuns and their music, *Spend It All.* Watch, too, for the big crayfish scene in his New Orleans Mardi Gras film *Always for Pleasure.*

---

Sacramento . * Catfish
ELK GROVE-FLORIN
CATFISH FARM

8047 Elk Grove-Florin Road, Sacramento 95823. Telephone (916) 682-3936. Hours: F–SUN 8:30–5:30.

On the weekends, the public can buy live catfish raised in earthen ponds at this seven-year-old catfish farm. They'll sell them to you from tanks or you can fish them out yourself.

---

San Francisco * Eastern Seafood
FISHERMAN'S WHARF
SEAFOODS

Pier 47, San Francisco 94107. Telephone (415) 776-6727. Hours: M–F 7–5, SAT 10:30–5.

This wholesaler deals in seafood, mainly shellfish, flown in from the East Coast. You can get live Maine lobster, oysters, clams, and mussels, all from the East Coast; also frozen Maryland blue crab and some fresh local fish like snapper or sole. Bushels (eighty pounds) get a discount. A bushel of oysters, a few volunteer experienced oyster shuckers, and you have the makings of a great party.

## GEODUCK CLAMS

The geoduck (pronounce "goo-ey-duck") clam is indisputedly the world's homeliest shellfish: a large fleshy trunk resembling that of an elephant's drooping sadly from a large ribbed clamshell. But ugly or not, this Puget Sound delicacy with a taste reminiscent of abalone is sought after by cooks who know a good thing when they see it.

Sliced thin, the raw meat can be eaten as *sashimi,* or can be tenderized and briefly sautéed. Much of the Pacific Northwest's catch is exported to the Orient, but you can generally find it in these San Francisco Chinatown markets: Lee Sang Market, 1207 Stockton Street, 989-4336; Sang Sang Market, 1143 Stockton Street, 285-0890; Hip Hing Market, 771 Clay Street, 982-9312.

---

**East Bay ✳ Eastern Seafood**
## THE GREAT ATLANTIC LOBSTER COMPANY

*95 Jack London Square, Oakland 94607. Telephone (415) 834-2649. Hours: M–TH 9-5, F 9-5:30, SAT 11-5.*

Oakland's the Great Atlantic Lobster Company specializes in eastern seafood. They have oysters (bluepoint and California-raised Belon), clams (littleneck and cherrystone), and East Coast mussels. Bushels get a discount. Succulent blue crab from the Chesapeake Bay are available in all months except December through March. October brings fresh soft-shell crabs; they stock them frozen the rest of the year. Live Alaskan or California Dungeness crabs fill one tank, while California spiny lobsters crowd another. Their live Maine lobsters run from tiny one- and two-pounders

up to fifteen- and twenty-pounders waving claws of terrifying proportions.

A variety of fresh fish are flown in from the East Coast; angler or monkfish, a favorite with Julia Child; scrod or haddock; Eastern swordfish, sole, and flounder. Seasonally there are sleek California salmon.

Sea urchins are sold live; the rich roe is wonderful spread on toast. Known as *oursin* in France, sea urchin appears as an ingredient in *bouillabaisse.* In May through September, the store often has live eel, a much sought-after delicacy for cooks from the Mediterranean countries. And conch, live in the shell, comes in briefly once a week. These sea snails come two or three to the pound. The meat is usually sliced and then cooked.

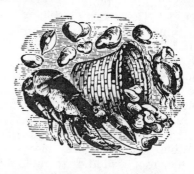

---

**East Bay ✳ Louisiana Fish and Shellfish**
## GULF COAST OYSTER BAR AND SPECIALTY COMPANY

*736 Washington Street, Oakland 94607. Telephone (415) 839-6950. Hours: M–F 9-3, SAT 11-3 (for retail sales; call for lunch and dinner hours).*

Located just down the street from the East Bay's mecca of Greek and Middle Eastern foods, G. B. Ratto's, the recently opened Gulf Coast Oyster Bar and Specialty Company is a sign of the regentrification of downtown Oakland. The oyster bar features "Louisiana Gulf cooking" with, of course, oysters on the half shell, seafood gumbos, jambalaya, shrimp *étouffée*, and red beans and rice prepared by owners Carolyn and Dan Wormhoudt. Gulf Coast also sells the makings of Creole cuisine. They import filé powder, cayenne, Creole tomatoes in summer, and, when they can get it, the rice they consider the tops, Crowley's rice from a little way up the Mississippi from New Orleans. They also bring in authentic *andouille* sausages from Louisiana. Much of the seafood sold here is flown in from the Gulf: redfish, a relative of bass (they have both the smaller "rat reds" and the regular redfish that comes in the five- to six-pound range); speckled trout, a trout that spends its entire life in the sea. This trout is used for some of the more subtle Creole dishes—trout *meunière*, for example. They have live blue crab year round and the softshells from late summer into the fall. The Gulf shrimp are browns, or "hoppers," and pinks, but the choicest are the Louisiana whites or blues, abundant in April and May, but superb in June. The shrimp come fresh or blast frozen, with heads on or off.

When available, they have Gulf oysters, too, in addition to bluepoints from Long Island (these are the same species, but since they've been grown in environmentally different conditions, the taste is different); the standard Pacific oyster in two sizes, petite and extra small; as well as local Belon oysters.

### East Bay ∗ Chinese
## HOP HING FISH MARKET

*716 Franklin Street, Oakland 94607. Telephone (415) 835-2274. Hours: 8–6 daily.*

Hop Hing Market sells fish, all clear-eyed and bright, as seen in the windows of the storefront on Franklin Street. Small pompano, silver and perfect, are

absolutely fresh. Milky squid, whole rock cod, halibut steaks—the pick of the catch—all wait to be admired.

Whole salmon are sliced into bright steaks at the fish-cutting counter. A live lobster, its claws held closed with yellow tape, is promenaded for a prospective customer.

### Sonoma County ∗ Oysters
## INTERNATIONAL SHELLFISH ENTERPRISES

*520 Cleveland Lane, Petaluma 94952. Telephone (707) 778-6712. Wholesale to the trade or in very large quantities only.*

In November of 1980, International Shellfish Enterprises harvested the West Coast's first commercial crop of the prized Belon oyster, which the French have been downing on the half shell with great relish for centuries. This is the flat-shelled, slightly astringent *Ostrea edulis*, indigenous to Europe.

The company's scientific facility located at Moss Landing has been researching and working for years on the problem of culturing the Belon oyster in Pacific waters. Though it had recently been successfully cultivated on the East Coast, there are problems with growing the oyster on the West Coast because the Pacific is more saline than the Atlantic Ocean—and, in general, oysters thrive in water with low salinity.

But ISE's research has paid off: California's new Belon oysters are as delicious, astringent, and briny as their European counterparts.

The company also cultivates the Pacific oyster and, using cultchless methods, produces a small, tender oyster with a long, sweet aftertaste, eminently delicious eaten on the half shell.

Future projects include experimentation with cultivating lobsters in California.

ISE's oysters are available at Bay Area fish markets.

### Marin County * Oysters
## JOHNSON OYSTER FARM

*Point Reyes National Seashore, Sir Francis Drake Boulevard (P.O. Box 68), Inverness 94927. Telephone (415) 669-1149. Hours: T-SAT 8-4:30, SUN 9-4:30.*

Among some San Franciscans, it's been a summer tradition for years to drive out toward Point Reyes and pick up dozens of Pacific oysters from Johnson Oyster Farm, then barbecue them on the beach. Grown in the warmer waters of Drake's Bay, these large, meaty oysters produced by traditional Japanese methods are delicious barbecued, fried, or used in oyster stews. They've just never been too appealing as raw oysters on the half shell.

At Johnson's you can buy them by the bushel, by the pound, or in quarts or six-pound cans.

Also available at local fish markets.

### San Francisco * Oysters/General
## LA ROCCA'S OYSTER BAR

*3519 California Street, San Francisco 94118. Telephone (415) 387-4100. Hours: M-SAT 11-8.*

La Rocca's is owned by Pat La Rocca, one of the original owners of Swan Oyster Depot, and, like Swan, it's both an oyster bar and a retail fish market.

You can get tiny Olympia oysters, eastern bluepoints, and delicious Pigeon Point oysters from Humboldt County, as well as small bay scallops from Long Island, shrimp, prawns, and fresh squid. Seasonally, you'll find fresh fish like snapper, petrale sole, swordfish, halibut, or sand dabs.

### East Bay * Louisiana Fish
## MOURA'S FISH MARKET

*818 Jefferson Street (inside Housewives' Market), Oakland 94607. Telephone (415) 444-8784. Hours: M-SAT 9-6.*

This fish market inside Housewives' Market in downtown Oakland specializes in fresh Louisiana fish: buffalo fish, tasty catfish, kingfish, garfish, gasper goo, speckled trout, black bass, and, in winter, drum and sheephead, plus fresh Louisiana crab and jars of Gulf oysters.

If you don't know how to pick a fish, just get behind one of the shrewd Louisiana women and watch how she does her buying. Wonder what is the best way to cook garfish or catfish? Just ask and you'll be deluged with recipes from everybody in line.

### Peninsula * Oysters
## PIGEON POINT OYSTERS

*921 Pigeon Point Road, Pescadero 94060. Telephone (415) 879-0391. Hours: 8:30-5 daily (closing hours variable).*

Pigeon Point Oysters was one of the first California oyster companies to try cultivating the Pacific oyster, *Crassostrea gigas*, by cultchless methods utilizing suspended raft culture. Since, unlike oysters cultivated by traditional Japanese methods, Pigeon Point's oysters are not bottom grown, their taste is clear and sweet, not muddy, and the texture silky rather than slightly gritty. Harvested at small sizes and rapidly maturing, the oysters are excellent eaten on the half shell.

Some of the delicious Pigeon Point oysters that were marketed in the last two years were a subspecies of *gigas* produced by cultchless cultivation. Grown in Humboldt Bay, these had a thinner shell, with a slightly different coloration and faint stripes.

---

**East Bay ＊ Smokehouse**
## SPORTSMAN'S CANNERY

*Sixty-seventh and Hollis, Emeryville 94501. Telephone (415) 655-2282. Hours: M-SAT 10-5; closed in winter.*

Cecilio Bustillos has been opening his Sportsman's Cannery in Emeryville during the sportfishing season for almost twenty years now. They close down during the winter months, usually starting at the end of October, and open up at the end of February.

Salmon fishermen and other sportspeople bring their catch here to be smoked. The old-fashioned smokehouse uses natural hickory smoke. No preservatives are added to the fish, which is smoked in long strips the way the Indians do it. Their smoked salmon is moist and delicate, the best you'll ever taste. Salmon, bass, and sturgeon are the usual fish they smoke, at a $5-per-fish minimum or by the pound. But if you don't have a fish to bring in, don't despair, for Sportsman's Cannery also sells smoked fish by the pound.

They'll also smoke your turkeys and pheasants, duck, geese, venison, pork legs, and ham. All poultry and meat is given a Morton sugar cure before smoking. Mr. Bustillos also does a dry cure with salt and no sodium nitrite for bacon. Bring him what you want smoked and he'll charge you by the pound.

By law, any sausages you've made and ask him to smoke should have saltpeter, or curing salts, in them. Remember to hang them to dry for a few days before bringing them in. They may lose up to as much as 40 percent of their weight during the smoking process.

---

**San Francisco ＊ Oysters/General**
## SWAN OYSTER DEPOT

*1517 Polk Street, San Francisco 94109. Telephone (415) 673-1101. Hours: M-F 8-5, SAT 8-5:30.*

This fine oyster bar will sell you oysters to shuck at home, two kinds: Olympia, the small West Coast oysters from Washington; and bluepoints from the East Coast. They also carry whatever fish is available fresh: steelhead salmon, swordfish, ling cod, red snapper. . .

---

**Marin County ＊ Oysters**
## TOMALES BAY
## OYSTER COMPANY

*Highway 1, seven miles north of Point Reyes Station (P.O. BOX 29), Point Reyes Station 94956. Telephone (415) 663-1242. Hours: F-SUN 8-5.*

Though this company has over two hundred acres in Tomales Bay seeded with Pacific oysters, they supplement their own harvest with oysters purchased from ISE and Pigeon Point, selling all of them under their own name. Their parent company is American Shellfish in Moss Landing.

Available at local fish markets.

# *Gourmet Markets*

## Contra Costa
### A LA CARTE

*2055 North Broadway, Walnut Creek 94596. Telephone (415) 932-4777. Hours: M–F 10:30–7, SAT 10:30–6, SUN 10:30–5.*

A la Carte started with an ambitious idea: lawyer Sandy Ress built a five-floor split-level building to house a wine, liquor, and gourmet food mart. The first floor is a wine store with imported wine and wines from California's small wineries, the next a liquor store with a selection including Armagnacs, cognacs, and over 180 beers. Upstairs, the delicatessen section sells over 150 cheeses including Armenian string, aged *asiago*, *bleu de Bresse*, Caerphilly, Chaumes, Gorgonzola, Derby, *pre clos*, farmer's cheese, *feta*, Gruyère, Limburger, Pont l'Evêque, and *raclette*; plus pâtés, freshly baked quiches, homemade salads, cured meats and sausages.

The gourmet foods section includes coffee and teas, crackers, chutneys, jams, olives, oils, mustards, and vinegars. Fresh pastries come from a variety of local bakeries, and the ice creams are from Bud's, Mary B. Best, and Häagen-Dazs.

## East Bay
### BALABOSTA SHOP

*824 University Avenue, Berkeley 94710. Telephone (415) 548-0382. Hours: M–SAT 10:30 –5:30.*

Manager Sandy Waters explains that the Balabosta Shop is a " 'scratch house.' Everything but the beverages is our own product, made here: chutneys, relishes, sauces, jams, vinegars, and frozen entrées from our restaurant next door."

The jams are made in small batches according to the season—fig, raspberry, peach and nectarine, fig-kiwi, and bourboned strawberries in pomegranate jelly—as are the peach and cranberry chutneys. Jellies are made from varietal grapes including Chardonnay, a dark-purple Zinfandel, and three kinds of Cabernet Sauvignon.

The unusual herb vinegars include basil, rosemary, and dill plus pink peppercorn, rose vinegar, and an Oregon blueberry-wine vinegar.

The shop makes three kinds of sausages: French pimiento, hot Italian, and garlic sausage, plus pâtés and *terrines.* Fish sausages are available by special order.

They cure their own fresh herring, make their own *gravlax* (salmon cured with spices and dill), and smoke their own eels. The shop's custom-designed smokehouse is filled with turkeys, pheasants, capons, chickens, ducks, quails, partridges, and squabs, each kind of bird smoked with a different combination of light fruit woods.

Seventeen kinds of cheesecake are available by special order.

## Sacramento
### CORTI BROTHERS

*5810 Folsom Boulevard, Sacramento 95819.*
*1755 Arden Way, Sacramento 95815.*
*5770 Freeport Boulevard, Sacramento 95822.*
*6111 Sunrise Boulevard, Sacramento 95826.*
*Telephone for all stores (916) 391-0300. Hours: Folsom, Arden, and Freeport stores M–SAT 9–7; Sunrise store M–SAT 9:30–7:30.*

Sacramento is usually thought of as a sorry wasteland for lovers of good food. It's true the restaurant scene is dismal, but lucky Sacramento cooks can shop at Corti Brothers markets and make their own splendid food.

The stores carry a complete stock of supermarket staples, but they also supply prime and choice meat, fresh poultry and game, and a large selection of imported and domestic cheeses. Seasonally, they have live crayfish from the nearby Delta.

The Corti family came originally from Liguria and since 1947 have continued one of their Italian traditions by making ravioli. The tender packets come stuffed with beef and spinach or with ricotta and Parmesan.

Wine expert Darrell Corti has expanded the family's wine-importing business. He makes frequent frips to Europe to select wines, Armagnacs, cognacs, sherries, and grappa.

He selects *extra-vergine* olive oil from two estates owned by Marchese Antinori in Florence—exceptional oil made from olives that are handpicked when ripe, crushed in a granite *frantoio*, and pressed lightly in a hydraulic press. Because the soil conditions differ at the two estates, the oil from the Orvieto estate is lighter and more delicate than the full-bodied oil produced on the Chianti estate.

When the price is not prohibitive and the crop is good, Corti Brothers brings fresh white truffles from Italy into the country.

For Christmas baking, Darrell Corti makes his own vintage mincemeat following a recipe he found in an 1825 English cookbook. He combines beef, beef suet, raisins, currants, oranges, lemons, citron, hard cider, sherry, and brandy. The heady mix is aged one year before it is sold.

And to spread on thick slabs of morning toast, he also makes a vintage marmelade using Seville oranges from the trees that line the streets of Old Sacramento. Capitol Marmelade comes either light or in a more concentrated darker type.

Both the mincemeat and the Capitol Marmelade are also available in San Francisco at the Oakville Grocery.

## San Jose Area
## COSTANTINO'S

*2666 South Bascom (corner of Union), San Jose 95124. Telephone (408) 377-6661. Hours: M–F 9:30–8, SAT 9–7, SUN 10–6.*

Costantino's started as a produce stand some twenty years ago. Though the store is still recommended for its high-quality produce, much of it from small farmers, it now also stocks a full line of gourmet groceries including prime meats; fresh poultry and game; Russian caviar; smoked salmon; domestic and imported cheeses; vinegars, mustards, and virgin olive oils; and bulk grains, nuts, and flours including such unusual flours as chestnut and garbanzo.

The deli section includes *charcuterie* such as pâtés and fresh Italian sausages along with salami, hams, and other cured meats.

The produce here is truly exceptional: local produce from small farmers, including many special ethnic items such as Persian herbs and vegetables and fresh Italian herbs, is mixed with produce grown all over the world. For example, the store imports fresh pineapple, *ti* leaves, and taro root from Hawaii. Picked ripe rather than green, the pineapples have a real tropical flavor. Depending on the season, you can choose from six different kinds of fresh mushrooms including *shiitake* and chanterelles.

## Peninsula
## DRAEGER'S SUPERMARKET

*1010 University Drive, Menlo Park 94025. Telephone (415) 322-2723. Hours: M–SAT 7 am–8 pm, SUN 7 am–6 pm.*

This Peninsula market has as many gourmet groceries as some of the city's finest: fresh truffles in season; fresh Russian, Iranian, and California's own

Tsar Nicolai sturgeon caviar; imported mustards, vinegars, olive oils, and pasta; and a wide variety of special flours and grains.

The fresh poultry includes Cornish hens, ducks, quail, and, at the holidays, geese. The meat here is all prime, including milk-fed veal, spring lamb, and some of the tenderest thick-cut lamb chops around.

The beautiful produce comes in from local sources and around the world.

## San Francisco
## EDIBLES

*I. Magnin, Union Square, San Francisco 94108. Telephone (415) 362-2100. Hours: T, W, SAT 9:30–5:30; M, TH, F 9:30–8; SUN 12–5.*

The new section of I. Magnin on Union Square includes a gourmet department, Edibles, where you can buy expensive high-quality gourmet foods. The *charcuterie* section is stocked with pâtés, sausages, take-out entrées, cheeses, caviar, smoked fish, and fresh pasta with sauces, all from Narsai's Market in Kensington. The bakery has croissants, baked right in the store, along with breads, cakes, and pastries. Edibles has,

of course, collected a gourmand's treasury of vinegars, olive oils, mustards, chocolates from European *chocolatiers*, imported candies, jams, champagnes, and dessert wines.

Edibles also includes a café serving breakfast, lunch, and high tea; the menu includes croissants, *sorbets*, and European-style pastries.

## Contra Costa
## NARSAI'S MARKET

*389 Colusa Avenue, Kensington 94707. Telephone (415) 527-3737. Hours: M–SAT 10–7, SUN 10–4.*

You see Narsai's distinctive black and white bags all over town, at the most urbane picnics and the best parties and in the most cosmopolitan kitchens. Narsai David's market, next door to his restaurant in Kensington, is a *charcuterie*, a bakery, a wine store, and a gourmet grocery.

In addition to his own sausages and pâtés, take-out entrées, and breads and pastries, Narsai has his own line of quality jams (over ten kinds including cranberry conserve with currants, Canadian blueberry, quince marmelade, Oregon blackberry) and handmade chocolates, plus canned smoked oysters and sturgeon, mustards, virgin maple syrup from the Minnesota woods, and vacuum-packed roasted cocktail nuts.

The store is stocked with gourmet vinegars, mustards, oils, and other gourmet ingredients. Fresh white truffles and black truffles are available in season, toward the end of November and mid-December respectively. He has caviar, smoked black cod, and moist Skagit River salmon from an Indian tribe in Washington. Try the Italian cookies and biscuits, traditionally from Abruzzi, made by the Di Camillo bakery in Niagra Falls.

The monthly cheese specials, always with a theme, introduce customers to some of the world's best cheeses. One month might present Fontina Val d'Aosta, buttery Bel Paese, velvety Gorgonzola, and rich *mascarpone*. Another month might feature a selection of little-known French cheeses.

In addition to providing take-home entrées, the market will also prepare elegant airline box lunches or picnic fare. The market's monthly newsletter has a schedule of take-home entrées, breads, and wine tastings. Watch for occasional food tastings of such specialties as fine olive oils from Italy and France, farmhouse cheese, or chocolate. Friday and Saturday afternoon wine tastings include an unusual January *nouveau* Beaujolais celebration.

For more details on Narsai's *charcuterie* and breads, see those sections of this book.

### San Francisco
## THE OAKVILLE GROCERY

*1555 Pacific Avenue, San Francisco 94109. Telephone (415) 885-4411. Hours: M-F 10:30–6:30, SAT 10–6, SUN 12–6.*

The sophisticated city cousin of the Oakville country store, the Oakville Grocery is San Francisco's food store *de luxe*, filled with a profusion of the very best cheeses, sausages, grains and legumes, pastries, exotic foodstuffs, and produce from California and the rest of the world.

Manager Clark Wolf's background is in cheese, so that department is particularly good. They have fresh cheeses flown in from Italy: crocks of *mascarpone, mozzarella di bufala*, baby *stracchino*. Then there is Taleggio, *asiago, caciocavallo*, Sicilian *pepato*, and *parmigiano*, sometimes aged three years, plus the best of the cheeses from France, England, Greece, Scandinavia, and Switzerland as well as our own local Teleme, Monterey Jack, and Laura Chenel's fresh goat cheeses.

The store sells their own *crème fraîche*; rich Devonshire cream flown in from England; fresh barnyard flash-pasteurized whipping cream from the Napa Valley; cream-topped milk; and Guernsey extra-rich milk, plus bulk sweet butter and Normandy butter.

The long stretch of *charcuterie* counter displays fresh sausages from the best of the local suppliers; pâtés and *terrines* from local chefs and *charcuteries*; and cured meats, salami, and dried sausages from local as well as East Coast sources. The Oakville Grocery staff did their homework when they chose the store's country hams. It's the best selection anywhere, with peanut-fed Smithfields, ashy country hams from the Ozarks and Tennessee, Oregon sugar- and pepper-cured hams, and five kinds of East Coast prosciutto. They're sold both whole and by the pound, so you're able to taste before you buy.

For sausage makers, with one day's notice the store can have casings, fatback, lardon, or caul fat.

It goes on and on: salads, fresh game, smoked game, fresh crayfish, Pigeon Point oysters, tiny bay scallops, golden caviar from California Sunshine.

Grains and chocolates are bought in bulk and then repackaged for better prices; so are flours, which include pastry flours, semolina, bread flours, corn meal, polenta, winter flour, gluten flour, garbanzo and chestnut flours. They stock old-fashioned products like sheet gelatin, Westbrae's natural malt syrup, and unsulphured molasses sorghum. For eating and baking they have chunks of satiny Belgian Callebaut white chocoate and milk chocolate and Guittard's French vanilla chocolate, plus marzipan and Dutch-process high-fat cocoa. The imported French nut pastes—hazelnut, pistachio, and almonds with orange—are wonderful mixed with chocolate and used as fillings in tortes and pastries.

Herbs and spices are also available in bulk. If you plan to do some cooking in the nouvelle style, they have eighteen-ounce jars of pink peppercorns in vinegar, plus bundles of long Ceylon cinnamon sticks, bags of sweet paprikas, dried Oriental and European mushrooms, and costly fresh truffles in season. Then vinegars—sherry, tarragon, shallot, garlic—march on through rows of shelves, followed by the olive oils—virgin Tuscan, Provençal, Spanish, Greek, California's best—plus walnut and hazelnut oils. The mustards number over one hundred.

It takes discipline to stop shopping here. You'll always find something else for your basket; convenient eight-pound tins of sweet *peperonata*; red and yellow jars of sun-dried tomatoes from Liguria, sweet and smoky, packed in olive oil; wonderful *biscotti* from an East Coast bakery.

Oakville has French-style *sorbets*, made in house (see Ice Cream section) and an outstanding selection of fine produce (see Produce section).

## Napa Valley
## THE OAKVILLE GROCERY

*7856 St. Helena Highway, Oakville 94562. Telephone (707) 944-8802. Hours: M-SAT 10-6, SUN 10-5.*

The San Francisco store's country cousin, the original Oakville Grocery in Oakville, looks like just another country grocery as you approach it from the road, with its big Coca-Cola sign painted on the side.

But open the wide front door and it's immediately evident how extraordinary it is. Salamis and Smithfield hams hang over the central counter. Shelves are packed with mustards, fine olive oils, crackers, luscious jams. A refrigerator case displays country pâtés and *terrines*. Crockery bowls hold olives from the south of France, locally cured olives, mixed candied fruits. French canning jars display spices and herbs: fresh thyme, tarragon, sage on the stem, little rolls of *bouquets garnis* tied with string. Heavy garlic braids festoon walls hung with green bay-leaf wreaths.

Wine country cooks rely on the Oakville Grocery for fine ingredients: game, produce, cheese, *charcuterie*, grains and legumes. Visitors can find the makings of a superb picnic lunch here: Passini baguettes, good local and imported cheeses, pâtés, fine beers and wines, and rich pastries from local bakeries.

**East Bay**
# G. B. RATTO,
# INTERNATIONAL GROCERS

*821 Washington Street, Oakland 94607. Telephone (415) 832-6503. Hours: M-SAT 8-5.*

Though Ratto's in Oakland claims to specialize in Greek and Middle Eastern foods, it is truly an international grocery, without any of the pretensions of some "gourmet" groceries.

For your French country cooking they have dried morels and *cèpes,* and chanterelles in cans; and little bundles of classic French *bouquets garnis* made of herbs from Provence wrapped in a bay leaf and tied with string. Thyme, tarragon, and fennel or sage come the same way. French baking chocolates are sold in uneven chunks, by the pound, and Ratto's makes their own oak-aged vinegar, sold in quarts, half-gallons, and gallons, both red and white. There are cans of goose fat to flavor your *cassoulet,* tiny black *niçoise* olives, *couscous* in bulk, saffron for your *bouilla-*

*baisse,* and three kinds of olive oil from Marseilles.

If you want to try the cooking of Martinique or the rest of the Caribbean, Ratto's stocks pigeon peas, Demerara sugar (raw cane sugar and cane molasses), and spices like *annato* seeds to stain your dishes red, whole Jamaican allspice, small dried chilies, and long-grain rice. For Brazilian food, there is manioc flour in bulk, black beans, *tasajo* (or dried beef), and Portuguese olives in brine, green or black.

Ingredients for African cuisines include melon seeds *(egusi),* canned jute leaves, red palm oil, potato flour, and cream of palm fruits from Ghana.

For Italy's varied cuisines there is pasta, domestic and imported; dried fava, *cannellini,* and *lupini* beans; short-grained Arborio rice for *risotto;* capers in salt; pine nuts, polenta, and semolina; cheeses; Graffeo's Italian espresso beans; *baccalà;* dried mushrooms; and big handfuls of sweet basil kept in water up by the cash register.

An exceptional store.

SOLON CADDY'S
FINE
GROCERIES, WINES,
&c. &c.

Spices once cost their weight in gold, but today's cooks have an unparalleled wealth of spices and herbs from all over the world at their disposal.

It really does seem a treasure—a whole world of taste aligned on the pantry shelf, in rows of clear glass jars filled with dusky dried leaves or hard, reticent seeds that release their flavor when crushed. Opening the jars, you can smell the warm hills of Provence fragrant with thyme, marjoram, lavender, bay, rosemary, and fennel; or the overpowering scent of wild thyme crushed underfoot beside a dusty road in Greece. Leave them unlabeled. Each spice and herb is distinct: paprika, bitter and earthy; cinnamon, sweet and dusty; rosemary, oily and fragrant. You'll soon recognize the warmth of nutmeg, the sharp scent of ginger and the autumn fragrance of juniper berries. The eye delights in the dazzling yellow-gold of turmeric, the red of *achiote*, and the fiery orange of cayenne or the bluish purple of poppy seeds.

My kitchen has two mortars. The first is a heavy brass one a friend carried back from Africa for me. It rings out like a bell when you crush seeds and spices in its deep bowl. The other is wide and spacious, cool white marble veined with gray, from the marble quarries of Tuscany. It has a different feel. In summer I use it to pound garlic and salt to a sticky paste before beating in dark olive oil for *aioli* or crushing fresh basil leaves for a *pesto*.

Spice measurements in any recipe can never be exact since the quality and freshness of spices and herbs determine their potency. Always buy ground spices and herbs in very small quantities, as their flavor will fade rapidly. Whole seeds and berries will keep longer, but light and heat both take their toll with time. Be sure to smell and taste spices before using them. Faded spices will not give the food you cook a clear taste.

Of course, for herbs like tarragon, basil, thyme, marjoram, chervil, and sage, the fresh herb is always incomparably better than the dried leaves. Here in California, fresh herbs can be grown year round. Those that die down in the winter can be moved inside in pots until the spring. To store fresh herbs, wrap in cloth or paper towels, then place in a plastic bag in the refrigerator.

*Note:* many of the stores listed in the Produce section, and all of the stores listed in Gourmet Markets, carry fresh herbs. For a wide variety of dried herbs and spices in bulk, see Gourmet Markets, ethnic markets (especially Indian), and Natural Foods. See also the Seeds section for sources for culinary herbs and spices.

## Dried Herbs and Spices
## ATTAR SPICES AND HERBS

*Playground Road, New Ipswich, N.H. 03071. Telephone (603) 878-1780.*

Attar Spices and Herbs sells over seventy culinary herbs and spices by mail, including whole white or green cardamom, star anise, allspice berries, chervil, fenugreek, flax seed, true Spanish saffron, sausage seasoning, and "pumpkin pie spice." Prices are reasonable by the pound; buy with friends and divide.
*Free catalog.*

## East Bay ∗ Fresh Herbs
## BURNAFORD'S PRODUCE

*2635 Ashby Avenue, Berkeley 94705. Telephone (415) 548-0348. Hours: M-T, TH-F, SAT 9-6; W 9-7:30; SUN 12-4.*

Burnaford's Produce has a special section well provided with fat bundles of Mrs. Poggi's herbs, fresh cut and available until quite late in the season.

Signora Luisa Poggi grew up in Savona, near Genoa, Liguria's great port city. This part of Italy is renowned for the use of fresh aromatic herbs, especially *basilico*, or sweet basil, in its cuisine. Genovese sailors returning home from months of monotonous ship's fare used to catch the fragrance of sweet basil growing on the hills behind the city before even sighting land. If you visit Genoa, you'll see sweet basil growing everywhere: in empty petrol or tomato cans, in window boxes, and in terra cotta pots outside doorways.

Here in California, Mrs. Poggi has a big backyard in Concord where she grows fragrant culinary herbs—marjoram, oregano, thyme, rosemary, tarragon, mint, sorrel and flat-leafed Italian parsley. The sweet basil is grown from special seeds she brings back from Italy.

Says Mrs. Poggi: "I just decided one day I would do it" and promptly plowed up her backyard to make room for planting. "Everything is natural," she asserts. "I don't use any pesticides."

She sells her herbs to just a few other produce markets in the Berkeley–North Oakland area.

---

**Monterey Area ✱ Dried Herbs and Spices**
## HERBAL EFFECT

*600 Lighthouse Avenue, Monterey 93940. Telephone (408) 375-6313. Hours: M–SAT 10–5.*

Send for this Monterey-based herb company's thirty-page catalog of top-quality herbs, spices, teas, and tea blends priced by the ounce or by the pound. The selection of over fifty herbs and spices for cooking includes star anise, African bird pepper, a strong and fragrant California basil, chervil, Spanish saffron, whole nutmeg, and vanilla bean.

They also have special seasoning blends: *fines herbes*; "super seasons" (a

Mediterranean version of *fines herbes*); *garam masala*; two kinds of traditional East Indian curry powders, one hotter than the other; and an aromatic fish seasoning with dill, lemon, and basil.

*Mail order. Free catalog.*

---

**East Bay ✱ Dried Herbs and Spices**
## THE LHASA KARNAK HERB COMPANY

*2513 Telegraph Avenue, Berkeley 94704. Telephone (415) 548-0380. Hours: M–SAT 10–6:30, SUN 12–6.*
*1938 Shattuck Avenue, Berkeley 94704. Telephone (415) 548-0372. Hours: M–SAT 10:30–6.*

The original Lhasa Karnak Herb Company on Telegraph Avenue in Berkeley is a romanticist's idea of an herb store. Small and impeccably neat, the store has dozens and dozens of gallon glass jars filled with herbs and spices, roots, and seeds. You feel close to something elemental, buying up little packets of marvelously fragrant powders or leaves, colored in the whole palette of autumn and earth.

If you want a clear, piercing hot taste in your dishes, try the African bird's eye cayenne. Keep it in a shaker just like your salt and pepper to spice things up a bit. Stain your curries with pungent, deep-yellow turmeric powder.

*Mail order by UPS. Catalog 50¢.*

---

**San Francisco ✱ Dried Herbs and Spices**
## NATURE'S HERB COMPANY

*281 Ellis Street, San Francisco 94102. Telephone (415) 474-2756. Hours: M–SAT 7–4.*

The venerable Nature's Herb Company has been around since 1915, dispensing all manner of herbs, custom tonics, and herbal remedies to generations of health-conscious San Franciscans.

The store has literally hundreds of herbs, roots, and seeds filed away. Those of interest to cooks include anise seed, arrowroot powder, bay leaves, bitter orange peel, black caraway seed, borage leaves, cardamom, chervil, chicory root, dill weed, *galangal* root (for Indonesian cooking), hops, marjoram, mugwort, sweet basil, tamarind pulp, turmeric root, and whole vanilla bean. All herbs are sold in leaf form; powdered herbs cost a bit more per pound.

Along with all manner of soothing herbal teas, Nature's Herb Company espouses *yerba maté*, a South American drink.

If you're not feeling at your best, you might try one of the company's dozens of tried and true tonics and herbal remedies.

*Mail order.*

San Francisco ✷ Dried Herbs
and Spices
## SAN FRANCISCO
## HERB COMPANY

*367 Ninth Street, San Francisco 94103. Local telephone (415) 861-7174, California telephone 800-622-0768, U.S. telephone 800-227-4530. Hours: M–F 10–4.*

The San Francisco Herb Company is a source for quality herbs and spices in bulk. All the most common culinary herbs and spices are here, plus such uncommon items as *annato* seed for Caribbean dishes, pickling-spice blends to put up the summer's baby cukes, chicory root for your New Orleans-style coffee, and cinnamon sticks.

Spices of special interest include whole allspice; California sweet basil and Egyptian basil; fancy green cardamom; cayenne; gumbo filé blend; whole vanilla beans. Among the herbs you'll find borage, juniper berries, lemon grass,

mugwort, orange flowers, orange peel, peppermint, spearmint, and *yerba maté*. They also sell seeds for sprouting: alfalfa, cabbage, lentil, mung, radish, and red clover.

The best way to buy from San Francisco Herb Company is to get together with other cooks and make up one order; herbs and spices are all sold in one-, five-, or twenty-five-pound quantities. Whole seeds will stay fresh when stored properly, but smoke, heat, and sunlight will cause ground spices and dried herbs to lose their potency over a period of time. Buy whole whenever you can; use a retired electric coffee grinder to grind small quantities of spices as you need them.

*Mail order.*

Sonoma County ✷ Dried Herbs
and Spices
## TRINITY HERB

*P.O. Box 199, Bodega 94922. Telephone (707) 874-3418. Mail order by UPS.*

Bodega's Trinity Herb is a small cottage-industry–style distributor of botanicals and seasonings, plus a few related items.

Trinity Herb's order list is coded by symbol: some herbs are organically grown (basil leaf, tarragon, dill weed, parsley, alfalfa seeds and flax seeds, peppermint and spearmint), while others grow wild and are gathered by hand in the area. These are generally the botanicals, or medicinal herbs, but juniper berry is among them. Other culinary seasonings include fiery African bird pepper, fresh-ground cinnamon, cumin, whole nutmeg, rosemary, and sage.

Bulk botanicals and seasonings are available in not less than one-pound quantities. Join with fellow cooks to make up your order, which will be shipped UPS. Order by Wednesday night for delivery during the following week. Minimum order $25.

# Ice Cream

Just about everyone now agrees that Marco Polo didn't bring the noodle back from China. But when he came home to Venice in the early fourteenth century, he did bring a recipe for a frozen ice milk. Jaded Venetians quickly adopted the exotic new dessert that he had eaten in the streets of faraway China. Very soon, members of the new *mestiere* began to improvise ice creams, or *gelati*, flavored with fruits and nuts and lavished with liqueurs.

In southern Italy, the Sicilians had been introduced to water ices by the Saracens as early as the ninth century. During the Crusades they learned to make fruit ices flavored with lemon, orange, coffee, pomegranate, and rose water from the Persians and Arabs. To this day in Italy, it is the southern Italians who are renowned for their tradition of fine *sorbetti* (water ices) and *gelati* (ice creams).

When Catherine de Medici married Henry II of France, the greedy gourmande brought dozens of Florentine cooks with her to train the "primitive" French in the fine art of cookery. She introduced them to sauces, spinach, and *gelato*. At first the frozen dessert was strictly reserved for the court, but by 1660, the closely guarded secret was out. An enterprising Sicilian named Francesco Procopio opened the first *gelateria* in Paris, Café Procope, where he served ice cream and *sorbet* (*sorbetti*). The Parisians liked it so much that only sixteen years later Paris had 260 establishments making and selling ices.

Ice cream crossed the English Channel in the seventeenth century when Charles I brought a French cook privy to the secret back with him from Normandy. Like Catherine, he tried to make it the exclusive royal dessert and paid the cook a yearly fee to confine the secret to the court. But by 1740, the recipe was published, and cooks in upper-class households instructed themselves in the laborious art.

Of course the English brought ice cream with them to America. But it wasn't until 1840 that an American woman showed a little of that famous Yankee ingenuity. Nancy Johnson invented the hand-cranked ice cream freezer, and making homemade ice cream became a family pastime. It was a man from Baltimore, Jacob Fussell, who opened the first wholesale ice cream plant. But through the years, that same irrepressible ingenuity has tampered with a good thing. Today, much of America's ice cream is pumped full of air, emulsifiers, stabilizers, and artificial flavorings. Real ice cream has to call itself "old-fashioned."

The Bay Area, however, has no lack of good ice cream, *gelato*, and *sorbet* made from fresh cream, eggs, fruit, and real chocolate and other flavorings right in the store where it's sold.

## Peninsula ✳ Italian
## BRAVO FONO

*99 Stanford Shopping Center, Palo Alto 94304. Telephone (415) 322-4664. Hours: M–SAT 11–9, SUN 12–5.*

The Stanford Shopping Center boasts a *gelateria* to rival the best in Italy. Decorated in tones of straw and off-white, Bravo Fono is filled with light. It falls in intricate patterns on the polished granite counters and tables flecked with salmon and gray, and on the hand-cut travertine floors, pale as watered silk. Mirrors reflect stacked glassware, tiered *gelato* cones, bottles of liqueurs, vases of flowers, and baskets heaped with fruits and lemons. But the store's centerpiece is the spectacular display of *gelati* set in rectangular steel containers like watercolors in a child's paintbox. Displays of fresh fruit indicate the flavor of each cream or ice.

Paulette and Lazlo Fono, also the proprietors of Paprikás Fono, the Hungarian restaurant in Ghirardelli Square, wanted an ice cream place like those they grew up with in Europe. Hungary has a long tradition of Italian ice cream making; immigrant *gelatai* used to peddle their fresh-made ices through the streets of Hungarian towns and villages.

Armed with maps and the addresses of respected *gelato* craftsmen, Paulette and Lazlo scoured the Italian countryside, stopping to work with the masters of the trade. Home again with notebooks overflowing with recipes and ideas, they began experimenting with American cream and Italian machines. Paulette Fono is a perfectionist: the recipe for each flavor is built from scratch.

From the outside, you can look right into Bravo Fono's *gelato laboratorio* and see *gelato* in the making. The small batches are made in special Italian machines using only fresh eggs and cream and natural flavorings. From there, the freshly made *gelato* goes straightway into custom freezers to chill it quickly in order to preserve the silken texture.

The *nocciola* is outstanding, made with two hazelnut pastes from Piemonte, one smooth, the other chunky. The seductive pistachio has whole Iranian pistachios in a base flavored with imported pistachios, but the *capolavoro* is *moca*: barely sweet, made with strong espresso and finely ground espresso beans. The chocolate has an exquisite balance of sweet and bitter, while the *amaretto* has the wonderful grittiness of crushed almonds, their flavor heightened with a splash of Amaretto liqueur. The definitive test of any ice cream maker, the vanilla (*crema*), is full and voluptuous with both extracts and ground vanilla bean.

The ripe fruit flavors of the *sorbetti*, or ices, are livened with lemon juice.

The orange concentrates the taste of sun-warmed citrus, without a trace of bitterness; the pear keeps its granular and fleshy texture. The lemon is clear, aggressive, delicious, and the banana is a revelation, made only with ripest fruit. Try the *cassis*, a deep stain of violet, made from whole imported Polish black currants.

Outside under big white canvas umbrellas, you can enjoy a traditional coffee or lemon *granita*, a rough slush of cold crystals enjoyed by southern Italians in the summer. Or Bravo Fono will make you a plate of "spaghetti" ice cream: *crema* extruded from a special machine in thin strands and sauced with raspberry.

Even Bravo Fono's *coppas*, or sundaes, are Italian style: splendid fantasies of *gelati*, *sorbetti*, and toppings. Try the *amarena*: *crema* and *nocciola gelato* topped with a Bolognese wild-cherry sauce and *panna montata*, unsweetened whipped cream.

Then there are the *semifreddi*, or desserts made with ice cream: a plate of *profiteroles*, miniature cream puffs filled with vanilla ice cream and drowned

in a satin chocolate sauce; or a Sicilian *cassata,* layers of ice cream and cake molded and frozen.

Bravo Fono is a complete *gelateria*: a caffè serving *tremezzini,* layered triangular sandwiches filled with cheese, Polish ham and other fillings; *panini,* little breads with various fillings; and desserts and espressos.

The Fonos' future plans include *salatini,* tiny finger pastries to be eaten with aperitifs, and *frulatti,* thick drinks of blended fresh fruits and milk.

A second store is opening in San Francisco soon on Fillmore Street at the site of the Fonos' original Magic Pan restaurant.

## San Francisco * American
## BUD'S ICE CREAM

*1300 Castro Street, San Francisco 94114. Telephone (415) 648-2837. Hours: M-TH and SUN 11 am-11 pm, F-SAT 11 am-midnight.*

"Bud" is Al Edlin, who has been making ice cream for fifty years and will continue to do so as long as he is the "flavor designer" and "quality controller" of this veteran among ice cream stores. Recently the company changed hands; the new owner, Tony Garcia, vows to maintain close ties to the Edlin family and their tradition of quality.

We have entered the New Age of Ice Cream, to be sure. We need no longer steal furtive glances at the "sweet shoppe" as we pass by, running away from temptation. Ice cream is now a health food. Just look at the people crowding the stores: joggers in sweatsuits after a sixteen-mile run, diet-conscious freshman girls, young men undisturbed by the possibility of acne.

Bud's Ice Cream is still hand-cranked and ungimmicky, the way it was and still is made at the original Twenty-fourth and Castro location. It is also available at the following Bay Area locations:

Clift Hotel, Geary and Taylor, San Francisco

The Konery, 3208 Scott, San Francisco

Le Scoop, 2 Embarcadero, San Francisco

Wim's Restaurant, 141 Columbus, San Francisco

Corner Creamery, 3580 Alameda de las Pulgas, Menlo Park

Barbary Coast, Strawberry Shopping Center, Mill Valley

Bud's, 7991 Old Redwood Highway, Cotati

Lickety Split, 3141 Crow Canyon Place, San Ramon

## San Francisco * American
## DOUBLE RAINBOW

*1653 Polk Street, San Francisco 94109. Telephone (415) 775-3220. Hours: M-F 11 am-midnight, SAT-SUN 11 am-1 am. 3933 Twenty-fourth Street, San Francisco 94114. Telephone (415) 821-3420. Hours: noon-midnight daily. 407 Castro Street, San Francisco 94114. Telephone (415) 621-2350. Hours: SUN-TH 11 am-midnight, F-SAT 11 am-1 am.*

Steve Fink and Mike Sachar run this excellent shop in the heart of San Francisco's Polk Gulch, with branches on Twenty-fourth Street and Castro. They are cozy places that also sell espresso drinks and "mix your own" sundaes. By traditional American standards their ice cream colors are subdued, and there are no fantasy flavors. A soft purple-gray envelops plump blueberries in an ice cream with the texture of *gelato.* The taste of orange in the delicate Orange Blossom persists long after the last bite. Ultra Chocolate has the direct, comforting flavor of Dutch cocoa, with a velvety aftertaste. Among the twelve or so other traditional flavors, pistachio

is the *pièce de résistance*: musky and creamy, not too sweet, studded with whole nuts. Vanilla, a bit sweeter than the rest, comes across evenly, clear and custardlike.

## San Francisco/Peninsula ✳ Italian
## GELATO

*2211 Filbert Street, San Francisco 94123. Telephone (415) 929-8666. Hours: SUN–TH noon–11 pm, F–SAT noon–midnight. 201 Parnassus Street, San Francisco 94117. Telephone (415) 566-9696. Hours: noon–10 pm daily. 421 Alma, Palo Alto 94301. Telephone (415) 321-4875. Hours: noon–11 pm daily.*

After a Roman dinner of *agnolotti al sugo* and *fritto misto* at Osteria Romana, and a stop at Il Fornaio for your next morning's *biscotti*, stroll down Filbert Street to Gelato, the tiny shop at the heart of San Francisco's newest—and very fashionable—Italian shopping area. The original store on Parnassus can be blamed for starting the city's romance with *gelato*.

The local favorites are *torta di mele*, made with apples, and Joseph St. Almond, rich with toasted almonds. Chocolate, vanilla, almond, and pistachio can be sampled together in the *coppa mista*.

"Questo gelato è veramente buono," remarks an Italian gentleman spooning the silken *gelato* from his paper cup. Gelato's ice cream is compact, sweet, but not overwhelming.

As fresh fruit comes into season, so do fresh apricot, strawberry, and *arancia* (orange), all made every day. And owner John Hefferman makes frequent trips to Italy for flavor inspiration.

A la Carte in Walnut Creek also sells Gelato's ice cream as a dessert or by the pint.

## San Francisco/Peninsula ✳ American
## HÄAGEN-DAZS

*2066 Union Street, San Francisco 94123. Telephone (415) 563-4495. Hours: SUN–TH 11 am–11 pm, F–SAT 11 am–1 am. 700 Welch Road, Stanford Shopping Center Barn, Palo Alto 94304. Telephone (415) 326-1638. Hours: SUN–TH 11 am–11 pm, F–SAT noon–midnight. 2228 San Mateo Fashion Island Mall, San Mateo 94404. Telephone (415) 349-5331. Hours: M–TH 9:30 am–10:15 pm, F–SAT 9:30 am–11:30 pm, SUN 11 am–10:15 pm.*

Weighing in at a hefty pound per pint, with 15 percent butterfat, HD is the favored heavyweight for the ice cream title.

Though HD is meant to sound imported and Danish, expensive and sophisticated, a chance comment by a friend that the Danes had rich ice cream suggested the name to founder Reuben Mattus. When he started in 1960, Mr. Mattus made only a few flavors and sold them in cartons to delis and liquor stores. To tastebuds battle shocked by such inconceivable flavor combinations as pumpkin licorice, root beer horseradish, chile con carne, and other "fantasy" flavors, his "plain" well-made vanilla, chocolate, and coffee were a taste revelation.

He couldn't make enough of it at first. Twenty years later, HD is a familiar sight all over the country. All the ice cream is still made in one plant in New Jersey under the personal supervision of Mr. Mattus. He is now offering franchises for "dipping" stores and has expanded his flavors from nine to eighteen. At this writing California has seventeen HD parlors, three of them in northern California.

To stress the purity of their ingredients, the HD parlors put everything up front. Every ingredient—and they're all natural—is listed beside the name of the ice cream. The raspberry and lemon *sorbets* are not just made with *any* water, but with *mountain spring* water.

HD's superior vanilla chip is packed with a rubble of broken bittersweet chocolate. The strong coffee version is as sophisticated as they come. But for professed chocolate addicts, the chocolate chip puts the same choice rubble in a dark fudgy base.

A good strawberry ice cream is hard to find. Our overbred strawberries just don't have an intense flavor. Mattus spent six years developing his recipe for strawberry ice cream. Fragile pink, it is set with chunks of quartered berries in delicious contrast to its slightly sweetened cream base.

HD's fruit ices are firmly in the European tradition. The finely iced crystals of the wine-colored *cassis* carry the tart, full flavor of black currants. The lemon shows a pleasing balance of tart to sweet, but the flavor of the boysenberry and raspberry ices is dulled by oversweetening.

## Peninsula ✳ Italian
## LA MODERNE

*980 Woodside Road, Redwood City 94061. Telephone (415) 367-9230. Hours: SUN–TH 11–10, F–SAT 11–11.*

If you find yourself in Redwood City on a hot summer day, stop and cool down with a scoop or two of fresh fruit ices at La Moderne. The orange is smooth, a refreshing pale amber. The watermelon has chunky bits of pulp, even an occasional seed.

## San Francisco ✳ Italian
## THE LATEST SCOOP

*4077 Eighteenth Street, San Francisco 94114. Telephone (415) 864-5055. Hours: noon–midnight daily.*

The nutty taste of the Latest Scoop *nocciola* (hazelnut), *gianduia* (chocolate and hazelnuts), or *torrone* (almond nougat) can satisfy any untoward cravings for *gelato.* The ingredients for these classic flavors come straight from Italy.

The selection of flavors at the Latest Scoop changes frequently. Another visit might present the *gelato* aficionado with pistachio, *marron glacé*, rice pudding, or lemon custard. *E mangia. . .*

*Gelato* from the Latest Scoop is also available at a new store in Berkeley called Scoops of Italy at 2430 Durant Avenue, telephone (415) 840-6740. The store is open seven days a week, noon to midnight.

**San Francisco * Latino**
## LATIN FREEZE

*3338 Twenty-fourth Street, San Francisco 94110. Telephone (415) 282-5033. Hours: M–SAT 12–6.*

Open just two years, Latin Freeze has become a required stop for the *paletas* addict. For the uninitiated, *paletas* are frozen fruit bars made of puréed fresh tropical fruit. On the rare days of Bay Area heat the *paletas* line might be long and slow, filled with young schoolchildren, dark-haired Latin beauties, and khaki-clad revolutionaries from Casa Salvador. But it is a worthwhile wait. *Paletas* flavors are undeceivingly seasonal, and their colors match the warm tones of the Mission's outdoor murals: pineapple yellow, rosy melon, *jamaica* (hibiscus flower) scarlet, pearly coconut, autumn leaf *cacahuate* (peanut). You will be easily tempted by the fleshy mango, refreshing sour tamarind, or luscious papaya. However, young Latinos often prefer strawberry. The girl behind the counter shrugs and smiles: "A todos les gusta fresa." Yes, everyone likes strawberry. We are in *los estados unidos,* after all.

Jose Montes, Jr., heads this part of the family business. His father, Jose Montes, Sr., from Guadalajara, runs Paletas Polar, a sister store, in San Jose.

---

**East Bay * International**
## MARY B. BEST

*3794 Grand Avenue, Oakland 94610. Telephone (415) 451-6059. Hours: TH–SAT 12:30–4:30.*

Despite the increasing number of ice cream lovers making pilgrimages to her door, Mary B. Best certainly hasn't gentrified her store. Her "administrative and manufacturing office" is still a crowded storefront on Grand Avenue, tiny and difficult to find, where she makes small custom batches of ice creams for fine restaurants as diverse as Trader Vic's or Gaylord Indian restaurant, or for the Sweet Dreams candy shop. To the public, she's open just three days a week when she sells overruns of her custom flavors. You never know what you'll find, but that doesn't mean the selection is limited. Go behind the counter to survey the day's choices. The hand of Mary B's husband and front man, Jeff Best, can be detected in the collaged labels describing flavors like Bleu Berry, "quintessence of northern blueberries waltzed into rhapsody of creamed base"; or La Vie en Rose, "crushed petals of the hauntingly beautiful American Beauty Rose w/out butterfat."

While Mary B. works her magic in the back, devising ice creams and ices lavished with the richest cream and the finest chocolates, flavorings, and liqueurs, Jeff will give you a scoop of your choice, but not without insisting you "extend your taste experience" with a few of that day's more remarkable flavors. Let him be bossy. It may be your last chance to taste Virgo St. Vienna or Juliet et Paris. At this accounting Mary B's imagination has created 370 flavors, over 60 different vanillas alone. If there's one you fall in love with and can't bear to think of never tasting again, Jeff will inform you the next time it's made.

Mary's expertise with fruits is not accidental. She experiments until she's found just the right variety for the flavor she has in mind. Polly Peche is made from a rough purée of Yakima Valley peach, Figaro Fig from fresh California figs, and the tart Klondike Cranberry ice from fresh northwestern cranberries.

Indian restaurants serve her tropical mango, coconut, and lychee nut flavors. Her ginger, dosed with the scraped and dried root of pungent Indian ginger, duplicates the comforting taste of Indian desserts. Mary B. loves a challenge—she's even making a taro root ice cream for a Polynesian restaurant.

No one makes better coffee flavors. Café Brûlot is made from Guatemalan coffee, fresh orange peel, 40 percent cream, and 80 proof brandy and cognac. For her Sequidilla, she mixes roasted Brazilian coffee beans with Spanish cocoa and butter-roasted almonds.

In another age her rich ice creams would have been banned under sumptuary laws. But to balance all that, she does a delightful penance with her "no butterfat" glacés, or ices. The Lemon Glacé has thin strands of zested lemon suspended in a fine-spun lemon ice. She makes a classic Grand Marnier ice and a spectacular *framboise* ice made with raspberry brandy. Her Blackberry Belgique Glacé uses Oregon blackberries. Imported cherry blossom wine makes an intriguing Oriental ice.

The woman is a genie of ice cream. When she's not concocting new flavors, she's designing new ice cream confections like Tortoni La Scala, an imperial Baked Alaska, or a Russian Rum Cake. Over the years she has collected hundreds of ice cream molds in the shape of pheasants, fruit baskets, fluted domes, melons—even a wishbone. She'll make ice cream for you in any of their shapes.

Other places where you can find Mary B. Best ice cream:

Sweet Dreams, 2901A College Avenue, Berkeley

Au Coquelet, 2000 University Avenue, Berkeley

Fudge Alley, 376 Park Street, Moraga

Best Ice Cream, 1352A Ninth Avenue, San Francisco

Cafe de Young, de Young Art Museum, San Francisco

## San Francisco * French
## OAKVILLE GROCERY

*1555 Pacific Avenue, San Francisco 94109. Telephone (415) 885-4411. Hours: M–F 10:30–6:30, SAT 10–6, SUN 12–6.*

A feast of good things to eat is gathered together under the Oakville Grocery's roof: perfectly ripened fruit, mellow cheeses, fragrant sausages, elegant pastries, dense dark breads. Add to this a collection of ice creams made from the finest ingredients: Häagen-Dazs, Vivoli, and the store's own *sorbets*, made in the strict French tradition.

"At first we made the most amusingly awful *sorbets*," explains manager Clark Wolf. Making *sorbets*, like making wines, requires thought and experimentation. There are a number of capricious variables: the ripeness of the fruit, the ratio of sugar to water, and freezing and sealing techniques. Time and devotion play a major role, but look how California wines have paid off. Taste Oakville Grocery's *sorbets*.

At the peak of summer, raspberries are puréed to make a sumptuous, velvety-red ice with a deep and clinging taste. A lemon lime fills the mouth with a slush of cold, tart crystals; and another lemon, flavored with maple sugar, is the color of polished ivory. Gordon Smith and Rick O'Connell make the *sorbets*, using only fresh fruit purées sweetened with sugar syrup. Produce man David Findley finds the ripe fruit for the luscious pear *sorbet*. Late winter brings superb Mexican blood oranges and a delicate *sorbet* stained with red. And in the early spring, when the fruit is at its creamy sweetest, they make their favorite, a papaya *sorbet*.

Oakville's *sorbet* makers make no fantasy flavors spiked with liqueurs. Their ideal is a *sorbet* with the intense straightforward flavor of ripe fresh fruit.

**San Jose Area \* Latino**
## PALETAS POLAR

*1175 South White Road, San Jose 95127. Telephone (408) 251-3260. Hours: 11– 5:30 daily.*

Latino *paletas.* See Latin Freeze, above.

---

**San Francisco \* American**
## POLLY ANN ICE CREAM

*3142 Noriega Street, San Francisco 94122. Telephone (415) 664-2472. Hours: SUN– TH 12-10, F–SAT 12-11.*

Good humor and fun fill this foggy corner of San Francisco where for the last fifteen years Polly Ann's Ted Hansen has been defying the imagination of children and grownups with his fantastic concoctions. For those easily plunged into crises of indecision, he has installed a roulette wheel to help them choose from the 330 flavors, 50 of which are available at one time. The A's lead the extravagant parade with American Beauty, Apple, Apricot, Apple Berry, Ambrosia, Angel Plum, Appleanna, Apple Ginger . . . . The B's come marching in with Black Night, Bulgarian Buttermilk, Bicentennial, Black Rhiza, Bumpy Freeway. . . . The list of sweet acrobatics goes on as flavors file past the entire alphabet.

Children love the place with its festive mood and wall of hand-painted signs designed by Ted to illustrate his far-flung flavors: King of Hearts, a buttery mix of strawberry, peach and banana; Kohoutex (*sic*), a cherry and pineapple; or Arab's Lunch, an insolent blend of dates and cheese. A disquieting piece of edible pop art, the vegetable ice cream—a wholesome ice cream?— actually contains twelve different vegetables. Who said you couldn't have your V-8 and lick it too?

**East Bay \* Italian**
## VIVOLI'S

*2115 Allston Way, Trumpetvine Court, Berkeley 94704. Telephone (415) 845- 6458.*
*2122 Vine Street, Walnut Square, Berkeley 94709. Telephone (415) 540-0522. Hours for both stores: SUN–TH noon– 11 pm, F–SAT noon–midnight.*

It's not quite like sitting at Tre Scalini watching sun-drenched Romans stroll through the Piazza Navona, but the sunny brick court draped with trumpet-vines invites sitting down, eating *gelato,* and watching the Berkeley chic go by. The three proprietors of Vivoli's—Mary Ann Frey, Jean Howe, and Beverly Sullivan—were attracted by the possibilities of making a dense creamy *gelato* in this country as good as their famous namesake Vivoli's in Florence (although there is no other connection to the Italian store). But if you come expecting the experience of Florentine *gelati*— the constant play of seasons and flavors— you'll be disappointed. Though the quality of Vivoli's *gelato* is consistent, it lacks passion, and sometimes even flavor. There are few surprises in the eight to ten flavors available.

The *gelato* here is good, but it's not inspired. Try their big seller, the deep dark Chocolate Correa named for Shelley, the designer-carpenter of both stores, or the Vanilla Bean, peppered with ground bean. A minty invention, Excite-Mint is as popular as the more decorous Espresso.

On weekends Vivoli's stays open till the civilized hour of midnight. And from its small plant in Berkeley, Vivoli's ships ice cream to the Oakville Grocery in San Francisco and Le Pique Nique in Oakland.

# Meat

A good butcher is hard to find. There aren't many who still personally buy their beef and age it well before cutting it for their meat counter. And good meat is just as hard to find as a good butcher. There just isn't that much of it around these days, and the government is now considering grading down the categories of "prime" and "choice" once again.

In addition to good local butchers and stores that specialize in ethnic cuts of meat, this chapter includes listings for Jewish kosher meats as well as a store selling Mohammedan *halal* meats. In both slaughtering methods, the animals must be killed by an authorized person of the religion, and the blood entirely removed from the carcass by draining, soaking, and salting.

## RETAIL MEAT MARKETS

**East Bay * Islamic**
**ALMUBARAK**

*3338 Grand Avenue, Oakland 94610. Telephone (415) 451-3873. Hours: M-SAT 11-6:30.*

This Islamic store has beef, lamb, goat, and chicken, all killed in the prescribed Islamic manner. Though they regularly have both lamb and goat meat by the pound, you should call in advance to order whole lamb or kid or any of these meats in large quantities. The chickens come whole, with heads and feet.

**San Francisco * General**
**BRYAN'S QUALITY MEATS**

*Cal Mart Super, 3585 California Street, San Francisco 94118. Telephone (415) 752-3430. Hours: M-SAT 8-6.*

A tiny old lady wheels a cart up to the meat counter and asks, "Is Bryan here?" A craggy Irishman with a lively gleam in his eye calls out "Hi, doll," and waves. If you're lucky enough to order from Mr. Flannery, Senior, you'll get a large dose of San Francisco history along with your beautifully aged steak: "It's called Bryan's because everybody downtown knew me by my first name."

There's something different about this butcher shop. Along the wide stretch of wooden chopping surface, thirty or so butcher's knives and boning knives of various sorts are lined up, tucked behind just so, as in a French *boucherie.*

"Well, you see, I learned to cut meat under a Frenchman, Henry Bercut. So did Frank Petrini. Bercut was from Limoisin, France. He was the best meat man around. When we were cutting meat, he used to tell us you have to treat it like a rose.

"You know how I became a butcher? My mother didn't want me to play football because I was so small. She shopped at Grant's Market downtown and she asked around to see if there were any jobs after school for me. So from the time I was fifteen I worked at the market after school and on Saturdays. Then when I got out of high school, it was 1931 and the Depression and I continued to work—thirty-five years at Grant Market and seventeen years at this location. But all my five kids (three boys and two girls) went to college."

It's not only the knives that look French at Bryan's Meats. Check the beautifully tied roasts; each piece of meat looks like a sculpture. The big walk-in is crowded with hanging quarters of beef. Bryan dates it by kill and ages it twenty-three days.

"When I first came to this neighborhood, I had to introduce customers to lamb. I had a lot of trouble selling it at first." But Bryan has exceptional lamb. It's all raised in California, and he ages it himself for tenderness. He buys the smallest lambs he can find for the spring lamb season from Easter through the end of September.

His pork is all eastern and corn fed. "Colder weather means better pork."

When Bryan was first learning the business, there were seven slaughterhouses in the vicinity of the city. Now there aren't any. Bryan buys from a slaughterhouse just outside Sacramento. With current gas prices, he's had to limit his former daily trips to three times a week. "I pick it all myself and have it stamped right there, then bring it in for aging."

If he can't get good veal Bryan just won't sell it. He complains he can't get the quality he used to get, young milk-fed veal weighing around ninety pounds. He says Provimi veal is "older than true veal—the calves weigh two hundred pounds each and the meat is pale only because it has been fed a formula to bleach the meat."

## San Francisco * Latino
### EL REY MEAT MARKET

*3182 Twenty-fourth Street, San Francisco 94110. Telephone (415) 647-6733. Hours: M–SAT 9–6.*

This friendly neighborhood meat market features Latino specialties like pigs' feet, tripe, brains, flank steak, and *carne adobada*, plus a small selection of fresh cheeses and basic canned goods.

## San Francisco * Chinese
### HOP SANG

*1199 Stockton Street, San Francisco 94133. Telephone (415) 781-1692. Hours: M–F 9–6, SAT 9–5.*

This busy corner store is highly visible from Stockton Street. On weekends, it takes some firm resolve to get close enough to the meat case to get a good look at the cuts of meat for sale. At the back, huge sides of beef and pork hang from overhead hooks. A team of butchers in hard hats are at work sawing and cutting meat to supply the cases at the front. The pace is brisk here; there's always a line, and no time to hem and haw. You may have to write down your order for yourself, so you won't be flustered when your turn comes: everybody else is waiting for you to hurry up with it.

All the parts of the pig are excellent here. The pigs' feet are big and beautiful. The liver is fresh each day. Hop Sang is also a source for fresh caul fat for pâté making.

## San Francisco * Chinese
### HOP YICK MEAT COMPANY

*1147-9 Grant Avenue, San Francisco 94133. Telephone (415) 989-0247. Hours: M–SAT 8:30–5:30, SUN 8:30–4.*

Hop Yick Meat Company is another shop stocked with every conceivable part of the pig. They even have some of it cooked and ready to take out. The barbecued pork snout is popular with Chinatown shoppers.

## San Francisco * Kosher
## ISRAEL GOLDANSKI

*5621 Geary Street, San Francisco 94121. Telephone (415) 752-3064. Hours: SUN–F 7–6.*

For almost forty years now, butcher Israel Goldanski has been supplying the Bay Area with strictly kosher meats and poultry. He has kosher beef, veal, and lamb as well as chicken, ducks, turkeys, and geese. The deli sells corned beef, pastrami, salami, and other kosher meats and foods.

*Free delivery all over the Bay Area.*

## San Francisco * Chinese
## GOLDEN GATE MEAT MARKET

*1101 Stockton Street, San Francisco 94133. Telephone (415) 392-0940. Hours: 9–6 daily.*

Golden Gate Meat Market may be small, but it has lots of customers buying pork and more pork and an occasional chicken. For savory bean curd dishes they have inexpensive ground pork, almost a full dollar below prices in meat markets in other neighborhoods.

## East Bay * Variety Meats
## JACK'S ECONOMY MEATS

*Housewives' Market, 819 Clay Street, Oakland 94607. Telephone (415) 451-6795. Hours: 9–6 daily.*

Jack's Economy Meats has a constant supply of the variety meats used in many ethnic cuisines. You can buy goat and lamb whole or by halves. Kid comes halved or quartered, and they sell both goats' livers and hearts. You'll see calves' heads; lambs' heads for the Greek Easter soup, *mayiritsa*; pigs' heads for making head cheese. Liver is beef, pork, lamb, or steer; tongue is beef, lamb, or pork.

Jack's has every possible part of the pig for sale, including snouts, ears, feet, fresh pork hocks, and pig tails for making a succulent dish of red beans. Both beef and pork chitlings are sold by the pound, but you can also buy ten-pound buckets of pork chitlings.

You'll find plenty of meaty soup bones, baby-beef neck bones, veal bones for stock, and fresh blood for blood puddings or *boudin noir*, plus whole lamb shanks for country stews, sirloin steaks, cross rib roasts, and veal legs and breasts.

## San Francisco * Aged Prime Beef
## JURGENSEN'S GROCERY

*2190 Union Street, San Francisco 94123. Telephone (415) 931-0100. Hours: M–SAT 9–6.*

Jurgensen's Grocery, a Union Street gourmet market, is a well-known, if high-priced, source for well-aged prime beef. The three resident butchers know what they're doing—each of them has over thirty-five years in the business. This means they buy their beef well. It's all eastern, all prime, and all aged five to six weeks before it graces the meat counter. Prices are hefty; you've got to pay for all the shrinkage from the aging, and all the extra fat that must be trimmed because the beef is grain-fed. But what you get is a memorable piece of beef. Just as much care is taken with their veal, pork, and lamb.

## East Bay * Kosher
## KOSHER MEAT MARKET

*3256 Grand Avenue, Oakland 94610. Telephone (415) 451-3883. Hours: M–F 7–4, SAT 7–2, SUN 7–12.*

This Oakland meat market has kosher veal, beef, and lamb as well as chicken and other poultry. No delivery.

### East Bay ∗ General
## LENNY'S MEATS

*1469 Shattuck Avenue, Berkeley 94709. Telephone (415) 845-0751. Hours: M–F 9–6:30, SAT 9–5:30.*

Lenny's Meats is one of a fast disappearing type, an old-fashioned over-the-counter meat market with quality meat. Beef carcasses are bought prime and aged by the shop; other beef cuts are choice. Lenny's also has good pork, lamb, and veal.

For the holidays, they'll prepare fancy cuts such as crown roasts. With advance notice, Lenny's will even get you a fresh suckling pig weighing between fifteen and twenty-three pounds.

### San Francisco ∗ Veal/General
## LITTLE CITY MEATS

*1400 Stockton Street, San Francisco 94133. Telephone (415) 986-2601. Hours: M–SAT 9–6.*

You can't miss Little City Meats, with its broad red and green canopy curving around the corner and the big hand-lettered signs hanging in the windows. Inside, it's strictly business, mostly veal business. Little City Meats specializes in veal, locally raised, weighing sixty to seventy pounds. Butcher Ron Spinelli says he cuts it New York style, that is, with the grain. You'll find fancy veal chops, veal cutlets, shoulder veal, boneless veal leg roast, veal shanks,

and breast of veal. Thursdays and Fridays he has veal fillet.

Any doubts about how to cook your purchase? Mr. Spinelli hands out free recipes for stuffed breast of veal; the windows are covered with more recipes. Pick up a package of their own blend of Italian spices, a heady mix of rosemary, basil, and oregano.

### San Francisco ∗ Pork/Latino
## LUCKY PORK

*2659 Mission Street, San Francisco 94110. Telephone (415) 285-3611. Hours: M–SAT 9–6.*

Right in the heart of busy Mission Street, this Chinese-owned shop has mounds of specialty cuts for the Latino market: big pieces of beef with the bone for boiling; cuts for stewing and then shredding to make a filling for tacos; meaty soup bones and slabs of tripe for *menudo*, the famous hangover restorative; beef tongue; fresh cows' feet; and flank steaks to be butterflied, rolled around a stuffing of sausages, greens, and olives, and braised Cuban style.

The pork section displays every imaginable part of the pig; nothing is wasted here. Since business is brisk, even the neglected and little-used parts of the pig look fresh. A couple of pig heads sit right on the counter, and, underneath, there are huge piles of pork ears, snouts, fresh pigs' feet, skin, and fresh pork hocks. For sausage making, there is fatback, net fat, calf blood, and hard-to-find fresh pork intestines to use as sausage skins. There is stewing meat, ribs, roasting cuts, and pork shoulder or fresh picnics, which are perfect for juicy sausages. Suckling pigs for barbecues are available on order, and most days you can find goat meat for an authentic Caribbean stew.

## Marin County * Whole Cuts
## THE MEAT DEAL

*1115 Third Street, San Rafael 94901. Telephone (415) 459-1066. Hours: M-SAT 9-6.*

One of Bryan Flannery's sons (see entry for Bryan's Meats), Peter, has opened his own special meat store in San Rafael. The Meat Deal sells big hunks of meat, which the customer takes home to butcher into the cuts normally seen for sale in butcher shops.

If you picture yourself in a big butcher apron with a metal guard, girded with a chain link belt supporting knives and cleavers at your waist, you have the wrong idea. You don't need to be an expert in order to cut this meat. Everything, with the exception of the prime rib, is boneless. Instructions are included, but the way to cut the meat is obvious. Mostly, it is a matter of deciding how thick you want to slice it.

These are the same bagged cuts that small butcher stores get from the wholesaler. Each piece of meat is an unsectioned individual cut. Mr. Flannery has every cut of beef and it's all choice: New York strip, fillet, top sirloin, prime rib either with or without the bones, top round, bottom round, brisket, chuck. Occasionally he'll have prime, but there isn't much of that around. He sells pork, plus some veal and lamb as well. Also available are veal liver, calf's liver, veal kidney, and veal sweetbreads.

## East Bay * Smoked Meats
## PRIME SMOKED MEATS

*220 Alice Street, Oakland 94607. Telephone (415) 832-7167. Hours: M-F 7-3.*

Large bone-in Iowa hams, sugar cured and smoked, run twenty to twenty-four pounds here, while the smaller ones weigh fourteen to seventeen pounds. They also have boneless hams, and bacon sold in fifteen-pound boxes.

## San Francisco * Chinese
## QUON SUN MEAT MARKET

*1215 Stockton Street, San Francisco 94133. Telephone (415) 397-3135. Hours: 8:30-6 daily.*

At Quon Sun Meat Market, all the meats are well labeled. You'll find whole calf's liver, delicious stuffed and braised; pork melt; and beef feet. If a dish using beef feet does not spring immediately to mind, consult Calvin W. Schwabe's wonderful book, *Unmentionable Cuisine*, which gives short recipes from all over the world for cooking parts of the animal generally ignored by cooks in this country.

## Peninsula * General
## ROBERTS OF WOODSIDE

*3015 Woodside Road, Woodside 94062. Telephone (415) 851-1511. Hours: M-SAT 8:30-6:30, SUN 9-6.*

The meat market here is one of the best in the Peninsula, featuring both choice and prime midwestern corn-fed beef. Bought whole carcass, all of the beef is aged three to four weeks before it is cut for the counter. The lamb is all choice and aged as well. In the spring you can special order whole spring lamb. The veal is Provimi veal from the East Coast. Favored by many chefs and cooks for its lovely pale color, in general it lacks the taste or texture of true baby veal.

The butchers at Roberts make a special Cambridge sausage of English pedigree, using pork shoulder and secret seasoning supplied by the Roberts family. Imported British bangers are sold as well.

For holiday feasts, they prepare crown roasts with a meat stuffing, whole strip roasts, and other special fancy cuts. Fresh local poultry raised without steroids or hormones, as well as frozen quail and pheasant, is also available.

### San Francisco * Corned Meats
## ROBERTS TURKEY BRAND

*1030 Bryant Street, San Francisco 94103. Telephone (415) 621-2624. Hours: M-F 8-11:30 am, 12:30-3:30 pm.*

Roberts Turkey Brand Corned Meats began business over seventy years ago in 1910. To produce their renowned corned beef, Roberts uses the brisket from the forequarter—that's the first five ribs of the steer. Employing a method introduced by his great-grandfather, G. H. Roberts, Jim Dixon cures the meat from the inside out by directly injecting the arteries of the beef with spice-laden brine. (Traditional curing methods soak the meat in a heavy brine for as long as forty days.)

In addition to their unique curing method, the Dixon family claims the San Francisco climate has something to do with the superb quality of their corned beef: they tried making it in Chicago and it just wasn't the same.

Roberts gives a variety of cuts the corned beef cure; you can buy rump and bottom round as well as the classic brisket. They also sell genuine New York pastrami, hams, smoked or pickled tongue, pork hocks, and bacon.

There's a $150 minimum for delivery, no minimum if you come in.

### San Francisco * General
## ROSSI'S MEATS

*476 Castro Street, San Francisco 94114. Telephone (415) 431-1128. Hours: M-F 9-8, SAT 9-6.*

Eddie Perea gets up at 4 am to buy fish for his butcher shop, Rossi's Meats. The seafood includes squid, octopus, clams, scallops, and tiny shucked Olympia oysters, plus finnan haddie and real kippers from Scotland. As for meat and poultry, he has all the esoteric items like duck livers, veal sweetbreads, young whole turkey breasts, veal shanks for *osso buco*. You'll find duck as well as game birds like pheasant and quail.

For sausage making, he has natural casings, and caul fat for your *crépinettes*. He'll grind you a mix of meats both fat and lean for your sausage and force-meats, and will even remove the skin of a chicken all in one piece so you can make a special chicken galantine.

Because parking is difficult in the Castro area, once he knows you and your car, you can call your order in and stop out front to pick up and pay.

Tell him what you need and he'll special order it for you. A good neighborhood butcher shop with good prices.

### San Francisco * Chinese
## STOCKTON MEAT MARKET

*1352 Stockton Street, San Francisco 94133. Telephone (415) 421-0707. Hours: M-T, TH-SAT 8-6.*

The large Stockton Meat Company has good-looking and inexpensive pork shoulder roasts, Boston butts, pork chops, huge pigs' feet, and other common cuts of pork, plus a full line of less usual cuts or parts including pork stomachs and pork kidneys. *Charcuterie* supplies include fresh pork liver and sausage casings, but no pig blood for *boudin noir*. But they do have a display of snowy honeycomb tripe and another, all gossamer, like dotted Swiss. In addition, there's a whole counter of beef, and a mound of Petaluma chickens.

## San Francisco ∗ General
## STONESTOWN MEATS

*Stonestown Shopping Area, Nineteenth Avenue and Winston Drive, San Francisco 94132. Telephone (415) 681-3521. Hours: M–SAT 8:30–8, SUN 9:30–6.*

Stonestown Meats must have the longest meat counter in northern California. Midway down the line of good-looking beef and pork, you'll find a whole case of corned meats, not only "point cut" brisket corned beef, but center cut and bottom round corned beef, corned tongue, and corned leg of pork.

Check the beautiful French-cut lamb chops, lamb shanks, lamb shoulder, and lamb neck bones for stews. Some of the veal is local; some of it comes from the Midwest. Try stuffing a breast of veal or using ground veal in meat loaves or *tortellini* stuffing. Sausage-making supplies here include both hog and sheep casings, caul fat, and fatback.

## Amador County ∗ Butcher
## SWINGLE'S MEATS

*P.O. Box 692, Martell 95654. Telephone (209) 223-0731. Hours: M–SAT 8–5.*

If you can find and persuade an Amador County farmer to sell you a pig, you can take that pig to the local butcher, Swingle's Meats. They'll slaughter and butcher it for a fee based on the live weight of the pig. For another fee they'll cut it into pieces, giving you a winter's worth of side pork, pork butt, pork chops, roasts, and plenty of fat-and-lean scraps for your sausage making.

## San Francisco/East Bay ∗ General
## VER BRUGGE MEATS

*3939 Twenty-fourth Street, San Francisco 94132. Telephone (415) 647-8723. Hours: M–F 9:30–6:30, SAT 9–6.*
*6321 College Avenue, Oakland 94618. Telephone (415) 658-6854. Hours: M–F 10–6:30, SAT 10–6.*

This straightforward butcher shop has been providing Noe Valley customers with good-quality meat at moderate prices since 1947. No frills, just good meat. Because of his fine reputation, Mr. Ver Brugge was recently asked to open another butcher shop in north Oakland, on a stretch of College Avenue already boasting a cheese and gourmet store, a produce store, a poultry shop, and a fine bakery. The butcher shop is beautiful, with a fine long stretch of counter.

The meat for both stores is bought together. Not only is it of consistently high quality, but the store has lots of specials: fresh eastern pork, lean pork butts, legs of lamb. Mr. Ver Brugge is a shrewd buyer and his butchers are skilled. Look at the chateaubriand, the fillets, the thick culotte steaks, the roasts, ribs, and stewing cuts.

The veal is midwestern. And for those who prefer their veal pale above all else, they have Provimi veal. The poultry is a local brand with no estrogens. The College Avenue store even sells chicken parts in a spicy marinade for the barbecue. Sausage makers can order fatback and caul fat a few days before they need it.

In springtime, you can order whole lambs weighing anywhere from thirty-five to seventy pounds, and, year round, they'll provide you with frozen suckling pig.

There's a small selection of good-looking seafood, too—everything that's in season—and a box of fresh lemons on top of the counter.

San Francisco ✴ Latino
## YORK MEAT COMPANY

*2794 Twenty-fourth Street, San Francisco 94110. Telephone (415) 824-5419. Hours: M–SAT 9–7.*

This small butcher store has a meat counter running down one side of the store and a small take-out deli counter on the other side. There are yard-long chorizo sausages made here with the traditional coarse mix of fat and lean, and *carne adobada*, beef steaks stained vermilion by a marinade of ground chilies, garlic, onion, and secret spices, to be taken home and pan fried. There are also the usual stewing cuts of pork and beef for *adobos*, to be cooked slowly with green chilies for *chile verde*; or to use in a *mole*, its dark sauce flavored with chilies and spices, thickened with ground nuts.

At the deli counter, there is *pollo rostizado* (spit-roasted chicken), *carnitas* (flaky chunks of roast pig), large twisted pieces of *chicharrón* (fried pork crackling), and, of course, *arroz y frijoles*.

# WHOLESALE MEATS

Some meat wholesalers will also sell to the public, but don't expect the kind of over-the-counter service you might get from your neighborhood butcher. You must usually call your order in a day ahead of time, buy it in certain standard whole cuts, and pay for it in cash when you pick it up. Expect to do some trimming yourself, but the meat you buy will be the same as that sold to restaurants and should be a higher quality for its price than meat bought in retail stores.

Meat wholesalers also keep their own kind of hours geared to the restaurant trade. This means they open at six or seven and stay open only until the middle of the afternoon, sometimes closing for lunch between twelve and one (weekdays only).

Most of the wholesalers will also sell you twenty-five-pound bags of bones for stock. You can freeze some of the bones, share them with fellow cooks, or make a very reduced stock *(glace de viande)* and freeze that to use as a base for your various mother sauces.

East Bay ✴ Pork
## C&M MEATS

*2843 San Pablo Avenue, Berkeley 94702. Telephone (415) 848-3460. Hours: M–F 6 am–2:15 pm.*

C and M Meats specializes in pork. A yard-long loin of pork is fourteen to seventeen pounds. If you ask them to bone it out, you'll have several family-sized pork loin roasts and a slab of ribs you can broil or barbecue. Pork shoulders here are less trimmed than the ones you see in the neighborhood butcher store, but with extra fatback ground in, they're a good cut for your sausage making. About twenty pounds of shoulder should get you started.

They do have beef as well. A New York strip weighs about fifteen pounds, but you can cut around twenty steaks from it, depending on how thick you like them. A fine cross-rib roast weighs in at fifteen pounds. If you like to make a lot of soups or sauces, you can order twenty-five-pound bags of either beef or veal bones.

## East Bay * Veal
## C R MEATS

*994 West MacArthur Boulevard, Oakland 94608. Telephone (415) 654-0237. Hours: M–F 6 am–2:30 pm.*

C R Meats specializes in veal. If you stop in some early morning on the way back from the Oakland produce market, you might see more veal than you bargained for: dozens of fresh sides of it hanging from overhead hooks. Speak to the man in charge, who will sell you boneless, molded veal legs (four to five pounds), frozen to make slicing your *scaloppine* easier. Veal breasts average three pounds. Stuffed with a forcemeat, they make a splendid and inexpensive main course. Both small and large rib eyes, taken from sixty-five-pound veal calves, are sold by the pound.

C R Meats is a sausage and pâté maker's delight. Make your own German bratwurst and pale *Weisswurst* or *Leberkäse*, a pork and veal meat loaf. Scraps can be used in a savory *salsa bolognese* for pasta.

Someone at C R Meats may tell you on the phone that they sell only to restaurants, but if you go there and are clear about what you want (don't expect them to explain for hours), they'll sell to you.

## Peninsula * General
## GOLDEN STATE MEATS

*317 Roebling Road, South San Francisco 94080. Telephone (415) 421-3416. Hours: M–F 6 am–2:30 pm.*

Golden State Meats deals in midwestern pork and local veal, along with Wisconsin's pale but bland Provimi veal. Most of the veal calves weigh in at a giant two hundred to three hundred pounds. Very rarely, they get the "drop calves" who've just milked a little and are killed at two weeks.

The pork is choice. Loins run about fifteen pounds. When you pick up your pork shoulder, they'll sell you the requisite sausage casings to turn it into links. Suckling pigs should be ordered a week in advance if you'd like them fresh.

The beef is choice for the most part: New York strips, fillets, cross rib roasts, top round, bottom round, etc. A long leg of lamb comes with the hip chops on it and weighs about ten pounds. Buy lamb shoulder for *couscous* and Moroccan *tagines*. They also have imported New Zealand rack of lamb.

Call first. Pick up the day after with payment in cash. A minimum order of $100 is preferred.

## East Bay * General
## MILLER DEL-MONTE MEATS

*206 Second Street, Oakland 94607. Telephone (415) 392-4700. Hours: M–F 7 am–3 pm.*

Miller Del-Monte Meats is located in the general area of Oakland's produce market. It's hard to find in the confusion of trucks loading and unloading in front, but deep inside the warehouse there is a tiny office. Walk in and give your order to the man in the hard hat. You can buy all kinds of meat—from beef tongue to whole fillets and strips of steaks, from hot dogs in ten-pound boxes to whole suckling pigs (order ahead).

## East Bay * General
## PRINGLE'S MEATS

*216 Seventh Street, Oakland 94606. Telephone (415) 893-7400. Hours: M–F 7 am–12 noon, 1 pm–2:30 pm.*

Pringle's Meats is a good source for wholesale beef, lamb, and veal; they also have suckling pig.

Call your order ahead and pay cash when you pick it up.

Good cooking of any kind requires fresh, natural ingredients. Whether you're a strict health food advocate or not, natural foods stores are wonderful places to shop for staples.

Breadmakers can find a wealth of high-quality grains and flours, often stone ground and organic as well. They are usually sold in bulk, so you can buy small quantities of the whole-meal flours for optimum freshness. Some stores even mill their own flours on a daily or weekly basis. And for fruit cakes and other baked goods using dried fruits, most stores have un-sulphured dried fruits.

You can buy milk raw, just as it comes from the cow or goat, and fresh fertile eggs tasting worlds better than those that have been stored in your supermarket's warehouse for weeks before reaching its shelves. There are all kinds of yogurts, *kefirs*, and *tofu*, as well as *tempeh*, the Indonesian fermented soybean cake. Look for cold-pressed nut oils and fruity green California olive oil along with natural soy sauce, rich nut butters, and luscious jams and honeys.

Some natural foods stores have "organic" produce so dispirited you're sure all the nutrition has fled with its color, but many of the stores listed here have marvelous produce, beautiful and well tended, most of it from very local sources and sometimes in old-fashioned varieties no longer considered commercial.

*Note:* For additional flours, nuts, legumes, dried fruits, honey, and oils, see the Staples section. For sea vegetables and seaweed, see the Japanese section.

## Marin County
## BASIC FOOD SHOP

*47 Tamal Vista Boulevard, Corte Madera 94925. Telephone (415) 924-5206. Hours: M–F 10–7, SAT 9–6, SUN 10–6.*

This eight-year-old Marin County health food store has a great selection of staples: over twenty-five kinds of organic stone-ground flours including garbanzo, corn, millet, and buckwheat; a few dozen bins for whole grains and beans, most of them organic, including red lentil, *adzuki* beans, buckwheat, and triticale; and nuts and seeds of all kinds. All the dried fruit is unsulphured, some of it organic.

In addition to all the basic staples, the store stocks organic *tofu*, water-packed, as well as baked or fried; *tempeh*; a full line of local dairy products including raw milk, fertile eggs, and raw milk cheeses; and fresh juices are delivered twice a week. The produce, almost entirely organic, covers all the basics. Herbs and spices, seventy-five kinds of them, are sold in bulk.

## East Bay
## BERKELEY NATURAL GROCERY COMPANY

*1334 Gilman Street, Berkeley 94706. Telephone (415) 526-2456. Hours: M–F 10–7, SAT 10–6.*

Beautifully crafted cabinets display dozens of beans, grains, and flours, plus all of the dark Westbrae whole-wheat pastas in bulk. The store stocks a full selection of all the Westbrae products: nut butters, juices, fruit butters, *tamari* and *shoyu*, plus imported *miso* (fermented bean paste) and several kinds of dried seaweed and sea vegetables. They also carry Sonoma County raw milk and whipping cream.

**San Francisco**
## BUFFALO WHOLE FOOD AND GRAIN COMPANY

*1058 Hyde Street, San Francisco 94109. Telephone (415) 474-3053. Hours: 10–8 daily.*

Check the small produce section here for high-quality organic produce. But the store's real strength is in its bins of bulk items, including sixty bins of grains, beans, and flours, organic when possible. Most of the grains and flours are milled at Giusto's in South San Francisco, but when spring comes, they also get grains from Idaho Organics.

Twice a week, dairy products such as raw milk, raw milk cheeses, rennetless cheeses, and yogurt are delivered along with *tofu, tempeh,* and *mochi.* Fresh natural chickens are available every Thursday.

**Marin County**
## CAMPOLINDO MARKET

*60 Red Hill Avenue, San Anselmo 94960. Telephone (415) 456-2622. Hours: 9:30–7:30, daily.*

This Marin County market has a broad selection of produce, a lot of which is organically grown. Most of the grains, too, are organic, including wheat, rye, rice, rye and wheat flakes. The store carries Giusto's organically grown products, including a wide range of flours. You'll find beans, nuts, and seeds in bulk; all the dried fruits here are unsulphured.

The store also has a vegetarian health food deli called Aramia, run by a former cook at the health food deli in Berkeley's Gilman Street Gourmet (now Berkeley Natural Grocery Company). The deli features delicious vegetarian versions of lasagne, enchiladas, stuffed eggplant and other vegetables, and such classic Mediterranean fare as *tabbouleh, hummous,* and stuffed grape leaves, plus sandwiches and *tempeh* burgers. Everything is made, as much as is possible, with organic produce. Desserts are sweetened with honey.

**East Bay**
## THE DISCERNING MOUSE

*P.O. Box 641, Berkeley 94701. Telephone (415) 658-6920. Wholesale.*

Don Wexler, the Discerning Mouse, is the distributor for the excellent Westbrae health food products. He sells wholesale to individuals as well as to restaurants and stores, but the minimum order for delivery on his regular route is $150. He sells the full line of locally made Westbrae products, including juices, nut butters, Oriental and sea vegetables, *miso, shoyu, tamari,* cold-pressed oils, and the wonderful whole-wheat and spinach pastas.

His flours are organic and stone ground in South San Francisco by the Giusto family (see in Staples). The Discerning Mouse distributes both domestic and imported cheeses, but you must buy them in full wheels or bricks. (See Cheese section.) Canned goods are also sold: pumpkin, sauerkraut, artichoke hearts, kidney beans, whole tomatoes in purée, and a variety of canned fruits.

## Marin County
## GOOD EARTH
## NATURAL FOODS

*123 Bolinas Road, Fairfax 94930. Telephone (415) 454-4633. Hours: M–SAT 10–8, SUN 10–6.*

This store has terrific organic produce. One of the store's owners is actively involved in the movement to define organic foods and is interested in becoming an organic farmer himself. This means the owners search out and investigate their own sources for produce. They personally know the small farmers who use organic methods to raise the produce sold at Good Earth.

They try not to carry produce out of season, so the winter selection is dramatically different from summer's bounty of melons, peaches, plums, berries, and watermelon. But they always have lots of apples, citrus fruits, root vegetables, and lettuces.

All the dried fruit is unsulphured. Some of it is commercially grown, but there's always a good variety of organic dates, Mission figs, raisins, and apricots.

Wherever possible, the grains and flours here are organic. The store has its own mill and produces fresh-ground flours on a daily basis from organically grown wheat, rice, millet, and corn. For maximum freshness, you should buy flours in small quantities and often. Sweet rice flour, soft and hard wheat flours, barley, soy and garbanzo flours are among those available here.

Good Earth also has beans in bulk: soy, pinto, kidney, lentil, and more, all organically grown; over one hundred dried herbs in bulk; fresh cheeses, raw milk cheeses, rennetless cheeses, and goat cheeses; and organic *tofu,* plus a wide variety of macrobiotic foods.

## Marin County
## LIVING FOODS

*149 Throckmorton Avenue, Mill Valley 94941. Telephone (415) 383-7121. Hours: M–F 9–8, SAT 9–7, SUN 9–6.*

Living Foods buys the pick of the organic produce in season. When high quality organic produce is scarce, they supplement it with the best of the commercial produce. Bulk bins display nuts, unsulphured dried fruits, granolas, whole grains, beans, and flours, all organic when possible. A large selection of spices and herbs are also sold in bulk.

Check the dairy case for raw milk products including goat butter, raw cow and goat milk cheeses, two kinds of Indonesian *tempeh,* and organic *tofu* fresh every day.

Organic chickens are available on special order.

## Contra Costa
## OPEN SESAME

*3543 Mount Diablo Boulevard, Lafayette 94549. Telephone (415) 283-2207. Hours: M–SAT 10–6:30.*

This natural foods store has a selection of their own grains and flours; fresh produce, much of it organic; frozen naturally raised beef in various cuts; raw milk dairy products; and fresh farm eggs.

The cheese selection is unusually large for a natural foods store, with over 130 kinds of domestic and imported cheeses.

On Fridays, fresh organic chickens are delivered to the store.

**Marin County**
## OUR STORE

*1218 San Anselmo Avenue, San Anselmo 94960. Telephone (415) 457-4686. Hours: M–SAT 10–7, SUN 12–7.*

Seven years ago Our Store started out as a small co-op. Changing format through the years, it's now evolved to a nonprofit corporation, with workers having some ownership in the business. The people who work here are knowledgeable and helpful and the prices continue to be low.

The large produce section features organic produce with some commercial produce as well. Some of it comes from very local sources: the several community gardens in the area, fruit trees in customers' back yards, small truck farmers. Twice a week the selection is rounded out with produce bought at the Farmers' Market in San Francisco.

Choose from over seventy-five grains, beans, and flours (from Giusto's) in bulk, most organically grown. The store tries to get as much unsulphured dried fruit as possible and also stocks bulk honey and molasses. Milk, raw milk, and other dairy products come from local sources. The low-priced cheeses are cut and packaged at the store.

Any produce bought in cases or grains bought in twenty- or fifty-pound quantities get a 10 percent discount.

**Peninsula**
## PALO ALTO NATURAL FOODS

*463 University Avenue, Palo Alto 94301. Telephone (415) 328-5810. Hours: M–SAT 9:30–6:30, SUN 12–5.*

Dating from 1954, this small natural foods store stocks the inventory of a much larger store on its well-organized shelves: a basic selection of quality produce, as much as 80 percent of it organic; over one hundred bins of bulk items including grains, flours, nuts, and seeds (specialty flours are kept fresh in the refrigerator); dried fruits, some unsulphured; and *tofu, tempeh,* raw milk, cheeses, and fertile eggs.

PANF's honey is wonderful, sold in bulk and purchased from a local beekeeper who sells exclusively to the store.

**San Francisco/Marin County**
## THE REAL FOOD COMPANY

*1023 Stanyan Street, San Francisco 94117. Telephone (415) 564-2800. Hours: 9–8 daily.*
*2140 Polk Street, San Francisco 94109. Telephone (415) 673-7420. Hours: 9–9 daily.*
*3939 Twenty-fourth Street, San Francisco. Telephone (415) 282-9500. Hours: 9–8 daily.*
*200 Caledonia, Sausalito 94965. Telephone (415) 332-9640. Hours: M–SAT 9–7, SUN 11–6.*

The beautiful produce at the four Real Food Company stores is part organic and part commercial, each clearly labeled and both of the highest quality. Everything in season is arranged for visual pleasure. Several kinds of fresh mushrooms and organic walnuts and peanuts are displayed in wide shallow baskets. The rest of the bright, healthy produce is piled high on the neatly arranged counters.

The bulk food section here is extraordinary, with over one hundred different bulk items, from bulk dog food to pasta, carob chips, and wheat berries. The flours include polenta, corn flour, rice flour, gluten, whole-wheat pastry, and just about every other organic flour milled at Giusto's in South San Francisco. Fresh raw wheat germ arrives once a week, milled the day before.

Fresh juices come in every day from the Santa Cruz Juice Club, and fresh

wheat-grass juice from another source. Cheeses include raw milk, rennetless, and no-salt cheeses from a variety of suppliers, even a 100 percent goat milk *feta.* You'll find locally made organic *tofu,* fresh eggs, and raw milks and creams.

The bread selection is good, too. Try the tortillas made from organically grown corn, the *chapatis* or *pita* bread made from organic whole-wheat flour. They even have natural whole-grain English muffins.

Wines and local and imported beers are sold as well.

### San Francisco
## THOM'S NATURAL FOODS

*843 Clement Street, San Francisco 94118. Telephone (415) 752-2371. Hours: M-SAT 10-7, SUN 12-7.*

Thom's features organically raised meats. Unfortunately, it's all frozen: top sirloin, fillet, stewing cuts, liver, ground beef, lamb chops, pork chops, ground meats (lamb, pork, and veal), and more, plus no-nitrite bacon, sausages, weiners, and bologna, all organic.

Organic chicken comes in fresh, and is sold whole or in parts. And at the holidays, they have whole organic turkeys.

Check the produce section for organic fruits and vegetables. Thom's has even

found sources for organic nuts: almonds, walnuts, and sunflower seeds. All the dried fruits here are unsulphured; some are even sun-dried. The dairy selection includes raw milk, *kefir,* cheese, and organic fertile eggs. The store buys a wide range of flours and grains in bulk and then repackages them in one-pound bags. Herbs are also bought in bulk from the San Francisco Herb Company, and sold in one-ounce bags or larger.

### Contra Costa
## WILLIAMS NATURAL FOODS

*12249 San Pablo Avenue, Richmond 94805. Telephone (415) 232-1911. Hours: M-F 9:30-8, SAT 9:30-6.*
*2133 Hilltop Mall Road, Richmond 94803. Telephone (415) 222-3115. Hours: M-F 10-9, SAT 10-6, SUN 12-5.*

The original Williams Natural Foods store in Richmond stocks just about everything in the health food line, except fresh produce. The bulk bins are the real find here in the remote reaches of San Pablo Avenue, with a big selection of nuts, dried fruits, beans, whole grains, and flours from a whole network of sources.

Organic chickens, turkeys, and certain cuts of beef are available only frozen.

# – SPECIALTY FOODS –

## East Bay ✳ Mochi
## GRAINAISSANCE

*800 Heinz Avenue, Berkeley 94710. Telephone (415) 849-2866. Wholesale to the trade only.*

*Mochi* is a traditional Japanese food made from steamed and pounded glutinous rice. A small Berkeley company called Grainaissance has been making their version of this versatile food for over two years.

In Japan the most common *mochi* is a snowy white, but Grainaissance makes a brown rice *mochi,* explaining that the Japanese made *mochi* from brown rice until four hundred years ago when the process of removing bran from the rice was discovered. The new white rice *mochi* was considered a more "refined" food. The founders of Grainaissance intend to "reintroduce *mochi* in its true traditional and natural form." Their *mochi* comes in several flavors: plain; alfalfa-spice with a touch of onion, cayenne, oregano, and cumin; sesame-garlic with *miso* and *arame* seaweed. The two sweeter flavors are raisin-cinnamon and carob date.

An explanatory sheet gives many suggested ways to use *mochi.* Bake one of the cakes in a hot oven until it puffs up. Then eat it plain or stuff it with butter and honey, grated cheese, *tofu,* or vegetables. It's delicious dipped in a sauce of soy and ginger, or it can be pan-fried, cooked in a soup, or deep-fried. Traditionally *mochi* is grilled over charcoal, then rolled in a mixture of *kinako,* or roasted soybean flour and sugar.

Grainaissance *mochi* is distributed all over the West Coast. In the San Francisco area, you'll find it at Co-op markets and natural foods stores.

## East Bay ✳ Tempeh
## PACIFIC TEMPEH

*1508 Sixty-second Street, Emeryville 94608. Telephone (415) 655-4441. Wholesale to the trade only.*

According to William Shurtleff and Akiko Aoyagi, authors of *The Book of Tempeh,* tempeh (pronounced TEM-pay) is "a popular Indonesian fermented (cultured) food consisting of tender-cooked soybeans... bound together by a dense cottony mycelium of *rhizopus* mold into compact 3/4-inch-thick cakes or patties." It originated centuries ago in central and east Java, and today its use has spread to include Malaysia, Singapore, and the Netherlands.

You'll see it in markets all over Indonesia, each piece wrapped in dark-green banana leaf. With a firm texture and an interesting taste (described as "cheesy," "mushroomy," or "nutty"), *tempeh* is a protein as concentrated as meat or fish; and, unlike *tofu,* it is a complete protein, providing vegetarian diets with essential vitamin $B_{12}$. As a popular Indonesian street food, *tempeh* is often steamed with spices and coconut milk in fresh banana leaf wrappers. *Tempeh* fried to a golden brown also appears in the famous Indonesian salad *gado-gado,* along with both cooked and raw vegetables, topped with a hot spicy peanut sauce. Another popular way of serving *tempeh* is to marinate slices in spice- and salt-laden water, then deep-fry them in coconut oil and serve with a blazing hot *sambal,* or chili paste.

Travis Burgeson, founder of Pacific Tempeh, first became interested in *tempeh* when he learned there was a type that could be made from *okara,* the lees, or by-product, of *tofu* production. He experimented with this and then went on to make his own soybean *tempeh.*

Pacific Tempeh packages their *tempeh* in eight-ounce cakes. These are vacuum packed, because while fresh *tempeh* is very perishable, with a three- or four-day shelf life, vacuum packing extends its shelf life up to three weeks. The flavor of *tempeh* intensifies as it ages; *tempeh* devotees come to prefer it at different stages of its ripening. The enzymes operate even in the refrigerator. As it matures, the mold puts out spores, which are gray or black and darken the color of the *tempeh.* At the same time, the cake continues to soften until at three or four days it has the ripe texture of Camembert, and the taste is richer and stronger.

Stores stocking Pacific Tempeh include Real Food in San Francisco, Open Sesame in Lafayette, and Co-op Natural Food Store in Berkeley.

### East Bay * Tofu
## TRADITIONAL TOFU

*6510 San Pablo Avenue, Oakland 94608. Telephone (415) 653-0990. Wholesale to the trade only.*

*Tofu* from Traditional Tofu is tender and creamy, with a bright fresh flavor even if eaten very plain, seasoned only with soy sauce and vinegar. When Ray and Gary Sato first started their business, they made *tofu* by hand the traditional way. But their desire to sell high-quality *tofu* for a low price to a large number of consumers led them to experiment with automated equipment purchased from Japan. They feel they've now developed a way to use the equipment to produce a *tofu* as good as their handmade version. Having gone to all the trouble to make the best *tofu* they can, they will only distribute to stores who will take the time and effort to handle their product with care.

Unbelievably, the small company is now making and selling one to two tons of fresh *tofu* a day. It's delivered to the stores the same day it's made. Some of it is vacuum packed and dated; some of it is sold in bulk and packaged by the individual markets.

They also supply some stores with *okara,* the bean curd pulp or lees produced in the *tofu*-making process. *Okara* may look like white sawdust, but it has many of the same nutrients as soybeans. You can use it in soup stock or cook it with black mushrooms and vegetables. It also adds bulk to meat loaves or *frittata* and can be used as roughage in breads. And another plus: *okara* is a gentle food, completely digestible.

To keep your *tofu* at maximum freshness, Nagai and Sato recommend that you change the water immediately after purchasing and daily after that (it will keep this way for about three days).

*Tofu* from Traditional Tofu is sold in bulk at Berkeley Bowl Market, Monterey Foods, and Tokyo Fish Market, all in Berkeley. You can also find it packaged in Co-op markets, ethnic food markets, and in Japantown.

Call Traditional Tofu for the location nearest you.

### Marin County * Tofu
## WILDWOOD NATURAL FOODS

*135 Bolinas Road, Fairfax 94930. Telephone (415) 892-5109. Wholesale to the trade only.*

Wildwood Natural Foods has been making *tofu* since 1980 using the traditional methods of small Japanese family *tofu* shops. Their excellent product is made from organic soybeans and filtered water and is curded with the traditional *nigari* (magnesium chloride extracted from sea water).

Because production is small, Wildwood Natural Foods *tofu* is distributed only in Marin and San Francisco. You can find it at many natural foods stores.

# Pasta & Dough

For a very long time popular history credited Marco Polo with the discovery of the noodle in China during his travels in the fourteenth century. But it is now believed that pasta was known in Italy as early as the time of the Etruscans. Some historians even put in a vote for the early Germans or the Arabs as inventors of the noodle.

Whatever its origin, the Italians have perfected the art of making pasta and have invented hundreds of varieties. Much of it is *pasta secca*, or dried pasta, in wonderful imaginative shapes, but in the north of Italy it is the fresh egg noodle, *pasta all' uovo*, that reigns supreme. San Francisco has many delicatessens, founded by northern Italian immigrants, that still make fresh pasta. And in the last year, with the renewed interest in regional Italian food, many new pasta shops have opened all over the city.

The Chinese have an equally long history with the noodle. Here in San Francisco, Chinatown noodle factories make as many as twenty-five different kinds of noodles and dumpling skins to supply the Chinese community.

Also included in this chapter are sources for doughs: puff pastry, strudel dough, *filo* dough, and *masa* dough for making your own tortillas.

## CHINESE NOODLES

**San Francisco**
**MON SING NOODLE COMPANY**

*1392 Pacific Avenue, San Francisco 94109. Telephone (415) 776-5273. Hours: M–SAT 8–2.*

This noodle company makes just two items: Chinese egg noodles and *won ton* skins, both of superior quality. Flecked with darker wheat, they are thinner and more tender than other noodles of this type because they're made with lots of eggs and entirely without preservatives. You can buy them here at the factory or at Ping Yuen Drugstore.

**San Francisco**
**NEW HONG KONG NOODLE COMPANY**

*874 Pacific Avenue, San Francisco 94133. Telephone (415) 982-2715. Hours: M–SAT 7–6, SUN 9–5.*

This store is the retail outlet for New Hong Kong Noodle Company. The fresh Chinese noodles—regular, thin, and extra enriched–resemble a semolina pasta and can be used in place of one. They're also good in soups and in spicy, cold Hunan-style noodle dishes. The store also stocks thicker discs of dough for making *kuo teh*, or pot stickers, and dough for meat dumplings, too.

The noodles are made on Pacific Avenue in twenty-five different sizes and types including the regular fresh Chinese noodles most widely sold; fresh Shanghai noodles (made only with flour and water, no eggs); extra-thin noodles (made with a darker wheat flour, Hong Kong style); fresh wide noodles (Shanghai style); several kinds of dried noodles; long-life noodles (deep-fried fresh noodles); regular *won ton* skins and Hong Kong style *won ton* skins; egg roll skins; pot sticker skins; and several other kinds of special dumpling skins.

The retail price at the factory is slightly above wholesale.

**San Francisco**
**PING YUEN DRUGSTORE**

*1109 Grant Avenue, San Francisco 94133. Telephone (415) 433-1357. Hours: M–SUN 9:30–6:30.*

Ping Yuen Drugstore in San Francisco's Chinatown is the only retail outlet for the very good *won ton* wrappers made by Mon Sing Noodle Company. Go right up to the drugstore cashier and ask for the *won ton* skins—kept near the cash register.

### East Bay
## YUEN HOP

*824 Webster Street, Oakland 94607. Telephone (415) 451-2698. Hours: M-SAT 8-6:30.*

This Oakland Chinatown noodle factory wholesales to East Bay Chinese restaurants, but they will also sell to passersby. To avoid any language problem, everything is clearly labelled and priced: fresh egg noodles "for chow mein," another type for soup; square and round *won ton* skins; egg roll skins and crispy noodles, plus several kinds of *tofu*; small flat squares of "fresh bean cake"; boxes of "soft" *tofu* and deep-fried bean cakes; and—their own bean sprouts, rice, and some produce.

## ——PUFF PASTRY——

### East Bay
## PIG BY THE TAIL

*1512 Shattuck Avenue, Berkeley 94709. Telephone (415) 843-4004. Hours: M 11:30-5:30, T-F 10-6, SAT 10-5:30.*

This excellent Parisian-style *charcuterie* sells *pâte brisée* in one-pound balls, enough for an eleven-inch quiche, and *pâte feuilletée* (puff pastry) in one-pound balls, enough to make a cookie-sheet-sized fruit tart.

### Marin County
## TRUE CONFECTIONS

*17 Madrona Street, Mill Valley 94941. Telephone (415) 383-3832. Hours: T-SAT 8-6.*

True Confections will sell puff pastry by the pound with two days' notice.

## ——FILO DOUGH——

### San Jose Area
## INTERNATIONAL DELICATESSEN

*495 The Alameda, San Jose 95126. Telephone (408) 286-2036. Hours: M-F 9-5:30, SAT 11-3.*

The Greek wholesale bakery Hun-i-nut stretches its own *filo* dough by hand. You can buy it next door at the International Delicatessen in one-pound packages of the plain, large sheets, or prebuttered in four-layer strips for use in elaborate layered pastries.

### San Francisco
## SHEHERAZADE BAKERY

*1935 Lawton Street, San Francisco 94122. Telephone (415) 681-8439. Hours: T-F 9-6; M, SAT 9-5.*

Sheherazade Bakery makes its own *filo* dough. Fresh and unadulterated with preservatives, it is supple and tender as a bolt of silk and can easily be folded and rolled into complex shapes. It is more expensive than the better-known brands sold frozen, but it is well worth buying for your most beautiful *filo* dough confections.

# —ITALIAN PASTA—

### San Francisco
## AUNTIE PASTA

*1501 Waller Street, San Francisco 94117.
Telephone (415) 681-4242.
741 Diamond Street (at Twenty-fourth),
San Francisco 94114. Telephone (415)
282-0738. Hours: 11–7 daily (both stores).*

David and Pat Howell had been making
pasta at home for years when they
decided to try it as a business. Their
first Auntie Pasta store opened on
Waller Street in 1981; the second store
at Twenty-fourth and Diamond opened
in February 1982.

Auntie Pasta is strictly a pasta store.
They do sell a few condiments—olive
oils, dried herbs, and some emergency
stores of dried pasta—but that's it.
They have no intention of becoming a
deli.

It's lovely walking into the radiantly
sunny corner store. Behind the counter
are big wooden mesh-bottomed trays
filled with loose coils of freshly made
pasta—pale gold, grass green, darker
whole wheat, and a beautiful orangey
tomato—all made with semolina, fresh
eggs, and olive oil and cut into *fettuccine,
linguine,* or *tagliarini* widths. Occasionally they make a lemon-spiked
pasta; a fresh herb pasta flecked with
green; and even a dark chocolate pasta,
delicious in winter with a rabbit or beef
sauce *agrodolce.*

They also make ravioli from their
fresh pasta, with two different fillings:
one is ricotta, romano cheese, parsley,
and egg; the other beef, Italian sausage,
spinach, ricotta, and cheese.

Take-out sauces are chalked on the
wall behind the counter: tomato basil;
a butter, cream, and cheese sauce (really
an Alfredo); a sour cream and dill; a
clam sauce lively with garlic; and a
walnut-ricotta sauce with Parmesan
and fresh nutmeg.

### San Francisco
## CAFFERATA RAVIOLI FACTORY

*700 Columbus Avenue, San Francisco
94133. Telephone (415) 392-7544. Hours:
M–SAT 10–10, SUN 5–10.*

Since 1896, Cafferata Ravioli Factory
has been making plump packets of
fresh pasta stuffed with meats and
cheeses. They still use a ravioli machine
over a hundred years old. Look in their
windows between 10 and 3 to watch a
succession of fresh egg pastas—ribbons
of *fettuccine, linguine, trenette,* and the
finer *tagliarini*—emerge from the pasta
machine. The Hollywood Pasta (100
percent whole-wheat pasta) is the rage
in Italy too now, where it is called *pasta
integrale.* Exuberant Genovese Gino
Biradelli also makes that Bolognese
delicacy, *tortellini:* little squares of dough
stuffed with meats and cheese, folded
over, and then twisted around a finger.
Serve them *in brodo,* in a clear broth; or
sauced like a pasta; or simply with a
browned butter suffused with fresh
sage leaves. In Bologna, these delicious
pasta morsels are affectionately known
as "Venus's navels."

Inside there's a small café with red
and white tablecloths, where you can
eat fresh pastas prepared with sauces
according to Gino's own recipes.

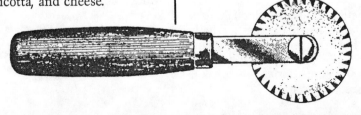

Buy some boxes of *tortellini* to take home to your freezer. If you're the type who feels insecure without a hefty stock of pasta in the house, Cafferata sells five- and ten-pound boxes of dried pasta.

## East Bay
## CAFFE VENEZIA

*1903 University Avenue, Berkeley 94704. Telephone (415) 849-4681. Hours: M–SAT 11:30 am–10 pm, SUN 4–10.*

This Berkeley caffè dishes up plates of pasta made Italian-style right on the premises. But Caffé Venezia also sells their pasta by the pound. The shape of the pasta made changes daily: it may be *fettuccine, linguine,* spaghetti, or *rigatoni* or shells. If you need more than three pounds of pasta, call a day ahead.

Their *marinara* (tomato) sauce and a *bolognese* (meat) sauce are available for take-out also.

## San Francisco
## EDUARDO'S PASTA AND TORTELLINI FACTORY

*7 Vandewater, San Francisco 94133. Telephone (415) 981-5082. Wholesale to the trade only.*

When Eduardo Moretoni, a native of Rome, came here from Venezuela almost fifteen years ago, he opened a very successful restaurant on Chestnut Street where many San Franciscans tasted their first fresh *fettuccine* and lovely fresh *tortellini* filled with *mortadella* and cheese. His excellent pasta, made with semolina flour and fresh eggs, was so popular that he began to dry it and sell packages of it in his restaurant. Four years ago he closed his restaurant and went full time into making dried pasta, including *fettuccine* and *tagliarini,* both plain and spinach, as well as squares of flat, unruffled

lasagne noodles, just like homemade, and a variety of molded pasta shapes: shells, *rigatoni,* and the tiny *pastina* for soups.

Eduardo's-brand pasta is distributed to fine food stores from Hillsdale to Santa Rosa, and it is also sold in some supermarkets.

## San Francisco
## FETTUCCINE BROTHERS

*2100 Larkin at Vallejo, San Francisco 94109. Telephone (415) 441-2281. Hours: T–F 11-7, SAT–SUN 10-6.*

The walls of this cozy pasta shop are decorated with poster-sized prints of Napoli's famous "i mangia maccaroni." As mentioned in every Victorian traveler's account of Italy, the citizens of Napoli had the notorious habit of purchasing plates of spaghetti from street vendors and eating it out of hand with grand dramatic gestures right on the street. Though Fettuccine Brothers has pasta to take out, it's not *that* take-out.

Come for lunch (any day but Monday) when you can sit down at one of the few simple tables and enjoy a plate of tender *fettuccine* sauced with any of the shop's fresh-made sauces.

The fresh pasta, made daily from durum and semolina flours, whole fresh eggs, and filtered water, comes either plain or colored a beautiful green with spinach leaves. You can buy it cut as *spaghettini,* spaghetti, *linguine,* or in ribbons of *fettuccine.* They'll also sell you uncut sheets for making your own *cannelloni* and lasagne.

They also make *tortelloni:* packets of green or yellow pasta with a classic stuffing of ricotta, Parmesan, and spinach. Cook them *al dente* in lightly salted water and serve in a butter browned with some fresh sage leaves for a simple supper.

The machine that turns out the pasta sits just behind a small deli case filled with cheeses, cold meats, and freshly made salads. The selection of Italian cheeses includes Taleggio, goat *caprini*, Fontina Val d'Aosta, *mozzarella di bufala*, Bel Paese, and Gorgonzola. Meats include salami, *mortadella*, hot *coppa*, prosciutto, *pancetta*, and *zampone*.

Fettuccine Brothers makes its own *peperonata* (roasted and marinated sweet red peppers), *caponata* (Sicilian eggplant antipasto with onions, capers, tomato), and *calamari* salad.

The sauces made here include a basic *marinara* sauce made from plum tomatoes lightly flavored with garlic, onion, and Italian herbs; and a traditional *bolognese*: a light tomato-based meat sauce made with beef, veal, prosciutto, *pancetta*, red wine, and finely diced vegetables. But then there is a *vongole*, or baby clam, sauce made with white wine; a northern Italian walnut sauce; and a *primavera* sauce lavished with the season's best fresh vegetables in a *marinara* base. *Pesto* is made here only during the sweet basil season, and rightly so.

The winner among the sauces is the Marco Polo, made from fruity olive oil, tangy olives, Parmesan, and a secret blend of herbs and spices.

### East Bay/Contra Costa
### GENOVA DELICATESSEN

*4937 Telegraph Avenue, Oakland 94609. Telephone (415) 652-7401. Hours: M–SAT 9–6, SUN 8–4.*
*1105 South California Boulevard, Walnut Creek 94596. Telephone (415) 939-3838. Hours: M–SAT 9–6, SUN 9–5.*

Genova's egg and spinach pastas are sold as *fettuccine* or *tagliarini*, or you can buy sheets of uncut pasta, for making *cannelloni* or a delicate fresh-pasta lasagne.

### San Francisco
### IL FORNAIO

*2298 Union Street, San Francisco 94123. Telephone (415) 563-3400. Hours: T–SAT 8–7, SUN 8–5.*

In addition to regional country breads, *pizza al taglio* (trays of pizza by the slice), *pizzette* (individual snack pizza), and traditional Italian pastries, this Italian *panificio* makes semolina pasta: whole egg, spinach, rosy tomato, and a wonderful *pesto* (with *pesto* sauce in the dough). Their own delicate ravioli, made of egg or spinach pasta, are classically stuffed with ricotta, spinach, and Parmesan.

### Marin County
### LET'S EAT

*1 Blackfield Drive, Tiburon 94920. Telephone (415) 383-3663. Hours: M–SAT 10–7, SUN 10–6.*

Fresh pasta—*fettuccine* and *linguine*, both spinach and egg—is made every day. Sauces available for take-out are *marinara*; *bolognese*; *pesto*; wild Italian mushroom, or *porcini*; and sausage with sweet red bell pepper.

The store also sells *filo* dough in one-pound packages and puff pastry by the pound.

### East Bay
### MADE TO ORDER

*1576 Hopkins Street, Berkeley 94707. Telephone (415) 524-7552. Hours: M–SAT 10–6.*

Made to Order makes pasta daily with fresh eggs and a mix of semolina and golden durum wheat. The usual cut is *fettuccine*, but owners Linda Briganti and Sylvana La Rocca will sell you whole sheets of uncut pasta or cut it to order for you. Their pasta is thin enough for making your own ravioli, too. Just seal the edges with water.

And in true Italian tradition, they sell *maltagliati*, literally "badly cut" pasta and pieces and scraps for soup noodles. The store also stocks homemade *pesto* sauce and *salsa casalinga* (a hearty meat and tomato sauce), as well as an authentic version of *salsa bolognese* made with veal, chicken and prosciutto, cream, and a touch of tomato.

Also there are occasional specials: at Christmastime, a tuna sauce with capers and a squid sauce for the traditional meatless Christmas Eve dinner. Puff pastry is also sold by the pound. And for your own pasta making, there are bags of durum wheat flour and coarser semolina flour.

### San Francisco
## MOLINARI DELICATESSEN

*373 Columbus Avenue, San Francisco 94133. Telephone (415) 421-2337. Hours: M–SAT 8–5.*

G. B. Molinari sells fresh pasta, close to five thousand pounds of it a week in both egg and spinach varieties. A lot of it goes to North Beach restaurants—it's not all walk-in trade. They also make two kinds of ravioli in their factory in back, one stuffed with ricotta, Parmesan, and eggs; another with beef, veal, Parmesan, and eggs; plus boxes of handmade *tortellini*, too.

### East Bay
## THE PASTA SHOP

*5940 College Avenue, Oakland 94618. Telephone (415) 547-4005. Hours: M–F 10:30–6:30, SAT 10:30–6, SUN 12–5.*

Behind the counter, a crew of women is busy making pasta with fresh eggs and semolina. A rustic basket displays the pale-yellow and dusty-green coils

of fine *spaghettini*, *tagliarini*, *linguine*, and wide *fettuccine*. Sometimes they make a pasta tinted pink with tomato, or a gorgeous fresh herb-flecked one, or a pasta stained red with beets or streaked with golden saffron. Buy the red pasta by the sheet and use with spinach and egg pasta to make a *lasagne tricolori* in the colors of the Italian flag. Any of the pastas can be made by special order. The pasta makers are experimenting with buckwheat noodles from the hearty cuisines of southern Italy, and the popular *pasta integrale*, or whole-wheat noodles.

And to sauce your pasta, they sell spinach *pesto*, basil *pesto*, garlic butter, a walnut and garlic sauce with cream, a traditional *marinara*, and a sauce of mushrooms reduced in cream.

Garlic and shallots are sold from baskets, and for your own *salsa puttanesca* there are big crocks of tiny green *picholine* olives with firm, bitter flesh; the small tasty black *nyons* olive; pointed Greek *Kalamatas*; and big meaty Sicilian-style green olives.

For your *antipasti*, the Pasta Shop has *coppa*, salami, local Iacopi prosciutto aged six months on the bone, a wonderful smoked pork loin, and a selection of cheeses.

You can have a lunch of their pasta salads or lasagne and other pasta dishes.

## Contra Costa
## RAPALLO DELICATESSEN

*1922 Oak Park Boulevard, Pleasant Hill 94523. Telephone (415) 937-5477. Hours: M–SAT 9–6, SUN 9–5.*

Fresh spinach and egg pasta as well as meat and cheese ravioli.

## Sonoma County
## RAVIOLI DELICATESSEN

*1422 Fourth Street, Santa Rosa 95404. Telephone (707) 526-3435. Hours: M–F 10–6, SAT 11–5.*

Every other day from 2 to 4, watch pasta makers make fresh ravioli stuffed with spinach, cheese, and chicken, using the traditional wooden ravioli rolling pin. You should take home about one dozen for each person as a main course, half a dozen as a first course.

## San Francisco
## VIVANDE

*2125 Fillmore Street, San Francisco 94115. Telephone (415) 346-4430. Hours: M–F 11–7, SAT 11–6, SUN 11–5.*

This new Italian *salumeria* and take-out shop has pasta *fatta in casa* of durum flour and eggs. Regular or green with spinach, it is sold as *fettuccine*, hand-cut lasagne, or in pasta sheets for your own *cannelloni.*

Sauces to take out include a basic *marinara*, or light tomato sauce; a *bolognese*, or meat and tomato sauce; a *balsamella*, or béchamel sauce; and their own *pesto* made with pine nuts.

They also have prepared pasta dishes that you can take home and heat in your own oven: *cannelloni* with a variety of fillings and sauces; *conchiglie*, large shells with a ricotta and prosciutto filling; lasagne; golden *gnocchi* made

from polenta, or small ricotta and spinach nuggets served with butter and cheeses; and pricey *arancine*, a popular southern Italian street food sold in *tavola calda* establishments all over Italy: deep-fried balls of rice filled with cheese, meat, or chicken and sauced with tomato.

# —— LATINO ——

## San Francisco
## CASA SANCHEZ

*2778 Twenty-fourth Street, San Francisco 94110. Telephone (415) 282-2400. Hours: 9–6:30 daily.*

Prepared *masa* dough.

## East Bay
## MI RANCHO MEXICAN STORE

*464 Seventh Street, Oakland 94607. Telephone (415) 451-2393. Hours: M–SAT 8–6.*

The tortilla-making section of this Mexican food emporium in Oakland will sell their own *masa* dough quite inexpensively. The process of preparing the *masa* is quite long: whole dried hominy is first soaked in lime, then cooked and stone ground—coarse for tamales or finer for tortillas.

They'll sell you *masa* flour, too, ground any way you like. And if you insist on starting from scratch, they have whole dried hominy.

## San Francisco
## LA PALMA MEXICATESSEN

*2884 Twenty-fourth Street, San Francisco 94110. Telephone (415) 648-5500. Hours: 8–6 daily.*

Prepared *masa* dough for making your own tamales, tortillas, *gorditas*, and other Mexican foods.

# —CHINESE·PASTRY—

### San Francisco
### EASTERN BAKERY

*720 Grant Avenue, San Francisco 94108. Telephone (415) 392-4497. Hours: 8–7 daily.*

Outside, passersby stop to admire the shiny, fried golden twisties piled in the front window next to chocolate cupcakes and pound cake. The side window, facing the alley, displays trays of gelatinous white-and-beige diamonds—a pastry made from sweet rice—and big slabs of a fluffy sponge cake, unfrosted, also cut in diamonds.

Inside, you can take a seat at the counter and indulge in some of the individual sponge cakes, like oversized cupcakes; the butter cupcakes; or the pineapple turnovers. The high, round moon cakes, each with a dab of glaze, are made with a variety of fillings: black bean, fruit and nut, melon, lotus. But the richest are filled with yellow soybean paste and the yolk of a preserved egg.

Like all the Chinese bakeries, Eastern Bakery proudly displays its rococo cream cakes.

### San Francisco
### THE FORTUNE BAKERY

*570 Green Street, San Francisco 94133. Telephone (415) 421-3713. Hours: 8:30–5 daily.*

The Fortune Bakery makes fortune cookies and almond cookies, plus Chinese wedding cakes.

### San Francisco
### GOLDEN GATE BAKERY

*1029 Grant Avenue, San Francisco 94133. Telephone (415) 781-2627. Hours: 7:30 am–7 pm daily.*

Golden Gate Bakery has a good selection of airy giant cupcakes, spiraled snails, layered cream-filled cakes, and sponge cakes.

### East Bay
### KAR MEE BAKERY

*1015 Webster Street, Oakland 94607. Telephone (415) 835-0520. Hours: M–SAT 7–10 (closed some Saturdays).*

Kar Mee Bakery makes giant, colored, or plain fortune cookies.

### San Francisco
### KAY WAH PASTRY COMPANY

*1039 Stockton Street, San Francisco 94133. Telephone (415) 781-0096. Hours: 7–6 daily.*
*1426 California Street, San Francisco 94109. Telephone (415) 885-3051. Hours: 9–6 daily.*

Several years ago, the *Bay Guardian* touted the egg custard tartlets at Kay Wah Pastry Company as the best in the city. It's true; Kay Wah does have wonderful egg custard. Made with a crumbly "short" pastry and filled with a high yellow custard, eggy and not too sweet, you can buy them still warm from the oven, when they're especially delicious. Saturdays, take your tasty egg custard outside to eat while watching the lively buying and selling of game birds from vans parked on this block of Stockton Street.

Kay Wah also makes fat moon cakes, sponge pastries, a few kinds of steamed *dim sum*, and western-style Danish pastries.

## San Francisco
## MEE MEE BAKERY

*1328 Stockton Street, San Francisco 94133. Telephone (415) 362-3204. Hours: 9–6 daily.*

Mee Mee Bakery is an old-fashioned fortune cookie factory and store. A serene Chinese woman in a candy-pink smock presides here in front of an old rolltop desk, its every cubbyhole stuffed with notes, bills, and orders. She'll sell you bagged sesame cookies or classic fortune cookies. One a day is guaranteed to remove indecision and uncertainty from your life.

They also sell "adult" fortune cookies.

## San Francisco
## THREE STAR BAKERY

*1131 Grant Avenue, San Francisco 94133. Telephone (415) 391-1133. Hours: 7–6 daily.*

There are more western-style pastries here than Chinese style, but they seem to be more like dream cakes than real ones: all airy confections of light cake and whipped cream. A whipped cream and strawberry cake sells at this writing for $3.95, and they're selling dozens of them.

The Chinese-style cupcakes are huge, light, and spongy. A Chinese friend says the first time she tasted *génoise,* she just thought how much it tasted like Chinese cupcakes.

# EUROPEAN
# INTERNATIONAL

## Contra Costa
## ALANO'S PASTRIES

*1237 Boulevard Way, Walnut Creek 94595. Telephone (415) 938-7277. Hours: T–SAT 8:30–4:30.*

Walnut Creek's Alano's Pastries is a special, homey kind of bakery where Alan Oswald produces an impressive number of delectable baked goods. The cases are stuffed with chocolate éclairs, napoleons and cream puffs, brownies, individual tartlets, buttery Scotch short-bread, and assorted cookies. His collection of carved cooky molds from all over the world finds its way down off the walls into the kitchen, too. Try the charming Arabic *mamool,* stuffed with date filling.

In summer, he makes fresh-fruit tarts; lighter sponge-based cakes layered with strawberries or lemon curd and whipped cream; silky strawberry mousse; wonderful fresh-fruit turnovers in such old-fashioned flavors as rhubarb, plum, and apricot; and even more cookies.

In winter, he opens up the spice box. One of his favorites is a Jewish honey-cake, made entirely from rye flour, sweetened with honey, and lightly spiced with nutmeg, anise, and cardamom. Another of his winter cakes is a date-cranberry-walnut buttermilk cake, with orange rind soaked in orange syrup. And, of course, there's a comforting, spicy gingerbread.

At Christmas, he bakes rich fruitcakes and a special *stollen* made with wine-soaked raisins, fresh cranberries, and citrus peel he candies himself.

As a service to his customers with food allergies or special diets, Mr. Oswald experiments with such desserts as unsweetened *mamool* cookies for diabetics, a chocolate pecan torte made without wheat flour, and a sugarless fig pie, sweetened with honey and crunchy with walnuts.

### San Francisco/East Bay
# COCOLAT

*3324 Steiner Street, San Francisco 94123. Telephone (415) 567-9957. Hours: T–SAT 10:30–6:30, SUN 12–5.*
*1481 Shattuck Avenue, Berkeley 94709. Telephone (415) 843-3265. Hours: M–SAT 10–6, SUN 11–5.*
*3945 Piedmont Avenue, Oakland 94611. Telephone (415) 653-3676. Hours: T–SAT 10–6.*

When Alice Medrich's Paris landlady, Madame Lastelle, gave her a recipe for home-style chocolate truffles, she couldn't have envisioned the prospering three-store truffle empire that would grow from such a modest beginning. Back home in Berkeley Alice experimented with American ingredients until she got the recipe right, then she approached the then newly opened *charcuterie* Pig by the Tail to see if they'd like to sell her truffles. They ordered thirty-six dozen right away, then more and more. The rest is truffle history. Now there are three of Alice's Cocolat stores, a thriving mail order business, and a veritable truffle-making factory.

The home-style truffles are a mix of chocolate, sweet butter, nuts, and a liqueur such as cognac or rum. Shaped by hand, they are then rolled in un-sweetened dark cocoa. Their irregular shape is meant to imitate that of the famous black truffles of Perigord. Other types are dipped in dark or white chocolates. Her best sellers are the large rum-drenched truffle and a smaller bittersweet truffle *maison* available every day along with a rotating selection of a half dozen other truffles from her full repertoire of almost thirty: blanc de blanc, dark on dark, brandy, mint, hazelnut, Grand Marnier, chestnut, Kahlúa, Brazil nut, framboise, pistachio...

Then she has cakes—chocolate cakes—sold whole or by the slice. The pastry case holds the tortes: a cognac-soaked *reine de saba; le petit prince*, made with ground almonds and innocent of liqueurs; a hazelnut torte substituting hazelnuts for almonds. The *gateau au chocolat* is a fudgy chocolate cake rather than a torte, glazed with dark chocolate, while the *royale* alternates layers of marzipan and raspberry preserves with layers of the same cake.

The delicate *génoise* and butter-cream cakes are refrigerated. The chocolate Grand Marnier is a *génoise* soaked in orange liqueur and filled with apricot jam and chocolate butter cream. The *gâteau des iles* is a pale *génoise* drenched in Curaçao and layered with apricot jam and coffee butter cream. They also bake the notorious Chocolate Decadence, a dense, bittersweet chocolate layer frosted with whipped cream and decorated with bittersweet chocolate truffles. It comes with a seasonal sauce: raspberry, strawberry, or cranberry.

Each Christmas her bakers whip up Alice's inspired holiday offerings, different every year but usually including ceramic bowls of Alcoholic Aggie's Oxfordshire Christmas Pudding, made with several kinds of raisins, fresh apples, candied fruit, suet, brown sugar, Guinness stout and California brandy.

*Truffles available by mail order.*

**San Francisco/Napa Valley**
## COURT OF THE TWO SISTERS

*2030 Union Street, San Francisco 94123.
Telephone (415) 921-1698. Hours: M–F
8–6, SAT 8:30–6, SUN 10–5.
6530 Yount Street, Yountville 94599.
Telephone (707) 944-2138. Hours: 9–
5:30 daily.*

Helda Auster-Muehle and her sister
Leona Burns have been making pastries
and cakes since their girlhood in St.
Gallen, Switzerland, but it wasn't until
they moved to the Napa Valley, after
retiring from other careers, that they
set to work in earnest as professional
pastrymakers. They made a lot *more* of
the enticing European pastries they
had been making all along. Their
Yountville bakery, the Court of the
Two Sisters, quickly won favor with
Napa Valley residents attracted by the
restrained elegance of their pastries.
But those who come to buy the petits
fours, cakes, and tortes, all made with
sweet butter, come away charmed by
their zany rococo "frog torte," covered
with little green frogs' heads.

Their second store is on Union Street
in San Francisco.

**San Francisco**
## FANTASIA BAKERY

*3465 California Street, San Francisco
94118. Telephone (415) 752-0825. Hours:
T–SAT 8–6:45, SUN–M 9–6.*

When German-born Ernst Weil had to
leave Germany just before the war, he
made his way to France where he
studied at the Cordon Bleu. When he
moved on to San Francisco, he opened
Fantasia Bakery.

Greatly expanded from its tiny beginnings, the bakery is now located on
California Street, but the actual baking
is done at a big central bakery in South
San Francisco. The store's first employee,

Ted Sufern, still works there along
with twenty other bakers from all over
Europe: Germany, Switzerland, France,
Czechoslovakia. Though Fantasia sells
countless pastries to the city's large
hotels and airlines, the quality of their
products remains remarkably high.

The bakery is best known for its
*Sachertorte,* a moist chocolate cake
layered with raspberry and apricot jams,
and for the *Doboschtorte* from old Budapest iced in chocolate and crumbs. But
dozens of other cakes and petits fours
are available year round.

Fifteenth-century legends credit the
gypsies with the invention of one of
Fantasia's specialties, *Baumkuchen,* a
cake cooked on a spit over an open fire.
The batter, a rich, refined pound cake,
is poured onto the rotating spit of a
special oven fitted with a row of gas
flames and cooked, layer by layer, to
resemble the rings of a tree. Joe Schmidt,
Fantasia's current master of *Baumkuchen,*
makes a cake rich with egg yolks and
butter, and flavored with vanilla, lemon,
and marzipan. Fantasia's *Baumkuchen*
are sometimes five feet long, but the
cake is sold by the pound and can be
cut into various lengths. Fill the hollow
cavity with ice cream or sweetened
whipped cream.

For Christmas in Germany, the
centerpiece of the holiday table is *der
bunte Teller,* a plate of fruits, nuts, and
cookies. To provide the last, Fantasia's
European bakers make *Nürnberger
Lebkuchen,* big rounds of nut dough
dark and spicy with mace, cardamom,
cinnamon, and allspice; *Basler Leckerli,*
chewy squares of honey dough; and
their own *Basler de luxe,* honey dough
sandwiched with marzipan and fruit
jams, then dipped in bittersweet chocolate.

Ernst Weil spends most of his time
supervising his giant bakery now, but
he still puts on his apron to experiment
with new fantasies. Last year he made
edible chocolate valentine boxes filled
with an assortment of chocolate truffles.

**East Bay**
# THE FRENCH CONFECTION

*1584 Hopkins Street, Berkeley 94707. Telephone (415) 526-8188. Hours: M–SAT 10–6.*

The French Confection, a small bakery specializing in fine European pastries, opened in July 1980, on a strip of Hopkins Street in north Berkeley now devoted to food stores: a fish store, a coffee store, a produce market, a gourmet deli.

Owner Gail Harper never had any professional baking experience at all. A French major at UC Berkeley, she did go to school in Paris and studied with master *pâtissier* Gaston Le Nôtre. When she returned to the Bay Area, she began teaching cooking classes, but they soon focused more on pastry than cooking. She continued baking and experimenting; the cakes accumulated; even a horde of well-intentioned friends couldn't eat them all up. The only sensible solution that presented itself was to open a pastry shop and sell the cakes.

Her repertoire includes a half dozen sinfully rich chocolate cakes starring *le marquis royal* made with hazelnuts. An array of *génoise* confections layered with butter creams and scented with liqueurs is led by a gorgeous *boule di neige* (snowball): a dome-shaped cake of *génoise* soaked in Amaretto, with whipped cream, chocolate, hazelnuts, and *amaretti.* Seasonal fruit tarts include the French bistro's winter favorite, a classic *tarte Tatin,* or caramelized upside-down apple tart.

The French Confection is one of the few bakeries to take the care and time to make a true Danish pastry dough, with all the turns. Made with sweet butter, it is flaky and light, fragrant with freshly ground cardamom.

Holidays bring an abundance of specialties; for brunch, an irresistible marzipan brioche strewn with sliced almonds and pearl sugar; a Dresdner *stollen;* a Four Seasons white fruitcake, drenched in rum and wrapped with a thin layer of marzipan; a proper English toffee made using only sugar, sweet butter, milk chocolate, and fine pieces of walnuts and almonds; *bûche de Noël* in several flavors; a rococo *gâteau St.-Honoré* (a round of *pâte brisée* ringed with cream-filled *profiteroles* glazed with caramel, the whole filled with Grand Marnier praline mousse and topped with *crème Chantilly*).

**San Francisco**
# JUST DESSERTS

*248 Church Street, San Francisco 94114. Telephone (415) 626-5774. Hours: M–TH 8 am–11 pm, F 8 am–midnight, SAT 9–midnight, SUN 9 am–11 pm.*
*1469 Pacific Avenue, San Francisco 94109. Telephone (415) 673-7144. Hours: T–TH 9 am–11 pm, F–SAT 9–midnight, SUN 9 am–11 pm.*
*3 Embarcadero Center, San Francisco 94111. Telephone (415) 421-1609. Hours: M–F 7:30–6, SAT 9–5.*
*836 Irving Street, San Francisco 94122. Telephone (415) 681-1255. Call for hours.*

Just Desserts, a San Francisco–based company with four pastry shops and a large wholesale business, started in 1974 with three friends and a cheesecake recipe. Elliot Hoffman, his wife Gail Horvath-Hoffman, and Barbara Radcliffe were baking cheesecakes at home and supplying them to city restaurants. They soon opened their first store on Church Street, then, in 1976, the Pacific Avenue store where the three partners were joined by Jane Fay-Sills. Two years later, there was an Embarcadero Center shop and in June '82 one on Irving Street.

In addition to the walk-in, sit-down, or take-out business at the four shops, Just Dessert's central kitchen now

supplies over six hundred restaurants between Monterey and Sacramento. This is big business. You'll see huge semi-trailers pulled up at the Church Street store unloading bag after hefty bag of sugars and flours to supply the busy bakers behind the scenes.

Just Desserts' forte is the kind of traditional American dessert you'd bake yourself if you had the time.

Of course, there's the New York-style cheesecake that started it all (with almond-butter crust); at least five kinds of fruit or nut-filled Danishes, all topped with orange-honey glaze; blueberry muffins; honey-sweetened bran muffins; sour cream coffee cake with fresh apple filling. Their best-selling carrot cake is made with cream cheese frosting, while the banana nut bread is rich with sour cream and walnuts. They bake dozens of lemon buttermilk cakes, poppyseed cakes, southern pecan pies and apple crumb pies, plus fudge brownies, chocolate chip cookies, and shortbread.

Christmas brings festive specials such as pumpkin-orange cake, Christmas cookies, Linzertortes, upside-down ginger pear cake, cranberry-orange nut bread, and cranberry tarts.

---

**East Bay**
**LA FARINE**

*6323 College Avenue, Oakland 94618. Telephone (415) 654-0338. Hours: W-SAT 10-6, SUN 10-2.*

Irresistible smells steal out onto the street from the lovely College Avenue bakery, La Farine, where Lili Le Coq recreates the delicious cakes, pastries, and breads of her European childhood.

The old-fashioned wood and glass pastry cases display her fancy dessert cakes, French *gâteaux* and tortes, and her seductive chocolate desserts—rich, but not overly sweet. All year round

she makes her beautifully crafted fruit tarts, but in spring and summer the store blossoms with them in every available fruit: overlapping whorls of apple, glistening rounds of clear-green kiwi fruit, perfect raspberries, a heap of blueberries, mixed fruits in elaborate patterns.

At the holidays, Lili takes extra pains, with her classic *bûche de Noël* graced with marzipan mushrooms and other woodsy creatures, a *gâteau familial* rich with almonds, and a giant croissant-shaped bread that feeds the whole family. Just after New Year's, Lili starts making *galette des Rois*, the traditional French cake to celebrate the arrival of the magi on January 6. It is a crown of feather-light puff pastry layered with marzipan, covered with a sugar glaze, and topped with gilt-paper crowns.

For La Farine's breads, see Bread section.

---

**East Bay**
**LA VIENNOISE**

*5940 College Avenue, Oakland 94618. Telephone (415) 655-3209. Hours: T-F 11-7, SAT 10-6.*

La Viennoise is Karen Shapiro's tiny jewel of a bakery in North Oakland, where this petite wizard of the pastry arts works from early morning till late at night concocting her splendid tortes, cakes, and tarts. A former art student who later studied at the Culinary Institute in New York, she now works entirely with a palette of fine flours, sweet butter, fresh eggs, chocolates, marzipan, and nuts. The results are such tempting examples of the pastry-maker's art as a chocolate-pecan torte, a rich torte layered with raspberry jam and iced with chocolate *ganache*; her lovely spring marzipan torte, a chocolate *génoise* layered with chocolate cream, strawberries, and whipped cream, then blanketed with marzipan; the marvelous Thalhof torte, a luscious chocolate-almond torte, doused with brandy and orange liqueur, covered with chocolate *sabayon* cream, and topped with chocolate wafers; or the masterful hazelnut torte, filled with apricot purée and chocolate *ganache* and glazed with dark chocolate. And just as European *pâtissiers* do, she makes lots of individual desserts such as her Engadiner tartlets: almonds, pecans, and hazelnuts in a sticky rum caramel.

Karen loves the holidays. Valentine's finds her making all kinds of heart-shaped pastries and cookies, even a heart-shaped *gâteau St.-Honoré*. Christmas baking commences with lovely rounds of Vienna's beloved *Linzertorte*; decorated with pastry holly, the superb sweet butter and almond pastry has a luscious raspberry jam filling. Her edible personalized Christmas cards come in two versions: a *speculaas*, or Dutch honey gingerbread (sandwiched with sticky honey-almond paste), or an embossed buttery shortbread, both seasonally decorated.

She takes special pains with her fruitcakes, which are aged in brandy and packed with dried apricots, pears, pineapples, and other California dried fruits, plus a winter's hoard of walnuts, almonds, and other nuts.

(If you've fallen in love with some of the sumptuous pastries in the cases at the Oakville Grocery, they're Karen's. They are also sold at A la Carte in Walnut Creek and Valentine's fine chocolate shop in San Rafael.)

## Napa Valley
## LE GATEAU

*3078 Jefferson Street, Napa 94558. Telephone (707) 252-1414. Hours: M–SAT 7–6.*

A small shopping center in the middle of Napa is an unlikely location for a fine European-style pastry shop, but Le Gateau has wine country residents driving in from all the neighboring valleys to buy their sumptuous sweets. The bakery's partners, Regina Petruzziello and Donald Mason, both attended the Culinary Institute in New York. Donald was working at the Silverado Country Club, Regina in San Francisco, when this bakery came up for sale.

Best known for their lavish tortes, Le Gateau has my vote for the most delicious in their Maniaci Torte. made of filberts, almonds, and chocolate butter cream, the whole cake is cloaked in marzipan. But the lemon-citron, chocolate-sherry, and Grand Marnier tortes are not far behind.

Among the changing array of individual desserts, the apple puff-pastry tarts glazed with apricot would make any Parisian *pâtissier* proud. The tiny Florentines are as delicate as their Tuscan counterparts, thin lacy discs coated with chocolate. One secret of Le Gateau's success is the local sweet butter used in all their pastries. You can taste it in the tender, flaky croissants and the *pain au chocolat.*

Try to visit Le Gateau close to noon-time when the quiche emerges from the oven. If the very idea of quiche has lost your interest, don't follow your instinct. Theirs is spectacular, with a sweet buttery dough, lots of bacon, and a creamy, substantial taste. The high individual quiches are made with spinach or bacon.

At Christmas, they make a *stollen* with their own fresh candied peel and brandy-swollen raisins; a traditional *panettone;* a *bûche de Noël,* usually in three flavors and sizes; fat gingerbread boys with black currant eyes; and, on special order, pretty gingerbread houses.

Le Gateau's pastries are also sold at the Oakville Grocery in Oakville.

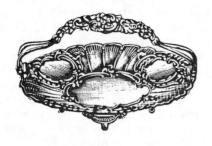

## Contra Costa
## NARSAI'S MARKET

*389 Colusa Avenue, Kensington 94707. Telephone (415) 527-3737. Hours: M–SAT 10-7, SUN 10-4.*

From Narsai's Market in Kensington, you can take home some of the same elegant pastries served in the well-known restaurant: individual *tartelettes,* rich cakes and tortes by the slice, honeyed Middle Eastern confections made with fine layers of *filo* dough.

On Sundays, they have an even bigger selection of assorted pastries to tempt you: homemade strudel, a marvelous quince Danish, or a cheese *schnecken* with caraway and cheddar. At Christmas, you can take home plum puddings with Cumberland sauce, persimmon puddings, traditional English fruitcakes, and French *bûche de Noel.* For Passover, the market prepares kosher-style chopped liver, gefilte fish, fresh horseradish, and matzo spice cakes. Lenten hot-cross buns are baked until Easter. Then the market has handmade sugar eggs, individually decorated, the kind you can keep from year to year; egg-shaped cakes, all decorated in spring's pastels;

and glazed whole apple-smoked hams for your Easter morning breakfast.

Narsai's also supplies I. Magnin's new gourmet market with fresh croissants and an array of Narsai's own pastries.

## Marin County
## SWEET THINGS BAKERY

*1 Blackfield Drive, Tiburon 94920. Telephone (415) 388-8583. Hours: M–F 8:30–6, SAT–SUN 10-6.*

All the desserts at Sweet Things Bakery are made from the best flour, butter, nuts, chocolate, and other natural ingredients. Proprietors Sharon Leach and Marsha Workman say their best seller is the carrot cake that launched the business from Ms. Workman's home kitchen. Then they dreamed up a Chocolat Mousse Torte that has Marin County chocaholics standing in line (there's a pound of bittersweet chocolate in every cake).

Comfort yourself on cold winter mornings with one of their apple-cream coffee cakes. The banana cake and the Grand Marnier Truffle Torte are perfect for late afternoon high tea.

For kids, they have brownie cake, peanut-butter cake, and heaps of cookies just like mama bakes when she has the time: chocolate chip with walnuts, oatmeal with raisins, ginger crisps, crunchy butter cookies, and sand tarts. Sweet Things delivers its sweets to over ninety Bay Area restaurants and food stores, as well as supplying them to Bloomingdale's in New York and a restaurant in Hong Kong!

## San Francisco
## TARTS, INC.

*509 Laguna Street, San Francisco 94102. Telephone (415) 863-5572. Hours: T–F 11-6, SAT 11-5.*

If you're not already familiar with the shop, you might miss the simple blue and white sign. At first it's not entirely clear what a store called Tarts, Inc. could be, but a step inside leaves no doubt. The unpretentious storefront contains only a large glass case filled with rows of perfectly executed pastries, each sitting on a cut-paper doily. With its spacious presentation and serene atmosphere this seems more like a museum of tarts than a store selling them.

Owners John Sutherland and Jim Stacy do their main business with San Francisco restaurants, but they'll sell you the same elegant pastries served in local pillars of gastronomy for just 50¢ above wholesale. They caution: if you have your heart set on a particular pastry, order a day ahead to be sure it will be available.

Customers spend a long time musing in front of the case, scrutinizing the perfect circles of tarts in every shade and texture: bright raspberry and strawberry, pastel lemon, pale chocolate mousse, tawny caramelized almond or macadamia nut.

Then come satiny dark chocolate-glazed rounds of chocolate truffle, *reine de saba*, and Chocolate Decadence or double espresso cakes, plus Vienna's *Sachertorte*, or a raspberry Bavarian torte. Next consider the lovely layer cakes with exotic names like Ivory Coast and Mocha Kahlúa, the cheese-cakes, and *Linzertortes*.

At holiday time the bakers strut their stuff with a big lineup of Christmas goodies such as a pumpkin mousse torte silky with sweet pumpkin, rum-spiked cream, and pungent fresh ginger; a praline tart with caramelized pecans; a Seville orange–almond tart; or a snowy coconut tart with apricot. The Florentine is a delicious sticky mix of hazelnuts, chocolate, and bright candied fruit. You can also order a classic *bûche de Noël* and rum-drenched fruitcakes.

## Marin County
## TRUE CONFECTIONS

*17 Madrona Street, Mill Valley 94941. Telephone (415) 383-3832. Hours: T–SAT 8–6.*

For almost four years now, partners Jo Ann Cuffino, her husband Bob, and Mary Culp have been baking up a storm of delectable pastries at their small bakery in Mill Valley, True Confections. (Jo Ann and Mary, the pastry chefs behind the scenes, first met when both were baking desserts at Larkspur's 464 Magnolia restaurant.)

Don't resist the tempting Walnut Lutetia, a splendid torte made from hand-ground walnuts rather than the more usual almonds, filled with a rum-spiked toasted-walnut butter cream, and glazed with semisweet chocolate. Coffee lovers should try the mocha torte, a spongecake soaked with brandied syrup, layered with chocolate mousse and covered with a superb mocha butter cream. The dark Black Forest cake is filled with Royal Ann cherries soaked in kirsch. Chocolate lovers will enjoy the chocolate cake, glazed with dark chocolate, and the dense chocolate pie with Grand Marnier and cream.

In the fall, the bakers can't bake enough of the apple tarts made with brandy custard filling in a flaky pastry. The pear tart, equally as good, has an almond-rum filling with a layer of apricot preserves. Summer tarts are made with all the season's fruit.

During the season, they make a spectacular strawberry cake: a light *génoise* soaked with kirsch, filled with fresh berries and cream, and layered with meringue and red currant jelly, the whole smothered in whipped cream.

In the mornings there are impeccable fresh-baked croissants, *pains au chocolat*, and *brioches*.

At Christmas, they make *bûche de Noël*; big wreaths of Christmas bread from a rich buttery dough filled with sweet ground almond paste; a regal *kugelhopf* made of briochelike dough flavored with orange rind, almonds, and rum-soaked raisins and baked in the traditional tall fluted ring mold; and moist loaves of French *pain d'epice* rich with butter, rum, and lots of spices.

# —GREEK PASTRY—

San Francisco
## ACROPOLIS BAKERY AND DELICATESSEN

*5217 Geary Boulevard, San Francisco 94118. Telephone (415) 751-9661. Hours: T-SAT 8-7, SUN 8-4.*

Gregory and Christina Triantafillidis own a special kind of store: it is both Greek and Russian because they are Greek and Russian. There is a tempting assortment of *baklava*, birds' nests, and other *filo* and honey pastries. Order your braided Greek Easter bread in advance, decorated with eggs dyed red for the blood of Christ.

Try the *dolmadakis, tiropites* (*filo* triangles stuffed with cheese), and the *spanakopita* (spinach pie). Gregory's excellent *kasseri* cheese, kept in the back, is the real thing, made of sheep's milk, crumbly like *halvah*, slightly sharp and aged two years.

San Francisco
## OLYMPIC GREEK AMERICAN PASTRIES

*3719 Mission Street, San Francisco 94110. Telephone (415) 647-6363. Hours: M-SAT 8:30-7:30, SUN flexible but usually 8:30-3.*

The warm smells of cinnamon, butter, and vanilla pull you through the door into the cool and dark of this small store crowded with every kind of Greek foodstuff. Just inside there are sacks of flours, sesame seed, semolina for pastries, rice, and roasted chick-peas for snacks. Owner Pete Panagiotides is from Athens and proudly shows you his goods:

"We have *feta* from Greece and from Bulgaria—both sheep's milk—and the best olives from Kalamata [sleek and purply-black, slit at the pointed end], dry-cured olives [wrinkly black, slightly bitter] and the green *megales*. We have tins of imported octopus and jars of *volvi*, tiny wild Greek onions." Gallon jars of much used spices such as oregano, nutmeg, and anise seed sit above the cheese and olive counter along with lumps of *levani* (frankincense) to perfume your home.

In the adjoining baking room Pete's radiant wife Teta butters tissue paper-thin sheets of *filo* dough, spreads them lavishly with nuts and rolls them into her exceptional *strifto, trigona, natras,* or *baklava*. "My wife is from Mykonos and makes all the pastries. Everything is expensive that we use: the sweet butter (we make our own from country cream), the nuts (walnuts, almonds, cashews, pistachios), and the honey. We used to make our own *filo* dough, too, but we can't afford to anymore."

Teta also caters trays of her pastries and *dolmadakia* (grape leaves stuffed with rice and meat) or *moussaka* (the eggplant and lamb casserole). On Friday she bakes long crusty loaves of bread sprinkled with sesame seeds.

Sometimes their son George serves cups of strong sweetened Greek-style coffee (the store carries several brands) to friends and customers who drop by to chat. The sound of Greek envelops the baking room as they dip pieces of *paxamalia* (a whole-wheat "toast" accented with anise) or *koulouraika* and *paximaraika* cookies in their coffee. Soft-eyed Greek children hide behind their mother's skirts eating powdery *kourabiethes* (butter cookies with nuts).

# —ITALIAN PASTRY—

### San Francisco
## BOHEMIAN CIGAR STORE

*566 Columbus Avenue, San Francisco 94103. Telephone (415) 362-0536. Hours: T–SAT 10 am–1 am, SUN 10–6.*

You can get one of the best *cappuccinos* in North Beach at Mario and Liliana Crismani's Bohemian Cigar Store at the edge of Washington Square. Late afternoons, nostalgic Italians read newspapers from home at the long counter, listen to sentimental *napoletano* songs, and enjoy a slice of Signora Crismani's homemade cheesecake. Rich with eggs and ricotta cheese, fresh with lemon peel and light on the sugar, it's a real *torta di ricotta*, custardy and dense at the bottom, light and honeycombed toward the top. She also makes *crostata*, big trays of buttery cooky dough spread with raspberry or apricot filling and crisscrossed with strips of dough.

### San Francisco
## CUNEO ITALIAN FRENCH BAKERY

*523 Green Street, San Francisco 94133. Telephone (415) 392-4969. Hours: 7–6 daily.*
*3155 Scott Street, San Francisco 94123. Telephone (415) 567-4408. Hours: 7:30–6 daily.*

The Green Street bakery has been a fixture in North Beach since 1880; now there is a branch on Scott Street, too. The original owners of Cuneo Bakery were from Cuneo and sold it to three partners from Tuscany, from the towns of Carrara, Lucca, and Viareggio. The big plate-glass window is stocked with bags of hardtack and hearty semolina *farfalle, fusilli,* and *tagliarini*

pastas from Salerno in southern Italy. But who'd want to eat hardtack when the real goods are the breads and sweets? Inside, Cuneo's hundred-year-old wooden bins hold good country bread in thick crusty rounds (baked a block away at the old Italian French Baking Company, now owned by Cuneo, too), *torcetti* or *sfogliate* (twists of puff paste with a sugar glaze), assorted *biscotti,* and some cookies. Feni Marchetti, one of the saleswomen, makes real *torta di toscana* for those who like heavy pastries. Very rich and dense, it is made with rice cooked in milk with chocolate and eggs, and flavored with whiskey, Marsala and Amaretto liqueurs, lemon, orange peel, and raisins.

All through October and November, the women in the back bake, cut, and fit together dark slabs of gingerbread to make lovely old-fashioned gingerbread houses for Christmas.

### San Francisco
## DANILO BAKERY

*516 Green Street, San Francisco 94133. Telephone (415) 989-1806. Hours: 7 am–6 pm daily.*

The Di Piremo family from the walled city of Lucca, in Tuscany, have owned this cozy neighborhood bakery for nine years. It feels like a small village bakery in Tuscany, with even a long, sprigged white curtain in the doorway to pull closed in the summer heat. The display of baked goods in the picture window changes all through the day as fresh batches come out of the oven. *Grissini* (the fat bread sticks with olive oil in the dough, a specialty of Turin) are stacked like cordwood—the best in North Beach. A pair of plump bread hands made from the same dough gesture toward a plate of tomato-red pizza wedged between big loaves of country-style bread. Later in the day there might be a warm *torta di legumi* (a latticed sweet pie with a Swiss chard filling and sprinkled with *pignoli*) or a *torta di mandorla* (a moist, low cake made with ground almonds). Inside, you'll find homemade *biscotti*, imported candies, and shelves of basic groceries like pasta, canned tomatoes, *acqua minerale*.

While the dark-eyed young beauty at the counter bags your order, try an imported *sapori di cioccolata* (a small oval chocolate-coated cookie) from northern Italy. For a Lucchese version of *pan bagna* (bathed bread), buy one of the *friselle*, pale wreathes of bread split, then tied together with fine string. Dampen the two halves with fruity green olive oil, rub with garlic, then spread with prosciutto, salami, olives, and marinated vegetables. Danilo's *pan dolce alla genovese* (Genoan-style *panettone*), generous with candied fruit, orange rind and real currants, is light and moist, with characteristic anise seeds set in the crumb. Their Milanese version (no anise) is crowned with slivered almonds. The *cialde* (very large, patterned anise-flavored cookies made with an old-fashioned iron) are sold flat or rolled for filling with thickened cream or sweetened ricotta.

## San Francisco/Peninsula
## DIANDA ITALIAN AMERICAN PASTRY

*2883 Mission Street, San Francisco 94110. Telephone (415) 647-5469. Hours: 7–6:30 daily.*
*49 West Forty-second Avenue, San Mateo 94403. Telephone (415) 341-2951. Hours: M-T, SAT 9-7; W-TH 9-8, F 9-9, SUN 10-7.*

Dianda Italian American Pastry sits isolated in a neighborhood in San Francisco that was largely Italian at the turn of the century. Until a recent move across the street, the shop had been at the same site for eighty years and in the hands of the Dianda family for eighteen. Before coming to San Francisco, Elio Dianda was the pastry chef at Salza, the finest *pasticceria* in Lucca.

Elio's widow, Signora Erica, presides in the store and ensures that the highest tradition of baking is maintained. Everything is cooked with care and with the best ingredients: the tiny *allumette*, absolutely light and crunchy, with almonds and powdered sugar; the small *palmine*, crisp and tacky with sugar; the *amaretti*, shaped like miniature cupcakes, the almond crumb moist at the center. The flowery scent of *torta di mandorla* baking perfumes the whole store and the street outside. As is everything here, the *zabaglione* is made by Signora Erica's sons: Armando, Pasquale, and Floriano. This rich, creamy sauce, still whisked by hand in a huge copper bowl, goes into the *torta di zabaglione e rum* and the *zuppa inglese* (layers of *pan de spagna*, *génoise* cake, puff pastry, and the golden cream).

But the *capolavoro* is *panforte*, Siena's claim to culinary fame. Normally this fruitcake makes the rounds in every Italian household at Christmas time; at Dianda it is always available whole or in bite-sized pieces. Instead of the dry, heavy sweet eaten in most of Italy, Dianda's is a moist and chewy, not-too-sweet morsel filled with nuts and covered with a melting wafer. No wonder Elio Dianda won first prize in Siena's *panforte* contest.

*2 Cambriaro*

**Peninsula**
## MAZZETTI'S BAKERY

*101 Manor Drive, Pacifica 94044. Telephone (415) 355-1007. Hours: T–SUN 7:30–6.*

*Focaccia, panettone,* and other Italian baked goods.

**Peninsula**
## NEW GENEVA BAKERY

*29 San Pedro Road, Colma 94014. Telephone (415) 755-0119. Hours: W–TH, SAT–SUN 7–7; F 7–5.*

*Panettone.*

**San Francisco**
## STELLA PASTRY

*446 Columbus Avenue, San Francisco 94133. Telephone (415) 986-2914. Hours: M–SAT 8–6, SUN 8–2.*

Franco Santucci and his wife Mercedes own this lovely blue and white store; Franco is from Lucca, not surprisingly, since there seem to be *lucchesi* in every bakery in North Beach. Before buying the store from its original owner, a Piemontese widow, Claudina Zanello, Franco worked as a baker here for four years. The well-provided store features *sacripantina,* a heavenly adaptation of a dessert that was a specialty of an old pastry shop in Genova. It is a velvety molded *semifreddo* that combines light sponge cake, *zabaglione,* and whipped cream. It comes in a variety of sizes and should be ordered in advance. The *cannoli* are filled with sweetened ricotta and bits of candied fruit. These popular Sicilian "pipes" were originally served at weddings to induce fertility in the young newlyweds.

Franco's *panettone* sits solid and tall and fine textured, topped with almonds, sugar, and *pignoli.* Cookies and small pastries are sold by the pound: delicious *parigini* or *crostatine,* tiny buttery raspberry fruit bars; *occhi di bue,* or "ox eyes," round cookies with a glistening ruby-colored center, every bit as good as in Rome's *pasticceria* Euclide; lacy arabesques of crisp *fiorentini* covered with caramel; *amaretti,* fragrant almond and egg white cookies with or without *pignoli; bignè,* deep-fried pastry puffs, some cream filled; or *pasticiotti,* small crumbly tarts filled with the sweet pastry cream typical of southern Italy, and exquisite *savoiardi* (lady fingers) delicate with sugar and beaten egg whites.

During the Easter season you'll find the *colomba pasquale,* the Easter dove, bread in the shape of a bird made from the same sweet dough as *panettone,* decorated with toasted almonds and a powdering of sugar; and *uova di pasqua,* enormous chocolate Easter eggs. At holiday time, Stella also sells imported Alemagna brand *panettone,* which, despite its reputation, can't compare to the fresh homemade version you find here or in any other North Beach bakery. You can also find imported *pandoro Bali,* Verona's sweet bread, lighter than *panettone,* tall and ribbed like a Gothic cathedral.

## San Francisco
# VICTORIA PASTRY

*1362 Stockton Street, San Francisco 94133. Telephone (415) 781-2015. Hours: 7–6 daily.*

Established in 1914 during the surge of enthusiastic rebuilding after the earthquake, Victoria Pastry is one of the oldest bakeries in North Beach. In the early years of this century, newly arrived immigrants to San Francisco banded together according to skill and origin to open businesses in this thriving Italian-American community. Unlike some of North Beach's delicatessens, all the Italian bakeries are still owned by first-generation Italians who learned their trade in the mother country. Victoria's current owners first worked as bakers at the shop, later becoming partners. Signor Renzo is Genoese, Signor Gianni is Sicilian, and Signor Romano is Tuscan. They have each brought the specialties from their own regions: Genoese-style *panettone* (a holiday sweet bread), Sicilian *cannoli* (crisp rolls of pastry filled with a sweet thick *crema*), and Tuscan *ossi di morto* ("dead man's bones"), meringue cookies baked rock-hard with chunks of almonds.

With its black-and-white–tiled storefront featuring a formal display of pastries, fancy bouquets, and framed photos of couples cutting wedding cakes, Victoria has the feeling of a small-town *pasticceria*. In Italy it would sit squarely on the main *piazza*, where the Sunday promenade would pass and repass its windows.

Downstairs in the old-fashioned bakery kitchen, bakers all in white spread slabs of *génoise* with rich fillings to form tall, elegant cakes. (Catherine de Medici's pastry chefs introduced the cake from Genoa, known there as *pasta genovese*, to the French when she married Henry II.) Tall rolling racks are stacked with trays heaped with the many cookies to stock the pastry cases upstairs: *biscotti* (sweet cookies sliced from a long rope of dough imbedded with nuts or candied fruit); *palmettes* (paired spirals of fine buttery puff paste glazed with sugar, copies of the ornaments on Ionian columns); *allumettes* (bars of unsweetened puff pastry topped with a pale meringue striped with raspberry jam); *sfogliate* (elongated twists of the same pastry simply sugar glazed); and little meringue cookies with walnuts, which break to a delicious powder with the first bite. They're all sold by the pound.

Victoria's *brioschi* (plump crescents glazed with sugar) are completely delicious, and with their rich, eggy dough, they're ten times better than any *cornetti* you're likely to find in Italy. *Panettone* is the traditional Easter and Christmas bread, its sweet dough enriched with eggs, candied fruit, and almonds. The Lombardians claim it originated in medieval times as "pan de Tonio," the bread made by a young apprentice baker to court his boss's daughter. But the *genovesi* assert that their version, with fennel seeds and often pistachios, is the original. In Italy, *panettone* is sold only at holiday time, and most of those sold are commercially made, boxed and slightly stale. In North Beach, the demand for *panettone* is so great that all the bakeries make it year round, sometimes as often as two or three times a week. Victoria's is a round, home-style loaf.

Victoria's refrigerator case is plastered with shocking-pink stickers announcing that ZUCCOTTO IS HERE. Inspired by the specialty of Florence, said to take its form from the dome of Brunelleschi's cathedral, it's a *semifreddo*, or chilled molded dessert, made of light cake, custard, and chocolate creams

drenched with secret liqueurs and flavorings. You won't find a Florentine
version as flashy as this customized
American one.

# —JAPANESE PASTRY—

When visiting the home of friends, the
polite Japanese visitor brings his hostess
a box of *manju*, sweet rice cakes made
of pounded glutinous rice and filled
with *an*, a sweetened bean paste made
from tiny red *azuki* beans.

In Japan, *manju* reflect the changing
seasons with different shapes and flavors.
One of the first signs of spring is the
bird-shaped *uguisu mochi*, made to
celebrate the day when the nightingale
breaks his winter silence. And just
before the cherry trees blossom, the
pastry shops make *sakura-mochi*, a
lovely pale-pink rice cake wrapped in
cherry leaves. In autumn there is *ohagi*
with its heart of *mochi* covered with
red bean paste.

Unlike western desserts, *manju* are
usually not eaten at the end of the
meal, but are served on their own with
strong green tea to cut the sweetness.

## San Francisco
## BENKYODO COMPANY

*1747 Buchanan Street, San Francisco
94115. Telephone (415) 922-1244. Hours:
M–F 7–6, SAT 8–6.*

While some of the other Japanese bakeries' clerks might sometimes be puzzled
as to why a westerner would want to
try *manju*, Ricky Okamura, the *manju*
maker at Benkyodo, is delighted to
introduce his pastries to those unfamiliar with them. Stop by in the late
afternoon, when the shop is less busy,
and try some of the many delicious
*manju* with a refreshing cup of green
tea.

At the new year, Japanese families
buy several sets of fresh *mochi* or rice
cakes called *okasane*. Made of pounded
sweet rice, Benkyodo Company's round
cakes look like pristine snowmen. The
custom is to display them in the kitchen
or living room throughout the holidays
and then eat them just after the new
year.

## San Francisco
## KANSENDO
## JAPANESE PASTRY SHOP

*1825 Post Street, San Francisco 94115.
Telephone (415) 346-5083. Hours: 10–
5:30 daily.*

Though it's situated just off a concrete
hallway on the bottom floor of the
Japan Center, Kansendo Japanese Pastry
Shop, with its *shoji*-screen windows,
looks as if it's been lifted intact from
the Japanese countryside. Inside, groups
of Japanese are relaxing and talking
with each other over pastries at the
tiny tables. At the side counter, a
Japanese woman pours familiar American restaurant coffee into mugs and
gossips in Japanese with the shop's
regular customers.

There are usually a dozen different
bean pastries, or *manju*, all made with
the same materials but with different
flavorings, each snug in high, pleated
pastry wrappers and nestled in black
wooden boxes. Try the steamed rice
pastry mottled like a blueberry muffin,
or the pale green *manju* with three
indented fingerholes like a bowling
ball.

Kansendo also has *yokan*, candies
jelled with agar-agar. The long bars of
the mahogany-colored sweet bean paste
gel are sometimes flavored with persimmons or chestnuts. The soybean
nut clusters, bags of sugared soybeans,
and imported savory crackers also make
good snacks.

## San Francisco
## YAMADA SEIKA CONFECTIONERY

*1910 Fillmore Street, San Francisco 94115. Telephone (415) 922-3848. Hours: T–SUN 9–6.*

Yamada Seika is a miniscule Japanese pastry shop on Fillmore Street. A simple wooden pastry case displays the shop's exquisite *yokan* and *manju* in elaborate traditional forms: rounds of pale yellow, cracked like dry earth; white spheres of steamed rice incised with a maple leaf; mottled dark bluish-purple and white cakes; small golden-brown balls embossed with two little birds; *manju* bearing calligraphy and a dab of warm brown glaze . . . Nestled in a pink bakery box, these lovely Japanese sweets are a real treasure to take home to tea.

# —LATINO PASTRY—

## Peninsula
## AGUILILLA BAKERY

*3305 Middlefield Road, Menlo Park 94025. Telephone (415) 367-8851. Hours: 8:30–6:30 daily.*

Fresh tortillas and *panes dulces*, as well as homemade tamales and *carnitas*, tender flaky pork.

## San Francisco
## DOMÍNGUEZ BAKERY

*2953 Twenty-fourth Street, San Francisco 94110. Telephone (415) 824-6844. Hours: 9 am–11 pm daily.*

The fancy red and blue letters hand-painted on the window read Domínguez Bakery: Panadería Flor de Jalisco. Beneath them the window is filled with trays of pink pom-pon cookies covered with coconut, spicy gingerbread pigs, sugar cookies shaped like cactus flowers or a mosaic of colors—cookies *millefiori*—brown sugar candies, and fat meringues.

Domínguez's *panes* are extremely good and always fresh; they bake several times a day. You can often find fresh egg bread, sweet crescent rolls, and large leaf-shaped *ojaldre.*

And about 4 o'clock every day, they make *churros,* twists of crisp dough for dunking in creamy hot chocolate. With a fat fluted pastry tube, *la señora* squirts the sweet dough into hot deep fat in a big spiral. When it's golden, she cuts it into short lengths and rolls them in sugar.

For the Day of Epiphany, January 6, you can special order a festive *rosca de reyes,* a crumbly, dense, and faintly sweet egg bread set with bands of ruby-red glaze and glittering with tiny multi-colored sprinkles. A small doll is hidden inside. The person who finds the doll in his/her piece of cake will be prosperous enough to host the party next year.

Most Mexican bakeries sell a number of cheeses and other staples. Here they have *queso crema* (oblong-shaped cream cheese); large chunks of *queso fresco* (fresh cheese); and small tubs of *crema fresca,* the Latin American version of *crème fraîche*—homemade, expensive, and delicious, the classic accompaniment for fried golden ripe plantain slices. On the counter, there are handfuls of fresh herbs, chorizo, and stacks of tortillas. And crowded at the front door are crates of *plátanos maduros*, chilies, *tomatillos*, *tamarindo*, and pale-yellow fava beans.

### San Jose Area
### GUADALAJARA BAKERY AND MARKET

*1661 East Santa Clara, San Jose 95116. Telephone (408) 251-2120. Hours: 6 am–7:30 pm daily.*
*452 East Empire, San Jose 95112. Telephone (408) 294-0545. Hours: 6 am–7 pm daily.*

These two bakeries make *panes dulces*, flour and corn tortillas, and chorizo. They also carry a stock of Mexican-style cheeses, chilies, hot sauces, and canned goods.

### San Francisco
### LA MASCOTA BAKERY

*3254 Twenty-third Street, San Francisco 94110. Telephone (415) 647-7488. Hours: M–SAT 9:30–6:30.*
*199 Ocean Avenue, San Francisco 94112. Telephone (415) 587-7724. Hours: M–SAT 7:30–6:30, SUN flexible, usually 9–2.*

The tiny Twenty-third Street bakery has windows crammed with sensational paperbacks, faded photos, tinsel, and wonderful old junk. Inside, you can buy individual pieces of such Central American specialties as *quesadilla de mantequilla*, a powdery fine-textured pound cake; *torta de pelota*, a delicately spiced small loaf with raisins; and *semita poleada*, a heavy bread, its bottom sticky with a sweet layer of pineapple and raisins—all baked at the larger Ocean Avenue store.

### San Francisco
### LA MEXICANA

*2804 Twenty-fourth Street, San Francisco 94110. Telephone (415) 648-2633. Hours: 7 am–9 pm daily.*

La Mexicana is a little bakery that features small, basket-shaped *pastelitos* filled with apple or pumpkin. If you drop in on Wednesday, be prepared to see mostly empty shelves. As a rule, Mexican bakeries do not bake on that day.

On Fridays and Saturdays, they have bread baked in the shape of alligators.

### San Jose Area
### LA MEXICANA BAKERY

*3127 Story Road, San Jose 95127. Telephone (408) 258-6373. Hours: 8 am–8 pm daily.*

A selection of *panes dulces* and cookies.

### San Francisco
### LA VICTORIA

*2937 Twenty-fourth Street, San Francisco 94110. Telephone (415) 824-9931. Hours: 9 am–10 pm daily.*
*1205 Alabama Street, San Francisco 94110. Telephone (415) 824-9991. Hours: 10–10 daily.*

La Victoria, across the street from Domínguez, is the best-known bakery on Twenty-fourth Street. Their *cocadas* (macaroons) are fat and moist, and the large *polvorones* (Mexican wedding cookies) covered with powdered sugar are lovely, stacked alternately rose and white in the window. Go in, grab a tray and pair of tongs and help yourself to a mountain of baked goods that can be easily frozen. Don't miss Victoria's collection of exiting Mexican calendars

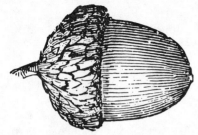

with Aztec warriors dressed in full battle attire and voluptuous virgins being offered to the gods while storm clouds gather above the snowy peaks of Popocatépetl.

### East Bay
### MIRAMONTES BAKERY

*1613 East Fourteenth, Oakland 94607. Telephone (415) 536-7600. Hours: 8 am–9 pm daily.*

Miramontes Bakery is East Oakland's Mexican bakery. Here you can load your tray with dozens of traditional *panes dulces* and cookies. At Christmas, try the *tamales dulces*, sweet compact packages eaten at the end of holiday meals. Crushed strawberries, pineapple, or bananas are enclosed in tender corn *masa*, wrapped in dried corn husks, and tied at the ends.

Though the baked goods remain the same high quality, Miramontes lost much of its appealing atmosphere recently when an adjoining store was annexed to make a vast, dim supermarket of Mexican foods.

### Peninsula
### MISSION BELL BAKERY

*2565 Middlefield Road, Redwood City 94063. Telephone 365-7001. Hours: 7 am–7:30 pm daily.*

Mission Bell makes their own tasty and decorative *panes dulces.* You can also find fresh chorizo sausages, *chicharrónes,* and ingredients for Mexican cuisine.

### San Francisco
### PANADERIA LA REINA

*3114 Twenty-fourth Street, San Francisco 94110. Telephone (415) 647-6502. Hours: 8–8 daily.*

Baking in one of my favorite bakeries begins early in the day. At least twenty-five different kinds of bread, rolls, buns, and *pasteles* emerge hot from the oven to be stacked on racks in the back room: *elotes,* shaped like small corn cobs; *nopales,* like the broad planes of the cactus; *cocadas,* coconut bread; and *quesadillas,* buttery cheesecakes with the texture of pound cake.

Curious about the kitchen that turned out such variety, one day I wandered into the back. Four or five young men sat around the enormous worktable eating a delicious-looking soup studded with fresh *cilantro* and vegetables. They were just about to go back to work so I stayed and watched them. Itinerant bakers who work and travel as a team, they never stay longer than a week or two in any one place, baking their way through the western states. "And where will you go from here?" I asked. "Y quien sabe!" said one of them, Joaquín ("Call me Jack"), kneading, weighing, and cutting cookie dough without missing a beat. Asked what they thought of the rival La Victoria, "Ah," burst Jack-Joaquín, "they are the kings, but we are the aces."

# MIDDLE EASTERN PASTRY

See Greek, above; see International Delicatessen, Istanbul, Middle East Foods, and Sheherazade Bakery under "Middle Eastern" in the Ethnic Markets section.

I buy poultry in Chinatown whenever I can because it's always very fresh and because it's the only place where you can buy *whole* poultry. A Buddhist exemption from the Department of Agriculture allows Chinese markets to sell poultry with its head and feet (these are excellent additions to your stockpot). On weekends, you can even buy live chickens and game birds from street vendors parked on Stockton Street. Watch for a crowd gathered round a truck or van. The owner will take a live bird from its cage, tie its wings, and hand it to you to take home in a brown paper bag.

Many local poultry stores sell fresh poultry raised in the Santa Rosa–Petaluma area as well as game birds in season. They'll also provide you with duck and chicken livers for your pâtés; some of them will even bone out whole chickens or ducks for *galantines.* Read the Otto H. Reichardt duck farm entry for information about the local Pekin ducks sold in Chinatown.

Since much of the poultry sold today lacks flavor, organic chickens are a good buy because they taste better, even if you're not interested in the health implications of hormone-fed chickens. And with turkeys, there is no comparison: the organic birds are much tastier and juicier than the standard holiday bird.

Poultry stores also sell fresh country eggs, often delivered twice a week, and most health food stores carry organic fertile eggs, both brown and white.

Sources for game birds are also included here; these birds are most often available during the Thanksgiving and Christmas holidays.

*Note:* For roast duck and chicken, see the Take-Out section.

# RETAIL POULTRY MARKETS

## San Francisco ✳ General/Boned Poultry
## ANTONELLI AND SONS

*Cal-Mart Market, 3585 California Street, San Francisco 94118. Telephone (415) 752-7413. Hours: M–SAT 8–6:30.*

Antonelli's poultry section has chicken parts, small whole broilers for *pollo al diavolo,* slightly larger broilers, frying chickens, and plump four-pound roasting chickens. The large roasting chickens weighing in at six pounds are not true capons: since it is illegal in California to castrate chickens, all true capons are from out of state. Fresh game birds include quail and squab raised locally in Hayward.

The ranch eggs sold here are very fresh: laid one day and sold the next.

Antonelli and Sons will do all the boning you like. For one customer/friend they boned out a whole series of poultry for this galantine: a squab inside a fryer inside a duck inside a large roaster inside a goose inside a turkey. Don, who was invited to dinner, says the center cut was superb.

And if you want to learn to do it yourself, Don Antonelli teaches classes in boning at Judith Ets-Hokin Cooking School.

## San Francisco ✳ Smoked Poultry
## BEAR-LION PRODUCTIONS

*P.O. Box 31405, San Francisco 94131. Telephone (415) 586-8059. Call one week ahead.*

With a week's notice, you can order smoked turkey, duck, pheasant, quail, or squab from the Borel family's Bear-Lion Productions in San Francisco.

The drier birds are first given a wet marinade, while larger birds like turkey are dry-marinated; then each kind of bird is smoked with a special combination of mesquite and light fruit woods. All the birds are stuffed with dried fruits and vegetables to keep them moist while they're smoking. The result is superb smoked poultry, tender and still moist.

On request, they will give hams, bacon, sausages, and suckling pig the smoky touch. You can also bring your own fresh game to Bear-Lion Productions to be custom smoked.

### Napa Valley ✴ Geese
### JOICE AND MIKE BEATTY

*150 Olive Avenue, Angwin 94508. Telephone (707) 965-3753. Call first; geese available from November to first of year.*

At holiday time, Joice and Mike Beatty sell the geese they've raised. Reserve ahead by writing or calling. State your size preference. (Angwin is eight miles east of St. Helena.)

### San Francisco ✴ Chinese
### CANTON MARKET

*1135 Stockton Street, San Francisco 94133. Telephone (415) 982-8600. Hours: 8–6 daily.*

You can get fresh duck, squab, and chicken; chicken backs and feet for stock; and chicken and duck livers for pâté making at Chinatown's Canton Market.

### San Francisco ✴ Pressed Duck
### HING LUNG COMPANY

*1261 Stockton Street, San Francisco 94133. Telephone (415) 397-5521. Hours: 9–6 daily.*

Hing Lung Company has row upon row of pressed duck high in the window. Behind them are oversized bottles of Sprite and Coca-Cola. Try the barbecued liver or whole roasted duck, too.

### San Francisco ✴ Chinese
### ITALIAN MARKET

*966 Grant Avenue, San Francisco 94108. Telephone (415) 982-6414. Hours: SUN –F 8–5:30, SAT 7–5:30.*

The Italian Market is strictly a poultry store, and, despite its name, a Chinese poultry store with some of the freshest birds in the city. From the right side of the store, choose whole chickens, ducks, pullets, and squabs, as well as chicken parts. Add some of the chicken feet to your stockpot, or braise them and serve with black bean sauce. The left side of the store is a deli selling Peking duck, roast squab, and whole pale-yellow chickens with their heads. They'll sell any of the roast poultry by halves, too. Save time on your holiday *cassoulet* by buying a duck already roasted from Chinatown.

### San Francisco ✴ General
### JURGENSEN'S GROCERY

*2190 Union Street, San Francisco 94123. Telephone (415) 931-0100. Hours: M– SAT 9–6.*

Jurgensen's has fresh game in season— partridge, quail, and pheasant—plus local grain-fed chickens, frozen Long Island ducklings and, on special order, fresh Pekin ducks. For Thanksgiving and Christmas, they have special organic turkeys, all grain-fed in the Palm Springs desert.

For those who want to cook and eat well, but whose time is more limited than their budget, not only will Jurgensen's deliver groceries, they'll even let themselves in with your key and put perishable items away in the refrigerator.

### Sonoma County ✱ Pheasants/ Partridges
### KROUT'S PHEASANT FARM

*Jack and Verna Krout, 3234 Skillman Lane, Petaluma 94952. Telephone (707) 762-8613. Hours: T–SAT 1–5, September 15 through January.*

A visit to Krout's Pheasant Farm is a unique experience. There are birds everywhere: eagles, wild turkeys, pet turkeys, birds in aviaries. Mr. Krout has many decorative pheasant varieties, but for best eating he raises the Mongolian ring-necked pheasant. The Krouts sell these delicious game birds from September 15 until the end of January. Last year, they sold over two thousand. Give them two days' notice to have the dressed birds ready for you. He says the birds are best if you then age them three to five days in the refrigerator. Hen pheasants weigh about two pounds and feed two people, while cocks average three pounds and will feed three more than adequately.

He also sells plump chukar partridges. Just under a pound, one lovely little bird will serve one person splendidly.

### Sonoma County ✱ Pheasants
### LA QUINTA GAME BIRD RANCH

*4015 Frei Road, Sebastopol 95472. Telephone (707) 823-3142. Hours: 1–5 in season.*

July through January, La Quinta Game Bird Ranch has dressed pheasants for sale; fresh geese are available beginning in October, and fresh turkey beginning in November.

### East Bay ✱ General
### MAGNANI'S POULTRY

*6317 College Avenue, Oakland 94618. Telephone (415) 658-1122. Hours: M– SAT 8:30–6.*

Babe Magnani knows a lot about poultry. He was born and raised in the business. His father and his uncles, all from Lucca, Italy, owned Magnani Brothers, one of the largest poultry wholesalers in the Bay Area before the war. Started in 1917, it was based in the old Housewives' Market in Oakland. A photograph on Magnani's wall shows Babe as a teenager working at the family poultry stand. It looks like something out of a present-day Tuscan market, with chickens hanging upside down in a regular pattern. Chickens were sold whole, then—that means with heads and feet. "In the old days," Babe says, "they used to grow the chickens right out in Hayward and had their slaughtering houses there, too."

These days Magnani Poultry is a small shop on College Avenue in Oakland. Babe sells you whole chickens, chicken parts, chicken liver, and fresh capon, and will even show you how to bone a chicken breast. He's one of the few sources outside Chinatown for fresh white Pekin duck from Petaluma. The standard Long Island duckling, fattier than the Pekin, is sold frozen here. Pâté makers can get fresh duck livers by calling ahead.

At holiday time, he has fresh pheasant and fresh geese, available by special order.

**San Francisco ∗ Chinese**
## MAN SUNG COMPANY

*1116 Grant Avenue, San Francisco 94133. Telephone (415) 982-5918. Hours: 8–6 daily.*

Man Sung Company has fresh chicken parts at good prices.

---

**San Francisco ∗ Game/Specialty Poultry**
## NIGHT BIRD GAME POULTRY COMPANY

*Wholesale: 537 Divisadero Street, San Francisco 94117. Telephone (415) 922-3090.*
*Retail: 1501 Haight Street, San Francisco 94117. Telephone (415) 552-4650. Hours: 9–6:30 daily.*

Young former chef Gerald Prolman started out selling game birds to the city's finest restaurants. He was a treasured source that chefs shared among themselves, until he opened a retail store on Divisadero Street last year. That store is now his wholesale outlet; the new retail store opened at Haight and Ashbury just before Christmas of 1981.

Private cooks can now buy locally raised quail, partridge, pheasant, squab, goose, Pekin duck, *poussin* (tender baby chickens, just one pound each), and organic chickens. The store has some poultry and game birds, custom smoked by Willie Bird in Santa Rosa, as well as Willie's own smoked chicken and turkey. Quail and squab are available both whole and boned; squab comes cut into breasts or double breasts.

In addition to fresh Pekin duck, you can buy frozen mallards and frozen *mulards* (a tasty duck with lots of breast meat, much prized in France), as well as frozen true capons. (There are no local capons, because castration of poultry is illegal in California.)

Caterers who wish to buy case quantities should call the wholesale store. Most poultry and game is available every week, but call for availability.

---

**San Francisco ∗ Chinese**
## ON SANG POULTRY

*1114 Grant Avenue, San Francisco 94133. Telephone (415) 982-4694. Hours: 8–6 daily.*

There is no question but that Grant Avenue's On Sang Poultry has really fresh poultry: you can buy it live from the few cages stacked in front. On Sang used to be the only place where you could get freshly killed chickens. Now there are lots of such sources, but On Sang is still a best bet for fresh whole chickens. And whole here means with the head and feet. The Chinese community has special permission, on religious grounds, to sell poultry this way.

On Sang also has fresh duck eggs. They're delicious used all the ways chicken eggs are used, but you can also make your own salted eggs with them. Chinese cooking teacher Janice Lo uses this method: Dissolve coarse salt in hot water until the water won't accept any more salt. Cool to room temperature, then add fresh duck eggs. Wait three weeks.

Take-out dishes at On Sang include duck and tongue, and there's also a selection of fresh fish.

### East Bay * Live Poultry
## THE SHADOW BOX

*20819 Nunes Avenue, Castro Valley 94546. Telephone (415) 881-5889. Hours: M-SAT 9:30-6.*

If you really want to be fanatic about fresh eggs and poultry, you can raise your own. The Shadow Box in Castro Valley can supply you with live chicks, ducklings, bantams, turkey poults, and goslings in season. If you'd rather skip their awkward adolescence, at the holidays there are live full-grown, eating-sized geese and turkeys for sale, all hatched by the store's owner.

### San Francisco * Cases of Poultry
## TERMINAL MARKET

*1925 Jerrold Avenue, San Francisco 94124. Telephone (415) 648-4667. Hours: M-F 8:30-5, SAT 8:30-3.*

Terminal Market is the retail store for American Poultry Company, a wholesaler. Here you can buy fresh whole chickens and chicken parts either by the pound or by the case. Whole chickens come twenty to a case; chicken parts are sold in forty-pound cases. For stock, you can buy ten-pound bags of chicken necks or sixty-pound cases of chicken backs. For forcemeats or stuffings, they sell boned chicken breasts as well as cooked or raw chicken meat off the bone.

Fresh rabbits weigh about 2-1/2 pounds and come six to the case or by the pound. Cornish hens, quail, pheasants, Long Island ducklings, and genuine capons are all available frozen.

### Sonoma County * Geese
## WELLS RANCH

*7677 Occidental Road, Sebastopol 95472. Telephone (707) 823-2769. Hours: W-SAT 9-12, 1-6; SUN 9-12, 1-3.*

All through November and December, the Wells family sells fresh-dressed geese for your holiday table. Their birds have been given no antibiotics or hormones. Fed on fresh corn and apples, these young geese are tender, with a good flavor. The dressed birds weigh in at seven to ten pounds; plan on one pound per person.

The Wellses caution buyers not to ruin the goose in the cooking. They say the secret to roasting a goose is a slow fire and a long cooking time. Every customer gets a recipe for Grandma Wells' Drunken Goose—the goose is doused with a can of beer during the last half hour of cooking, and the cook can have a bottle of beer, too.

### Sonoma County * Organic Turkey
## WILLIE BIRD TURKEYS

*6350 Highway 12, Santa Rosa 95401. Telephone (707) 545-2832. Hours: M-F 9-6, SAT 9-5.*

"Willie" is William Benedetti. He first started raising Willie Bird turkeys when he was in high school as a Future Farmer project almost fifteen years ago. The birds were such a success that he went into business. A juicy Willie Bird turkey roasted to a deep mahogany brown is the centerpiece of a memorable Thanksgiving dinner.

Why do they taste so good? Willie's birds are a special strain he's developed working with one of the biggest breeders in the business. The meat yield is greater than the average turkey, and the birds are big, though they come in all sizes from ten pounds to twenty-five-pound hens; males can reach thirty-five pounds. Willie's birds are raised on normal feed, unadulterated with hormones.

At holiday time, a phone call will reserve you a fat bird, but many Bay Area butchers stock Willie Bird turkeys for their customers. The turkeys are also available at the Co-op superparkets.

Besides the two turkey farms, the family now has Willie Bird Restaurant in Santa Rosa, where you'll be served all manner of turkey, from the traditional roast bird to turkey steaks and turkey *scaloppine* Italian style.

# WHOLESALE POULTRY

Some poultry wholesalers will sell to the public, but you must usually buy in full cases. Some, however, will sell split cases of chickens or parts for just a bit more per pound. You can also buy ten- or twenty-five-pound bags of chicken necks. Most of them can be used for stock, the rest for *charcuterie*. (There's a French country sausage that uses the skin of chicken necks as a casing.)

Like the meat wholesalers, most poultry dealers ask that you call ahead, pick up the next day, and pay in cash. They also usually keep restaurant trade hours, opening early (around six or seven), sometimes closing at the lunch hour, and reopening until two or three in the afternoon.

**East Bay * General**
## ALLIED POULTRY SALES

*333 Clay Street, Oakland 94607. Telephone (415) 763-6200. Hours: M–F 7–4.*

In addition to fresh chickens, Allied Poultry Sales has fresh rabbits, both 2-1/2-pound fryers and stewing rabbits for your autumn *civet*. The stewing rabbits, however, are only killed on order, so call ahead. The capons are genuine, run eight pounds, and are only sold frozen. Call in advance for fresh squab. Usually pheasant and guinea hens are sold frozen, as are Long Island ducklings.

A case is the minimum order here, but in some instances, they will break a case. Ask. They are friendly to cooks and caterers.

**San Jose Area * General**
## MELANI POULTRY

*985 Richard Avenue, Santa Clara 95052. Telephone (408) 777-4145. Call for times.*

You can buy chicken, chicken parts, turkey, duck, geese, squab, and rabbits by the case from this wholesaler. Call first.

**East Bay * General**
## PARENTI POULTRY COMPANY

*721 Seventy-seventh Avenue, Oakland 94621. Telephone (415) 568-7493. Hours: M–F 7–4.*

Parenti Poultry is an East Bay wholesaler of rabbits, chickens (from young broilers up to big roasters), and turkeys. They have frozen Long Island ducklings and fresh squab. Here they will sell you a split case of poultry and charge you just 3¢ more per pound to do it.

**Sonoma County * Kosher/Buddhist**
## PETALUMA POULTRY PROCESSORS

*4700 Lakeville Highway, Petaluma 94952. Telephone (707) 763-1904. Wholesale to the trade only.*

Because of a special Buddhist exemption granted by the U.S. Department of Agriculture, Chinatown markets are allowed to sell whole chickens with heads and feet intact. Called pullets, these birds are processed by Petaluma

Poultry Processors and come in medium and large sizes. Since both head and the feet enrich a chicken stock considerably, these birds are perfect for making *coq au vin* or cock-a-leekie soup.

A rabbi comes to the Petaluma Poultry Processors to kill poultry for those who keep kosher. These are then supplied to kosher stores in the Bay Area.

---

**Sonoma County ∗ Ducks**
# OTTO H. REICHARDT DUCK DUCK FARM

*3770 Middle Two Rock Road, Petaluma 94952. Telephone (707) 762-6319. Wholesale to the trade only.*

The history of the domestic duck goes back well over three thousand years to China, where the Chinese bred the colored feathers out of the mallard to produce a pure white bird known as the Pekin duck. Many of the masterpieces of this great cuisine have been built around this duck so beloved of Chinese gourmands.

The Pekin duck did not arrive in America, with its once-abundant supply of wild ducks, until the late 1880's, when a Yankee clipper ship on its way to the East Coast by way of South America docked briefly in San Francisco. Among its cargo were three dozen Pekin ducks destined for the East Coast, but sometime during the ship's stay, one dozen of the birds disappeared.

The clipper ship continued on to the East Coast where the remaining two dozen ducks formed the beginning of what was at one time the largest duck-raising co-op in the world. At its peak the Long Island duck co-op sold 14 million "Long Island ducklings" a year.

In San Francisco, these are only available frozen.

The missing dozen ducks who jumped ship in San Francisco, were, it seems, sold to a small poultry farm right in the middle of the city. Fifteen years later in 1901, Otto H. Reichardt bought the small concern with its stock of white Pekin ducks. Otto H's grandson, Donald, still runs the Otto H. Reichardt Duck Farm. Now located in Petaluma, the farm raises the white Pekin duck exclusively, one million of them a year, with most of these beautifully tender ducks going to Chinese customers all over California.

Raised without hormones or antibiotics, Reichardt's ducks are all fed on natural grains. When properly cooked, the flesh of the fresh Pekin duck is butter-tender and moist. In fact, when André Daguin, the chef from the Gasgogne region in France famous for its cuisine based on duck, was in San Francisco last year, he was entranced with our local Pekin ducks.

But some of California's French chefs, who find the Pekin too fatty for their tastes, have been producing here for use in their own restaurants a cross of the Muscovy duck and the Pekin. These ducks are known in France as *canetons mulards*, because, like mules, the offspring of this cross between two different species are infertile.

---

**East Bay ∗ Squabs**
# SQUAB PRODUCERS OF CALIFORNIA

*23682 Clawither Road, Hayward 94540. Telephone (415) 785-0344. Hours: M-F 8-5.*

Squab Producers of California has plump, tasty squabs both fresh and frozen. Though there is no quantity discount for retail customers, prices are still lower than at a poultry market and you don't have to buy a whole case from this wholesaler.

# *Produce*

See also Herbs and Spices and ethnic sections for additional ethnic produce. See the Natural Foods section for additional organic produce listings.

## GENERAL PRODUCE

### Contra Costa
### ARATA FRUIT AND VEGETABLE STAND

*Corner of Camino Diablo and Vasco Road, Brentwood 94513. Telephone (415) 634-1031. When: May to October, depending on growing season. Open M–F 8–6, SAT–SUN 8–6 or sometimes 7.*

Cookbook author Marian Cunningham claims she finds the summer's best peaches, cherries, and berries here at Arata Fruit and Vegetable Stand in Brentwood. Load the back of your car with flats of berries and fruit, invite your friends home to gossip, and consult Cunningham's revision of the classic *Fanny Farmer's Cookbook* for jams. Specialties of the stand include sweet white corn, melons, and tomatoes.

To sweeten your breads and cookies, the fruit stand sells the thick honey produced at an adjoining farm. On weekends, they sell a Portuguese sweet bread made by a Portuguese employee of the farm.

### East Bay
### BERKELEY BOWL MARKET PLACE

*2777 Shattuck Avenue, Berkeley 94705. Telephone (415) 843-6929. Hours: M–F 9–7, SAT 9–6.*

Glen Yasuda has taken the vast space of a former bowling alley and transformed it into a lively marketplace complete with produce, fish, meat, cheese, coffee, Oriental groceries, and a modest wine section stocked with Berkeley's own Numano sake and plum wine.

The produce is trimmed and well-tended and available in great variety. Oversized bundles of greens (mustard, kale, collard, turnip, dandelion), sweet and hot chilies, bundles of *daikon* radishes, Belgian endive, and fresh herbs compete for your attention. Big bins are filled with sweet Valencia oranges, Texas grapefruit, and the rest of the season's fruit.

In addition to an exceptional selection of Oriental vegetables, Berkeley Bowl Market Place has tropical produce, too: tiny finger bananas, red bananas, *plátanos* (cooking bananas), *jícamas*, *tomatillos*, *chayotes*, pineapples, fresh coconuts, and several kinds of mangoes.

Near the refrigerated Japanese foodstuffs, they have fresh Oriental mushrooms: *shiitake*, the most nutritious mushroom; grayish oyster mushrooms, and occasionally, the very rare Japanese *matsutake* mushroom, grown in Seattle. They buy Traditional Tofu in bulk and package it themselves. There are fresh Oriental noodles, *sukiyaki* noodles, Japanese pickles, and condiments, too.

Berkeley Bowl Market Place proves that large markets don't have to operate like supermarkets. They can carry a wide variety of perishable foodstuffs and still sell everything in top condition. Their secret? Knowledgeable buying and a real concern for quality. Even the checkout line feels different—it's clear the checkers like working here.

**East Bay**
# BURNAFORD'S PRODUCE

*2635 Ashby Avenue, Berkeley 94705. Telephone (415) 548-0348. Hours: M-T, TH-SAT 9-6, W 9-7:30, SUN 12-4.*

Burnaford's Produce is well provided with Mrs. Poggi's fresh-cut herbs (see Herbs and Spices) until quite late in the season: fragrant bundles of marjoram, oregano, thyme, rosemary, tarragon, mint, sorrel, Italian parsley, and, of course, sweet basil. You can find her pungent fresh horseradish root, too, and fat fresh fava beans in season.

Unlike some produce markets, at Burnaford's you can usually expect to find ripe fruit. No squeezing through dozens of stone-hard plums to find one that is slightly less hard. At the height of summer, piles of orangey-gold mangoes ripen in the sunny front window.

**San Francisco**
# CAL-MART MARKET

*3585 California Street, San Francisco 94118. Telephone (415) 751-3516. Hours: M-SAT 8-6:30.*

Gerry and Evano Dal Porto (junior partners with senior partner Joe Gianpaoli) have a reputation for being tough and shrewd produce buyers. They arrive early at the produce terminal—at an hour that to the rest of us is the middle of the night—and prowl through the newly arrived produce, showing no mercy to what they feel is inferior. They're both very much a presence in the store, carefully arranging fruit and dispensing advice. They wrap big bunches of herbs in sleeves of plastic like flowers: mint, basil, tarragon, dill—so fresh the brush of your fingers sends forth a deep fragrance.

The broccoli florets are tight and closed. The artichokes come in all sizes, including the tender baby arti-

chokes. The fancy asparagus comes in long and slender spears or as fat, tender tips. Blue Lake beans are crisp and unblemished, while new red potatoes are sorted into baby and regular. The root vegetables—carrots, beets, turnips—are sold in bunches with their tops. And the greens—chicory; escarole; oak leaf, butter, and red lettuces; sorrel; and delicate dandelion leaves—are as fresh as if you'd picked them yourself.

Fruits are ripe and offered in as many varieties as the market will bear. The display of berries is beautiful and may include olallies, raspberries, boysenberries, loganberries, blueberries.

**San Jose Area**
# THE FLEA MARKET

*12000 Berryessa Road, San Jose 95133. Telephone (408) 289-1550. When: Saturday and Sunday mornings starting at 7:30.*

Shop for fresh fruits and vegetables from stalls and trucks parked among all the confusion of this bustling flea market's regular wares. San Jose's Flea Market has one of the best selections of all the varieties of fresh chili peppers. The word is out among homesick Latin Americans, who regularly make an expedition here to find all the makings for authentic fresh *salsas* spiked with fresh green *cilantro*.

**Marin County**
# GREEN GULCH FARM

*Zen Center, Highway 1 (Shoreline Highway), Mill Valley 94941. Hours: Sunday morning beginning around 11, until sold out.*

On Sundays, some of the organic produce grown on the Zen Center's Green Gulch Farm is sold at a little roadside stand on Highway 1. Don't sleep late, though. It opens about 11 and is sometimes sold out by noon.

**San Francisco**
# GREEN GULCH GREENGROCER

*297 Page Street, San Francisco 94102. Telephone (415) 431-7250. Hours: M-F 9-7, SAT 11-6.*

Green Gulch Greengrocer has organic produce purchased directly from truck farmers and farmer-friends of the Zen Center at reasonable prices. Since the store is connected with the Center's fine vegetarian restaurant, Green's at Fort Mason, the buyers shop for produce daily, rather than every two or three days as some produce markets do.

Some of the luscious produce is overflow from the model gardens at the Zen Center's Green Gulch Farm in Marin County, where French intensive gardening methods are used. In summer there are bundled fresh herbs, tender lettuce, and sun-ripened fruit.

Watch for frequent cheese specials at very good prices. You can also buy the whole line of delicious Tassajara Bakery breads here.

**East Bay**
# MONTEREY FOODS

*1550 Hopkins Street, Berkeley 94707. Telephone (415) 526-6042. Hours: M-SAT 9-6.*

Shopping at Monterey Foods is a pleasure to be savored. You may start with a shopping list, but it's better to let yourself be inspired by the bountiful produce itself. Since much of the high-quality produce comes from small truck farmers, you'll find vegetables in varieties you may not have seen in markets.

Want to make a Provençal *ratatouille*? You can find baby zucchini as slender as your finger—some even with the bright blossom attached—and their cousin, a brilliant yellow zucchini. There may be some satiny white summer squash to add to the pot. You can sometimes choose from four kinds of eggplant: regular, Italian, Japanese, and an albino variety washed with violet. Tomatoes? They have them, ripe and red. Besides the overused and abused green bell pepper, they have sweet yellow Italian peppers, true red pimientoes, and sweet red bells.

In summer, there are heaps of small pickling cucumbers, bundles of fresh herbs, and crates of all the kinds of fruit grown in California: grapes, pears, plums, nectarines, peaches, apricots, kiwis.

Pick up a crate of the truly luscious oversized strawberries, still with their stems. They're wonderful dipped in a barely sweetened sour cream or, if you want to be really fancy, in bittersweet or white chocolate.

Prices at Monterey Foods are low. There's nowhere else you can buy such a lavish stack of groceries for so little money.

## San Francisco/Napa Valley
# THE OAKVILLE GROCERY

*1555 Pacific Avenue, San Francisco 94102. Telephone (415) 885-4411. Hours: M-F 10:30-6:30, SAT 10-6, SUN 12-6.*
*7856 St. Helena Highway, Oakville 94562. Telephone (707) 944-8802. Hours: M-SAT 10-6, SUN 10-5.*

The produce departments at both of the Oakville groceries are as elegant as that of any *épicerie de luxe* on the fashionable Place de la Madeleine in Paris. Perfectly beautiful, perfectly ripe fruits and choice vegetables are displayed in country baskets, the bounty of the whole earth's harvest: local artichokes, Mexican melons, tropical coconuts and mangoes, Washington apples. None of it is inexpensive; you've got to pay for such earthly splendor.

Produce man David Findley works hard to procure the grocery's exceptional produce. His day starts at midnight when he sets out for the produce terminal. He wants to be there *early*; he doesn't want to take a chance of not getting his pick of the produce that's both good-looking and good tasting. But he doesn't stop there—he cultivates other sources for varieties of vegetables and fruits that are beloved by cooks, but are too delicate or not profitable enough for big commercial growers. Sometimes this means buying from local truck farmers or private gardens. He's planning to hire small farmers to grow special vegetables just for the store: *arugula*, an Italian salad green; or maybe even *radicchio*, a red chicory from Treviso.

In the springtime, you'll find fresh Half Moon Bay peas, thumb-sized baby carrots, tender blades of asparagus. Summer brings tiny sweet cantaloupes from Mexico and strawberries from the few growers whose fruit still has flavor. Fill your basket with fully tree-ripened peaches from one grower who brings in twelve varieties throughout the season; vine-ripened tomatoes from St. Helena; hybrid blackberries from the Napa Valley; and lovely old-fashioned icicle radishes.

Deep-fry a bouquet of golden squash blossoms as part of your *fritto misto*. Lay in a winter's hoard of local braided garlic at the end of the summer. Look for midwinter jumbo cranberries from Wisconsin, waxy yellow potatoes, small rose-skinned boiling potatoes, and tiny matched-pearl onions for stews.

## San Francisco
# ORANGE LAND

*1055 Stockton Street, San Francisco 94133. Telephone (415) 392-3236. Hours: 8 am-8:30 pm daily.*

Everything is in bins outside the store— a mountain of oranges, apples and lemons, plus grapes or persimmons— all for so many to the dollar.

Just drive by, wave your dollar out the window, and one of the crew will bag your oranges or apples and take your money, all before the light changes.

## East Bay
# THE PRODUCE CENTER

*1500 Shattuck Avenue, Berkeley 94709. Telephone (415) 848-8100. Hours: M-SAT 9-6:30.*

This corner produce market near Walnut Square in Berkeley has plentiful, well-tended vegetables with a particularly good selection of salad greens— lettuce, curly endive, Belgian endive, watercress, spinach—and fresh herbs, including sorrel, all in top condition.

Toward spring you can find the makings for an inspired *pasta primavera* here: fresh peas, snowy mushrooms, thumb-sized French carrots, baby zucchini, small heads of cauliflower, and broccoli with closed, tight florets. In summer, they sell small herb plants for your kitchen garden or herb box and a classy selection of the season's berries for pies and *sorbets*.

## Peninsula
### WEBB RANCH

*2720 Alpine Road, Menlo Park 94025 (on the corner of 280). Telephone (415) 854-6334. When: about mid-April through October, 9:30-6 daily.*

Webb Ranch has a roadside stand to the west of the Stanford Shopping Center in Palo Alto where you can find wonderful Blue Lake beans; "ranch" tomatoes, red on the outside *and* the inside; flats of bright, tasty strawberries and all the pie berries: raspberries, loganberries, olallie berries, all grown at the ranch. Go-fers for Berkeley's Chez Panisse restaurant are often sent here to pick up baby sweet corn, baby green beans, and other choice vegetables for the restaurant's menu.

## East Bay
### YASAI PRODUCE MARKET

*6301 College Avenue, Oakland 94618. Telephone (415) 655-4880. Hours: M–SAT 10-6.*

Yasai Market is part of the complex of shops near Alcatraz and College avenues in Berkeley that includes Curds and Whey, Ver Brugge Meats, and Magnani Poultry.

The produce at this colorful market spills out onto the street, where it vies for attention with a flower stand's vivid blooms.

Piles of melons, curly-headed endive, fat bunches of impeccably fresh herbs, baby red potatoes, miniature boiling onions, *jícamas*, baby zucchini, sleek Japanese eggplants, and the season's sampling of quality fruits are all beautifully displayed.

In addition, the market carries a careful selection of ingredients for Oriental cuisines: several kinds of *tofu*, *won ton* wrappers, fresh noodles, rice vinegar, *beni-shoga* (pickled ginger), and *wasabi* (horseradish).

# SPECIALTY PRODUCE

## Central Valley * Olives
### ADAM'S OLIVES

*Adam's Olive Ranch, 19401 Road 220, Strathmore 93267. Telephone (209) 568-2626. Call first.*

On Saturdays, Fred Adams loads up his van with olives grown and cured on his small organic farm in Strathmore near Fresno and drives all the way in to the San Francisco Farmers' Market. You'll find him in front of his stall calling out to the crowd to come try some olives. A big, friendly man weathered by the seasons spent working the olive trees, he'll scoop out a few of the firm-fleshed beauties for you and tell you how they're made.

"The olives are pickled Spanish style, that is, still green, and, instead of using the usual lye, we use the old process of wood ash. Our olives are made entirely without preservatives." The Adams family has had a lot of experience: "The last batch we made was eighty tons!"

They make a classic, tangy Sicilian-style olive, as well as a smoked version, but the most popular is their green-spiced olive cured with cloves of garlic, hot red pepper, and secret spices.

The price is low, but you can get an even better price by buying two-gallon tubs or even thirty-pound buckets. He'll also sell you cases of olives in jars at wholesale prices.

Adam's Olives are distributed to many Bay Area food stores and are also sold at the Alameda flea market on the weekends.

### Sonoma County * Truffle Trees
### AGRI-TRUFFLE, INC.

*P.O. Box 6801, Santa Rosa, CA 95406. Telephone (707) 525-8334. Wholesale only.*

Most American food lovers have had more contact with chocolate truffles than with the real thing. Fresh truffles appear in this country at Christmastime, flown in from their native region of Perigord in south central France. They're rare, are getting even more so all the time, and cost the earth. Prices have been known to reach an astonishing five hundred dollars a pound. Hardcore addicts will pay the price, but as legions of American gourmets cook and eat their way through the classic French cuisine and long to taste the fabled subterranean mushroom they've read about, the demand (and price) goes up.

The homely object of all this passion is a black gnarled lump of fungus, usually one to six inches across. Covered with miniscule diamond-shaped facets, the Perigord truffle is also known as the black diamond. Its musky, primeval aroma is overpowering and intoxicating, its taste earthy and seductive. Yes, they're rare. Hard to find, scattered in the wild, they spend their entire life cycle underground near roots of certain trees, usually filberts or oaks at the edges of clearings. Why some trees are host to the fungus and others are not

has always been a mystery, and attempts to cultivate truffles have failed until recently. In the late 1970s, French scientists were able to artificially innoculate seedling oaks and filberts with truffle spores. Agri-Truffe, a company licensed by the French government, then developed a workable method for propagating the trees and has successfully produced truffles in France for the last four years.

This is where transplanted Frenchman François Picart, an entrepreneur best known for transforming California's basic backyard snails into succulent escargots, enters the American truffle picture. A native of Perigord, Picart dreamed of growing truffle trees in his adopted land—the California wine country. He entered into partnership with the French Agri-Truffe firm to form the Sonoma-based company, Agri-Truffe, Inc.

While Sonoma County has the right climate for growing truffles, it doesn't have the right soil. Hence, Picart moved his site down the coast to Paso Robles, near San Luis Obispo, where he planted an initial five thousand truffle trees. His plans are to plant twenty thousand trees annually here and at other sites with the proper soil and climate throughout California.

Since Federal regulations prohibit directly importing the French seedlings into this country, Picart's trees are started from seeds and, at three months, innoculated with truffle *mycelium.* The seedlings are placed in containers with sterilized dirt and then coddled in greenhouses for a year before planting outdoors.

Since it takes three to seven years before these trees begin to produce truffles, Picart doesn't expect the first California crop until 1985. Until then, there's a lot to do, he says. For example, training dogs (or pigs) to sniff out buried truffles is expensive and time consuming. "My dog is half trained now," says Picart. "He can tell the difference between a truffle and a snail."

Picart's company will also sell innoculated seedlings and will advise people who are interested in growing their own truffle crops.

## Peninsula * Garlic
## BLOOMFIELD FARMS

*175 South San Antonio Road, Los Altos 94022. Telephone (415) 941-0410. Hours: M–F 8:30–12.*

Bloomfield Farms, an independent garlic grower, sells traditional garlic braids in California Ponderosa pine crates that are suitable for shipping and reusable. Buy your year's supply in the summer—the crop is often sold out by late fall.

The farm's useful booklet *For the Love of Garlic* gives some historical notes on garlic and includes "The Golden Rules of Garlic," a list of techniques including how to make and use a fresh all-purpose garlic purée.

The first Gilroy Garlic Festival was held on the grounds of the Bloomfield Ranch in 1979.

*Mail order.*

## San Francisco * Chinese
## BULL'S PRODUCE

*720 Pacific Avenue, San Francisco 94133. Telephone (415) 956-3381. Hours: M–SAT 8–5:30.*

It's difficult to pass through on the sidewalk, so many Chinese shoppers are pinching fruit and sorting through vegetables in front of Bull's Produce on Pacific Avenue. This small store is always crowded because Bull's has good prices and well-groomed produce: ropes of garlic, mounds of fresh ginger, rows of stately winter melons, bundles of long beans.

## San Francisco * Latino
## CALIFORNIA FRUIT MARKET

*3104 Twenty-fourth Street, San Francisco 94110. Telephone (415) 826-5663. Hours: 9–7 daily.*

An old-fashioned green and yellow striped awning shades a profusion of vegetables piled high in front of the store: oranges, grapefruit, lemons and limes, fat tomatoes from Mexico, and mounds of dark, leathery-skinned avocados. Heavy bunches of green *plátanos* (large cooking bananas) can be sliced in rounds and fried to make chips or cooked with other vegetables in tropical stews. Golden-ripe *plátanos maduros* are delicious fried and served with slightly sour *crema fresca*, or Guatemalan cream.

Inside, you can find all the makings for the delicious fresh *salsas* made all over Latin America: parsley, *cilantro*, sweet green pepper, lemon, and all the kinds of fresh hot peppers—small, pointed, dark-green *chiles serranos*; long, mild *chiles poblanos*; *chiles Californias*; and *chiles jalapeños*.

## East Bay * Garlic
## DELEGEANE FARMS

*1092 Amito Drive, Berkeley 94705. Mail order only.*

Berkeley's own Delegeane Farms sells popular elephant garlic: the giant, but mild variety that eliminates the tedious peeling of tiny cloves.

## Peninsula * Fruits
## DE MARTINI ORCHARD

*66 North San Antonio Road, between El Camino Real and Los Altos, Los Altos 94022. Telephone (415) 948-0881. Hours: 9-6 daily.*

The pick of the summer's crop of ripe melons, juicy strawberries, plums, and peaches are available at De Martini Orchard, at prices competitive with or well below supermarkets. Check their nuts, dried fruits, and grains, too. In late fall and through Christmas, fresh mincemeat and candied fruits are sold for holiday baking. They have organic honey as well.

## Sonoma County * Shiitake Mushrooms
## GOURMET MUSHROOM

*3620 Frei Road (P.O. Box 391), Sebastopol 95472. Telephone (707) 823-1743. Retail orders by mail; otherwise wholesale to the trade only.*

Many cooks are familiar with the imported dried mushrooms known as *shiitake.* A prime ingredient in both Chinese and Japanese cuisines, this nutritious, wonderfully flavored mushroom has an astounding 14 percent protein and is rich in B-complex vitamins.

A small Sebastopol-based company, Gourmet Mushroom, is successfully cultivating the temperamental *shiitake* mushroom in California.

The researchers at Gourmet Mushroom first began experimenting with the *shiitake* over ten years ago in Toronto, where they were the first to grow them in the western world. Three years ago they set up an operation in California, where the technology for growing the mushrooms was further refined. Their experiments developed methods to cultivate the mushroom year round and decreased the growing cycle from two years to four months. In the Orient, *shiitake* mushrooms grow on oak logs, but in Gourmet Mushroom's environmentally controlled process, oak wood chips and sawdust are used as a base.

Most of the *shiitake* mushrooms produced here are sold to fine Chinese restaurants in Los Angeles, San Francisco, and New York. Though Gourmet Mushroom's business is technically wholesale, and they haven't encouraged people to buy directly from them, you can order the dried mushrooms by mail in one-pound quantities. The fresh mushrooms do occasionally turn up in Bay Area markets, too. If you see fresh *shiitake,* be sure to buy some. You don't need an elaborate recipe. They're a wonderful treat simply sautéed or added to any stir-fried dish.

Gourmet Mushroom's dried *shiitake* are considerably fresher than the imported Oriental mushrooms and hold considerably more flavor. Imported mushrooms available in Chinatown often sit for long periods of time in huge warehouses, sometimes reaching your store only after a period of two years. This causes a noticeable deterioration of taste.

Gourmet Mushroom also cultivates the delicate pale-gray oyster mushroom, a native of Europe that is much easier to grow than the *shiitake.*

## East Bay * Mushrooms
## THE KINOKO COMPANY

*8139 Capwell Drive, Oakland 94621. Telephone (415) 562-3671. Hours: M-F 1-6.*

The Kinoko Company has kits available for growing your own fresh mushrooms at home: common buttons, velvet stems, tree oysters, wood ears, and *shiitake.* They also have dried Oriental mushrooms for sale, as well as books and mushroom herbal teas.

Occasionally, the company also has a small quantity of fresh mushrooms available to restaurants and to the public.

*Mail order ($15 minimum, $2 shipping charge).*

### San Francisco * Oriental
### LEE YUEN

*1131 Stockton Street, San Francisco 94133. Telephone (415) 956-0216. Hours: 9:30–6 daily.*

Lee Yuen has a lot of good produce impossibly fitted into the long, narrow store—all the Oriental vegetables plus herbs and Oriental groceries. You can even buy the tiny fresh red peppers, fiery hot. Look around. You'll find a big burlap sack of pine nuts in the shell, and fresh lemon grass for Indonesian cuisine sits in a bucket right by the cash register.

### Mendocino County * Garlic
### GUINNESS McFADDEN

*Potter Valley 95469. Telephone (707) 743-1614. Mail order only.*

The McFadden Farm sells their own high-quality garlic by the braid, by the pound, or in one-pound net bags. One-pound bags of their large shallots and half-pound boxes of wild rice from Mendocino County's mountain valleys are also available.

At Christmas they make fragrant bay leaf wreaths, sixteen inches in diameter, from leaves gathered in the hills above the farm's vineyard.

Send a self-addressed stamped envelope for an order card. All prices include shipping costs.

### San Francisco * Latino
### MISSION FARMERS' MARKET

*2076 Mission Street, San Francisco 94110. Telephone (415) 285-6634. Hours: M-SAT 9–6, SUN 10–5 (hours may vary).*

The Greek-owned Mission Farmers' Market is filled with the sweet smell of tropical produce: papayas, pineapples, mangoes, bananas. The *plátanos* here are in various degrees of ripeness, and there is a crate of delicious, tiny *bananos manzanas* (finger or apple bananas) right outside the door. In the back there are *chayotes* with thick dimpled skins and satiny green *tomatillos* with their papery, olive-brown husks.

### Marin County * Mushrooms
### MUSHROOMPEOPLE

*Bob Harris/Jennifer Snyder, P.O. Box 158, Inverness 94937. Telephone (415) 663-8504. Mail order.*

Mushroompeople is a mail-order source for information and supplies for cultivating mushrooms at home. They can supply you with mushroom cultures (*agaricus brunescens*, wood blewits, and the Oriental *shiitake* mushroom), culture supplies, tools for sterile work with mycelial culture, and compost supplies.

Write for a free catalog that includes books on mushroom cultivation, mushroom hunting, ethnomycology, and mushroom lore.

## San Francisco * Organic
## VERITABLE VEGETABLES

*233 Industrial Street, San Francisco 94124. Telephone (415) 468-0960. Hours: W–TH and SAT 7 am–9 am. Cases or half cases only.*

Veritable Vegetables is run by an all-woman collective. (Ten years ago when the store was first founded, a woman at the produce terminal in the early hours of the morning was a rare sight.) The experienced buyers at Veritable Vegetables look for quality produce at low prices. They want to support the small farmer who takes the extra care to grow organic produce. Veritable Vegetables in turn services collectives and small co-op stores, restaurants, and buying groups. Though most of their business is wholesale, the public can buy the mostly organic produce by the case or half-case at wholesale prices. Call in your order if possible.

## San Francisco * Chinese
## WO SOON
## PRODUCE COMPANY

*1210 Stockton Street, San Francisco 94133. Telephone (415) 989-2350. Hours: 7:30–6 daily.*

This big, open-fronted store with boxes of Chinese vegetables stacked both outside and inside is one of the most popular Chinatown produce stores. Business starts early, when awesome quantities of *bok choy*, Chinese mustard greens, and Chinese spinach stacked five feet high line the street waiting to be unloaded.

The old wide-slatted wooden floors make this one of the most appealing produce stores in town. They have Chinese watercress flown in from Hawaii, where it grows big leaved and full of flavor; gorgeous white ginger from Hawaii, blushed with rose at its edges; two kinds of long beans, one pale green and fat, the other slender, an elegant dark green.

Enormous winter melons, large enough to last the entire season, are lined up on the back wall. Buy some bunches of the curly Chinese mustard greens for pickling, or use it in lion's head soup with pork meatballs.

# FARMERS' MARKETS

## San Francisco
## PRODUCE MARKET

*United Nations Plaza at Seventh and Market streets, San Francisco 94103. When: Sundays 10–3.*

Since 1981, the Market Street Development Project and the American Friends Service Committee have jointly operated a downtown produce market Sundays from 10 to 3, to give the elderly and low-income residents of the Tenderloin and south of Market neighborhoods fresh low-priced produce.

## Peninsula
## SAN MATEO COUNTY
## FARMERS' MARKET

*Corner of Hamilton and Broadway in downtown Redwood City 94063. Telephone (415) 364-8181. When: Usually May–October, Saturdays 8–12.*

The San Mateo County Farmers' Market, located at the corner of Hamilton and Broadway in downtown Redwood City, opens at 8 on Saturdays during late spring, summer, and early fall. Early birds have the pick of the fresh produce from local truck farmers. By noon, most stalls are sold out.

**East Bay**
## WEST OAKLAND FARMERS' MARKET

*Market and West Grand, Oakland 94607. Telephone (415) 654-1084. When: Saturdays 8–2, summer only.*

Sponsored by the West Oakland Food Project, this farmers' market offers produce direct from farmers every Saturday from 8 am to 2 pm, starting at the end of June and continuing through the growing season.

# WHOLESALE PRODUCE

To get a real feeling for the resources of a city, get up at 4 or 5 in the morning and head for a wholesale produce market. Here you must buy full cases or boxes of any produce you purchase, but much of it comes in manageable quantities: strawberries are packed twelve little baskets to a flat, onions in fifty-pound sacks (they will keep for months stored in the dark); asparagus is sold in twenty-pound crates, and some vegetables come in cases as small as fifteen pounds each.

It's a wonderful excursion to make once, just to look, but if you go to buy, either organize your shopping with friends or save the produce terminal for the time when you'd like to make a big batch of chutney or jam or cook for a big party.

The markets begin to wind down between 6 and 7 am (with the exception of the smaller San Francisco Farmers' Market). Shopping done, car loaded with fruits and vegetables, join the rest of the produce market for a hearty breakfast in any one of a number of small restaurants in the area open to the early morning crowd.

**Peninsula**
## THE GOLDEN GATE PRODUCE TERMINAL

*131 Terminal Court, South San Francisco 94080. Telephone (415) 761-3360 or 583-4886. Hours: M–F 3 am–11:30 am.*

The Golden Gate Produce Terminal is the biggest and the most commercial of the produce markets. The best produce buyers get there at 3 am and have probably already gone home before you arrive at 5. The very best produce does go fast, so get there early.

**East Bay**
## OAKLAND PRODUCE MARKET

*Between Second and Fourth, Franklin and Broadway, Oakland. Hours: very early mornings, weekdays.*

Oakland Market is less formidable than the Golden Gate, with blocks of old-fashioned wooden buildings with roll-up fronts. It's wonderful in the early hours of the morning to stroll through the street crowded with trucks unloading crates of California's fruits and vegetables: artichokes, avocados, oranges, apples, lettuce, celery, beets, cucumbers, berries.

**San Francisco**
## THE SAN FRANCISCO FARMERS' MARKET

*100 Alemany Boulevard, San Francisco 94110. Telephone (415) 647-9423. Hours: T–F 7:30–4 or 5, SAT 6–6.*

For your regular produce buying, the very much smaller San Francisco Farmers' Market is more practical than the Golden Gate Produce Terminal (above). For one thing, it doesn't close down at the crack of dawn, but stays open until noon. For another, you can buy by the pound, rather than by the case. Prices are cheaper during the week than on the weekend, but Saturday is the big day, with many more people selling many more things.

This outdoor market, with stalls set up under an arcade, has the feeling of a real country market. Small truck farmers pull up to the selling areas, set up their scales, and display their goods just in front. Much of it you can taste before you buy: sweet oranges, home-cured olives, fresh almonds, dried fruit, coffee.

The San Francisco Farmers' Market is very international, too. You'll see bejeweled Indian women in colorful saris, Thai families in traditional dress, Latino women with long braids down their back. The banter between the sellers, the buyers, and the onlookers is lively and friendly. Two men selling inexpensive Colombian or French roast coffee may offer you a steaming cup in the early morning cold. One stand sells only the long sweet European cucumbers. Another deals in chili peppers and has garlands of them—red, gold, and green—strung as decoration all around and above the stand. Buy your winter's supply of garlic in thick heavy braids from the grower himself. An old Italian gentleman sells fava beans for planting, fat raisins, and quarts of his homemade basil-flavored vinegar as well as his homemade Tabasco sauce.

Some stands sell just dried fruits and beans, others just apples. There is a profusion of stands selling Oriental vegetables: tender hearts of *bok choy;* pale, thick-skinned snow peas and fuzzy-skinned ones, too; chilies; Chinese okra; bitter melon. Another stall offers perfect heads of broccoli, cabbage, or cauliflower.

## FARM TRAILS GUIDES

If you want the freshest vegetables and fruits possible, along with a big dose of country air, make an excursion to the country to pick up blueberries, peaches, and apples for pies, or cases of apricots, plums, or peaches for jam and chutney right at their sources. Fall is also the season for fresh game raised at a number of small ranches in the same areas.

*Note:* All guides are free, but be sure to send a self-addressed stamped envelope with your request.

## CALIFORNIA FARMER-TO-CONSUMER DIRECTORY
*Telephone toll free (800) 952-5272.*

County-by-county listings of farmers who will sell their produce directly to you.

## HARVEST TIME
*P.O. Box O, Brentwood 94513.*

A harvest schedule for apples, almonds, berries, melons, peaches, pears, walnuts, wine grapes, and other fruits and vegetables.

## NAPA COUNTY FARMING TRAILS
*4075 Solano Avenue, Napa 94558.*

## SONOMA COUNTY FARM TRAILS
*P.O. Box 6043, Santa Rosa 95409.*

## YOLANO HARVEST TRAILS
*P.O. Box 484, Winters 95694.*

# Seeds

The ideal way to supply yourself with the best-quality produce is to grow it in your own kitchen garden. Just step outside to collect a gorgeous *bouquet garni* for your stockpot. Gather up some pungent *arugula* and some tender baby lettuce greens for a salad. You don't need to drive clear across the city for a sprig of *epazote* to season your beans or a handful of lemon grass for a Thai soup. Following are a variety of mail order sources for culinary seeds.

## General/European
## BURPEE SEED COMPANY

*6350 Rutland Avenue, Riverside CA 92502. Telephone (714) 689-1191.*

Burpee, California's big seed company, carries all the American "garden-variety" seeds: five kinds of pickling cucumbers, three pages of corn varieties, and dozens of berries for making jam. But scattered in the eighty-page catalog you can find such culinary immigrants as garbanzo beans, celery root, Brussels sprouts, sweet Nantes carrots, Florence fennel, and Jerusalem artichokes.

The "Italian garden packet" has sweet basil, romano pole beans, eggplants, sweet peppers, roma plum tomatoes, and zucchini. Throw in some *arugula*

seeds (a distinctive bitter salad green) and you'll have all the ingredients for long late summer meals *al fresco*.

For down-home cooking, there is okra, black-eyed peas, plenty of greens, and thirteen kinds of watermelon.

Order the free catalog early; there's a big demand.

## European
## J. A. DEMONCHAUX COMPANY

*827 North Kansas, Topeka, KS 66608. Telephone (913) 235-8502.*

From Kansas (!) Demonchaux sells seeds for herbs, *haricots verts* (the very delicate type known as *filet*), green *flageolets*, cardoon, tiny Belgian carrots, French endive, Florentine fennel, several varieties of *mâche* (a tender salad green), *roquette*, sorrel, a long violet eggplant from the south of France, and seeds for miniscule French *cornichons*, or pickles.

They also carry a line of French comestibles and books on French cuisine, including French gardening books. A free planting guide and complimentary French flower seeds are enclosed with your order.

*Catalog 25¢ (free if you telephone long distance).*

Tropical
## EXOTICA SEED COMPANY

*1742 Laurel Canyon Boulevard, West Hollywood, CA 90046. Telephone (213) 851-0990.*

Owner Steven Spangler travels every year to Ecuador, Mexico, Hawaii, and throughout the Pacific collecting seeds, roots, and cuttings of tropical fruits and vegetables that can be grown in California. His catalog describes dessert banana, *chirimoya*, guava, papaya, and passion fruit varieties, with information on how to cultivate them in California. Exotica has seeds for carob, wild persimmons, European black olive trees, tamarind, Ecuadorean blackberries, Egyptian favas, and the Caribbean pigeon pea, too.

The long listing of live plants includes macadamia nut and cashew nut trees, *pignolo* (pine nut) and chestnut trees from Italy, and the cold-adapted Ecuadorean tree tomato.
*Catalog $2.*

General
## GURNEY SEED AND NURSERY COMPANY

*Yankton, S D 57079. Telephone (605) 665-1671.*

It's worth getting Gurney's catalog just for the glorious life-size illustrations of cucumbers, and for the pictures of varieties of corn that go on for pages: old-fashioned sweet, black Mexican, variegated honey, and cream. There are also soup peas and beans (black, fava, Swedish brown beans), two kinds of blue potatoes, and little yellow-flecked German potatoes for potato salad. For piemakers, there are cherries, raspberries, blackberries, strawberries, and three kinds of rhubarb. Gurney's has its own line of seasonings and herbs.
*Free catalog.*

General
## HENRY FIELD'S SEED AND NURSERY COMPANY

*Shenandoah, IA 51602. Telephone (712) 246-2110.*

Since 1892, Henry Field's has been sending catalogs of reasonably priced flowers, vegetables, and fruit trees to generations of avid gardeners. The many pear trees, peach and plum trees, black walnut trees, cherry trees (producing cherries for pies, like the Montmorency) are the stuff of summer reveries. And there are all the berries: gooseberries; red, purple, and black raspberries—even a fat golden raspberry.
*Free catalog.*

Chilies
## HORTICULTURAL ENTERPRISES

*P.O. Box 340082, Dallas, TX 75234.*

A blazing yellow poster-catalog of *Las Semillas Auténticas Mexicanas* lists thirty-two different chilies and peppers ranging in fire power from the tiny high-caliber *serrano* and the peppery *jalapeño* to the mild Roumanian. They've got all the Mexican and South American varieties, plus two from Taiwan and the fat sweet Italian *peperonata*, as well as *epazote* (the distinctive herb for seasoning *frijoles*), *chía*, *jícama*, green papery-husked *tomatillos*, and *cha yu* or *shia kuan*, Chinese tomatoes from Taiwan.
*Free catalog.*

Japanese
## KITAZAWA SEED COMPANY

*356 West Taylor Street, San Jose 95110. Telephone (408) 292-4420.*

Kitazawa offers over fifty kinds of Japanese vegetable seeds. Among them are *gobo*, or edible burdock; six varieties of Oriental cabbage; and nine types of the giant Japanese *daikon* radish. A single winter *daikon* may last you all season—it grows to 2-1/2 feet. The many greens include mustards; *mitsuba*, or Japanese parsley; and special greens for flavoring and coloring the pickled vegetables that appear at every Japanese meal. Try the sweet Oriental cucumber, pickling melons, and turban-shaped pumpkins, too.

*Free catalog.*

## Shallots/French
## LE JARDIN DU GOURMET

*West Danville, VT 05873.*

Specializing in shallots, Le Jardin du Gourmet sells standard shallot sets (one hundred for three dollars), gray shallots, the larger elongated type called "frogs' leg," Spanish shallots, and the same type of Egyptian onions as are seen in ancient tomb paintings.

They supply the most frequently used seeds for the family garden and even have about thirty varieties in mini seed packets for the very small garden (20¢ each).

Each year they get a limited number of the beautiful color catalogs from France's most illustrious seed company, Vilmorin, and regularly carry many of the French seeds in varieties not often seen here: Belgian endive, wild chicory, four kinds of *mâche*, *roquette* (another bitter green), turnip, cabbage, etc. They sell Vilmorin's *flageolet* beans for your winter *cassoulet*, and *petits pois* under their own label.

Order French seeds from Le Jardin du Gourmet—it's faster and simpler than ordering directly from France.

*Free catalog.*

## Herbs/Rare Seeds
## NICHOLS GARDEN NURSERY

*1190 Northwest Pacific Highway, Albany, OR 97321. Telephone (503) 928-9280.*

Nichols Garden Nursery has a wonderful seventy-page catalog for the gourmet gardener, filled with such rarities as pale-green *flageolet* beans (for *cassoulet*), white bush zucchini, Montezuma red beans (ancient Mexican dried beans), white broccoli, and lovely Sicilian purple cauliflower. Known for their fine-quality herb seeds, they offer six kinds of sweet basil, blue flowering borage, French sorrel, and true bay laurel seedlings. Nichols also sells hearty herb plants by mail, including many kinds of culinary thymes, mints, and rosemaries. The first commercial cultivators of elephant garlic, they sell French shallots and the Egyptian bunching onions depicted in pharaonic tomb paintings.

For gilding *paellas* or flavoring *bouillabaise*, plant their *crocus sativus* bulbs. The flower's dried orange stigmas are known as saffron.

*Free catalog.*

## General
## GEORGE W. PARK
## SEED COMPANY, INC.

*P.O. Box 31, Greenwood, SC 29447. Telephone (803) 374-3341.*

Since 1868, the Park family have been selling their excellent flower and vegetable seeds by catalog. For your kitchen garden, there is miniature butter lettuce, a golden tomato for hanging baskets, and an abundance of herbs including caper bush (the flower buds are pickled), carob, and holy basil. Burbank would have loved the Spanish and Valencia peanuts. Exotic foreigners include Cape gooseberry, *jícama,* a forty-pound Tahitian squash, sweet Florentine fennel, and Chinese cabbage. And there are pages of beautiful flowers in every shade and hue to grow from seeds.

*Free catalog.*

## Herbs
## OTTO RICHTER AND SONS, LTD.

*Goodwood, Ontario, L1C 1AO Canada. Telephone (416) 640-6677.*

This excellent herb catalog lists both common and old-fashioned varieties including carob, belladonna, and seeds for natural dye plants.

*Catalog 75¢.*

## Organic/Herbs
## SANCTUARY SEEDS

*2388 West Fourth, Vancouver, B.C. V6K 1PI Canada. Telephone (604) 733-4724.*

Sanctuary Seeds's lovely catalog illustrated with prints from old herbals has a good basic selection of vegetable seeds. They have avoided hybrids in favor of older, more traditional varieties, all entirely chemically untreated.

The dozens of culinary herbs include such old-fashioned varieties as angelica, bergamot (bee balm), costmary (an old favorite of English herb gardens), chicory (its roasted bitter root is used in New Orleans-style coffee), lovage, pennyroyal, and salad burnet. Medicinal herbs and fourteen kinds of healthy sprouting seeds are sold in quantities of one to fifty pounds: *adzuki,* rye, triticale, wheat, cress, etc.

The company has a line of packaged herbs and botanicals, too.

*Free catalog.*

## Rare Seeds
## SEED SAVER'S EXCHANGE

*Kent Whealy, Rural Route 2, Princeton, MO 64673. Telephone (816) 748-3785.*

Passionate gardeners from all over North America and many foreign countries exchange seeds here for rare or old-fashioned fruit and vegetable varieties neglected by commercial seed companies. To become a member, you must have seeds or cuttings to offer other members. The *Seed Saver's Exchange Yearbook* lists the members and their proferred seeds and explains how to collect and save seeds.

Nonmembers can participate, too, but must include $1 to cover the postage costs for each variety requested.

## Chinese
## TSANG AND MA INTERNATIONAL

*1306 Old County Road, Belmont, CA 94002. Telephone (415) 595-2270.*

Tsang and Ma first began bringing vegetable seeds out of mainland China when China-U.S. relations were renewed during the Nixon years. They now offer over twenty of the varieties most popular in Chinatown markets, including *mo gwa* (Chinese fuzzy gourd), *dow gauk* (yard-long beans), *doan gwa* (winter melon), and *see gwa* (Chinese okra). They're all easy to grow; you can pick choice, tender hearts of *bok choy* or baby Chinese broccoli from your own kitchen garden.

The seed packets have a clear photo of the plant with its botanical, English, and Chinese names; a brief description of its appearance and taste; and directions for cultivating it. The "cooking ideas" tell how it's best used: boiled in soups, steamed, or stir-fried.

Tsang and Ma plan to introduce Southeast Asian vegetables to their free catalog soon.

# Staples

## FLOUR, NUTS, LEGUMES, DRIED FRUIT, HONEY, OIL

Buying in bulk is a pleasure for the sensual shopper (akin to playing store when you were a kid). I like taking my paper bag and scooping up pearly grains of rice, tiny Louisiana red beans, or chalky corn flour. It's a pleasure to watch semolina pour into my bag like sand. I buy lovely gray buckwheat flour for hearty southern-style pasta; specially ground flour for *chapatis*, a kind of tender Indian flat bread; and the finest, silkiest pastry flour for my lightest confections.

Before it closed last year, Ohs Fine Foods on Mission Street was my favorite source for flours, grains, and legumes. The walls of this long narrow store were crowded with open sacks of every kind of bean or grain, from chestnut and pumpernickel-rye flours to bird seed for your kitchen parrot. Though it was sad to see this seventy-year-old San Francisco landmark disappear from the city, there are still good sources for high-quality staples.

By buying in bulk, you can buy specialty flours in quantities small enough to ensure that they'll be fresh when you use them. And you can buy just the amount of grains or beans you need for a recipe.

In addition to the stores listed in this chapter, many ethnic markets sell special flours and grains in bulk. Check the Natural Foods section for suppliers of organic grains and legumes and fresh stone-ground flours, along with bulk honey, nuts, and unsulphured dried fruits.

---

### San Francisco/East Bay
### BOMBAY BAZAR

*548 Valencia Street, San Francisco 94110. Telephone (415) 621-1717. Hours: T-SAT 10:30–6, SUN 12–5.*
*1034 University Avenue, Berkeley 94710. Telephone (415) 848-1671. Hours: T-F 10–6:30, SAT 10–7, SUN 11–6.*

This store has flours—flours for Indian breadmaking, yellow split-pea flour, corn flours—and a big selection of *dals*, both split and whole, as well as a flour made from *dal* for breads.

---

### East Bay
### DINO'S
### DRIED FRUITS AND NUTS

*Tenth and Washington streets, Oakland 94607. Telephone (415) 832-5647. Hours: M-SAT 9:30–5:30.*

You can buy lengths of old-fashioned flowered cotton remnants, do your vegetable shopping, have a doughnut and some coffee, and buy yourself some new socks, all at Swan's Department Store and Food Center in downtown Oakland, directly across from the Victorian Row Project area under renovation.

The dried-fruit-and-nut stand has been in place since 1917, with its bins of raw peanuts, filberts, Brazil nuts, and walnuts in the shell. For pies, choose between Spudnik pecans and paper-shell pecans with a longer, darker shell. Lazybones can buy them shelled as well.

For snacking or for a sumptuous holiday fruitcake, Dino Ramirez's dried fruits are lovely, with sticky subdued colors—name a fruit, he has it: apricots, pineapples, papayas, raisins, pears, figs, prunes; and citron halves, orange peel, and lemon peel.

**East Bay**
# THE FOOD MILL

*3033 MacArthur Boulevard, Oakland 94602. Telephone (415) 482-3848. Hours: M–SAT 8:30–6.*

Many local restaurants get deliveries of fresh flours, raisins, nuts, dried fruits, soup beans, and cooking oils from Oakland's Food Mill. The Food Mill has a reputation for consistent high quality of the many products they stock, from oils, nut butters, cereals, and dried fruit, to nuts, grains, and flours.

To assure maximum freshness, they grind all the whole-grain flours themselves. An attractive case displays all the many fresh-ground flours available at the Food Mill. The store is always crowded because the prices are low and the quality high. Sadly, rising gas costs have forced the Food Mill to discontinue their Friday night home deliveries.

**Peninsula**
# GIUSTO'S SPECIALTY FOODS

*241 East Harris Avenue, South San Francisco 94080. Telephone (415) 873-6566. Wholesale only.*

The Giusto family business started in 1940 as a small bakery behind a health food store in San Francisco. The demand for their high-quality natural breads

and baked goods was so high, they eventually became wholesalers. To ensure the consistent quality of their products, they decided to become millers of flours and grains.

The Giusto family actually visits many of the farms to talk to the farmers who grow the grain shipped to them for milling. They look for grains grown under the most natural organic methods.

Today, Giusto's supplies many local health food and natural foods stores with quality grain and freshly ground flours from their own South San Francisco mills.

Giusto's sells over forty kinds of bulk cereals and grains including toasted whole brown buckwheat groats, stone-ground corn meal, coarse polenta corn meal, yellow popcorn, steel-cut oats, whole dark northern rye, triticale (a cross between rye and a wheat grain), and hard red winter wheat berries.

The company has recently completed an air-pushed vacuum system for milling whole-grain flour, which they say enables them to mill flour with 20 percent less heat than most stone-ground mills. They claim this method retains more natural vitamins, minerals, and enzymes in the grain.

Giusto's natural whole-grain flours and regular flours include pure eastern buckwheat, garbanzo flour and meal, gluten, graham, lima bean, a coarse whole-grain rye pumpernickel, triticale, unbleached hard red wheat, and both unbleached and whole-wheat pastry flours.

**East Bay**
# MADE TO ORDER

*1526 Hopkins Street, Berkeley 94707. Telephone (415) 524-7552. Hours: M–SAT 10–6.*

Made to Order has both semolina and fine golden durum wheat in five-pound bags for your pasta making.

## Sonoma County
## NAPA VALLEY OLIVE OIL MANUFACTURING COMPANY

*835 McCorckle Avenue, St. Helena 94574. Telephone (707) 963-4173. Hours: 8–5:30 daily.*

Any visit to the Napa Valley should include Napa Valley Olive Oil Manufacturing Company, a wonderful old store on a back street in St. Helena.

If you want to eat a sandwich they have a few tables just outside. When you walk through the screen door, you'll find yourself in an old-world country store. Osvaldo Particelli and Policarpo Lucchesi are from a small town just outside Lucca in Tuscany where some of the finest virgin olive oil in Italy is made. Here in California, the partners are selling a heavy fruity oil made from olives grown in the Sacramento Valley. A dark golden green, it has a wonderful aroma when it's warmed. For those who prefer the even darker *extra vergine*, the closest you can get to the pellucid Tuscan oil that is the best in Italy, ask for the store's *extra vergine* kept in the back. They don't have it all the time; there's not even a label for it; and it costs just one dollar more per gallon than their regular oil. Guidi Brothers' olive oil is sold in many gourmet shops and delis, but it's much less expensive here at the source. Guidi Brothers Market, 1800 Filbert Street, San Francisco, has the oil, too, and distributes it to other Bay Area food stores.

Stock up on jars of homemade antipasto mild or hot, Diana brand ricotta cheese (the commercial brand closest to the light, fresh *ricotta romana*), bags of freshly grated *grana padano* (a grating cheese made in the same style as Parmesan) and the sharper *pecorino romano* (used mainly as a grating cheese, but in Rome, eaten with fresh fava beans in the early summer). Whole *prosciutti*

from the East Coast, Molinari salami, ten-pound boxes of domestic pasta from Fresno, and boxes of the best imported brand, De Cecco, with lovely maidens and sheaves of wheat on the box.

There are bags of nuts for *torta*, and one-pound bags of wonderful salt-cured black olives, dark and meaty; and little bags of precious dried *porcini* mushrooms and enormous barrels filled to the brim with South American mushrooms.

## East Bay
## G. B. RATTO

*821 Washington, Oakland 94607. Telephone (415) 832-6503. Hours: M–SAT 8–5.*

Ratto's has semolina, bulgur, *couscous*, manioc flour, polenta, buckwheat, and other flours in bulk, as well as *dals* for Indian cuisine; dried beans, including Italian *lupini* beans, Egyptian *ful medames*, and West Indian pigeon peas; Greek, Spanish, and California olive oils; and Greek honey and olives.

## Marin County
## TORN RANCH

*1122 Fourth Street, San Rafael 94901. Telephone (415) 457-2080. Hours: M–SAT 10–5:30.*

Don't be deterred by the rather touristy gift-shop decor of the Torn Ranch store in San Rafael. The packaged dried fruits and nuts are the same high-quality locally grown products that Milt and June Torn's family ranch in southern California has been selling since the twenties.

The perfect, sumptuous nuts are available both raw and roasted and, if you wish, unsalted. Raw nuts include walnuts, black walnuts, almonds, perfect pecan halves, pale-green *pepitas* (hulled pumpkin seeds), *pignoli,* and jumbo cashews. Fresh-roasted nuts include colossal California pistachios, macadamia nuts, filberts, and baby Brazil nuts.

They also have a full line of luscious sun-dried California fruits: smoky *medjool* dates, figs, apples, apricots, nectarines, peaches, pears, pineapples, prunes, kumquats, and papayas. Stock up on fine-quality glacéed fruits imported from Australia for holiday baking.

The store also carries custom-made vinegars, mustards, sauces, and ice cream toppings from New York's well-known Silver Palate food store.

*Mail order. Quantity discounts available. Write for order form.*

**East Bay**
## VITAL VITTLES

*1011 Heinz, Oakland 94710. Telephone (415) 845-3186. Wholesale to the trade only.*

The baker at Vital Vittles, frustrated in his attempt to find a high-quality, extremely fresh-ground bread flour, now imports carloads of winter wheat, grown in Deaf Smith County, from Texas's famed Arrowhead Mills. He stone grinds it himself every few days for his own baking needs and supplies it to a few other good bread bakeries like Tassajara Bakery in San Francisco and Bread and Chocolate in Marin County.

**San Francisco**
## WRIGHT POPCORN AND NUT COMPANY

*150 Potrero, San Francisco 94103. Telephone (415) 861-0912. Hours: M–F 8–12, 1–5.*

Ever run to the kitchen to pop a big bowl of popcorn just before the start of the late-TV movie to find there isn't any? No more buying popcorn in puny bags. Wright Popcorn and Nut Company will sell you a fifty-pound bag of unpopped yellow kernels at a very good price. And while you're there, you might as well haul away one of their twenty-five-pound bags of peanuts in the shell.

# HONEY

The Napa Valley with its wild flowers and stretches of open country is a prime site for apiculture. *Napa Valley* magazine published an article called "Combing the Valley for Honey" by Barbara Ostund-lang, with a listing of local beekeepers who sell their honey. The honey is generally extracted from the hives in May and or September. Call for availability:

K. Balsiger, (707) 224-4265
E. Grossi, (707) 226-5610
L. Jones, (707) 224-5261
H. Shimel, (707) 226-9264
R. Steltzner, (707) 252-0335

The Santa Cruz area is another important source for bees and honey.

# Take-Out Food

Once upon a time when you didn't feel like cooking and didn't want to go to a restaurant, there wasn't much hope of eating well. Take-out meant fast food of a fairly grim quality. The most you could aspire to was a prefab hamburger, soggy chop suey, or a flimsy pizza. But these days you can dine Italian, French, Indonesian, kosher, or Japanese in style. Take-out has stepped up in class, and some of the Bay Area's best cooks are in the business. (See Charcuterie for more *pâtés*, cured meats, etc.)

## BARBECUE

### East Bay
### EVERETT AND JONES BAR-B-QUE

*2676 Fruitvale Avenue, Oakland 94601. Telephone (415) 533-0900. Hours: M–TH 11 am–2 am, F–SAT 11 am–3 am, SUN 11 am–1 am.*
*1955 San Pablo Avenue, Berkeley 94702. Telephone (415) 562-4098. Hours: 11 am–7 pm daily.*
*9101 East Fourteenth Street, Oakland 94606. Telephone (415) 562-4098. Hours: 11 am–1 am daily.*

This is the baddest, hottest barbecue around, where, until 3 in the morning you can get big slabs of meaty ribs, succulent chicken, or tasty "links." If you bring your own container, Everett and Jones will sell you some of their special barbecue sauce. Just take it right on home and make your own "que" with it. But if you've never been there before and ask for the *hot* sauce, you might have to use all your powers of persuasion to convince the crew behind the counter you can take the heat. Marked with a skull and crossbones, the *hot* packs a lot of firepower and is laced with chili seeds.

Cooked over hickory wood, dinners come with potato salad and white balloon bread, or you can get an "order" of ribs, beef, chicken, or links.

## BRITISH

### San Jose Area
### THE MINISTRY OF FOOD

*1142 Saratoga Avenue, San Jose 95129. Telephone (408) 247-PIES. Hours: 10–6 daily.*

The Ministry of Food supplies her Majesty's San Jose expatriates with Cornish pasties, meat pies (steak and kidney, beef and mushroom, pork, or chicken), and pork sausages in buns, plus authentic British bangers, or lean pork sausages.

They also sell English jams, pickles, piccalilli, breakfast kippers, black pudding, and north-country sausage.

### San Francisco/East Bay
### NOBLE PIES

*4301 Twenty-fourth Street, San Francisco 94114. Telephone (415) 826-7437. Hours: M 12–8, T–SAT 12–9.*
*5422 College Avenue, Oakland 94618. Telephone (415) 653-2790. Hours: M–SAT 10:30–9.*

Australian Barbara Sutherland and Californian Robert Seymoure are partners in Noble Pies, the East Bay bakery and café continuing the British and colonial tradition of splendid savory meat and vegetable pies—high-sided, double-crusted, and decorated with cut pastry.

The domed Thistle Pie is covered with tiered pastry leaves to resemble an artichoke. When cut, its layers of artichoke hearts, black olives, cheese, and garbanzo beans look like geological strata. A South African customer told Noble Pies about Babootie Pie and even brought in a trial recipe. It's filled with curried beef, lamb, and fruit. A Jamaican customer introduced them to the spicy street food now sold at Noble Pies as Jamaican Beef Patty, hot with chili, onion, and tomato. The U.S. Turkey

Pie puts Thanksgiving dinner into a pie crust. It's all there: turkey breast, yams, and mushroom stuffing.

Individual pasties are sold hot, à la carte, or with a salad. The traditional Cornish pasty is filled with beef and vegetables, the Florentine with spinach, cheese, and mushrooms.

And for your final pie-out, they make old-fashioned fruit pies, several kinds each day. There are also scones, Scottish shortbread, and Lamington cake (a rich butter sponge cake spread with raspberry preserves, dipped in bittersweet chocolate, and rolled in coconut).

Don't forget a bottle of Foster's, the Australian beer, to wash it all down.

Whole or half savory pies and whole fruit pies should be ordered at least four hours in advance.

# ——— CHINESE ———

### San Francisco
## THE GOLDEN DRAGON

*157 Waverly Place, San Francisco 94108. Telephone (415) 398-4551. Hours: 8–midnight or 1 am daily.*

The take-out store for the Golden Dragon sells delicious Peking-style roast duck.
*Special order only.*

### San Francisco
## HONG SANG MARKET

*1136 Grant Avenue, San Francisco 94133. Telephone (415) 982-3603. Hours: 8:15–5:30 daily.*

Just across the street from Kwong Jow Sausage Company, this market is the place to buy excellent duck roasted in the Cantonese style. Fresh Pekin ducks are stuffed with *cilantro*, rubbed with spices and sesame oil, and glazed with sugared water. Then the chef uses an air compressor to inflate the skin away from the body of the duck. The skin then cooks to a delicious crisp while the duck itself stays tender and succulent.

The market has a small fresh fish counter, too.

### San Francisco
## JUNMAE GUEY RESTAURANT

*1222 Stockton Street, San Francisco 94133. Telephone (415) 433-3981. Hours: M–T, TH–SUN 8–6.*

Junmae Guey Restaurant does a brisk business in both roast pig and roast duck. Stop in for a bowl of noodles with some roast pig on the side, or *won ton* soup with pieces of roast duck. Be sure to visit the restrooms downstairs, because on your way down you can see dozens of bright pink pigs hanging ready to be roasted to a crisp.

### San Francisco
## SUN SANG MARKET

*1205 Stockton Street, San Francisco 94133. Telephone (415) 989-3060. Hours: M–SAT 9–5:30.*

Sun Sang Market is one of the best places around for roast pig, one of the oldest in San Francisco's Chinatown. Be sure you specify roast pig; it's not the same as roast pork (roast pig is the whole pig roasted; roast pork is pork

loin or butt treated with curing salts and roasted).

There's also boiled chicken, soy sauce chicken, roast squab. And they'll chop or slice your order any way you like. You can buy halves of either ducks or chickens. The ducks are delicious, roasted with anise and *cilantro*.

### San Francisco
## YONG KEE RICE NOODLE SHOP

*732 Jackson Street, San Francisco 94111. Telephone (415) 986-3759. Hours: T–SUN 8–5.*

Yong Kee Rice Noodle Shop has *dim sum* to go. If you don't read Chinese you'll have to point to what you want, but the odds are high you'll like what you pick.

There are the familiar steamed buns called *cha siew bao*, filled with barbecued pork, or a variation called *gai bao*, filled with chicken and mushrooms. The *shui mai* are savory steamed meat dumplings in a transparent pleated dough, and the *har gow* are stuffed with chopped shrimp. The dumplings are all delicious mouthfuls made with a variety of stuffings and wrapped in a dough made from wheat flour or glutinous rice.

# DUTCH INDONESIAN

### Contra Costa
## OTTEN INDONESIAN FOODS

*322 Key Boulevard, Richmond 94805. Telephone (415) 232-9511. Hours: M–SAT 8–4.*

Mary Otten, born in the formerly Dutch "Batavia" (Djakarta today), is famous in the Bay Area's Dutch-Indonesian community for her cooking. With her daughter Irena, also an excellent cook, and a former ballet dancer and circus performer, she makes Dutch-Indonesian specialties from her catering kitchen in Richmond, Otten Indonesian Foods.

She keeps a freezerful of prepared foods for take-out customers who come from as far away as Toronto and San Jose: *saucijsbroodjes*, or Dutch sausage breads, homemade sausage in a flaky pastry; *kroketten*, delicate, deep-fried potato croquettes; *kippen pasteijes*, individual chicken turnovers made with buttery pastry, a Dutch schoolchildren's treat; *bitterballen*, spicy meatballs. From the Indonesian tradition, try the *loempia*, a thin, crisp dough wrapping a savory filling of Southeast Asian vegetables; and *garnallen soesen*, shrimp puff pastries.

Mary and Irena cater in elaborate Indonesian style and often have some of the many dishes that make up a *rijsttafel* available for take-out. Their instant mini-*rijsttafel* is dinner for two.

You'll want to take home some of their homemade Indonesian condiments, too: a thick fragrant *ketjap*, an Indonesian cooking sauce of soy boiled with spices and molasses; several superb hot *sambals*, or chili pastes; and a wonderful, sticky tamarind chutney, sour and hot, good spread on fresh pineapple, apple, or avocado slices.

At Christmastime they make traditional Dutch cakes and pastries from

Mary Otten's grandmother's recipes: *spekkoek*, or "bacon" cake, thin alternating layers of dark and light spiced dough cooked one by one under a broiler (when cut it does resemble the dark-light striations of fat and lean bacon), and *kerstkransen*, wreaths of puff pastry dough filled with marzipan.

Call mornings before visiting their kitchen.

# EUROPEAN INTERNATIONAL

### Contra Costa
## A LA CARTE

*2055 North Broadway, Walnut Creek 94596. Telephone (415) 932-4777. Hours: 10:30–7:30 daily.*

It's understandable that Contra Costa County dwellers might sometimes be too tired to cook after that long commute from the city. That's why A la Carte, Walnut Creek's five-story gourmet emporium, includes a delicatessen well-provided with homemade pâtés, *rillettes*, quiches, *dolmas*, and fresh-made salads like *tortellini*, Provençal *ratatouille*, *paella*, *tabbouleh*, or an Oriental salad with snow peas and roast beef.

If you arrange beforehand, the catering chef will prepare entrées for you to take home and reheat, such as a roast chicken glazed with plum sauce, a *carbonnade* of beef *à la flamande*, or an orange-glazed ham.

### San Francisco
## ASHBURY MARKET

*205 Frederick Street, San Francisco 94117. Telephone (415) 566-3134. Hours: M-SAT 9–8, SUN 9–3.*

Ashbury Market is the Haight's mom and pop grocery store with an unex-

pected twist. Young Wilfred Wong, whose family has owned the market for over twenty-five years, has been making changes. A wine buff, every year he sets aside a portion of his California wine inventory for aging, and last year he opened a take-out kitchen with Mississippi-born chef George Lovette.

Chef Lovette makes a fresh soup every day, maybe an artichoke soup with hazelnuts or a fresh cream of tomato with cognac, and one or two entrées: perhaps *spanakopita*, spinach and *feta* cheese in *filo* dough; Belgian beef stew with dark beer; veal stew with walnuts and orange peel; or his special shrimp gumbo or roasted game hen stuffed with a vegetable pilau.

Wong and Lovette plan to publish each month's take-out menu in the store's flyer and will have wine specials each day to match the food. Reasonable and unpretentious.

### San Francisco
## EICHELBAUM AND COMPANY

*2417 California Street, San Francisco 94115. Telephone (415) 929-9030. Hours: T-F 11–7, SAT-SUN 11–4:30 (take-out).*

San Francisco's Stanley Eichelbaum has had what used to be called a "checkered career"—as a film and theatre critic, a student chef, a caterer, a restaurateur. In just a short time, his Eichelbaum and Company has become a neighborhood institution. And any of the food served in his tiny pink and white California Street storefront is available to go.

He regularly has a sumptuous Oriental chicken salad with mandarin oranges, a pasta salad with *tortellini* and *pesto*, spinach and mushroom quiches, and a selection of country-style pâtés. As one of the two fresh soups made daily, you might find tomato-orange, minestrone *or tortellini* soup; or, in summer, even a chilled peach soup made from Stanley's own Babcock peach tree on Potrero Hill. Or take home a plate of homemade *fettuccine Alfredo* or *fettuccine bolognese*.

Call for the daily special, which includes *fettuccine* and two *al dente* vegetables. It might be a roast leg of veal with *sauce madère*, braised ham with Cumberland sauce, cold poached salmon with a *sauce verte*, or sautéed chicken *fines herbes*. Desserts include a fresh raspberry or nectarine tart with *crème pâtissière* and a luscious apricot cheesecake.

Eichelbaum and Company prepares box lunches from four set menus using their pâtés, quiches, and salads. The weekend brunch special is *crépazes*, a stack of crêpes interleaved with prosciutto and ham, sauced with cream and cheese, and garnished with pistachios.

And every day San Franciscans take out dozens of the excellent croissants and flaky almond croissants.

## San Francisco
## GOURMET TO GO

*Tante Marie's Cooking School, 271 Francisco Street, San Francisco 94133. Telephone (415) 824-7590.*

Gourmet To Go is a unique take-out service offered through Tante Marie's Cooking School. Call to consult with graduate cook Sue Appelbaum on the menu. She'll shop for your meal, cook it in style and have it ready for you at Tante Marie's, packed to go straight into your home oven (or by special request, your microwave).

She'll make entrées for two to eight people, favoring one-dish meals, but you'll have to make your own salad and find your own dessert. You might order a hearty *cassoulet*, a roasted duck with wild rice, chicken breast in lemon with asparagus, or a lamb stew *prima-*

*vera* garnished with baby spring vegetables.

Because your meal is custom-cooked, Ms. Appelbaum can take into consideration special conditions such as an allergy to onions or an aversion to garlic.

Prices vary according to the season and the market. You pay by the dish: duck for two or *cassoulet* for six. Call at least twenty-four hours in advance.

## East Bay
## LE POULET

*1685 Shattuck Avenue, Berkeley 94709. Telephone (415) 845-5932. Hours: M-SAT 10-7.*

Le Poulet, the East Bay's chicken emporium, is really a *charcuterie*, but instead of specializing in dishes made with pork, owner Marilyn Rinzler specializes in chicken: chicken and duck pâtés and mousses; of course, chicken soup; and ten chicken entrées including chicken pie, whole roast garlic-lemon chickens, chicken crêpes, *cannelloni*, and enchiladas. But chef Bruce Aidells, a former research biologist and a passionate sausage maker, has managed to sneak in a few pork-based sausages: sweet fennel, hot Italian, Provençal, and a Spanish-style chorizo.

Of course there's chicken salad, this one a *niçoise*, but also garlic eggplant, rice *pesto*, and other fresh vegetable salads.

**San Francisco**
## LES JOULINS

*44 Ellis Street, San Francisco 94102. Telephone (415) 397-5397. Hours: M–F 7:30–7, SAT 9–7.*

This downtown *charcuterie* and bakery, owned by Simon and Betty Heyman, has a café area where you can lunch or have pastries and coffee. For your morning break, you can have *palmiers, pain au chocolat, pain au raisin,* croissants, and sugar-dusted almond croissants literally drenched in rum.

For lunch, take out slices of quiche—*épinards,* Lorraine, or mushroom—small double-crusted meat pies, or a fish-shaped pie with a salmon mousse filling or croissants stuffed with either ham and cheese or spinach mousse, cheese, and vegetables.

Have a picnic at the office with Les Joulins' baguettes or *pain de seigle* (rye) bread) and slices of their pâtés: *pâté de canard,* rabbit pâté, and a smooth chicken liver mousse. Occasionally, they have creamy pork *rillettes.* Near the holidays, there is richer fare—pâtés of quail or duck or pheasant, a subtle chicken liver mousse with a hint of truffle, a savory rabbit pâté *en croûte.*

Les Joulins also has French pastries.

**Marin County**
## LET'S EAT

*One Blackfield Drive, Tiburon 94920. Telephone (415) 383-3663. Hours: M–SAT 10–7, SUN 10–6.*

Sharon Leach and Marsha Workman change the menu at Let's Eat every two days. The take-out store's newsletter lists the planned menus, which include eight to ten salads: celery root with tarragon sauce, Chinese chicken salad, minted peas in mustard vinaigrette, and roasted sweet red peppers in olive oil and garlic.

Then there is soup, hot in cold weather, cold in hot weather. Fresh pasta is made every day. Among the sauces, choose a *marinara, bolognese, pesto,* wild Italian mushroom *(porcini),* or sausage with sweet red bell peppers.

There are two daily entrées. The first is pasta, such as lasagne Florentine made with turkey, spinach, and *béchamel;* or Sicilian *fettuccine* with pine nuts, tuna, tomatoes, and capers. In springtime, *pasta primavera* is tossed with tender baby spring vegetables. The second entrée is usually a chicken or meat dish.

You'll find a grand selection of desserts next door at Sweet Things.

**San Francisco**
## NANCY VAN WYCK CULINARY COMPANY

*3548 Sacramento Street, San Francisco 94118. Telephone (415) 921-6363. Hours: M–F 11–6:30, SAT 11–5:30.*

Nancy Van Wyck Culinary Company is well known as a caterer to San Francisco's high-society functions. The front of the culinary company is a small take-out shop where the regular bill of fare includes hors d'oeuvres (*dolmas, spanakopita,* stuffed mushrooms, Indonesian beef *saté*), eight to ten pâtés and meats, as well as a selection of salads (smoked chicken, potato and artichoke, pasta salad with pine nuts, Sicilian *caponata*), a daily quiche, and an array of pastries from *Linzertorte* to humble thumbprint cookies and shortbread.

The monthly schedule of carry-out cuisine lists the two daily entrées, which change twice weekly. Call after 11 am to reserve the day's entrée, usually a substantial dish like beef *pot au feu,* chicken *paprikás,* beef *carbonnade,* a comforting *coq au vin,* or *moussaka.*

Pasta lovers are plied with such dishes as molded pasta with eggplant, *cannelloni*, or *fettuccine* with smoked ham and cream sauce.

For orders of fifteen or more, you can choose from any of the month's menus.

Spring and summer, the staff makes up elaborate picnic baskets. Box lunches are also available, and wines are sold in the store.

## Contra Costa
## NARSAI'S MARKET

*389 Colusa Avenue, Kensington 94707. Telephone (415) 527-3737. Hours: M-SAT 10-7, SUN 10-4.*

The weekly entrées, most of them prepared in Narsai's restaurant kitchen, are listed in each month's *Market News*. You can take home dishes like *poulet farci*, boned chicken thigh stuffed with prosciutto, grated cheese, and basil; duck with Grand Marnier; salmon *coulibac*, a Russian dish of flaky pastry wrapped around a filling of salmon, dill, onions, and sour cream; *canard framboise*, duck with a delicate brown sauce flavored with raspberry vinegar; *daube de boeuf*; *navarin* of lamb; *coq au vin*; and even such plebeian attractions as Cornish pasties, *moussaka*, steak and kidney pie, or Narsai's own chicken pie.

The market always has a selection of freshly prepared salads: snow peas with exotic mushrooms, pickled Jerusalem artichokes, or a tangy celery root *remoulade*. Their pâtés are generally superb: duck liver pâté with port wine jelly, *pâté de volaille*, *pâté de campagne*, *ris de veau*, a *foie de porc*, and whatever other examples of the *charcutier's* art might inspire the resident chef. Their own fresh-baked breads complement the pâtés and cheeses available.

## San Francisco
## OPPENHEIMER

*2050 Divisadero off Sacramento, San Francisco 94115. Telephone (415) 563-0444. Hours: M-TH, F 7-7, SAT 9-6, SUN 9-5.*

The smart pink neon signs outside spell out Oppenheimer in tandem. Inside it's all Pacific Heights elegance in serene beiges and creams. "We wanted the food to be the main color," explain owners Eric Hamburger and Carl Haytcher. And it is beautiful: skinny baguettes; plump, flaky almond croissants; hand-shaped bagel twists and *bialys* in small baskets; fourteen different pâtés and *terrines*; first-cut kosher pastrami and corned beef; smoked game.

There are nine to twelve salads daily: two pasta salads, a *niçoise*, a *calamari* or crab, and one or more hot and spicy Hunan-style salads. Try the hot, shiny noodle or the pork and pasta salads. You can taste any of them before you buy.

They offer take-out entrées prepared by private chefs and caterers, and nine kosher dishes flown out from a kosher kitchen in Boston, including sweet and sour meatballs; knishes stuffed with meats, kasha, and onions; rolled cabbage; and Mother Oppenheimer's chicken soup with *kreplach* (meat-stuffed dumplings).

They plan to add eight to ten more entrées, available both fresh and frozen. You'll be able to take home a beef Wellington, a Cordon Bleu chicken, or a kosher roast beef brisket.

Oppenheimer has cadged an exclusive contract with Miss Grimble, New York's cheesecake queen, and has fourteen flavors of her very small, very rich, and very expensive creations, including her famous Grimbletorte (alternate layers of chocolate *génoise* and orange cheesecake, drenched in Grand

Marnier and covered with bittersweet chocolate).

And, like any mom and pop grocery, they stock necessities for the neighborhood—Tuscan olive oil, French vinegars and mustards, English preserves.

Expensive.

## Marin County
## TRUFFLES

*15 Madrona Street, Mill Valley 94941. Telephone (415) 388-3287. Hours: M–SAT 11–6:30.*

Call Truffles to be placed on the mailing list for the store's monthly menu of dishes available for take-out. Every day these include eight to ten fresh salads (tiny French lentils with ham, roast beef in horseradish sauce, beans mimosa, marinated Moroccan carrots); a selection of pâtés; fresh organic chicken roasted to a golden crisp; either a roast beef or a ham with hot pepper jelly glaze; a pasta entrée (lasagne with five cheeses or *fettuccine* with peas, prosciutto, and cheese); a second entrée such as curried chicken halves or *moussaka*; a daily soup (tomato with fresh basil); and a quiche made with fresh pastry.

Choose a dessert from the selection next door at True Confections.

And to stock your home freezer, Truffles also has a freezerful of frozen entrées.

## San Francisco
## LUCCA DELICATESSEN

*2120 Chestnut Street, San Francisco 94123. Telephone (415) 921-7873. Hours: M–F 9–6, SAT 7:30–6:30, SUN 8–6.*

This Chestnut Street version of an Italian *rosticceria*, a beloved spot in San Francisco for over fifty years, has the best roast chickens in town, fragrant

with herbs and flavored with vegetables stuffed inside. Ed Bosco roasts his own turkey and roast beef, too, and bakes high, round frittatas green with California's baby zucchini. His salads miraculously remain Italian, little Americanized. Try his home-cooked pigs' feet salad, the marinated kidney and garbanzo beans, or the lovely mixed fresh vegetable salad dressed with homemade mayonnaise.

Take home some boxes of his handmade ravioli and a carton of his frozen homemade minestrone, its rich stock flavored with prosciutto bones, for your emergency stores.

## East Bay
## MADE TO ORDER

*1576 Hopkins Street, Berkeley 94707. Telephone (415) 524-7552. Hours: M–SAT 10–6.*

Sylvana La Rocca and Linda Briganti have transformed Monterey Market's former storefront on Hopkins Street in Berkeley into a spacious and sunny gourmet delicatessen filled with wonderful food and wines with an Italian emphasis. There's a constant traffic of neighbors and customers stopping into the big kitchen here to say hello and make their orders.

Call in the morning to order their spectacular take-out specialty, Tuscan "chicken in a basket": a whole chicken roasted with lemon, garlic, and herbs, then wrapped in a bread dough suffused with the same herbs. It emerges from the oven a glazed ceramic brown, sculpted with bread-dough roses or grape clusters. Serving four to six, it can also be ordered with a bed of julienned sautéed vegetables beneath the chicken. Order the "original Caesar salad" to go with it: whole baby romaine leaves fanned out on a big platter with whole anchovies, Parmesan, and dressing.

Made To Order sells a fresh basil *pesto*, a *salsa casalinga* (a heavy meat and tomato sauce), and a *salsa bolognese* (with veal, chicken, pork, and prosciutto) to sauce their fresh semolina and durum wheat pasta.

And in the tradition of European *charcuteries*, Chef La Rocca often has marinated chickens or shish kebab ready for the grill, or thick, tender stuffed lamb chops for a quiet dinner at home. She also cures her own prosciutto the way her grandmother did it in Abruzzi-Molise, and the country pâté shows its Italian origin, too. There is a Florentine roll, a green and white spiral of top round, spinach, and cheese; a boned leg of lamb marinated in herbs and roasted; a pale pork loin cured in brine and spices; and an unsalted chicken galantine for those on low-sodium diets. The salads sold by the pound are made fresh every day and might include coleslaw, German potato, *ratatouille*, or French vegetable salad.

Made To Order will also create special take-out entrées and dinners.

---

**East Bay**
## THE PASTA SHOP

*5940 College Avenue, Oakland 94618. Telephone (415) 547-4005. Hours: M–F 10-7, SAT 10-6, SUN 12-5.*

The Pasta Shop, North Oakland's new *pastificio*, produces fresh egg and spinach pasta from whole eggs, semolina, and flour. You can make a quick pasta dinner with their *spaghettini, tagliolini, linguine*, or *fettuccine* and a spinach or basil *pesto*, a creamy Tuscan walnut and garlic sauce, a mushroom and cream sauce, or a *marinara* sauce, sold by the pint.

From that same tender pasta, they also make dishes to take out: a Molinari sausage lasagne made with the house *marinara* sauce and five cheeses, or a meatless lasagne with summer zucchini or eggplant. But the severe temptation is the lovely *torta di gorgonzola*: a mixture of Italy's seductive blue cheese and cream cheese encased in a pasta packet, then layered with sautéed tomatoes and topped with cheese.

Owner Bill Hughes (proprietor of John Brown's Cookware upstairs) believes in the basics: straightforward roasted or charcoal-grilled chickens every day, sold by the half or whole. Five salads are sold by the pound, and these change with the season: chicken curry with currants macerated in port, water chestnuts, almonds, and shallots; a Chinese tangy noodle dressed with black soy, vinegar, and chili oil; a green *tagliarini* with roasted sweet red peppers and pine nuts; or a curly *fusilli* pasta with spinach *pesto*, green peas, and imported sweet red and yellow *peperonata*.

For dessert, there's a lemon tart from La Viennoise next door, and Flo Braker's apple pie, "so good," Bill Highes testifies, "it brings tears to people's eyes."

---

**San Francisco**
## VIVANDE

*2125 Fillmore Street, San Francisco 94115. Telephone (415) 346-4430. Hours: M–F 11-7, SAT 11-6, SUN 11-5.*

The design of Vivande on Fillmore Street is spectacular, with a great open length of stainless steel kitchen at the back.

If you're having lunch at this new Italian-style take-out and delicatessen, the best seats in the house are at the two narrow marble counters looking right onto the action in the kitchen.

With its rope-tied provolone cheeses, some in the shape of little pigs, hanging overhead, Vivande's cheese case is immediately appealing, filled with the best of the Italian cheeses available in this country: rolls of cow's milk *caprini* as well as the authentic goat's milk *caprini; formaggio erbata,* ricotta cheese marinated in aromatic Italian herbs and olive oil; *mozzarella di bufala;* golden *wheels of parmigiano reggiano,* tubs of delicate *mascarpone,* wedges of *pecorino romano, caciocavallo,* Taleggio, and Gorgonzola.

The *salumeria* case displays pâtés and sausages, all made here. Their *salsiccie,* fresh pork sausages in casing or caul fat, come flavored with fennel, cheese, garlic, or hot red pepper. The pâtés include a creamy duck liver pâté scooped from a white ceramic dish, a smooth pork and liver pâté, and a savory country-style veal and pork pâté, as well as *terrines,* galantines, and daily specials *en croûte.* The stuffed breast of veal is beautiful, studded with pistachios. They also have a full line of Italian-style salami, *pancetta,* prosciutto, *mortadella,* and *coppa,* as well as corned beef, pastrami, *Bündnerfleisch* and Black Forest and Westphalian hams.

The store also prepares take-out specialities like rack of veal roasted with rosemary and garlic, *shiitake* mushrooms roasted on Vivande's grill, moist hickory-smoked ducks and chickens, crisp chickens roasted with rosemary, *cotechino* sausage with lentils, *pizza rustica,* and hearty soups.

The *antipasti* include artichokes prepared Roman-style, a lovely *insalata di fagioli con caviole, canellini* beans dressed with caviar; a squid salad; *caponatina,* the savory Sicilian eggplant relish with tomatoes, pine nuts, raisins, and capers; and *crostini,* thin toasts spread with mushrooms, garlic, olives, or sundry tomato toppings.

The store also stocks a small selection of ingredients for Italian cuisine: premium olive oils, Vivande's own wine vinegar in beautifully shaped glass bottles, jars of *mostarda,* anchovies packed in salt, and golden whitefish caviar. Near the front door there are bags of polenta, lentils, and dried beans in bulk, plus Arborio rice and imported pasta.

The *dolci,* all made on the premises, include fresh-fruit *crostate,* various tortas, even a *torta terremoto,* or chocolate "earthquake" cake with crackled crust; fragrant *amaretti* and crunchy *biscotti di Prato;* and wonderful *mele al forno,* baked apples with pastry cream.

For pasta and sauces to take out, see Pasta section.

# JAPANESE

**East Bay**
## BERKELEY FISH KITCHEN

*1504 Shattuck Avenue, Berkeley 94709. Telephone (415) 845-7166. Hours: T–SUN 11–6.*

Berkeley's sophisticated food esthetes have been stopping in their tracks to admire the windows of the Berkeley Fish Market where the Berkeley Fish Kitchen makes and displays trays of *sushi.* Koetsu Akasawa, a trained French chef and a veteran of Chez Panisse, Augusta's, and the Fourth Street Grill, always wanted to open a small Japanese restaurant. Berkeley Fish Kitchen features take-out Japanese food and specializes in *sushi.* Every day there are at least ten kinds of *makizushi* (rolled in seaweed): trays of *futomaki* (vegetables), *tekkamaki* (tuna), *sakemaki* (smoked salmon). There is *nigirizushi,* a finger's length of snowy rice topped with raw fish or a prawn and lined with *wasabi*

(horseradish); and the lovely *inari sushi,* golden pouches of deep-fried bean curd filled with rice, seafood, and vegetables; or the filling and popular *tawara sushi,* a large oval of the same rice secured with a waistband of dark seaweed.

From the tiny back kitchen comes *teriyaki* fish or chicken over rice; *sukiyaki* beef; squid and shrimp salads; or a briny *hijiki* salad (seaweed and *shiitake* mushrooms). *Bento* are Japanese lunchboxes filled with an assortment of *teriyaki* fish and chicken, prawns, Japanese omelet, pickles, and rice.

Ko also caters platters of *sashimi,* elaborate *sushi* arrangements, and *bento* for groups.

## LATINO

### East Bay
### JALISCO RESTAURANT

*1721 East Fourteenth Street, Oakland 94606. Telephone (415) 532-9484. Hours: M-T, TH-SUN 10-6.*

Friday, Saturday, and Sunday, Oakland's Jalisco Restaurant serves up some of the best *carnitas* north of Sonora when Bartolo Vasquez prepares great quantities of his buttery, flaky pig. The whole pigs are roasted deliciously *adobado*: caressed with lots of sweet onions, garlic, and a touch of cumin.

Sold by the pound, you can buy it *solo carnitas,* or *combinado,* with some of the coveted innards and liver sliced in along with the succulent meat. And if you like, you can sauce it with the fresh green *salsa* spiced with *cilantro* sitting in the black stone *mortero* on top of the counter. Bartolo's special *chicharrónes* are huge crispy planes of fried pork rind. From the counter, a package of fresh corn tortillas, some fat ripe mangoes, and a few limes to squeeze into your beer Mexican-style will supply you with the makings of a delicious *carnitas* feast.

### San Francisco
### LA TAQUERIA

*2889 Mission Street, San Francisco 94110. Telephone (415) 285-7117. Hours: 11-8 daily.*

The Mission District's La Taquería turns out authentic Mexico City–style tacos all day long. Two tender fresh corn tortillas enfold juicy *frijoles* and *carne asada* (grilled beef), *carnitas* (pork), chorizo (spicy sausage), chicken, or cheese, covered with a fresh *salsa* of tomato, onions, chilies, garlic, and lemon. The flour tortilla *burritos* come with the same fillings; they're just bigger.

La Taquería's *aguas frescas* are fresh fruit puréed with water to make a refreshing tropical drink: *plátanos* (green banana), melon, strawberry, pineapple, sometimes mango.

### East Bay
### TAQUERIA MORELIA

*4481 East Fourteenth Street, Oakland 94601. Telephone (415) 261-6360. Hours: 10-11 daily.*

Taquería Morelia is the East Bay's best *taquería.* The *quesadillas* are enormous, folded like handerchiefs, fried to the palest gold, and filled with molten cheese. Hearty eaters order the Super Burrito stuffed with *frijoles,* steak, *chile verde,* and sour cream and avocado.

The soft tacos and *burritos* can be ordered stuffed with savory *carne asada* (grilled meat), flavorful tender *carnitas* (roast pig), a wonderful *chile verde* with hot green chilies, a superior chorizo spiked with cloves and cumin, or *cabeza* (brain).

The *tortas*—Mexican sandwiches made on *bollilos,* or French-style bread— are filled with *carne asada, carnitas,* chorizo, or ham.

Inexpensive.

There are those, including even professed gourmets, who firmly state they don't want to know anything about wine. They'll drink it with pleasure, but learn about wine? It's too expensive. It's too complicated, and, once begun, there will never be an end to it. So they'll continue to pick labels by intuition or hearsay and not do too badly. But you don't need to acquire a great deal of knowledge to increase your wine-drinking pleasure dramatically.

Until recently, unless you were exposed to it by family or trained in it by profession, your chances of acquiring expertise in wine were slim. But for wine lovers, living in San Francisco has great advantages. The intense interest in food and wine here, the proximity to California's major wine regions, and the presence of sophisticated wine merchants have created thousands of wine enthusiasts. Wandering among the bins, you might meet a retired salmon fisherman with a passion for old Burgundies, a computer salesman interested in vintage ports, or a woman violinist who collects Cerruttis and reserve Chiantis.

Every year more and more tasting rooms and wine bars are opening in the Bay Area where you can sample and compare both California and imported wines. Wine classes are offered through adult education, specialized wine schools, cooking schools, and privately. And there needn't be a bit of tedium in the education of your palate.

Following is a selected guide to wine tastings, classes, wine societies, and wine-oriented bookstores and libraries in the San Francisco Bay Area.

## TASTING CATEGORIES

**Varietal** All the wines are made from the same grape variety; for example, the tasting may be a comparison of Cabernet Sauvignons from the different viticultural regions in California or Cabernet Sauvignons from farther afield, say Bordeaux or Australia.

**Blind** The wines included in the tasting are known by those participating, but the order of pouring is unknown. In both blind and double-blind tastings the wines are usually disguised in plain brown paper bags until their identities are revealed at the end of the tasting.

**Double-blind** The specific wines in the tasting as well as the order of pouring are unknown.

**Vertical** A comparison of different or successive vintage years of the same wine; for example, in a Château Ducru-Beaucaillou vertical, the ups and downs of vintage years in Bordeaux should be demonstrated as well as the wines' evolution with age.

**Horizontal** A comparison of wines from different vineyards or wine regions, but all of the same vintage and, usually, the same grape variety.

# INFORMAL TASTINGS

Informal tastings by the glass or the one-ounce taster's glass offer you a chance to sample a wine without buying (or drinking) a whole bottle. The price of the taste is based on the price of the bottle. Most wine stores and wine bars listed here pour new California releases and newly arrived European wines. Occasionally, there are rare old bottles, too. Informal tasting is one of the best ways to broaden your wine horizons.

## Contra Costa
### A LA CARTE

*2055 North Broadway, Walnut Creek 94546. Telephone (415) 932-4777. When: Late afternoons, weekdays and Sundays; all day Saturday.*

The three wines offered by the glass in the upstairs restaurant of this three-story gourmet market change daily and are poured later in the afternoon at the wine-tasting bar.

## San Francisco
### CRANE AND KELLEY

*2111 Union Street, San Francisco 94123. Telephone (415) 563-3606. Hours: M-F 10-6:30, SAT 10-6, SUN 11-6.*

Crane and Kelley offers tastings seven days a week at their miniscule stand-up bar and, after the lunch rush, at their few tables. On weekdays the new releases and other bottles change daily. Weekend offerings, listed in the store's newsletter, might be Louis Latour white Burgundies, the wines of Piedmont, fine California Chardonnays, or a festive tasting of Dom Perignon with delicate Pigeon Point oysters.

Dave Crane also selects the wines and presides over the tasting bar at their second shop inside the Oakville Grocery at Pacific and Larkin streets.

## East Bay
### CURDS AND WHEY

*6311 College Avenue, Oakland (4618. Telephone (415) 652-6317. Hours: M-SAT 10-6:30.*

The six or more wines poured daily at this small Oakland store change twice a week, with California varietals and new releases outnumbering imported wines. Once or twice a month on Saturday afternoons, wine makers like Jack Cakebread or Walter Raymond present their wines. Watch for the occasional Saturday featuring wines from home wine makers.
*Monthly calendar.*

## San Francisco
### EPICUREAN UNION

*2191 Union Street, San Francisco 94123. Telephone (415) 567-0941. Hours: S-TH 10-6, F-SAT 10-7.*

Epicurean Union is the tasting room for Windsor and Sonoma vineyards, with free samplings of all their wines.

## East Bay
### LAKE MERRITT WINE AND CHEESE REVIVAL

*552 Grand Avenue, Oakland 94610. Telephone (415) 836-3306. Hours: M-F 10:30-8:30, SAT 10:30-6.*

The small tasting bar at the back changes its scheduled tastings twice a week. Usually varietals, they range beyond the most popular varieties to white Rieslings, Merlots, and Cabernet Francs, or educational comparisons of

French Meurseults with California Chardonnays. Sherries, Sauternes, and champagnes are sold by the glass, along with eight ports. Try the excellent '70 Graham or the '75 Dow. Choose any of the more than six hundred wines in the store, including a big selection of tenths, at retail plus $2.50 corkage, to enjoy with escargots, or cheese and pâté boards at the small tables at the front.

### East Bay
## LE PIQUE NIQUE

*5620 College Avenue, Oakland 94618. Telephone (415) 654-9242. Hours: T-SUN, 11:30 am-2 pm, 5:30 pm-9 pm.*

The five wines offered each week may be medium-priced Cabernets, imported French whites, or other California varietals from boutique wineries. But the real point of visiting Le Pique Nique is to taste the wine with one of the *charcuterie's* sumptuous cheese and pâté boards. For a J. W. Morris retrospective, they even produced a blue cheese and walnut board to enhance his fine ports.

### San Francisco
## LONDON WINE BAR

*415 Sansome Street, San Francisco 94111. Telephone (415) 788-4811. Hours: M-TH 11:30-7, F 11:30-8. Lunch 11:30-2:30 daily.*

America's first wine bar, in the heart of the financial district, has established a sensible format for wine bars in this country. The fifteen wines posted daily over the bar include three reds, three whites, multiple specials, and at least one champagne. Choose from over a dozen ports, including Sandeman's '63, '66, and '67; and the '77 Dow, Quady, and Ficklin. There's a civilized stand-up bar with a brass footrail, and tables both upstairs and down. Quiche, salads, and sandwiches are served for lunch, pâté or fruit and cheese plates throughout the afternoon. Any bottle from their stock of 450 wines is available retail plus a corkage fee. Pick up a serving schedule at the bar.

### San Francisco
## MORRIS' FINE WINES AND SPIRITS

*605 Irving Street, San Francisco 94122. Telephone (415) 731-2429. Hours: TH-SUN 4-7.*

Morris's offers big two-ounce tasters' glasses of five to seven wines weekly, a bargain at 25¢ and up. The wines may all be from a single winery such as Château St. Jean, or varietals such as Fumé Blanc, comparing California wines to their French counterparts. Samplings hosted by the wine maker are listed in the printed tasting schedule.

### Contra Costa
## NARSAI'S MARKET

*389 Colusa Avenue, Kensington 94707. Telephone (415) 527-3737. Hours: F 3-6, SAT 12-6.*

Tastings here reflect Narsai David's avid interest in both French and California wines: clarets, French champagnes and California's sparkling wines, Alsatian Gewürztraminers, and the Napa Valley's late harvest. Don't miss the occasional event hosted by the wine maker. When Joseph Phelps presented his wines here, he brought a few old bottles along with his current releases.

The market added other wines, and Narsai couldn't resist bringing out older wines from his restaurant's extraordinary wine cellar to compare with the recent vintages.

The Bay Area's finest selection of aged French cognacs (35), Armagnac (12), brandies (15), and other eaux-de-vie are available by the glass at the adjoining restaurant's bar from five o'clock until midnight.

## East Bay
## NUMANO SAKE COMPANY

*709 Addison, Berkeley 94710. Telephone (415) 540-8250. Hours: 10–8 daily.*

This Berkeley-based Japanese company makes sake from a special rice strain grown in the Sacramento Valley. At their tasting room you can try the two types of sake made here, either straight or in a sake-based cocktail; a white rice wine; and an imported plum wine, all at no charge. Tours of the factory are Sundays from 12 to 4.

## East Bay
## PREMIER CRU WINE SHOP AND TASTING BAR

*4125 Piedmont Avenue, Oakland 94611. Telephone (415) 655-6091. Hours: M–SAT 11–7.*

Premier Cru opens two series of eight to ten wines weekly, including tastings of French and California Pinot Noirs, international sparkling wines, or new Sauvignon Blancs. Also by the glass are at least eight ports, including the local J. W. Morris, Quady, and Woodbury vintages, and Berkeley Wine Cellars' unusual Cabernet Sauvignon port; a gamut of sherries from *fino* to *oloroso* and cream; plus a golden Muscat from Spain.

A monthly newsletter lists scheduled tastings.

## Napa Valley
## SILVERADO RESTAURANT

*1374 Lincoln, Calistoga 94515. Telephone (707) 942-6725. Hours: 10 am–11:30 pm.*

The four wines by the glass or taster's glass scribbled on the chalkboard above the bar change daily. Or choose a bottle from the prize-winning wine list, which includes older California vintages, to share at the bar or enjoy with a meal in the restaurant.

## East Bay
## SOLANO CELLARS

*1580-A Solano Avenue, Albany 94706. Telephone (415) 525-0379. Hours: 11:30–8 daily.*

The daily tastings of California varietals at Solano Cellars change weekly. The wines may all be a single varietal such as Zinfandel, wines from the Sierra Foothills, a selection of good values, or wines from one winery.

*Monthly newsletter.*

## Peninsula
## THE TASTING ROOM

*Weimax Wines and Spirits, 1178 Broadway, Burlingame 94010. Telephone (415) 343-0182. Hours: M–SAT 11:30–9:02, SUN 11–5.*

The Tasting Room opens miscellaneous bottles and new releases of California wines weekdays. A schedule of weekend tastings is sent monthly to members of the store's wine club. The special Saturday tastings from 1 to 4 are not formal, but you should reserve your taste of the exceptional bottles featured.

Every few months owner Dave Bottles plans an all-day bus trip to the wine country which includes a lunch cookout.

*Printed tasting schedule.*

**Contra Costa**
## WALNUT CREEK WINE AND CHEESE CENTER

*1522 North Main Street, Walnut Creek 94596. Telephone (415) 935-7780. Hours: M-SAT 10-7.*

A series of eight wines is scheduled every week in an intelligently planned wine-tasting program. California Pinot Noirs might be followed by the big old-style red Burgundies of Marchand de Gramont, and then a tasting of other red Burgundies vs. the best California Pinot Noirs. (You learn to recognize the characteristics of the Pinot Noir grape, the difference in the wines it makes in Burgundy and in California, and the effect of different wine-making styles.) The daily tastings sometimes offer you a chance to taste fine wines like the '78 Chateau Margaux or Lafite (by the wineglass or taster's glass).

**San Francisco**
## WINE AND FOOD SHOP

*254 West Portal Avenue, off Nineteenth Avenue, San Francisco 94127. Telephone (415) 731-3062. When: Usually one day a week.*

Wine buyer Kim Baker pours six wines daily, usually varietals such as '78 Cabernets or '79 Chardonnays, and new releases.

**San Francisco**
## THE WINE MINE

*Wine and Cheese Center, 205 Jackson Street, San Francisco 94111. Telephone (415) 956-2518. When: One week a month, W-SAT 12-6:30.*

A recent change in wine-tasting policy has reduced the weekly wine tastings to one week a month concentrated on new releases and new arrivals from Europe.

In its former glory, the Wine Mine was a haven for serious wine amateurs. The wide-ranging and eclectic tastings changed weekly, and as each day progressed, new arrivals and interesting bottles from their "wine library" began to outnumber bottles on the scheduled tasting.

**East Bay**
## VINTAGE WINE CELLAR

*1000 B Street, Hayward 94541. Telephone (415) 886-8525. Hours: M-W 11:30-6, TH-SAT 11:30-11.*

Tastings of California wines from smaller producers change every week. On Friday night you can listen to live jazz, and on Saturday afternoon to classical music while you enjoy your glass of wine.

# FORMAL TASTINGS

Too much "tasting around" may be overstimulating, but it's a good way to discover the kinds of wines you like. Formal tasting explores one range of flavors at a time, such as Bordeaux from Saint-Emilion, 1978 white Burgundies, Ridge Zinfandels, or 1975 California Cabernets.

Because palates have a tendency to become snooty, most formal tastings are blind. The taster comes to the experience of the wines unprejudiced by labels. The test is in the glass. After swirling, sniffing, tasting, and gurgling each of eight to twelve wines, even the most unsophisticated palate can divine the best and the worst wines of the group. The hard part is evaluating the middle wines and finding a language to describe their subtle differences.

Most tastings use a simple point system to rank the wines. When everyone is finished, the group's results are compiled and the wines revealed one by one.

Formal tastings are by reservation only.

### Contra Costa
## A LA CARTE

*2055 North Broadway, Walnut Creek 94596. Telephone (415) 932-4777. When: Once a week, usually Thursday nights at 5 or 6.*

Inexpensive tastings of California varietals are led by wine buyer Lou Francone.

### San Francisco
## ASHBURY MARKET

*205 Frederick, San Francisco 94117. Telephone (415) 566-3134. When: Weekdays, once or twice a week at 7:30.*

Wilfred Wong, whose family has owned the Ashbury Market for twenty-five years, has a policy of reserving a small percentage of each year's California wine stock. This means he has a lot of older and hard-to-find wines for his small tastings with the store's staff and interested guests. Held in a private setting, there's no series of tastings more thorough. This year sixty-five '78 Cabernets were tasted over fourteen evenings, grouped by style, to ensure the ranking's significance. This fall, the group plans to taste eighty newly released Chardonnays over twenty evenings. The group begins evaluating the wines at 7:30 pm. At 9:00 they're tasted again with food to complement them: rabbit stew with the Zinfandels, stuffed roast veal with the Cabernets. Ask Wilfred Wong for details. Novices are welcome.

### Peninsula
## ASSU ENOLOGY CLUB

*P.O. Box 8943, Stanford 94305. Telephone (415) 328-8247. When: Sporadically September through June.*

Send $5 to the Enology Club to receive monthly announcements of wine tastings and classes for a year.

### San Francisco
## CRANE AND KELLEY

*2111 Union Street, San Francisco 94123. Telephone (415) 563-3606. When: Once a month, usually Wednesday night at 7:30.*

This small wine and cheese shop has formal tastings including '78 Bordeaux, '77 red Burgundies, and '78 white Burgundies. More expensive is a '70 Cabernet tasting comparing first-growth Bordeaux with the best of California's Cabernets, or a BV private reserve vertical tasting of selected vintages from '41 to '74.

### San Francisco
## DEGUSTATION

*P.O. Box 77233, San Francisco 94107. Telephone (415) 285-8019. When: Week nights as scheduled, 7-9.*

Watch the light fade over the city while you evaluate the eight to ten wines in front of you. Jean Wolfe Walzer, wine consultant and writer, conducts tastings in the specially designed glassed-in room at the back of her Victorian house on Potrero Hill. Her tastings are divided between European and California wines. Three tastings of different Burgundy vintages, '78 Grand Cru Beaujolais, and '71 Sauternes might alternate with tastings of legendary 1968 California Cabernets, pre-1970 Zinfandels, or older Chardonnays.

Since Dégustation is intended as a forum where the consumer can taste and inform him/herself about California wines, Walzer often invites wine makers and grape growers to conduct tastings of varietals, discussing their vinification and differences in style.

Call for information. Ms. Walzer will also give tastings to private groups on request.

## San Francisco
## ROBERT GOODHUE'S WINE TASTING

*55 Sutter Street No. 359, San Francisco 94104. Telephone (415) 956-1271. Tastings held at 660 Baker No. 505. When: Evenings 7-9.*

Robert Goodhue conducts popular varietal tastings such as '77 Zinfandels or '78 Chardonnays (eight best of vintage), but for those who'd like to inform themselves about German wines or Sauternes, he offers a fine series of tastings in both, including a tasting of the highest category of German wines, Trockenbeerenauslese; a comparison of Beerenauslese with their West Coast equivalents; and Kabinett wines. The Sauternes series has included a d'Yquem vertical, a Château Coutet, and a Rieussec vertical.

## East Bay
## JACKSON'S WINE AND SPIRITS

*3049 Ashby, Berkeley 94705. Telephone (415) 843-5840. When: SUN 3-5, bimonthly.*

This inexpensive series of tastings led by Chris Grossman introduces Jackson's customers to the bulk of the current releases. There's a Cabernet and Chardonnay series every month and occasional special-interest tastings such as a vertical St. Clement Chardonnay. See the store's newsletter for times and dates.

## San Francisco
## THE LONDON WINE BAR

*415 Sansome Street, San Francisco 94111. Telephone (415) 788-4811. When: Bimonthly.*

Twice monthly the London Wine Bar holds tastings downstairs in its brick-walled wine room. Tickets for the tastings, which include cheeses and bread, should be reserved. For instance, a series of Chardonnay tastings, the '76s, '77s, and '78s, shows how wine-making styles affect the aging potential of these big wines. A tasting of magnificent sweet botrytised Rieslings pits California late-harvest wines against their German counterparts.
*Schedule at the wine bar or by mail.*

## East Bay
## PREMIER CRU WINE SHOP AND TASTING BAR

*4125 Piedmont Avenue, Oakland 94611. Telephone (415) 655-6691. When: Weekday evenings as scheduled.*

This Oakland wine bar has special sit-down tastings in such "subjects" as 1976 Chardonnays, a comparison of different vintages of Heitz's "Martha's

Vineyard" Cabernet, or California Pinot Noirs followed the next evening by French red Burgundies.

## Napa Valley
### SILVERADO RESTAURANT

*1374 Lincoln, Calistoga 94515. Telephone (707) 942-6725. When: Tuesdays, 6 pm.*

Cellar master and owner Alex Dierkhising leads inexpensive comparative tastings of California varietals in the restaurant's back dining room.

## San Francisco
### TANTE MARIE'S COOKING SCHOOL

*271 Francisco Street, San Francisco 94133. Telephone (415) 771-8667. When: Every other Monday 2–4.*

Tante Marie's Cooking School sponsors educational tastings led by Peter Wilkins, an English wine consultant writing a book on the Napa Valley. The subject might be Cabernet Sauvignon, Pinot Noir, or Chardonnay. Tastings include cheese, bread, and hors d'oeuvres prepared by students.
*Monthly calendar.*

## Peninsula
### THE TASTING ROOM

*Weimax Wines and Spirits, 1178 Broadway, Burlingame 94010. Telephone (415) 343-0182. When: Monday, 7:30 pm, bimonthly.*

Tastings of California varietals. Choice tastings such as a comparison of the 1970 Cabernets including Heitz, BV, Chappellet, and Mayacaymus. Also a tasting of a 1971 German Riesling Eiswein and Beerenauslese (top year, top-of-the-line wines), or French champagnes.

## Contra Costa
### WALNUT CREEK WINE AND CHEESE CENTER

*1522 North Main Street, Walnut Creek 94596. Telephone (415) 935-7780. When: Twice a month, evenings.*

An excellent "meet the wine maker" series, designed to teach a lot more than just how the wine tastes. Grape grower Dick Steltzner has given a tasting of '74 Cabernets, all made from his grapes, but by different wineries. Michael Rhone, wine maker at Jordan winery, has presented a selection of his Cabernet aged in different oaks, and wines made from grapes grown in different vineyards on the property. Participants played wine maker and tried to make a blend to match Jordan's Cabernet.
    Regular tastings are often eclectic and inexpensive. A tasting featuring the Rhône wines of Marcel Guigal, including a white Hermitage and his fabulous '78 Côte Rotie "La Mouline," was a bargain. But there are also such luxurious evenings as a tasting of the 1966 first growth Bordeaux: $75 a ticket to linger over eleven of these fabled wines. Or a tasting of red Burgundies made by Monsieur Daudet-Naudin during the '50s in Savigny les Beaunes ($75).

## San Francisco
### THE WINE MINE

*Wine and Cheese Center, 205 Jackson Street, San Francisco 94111. Telephone (415) 956-2520. When: Tuesdays, 5:30 pm.*

Under Mel Knox's direction, the Wine Mine developed an ambitious formal wine-tasting program. The new wine buyer, Paul Moser, has discontinued the Saturday afternoon tastings, but Tuesday evening tastings still range from boutique Chianti Classicos, little-known Italian Brunellos, and '70 Bordeaux (including Becheville, Cos d'Estournel, Lynches Bages) to the best of the '79 Chardonnays. Luxurious tastings such as vintage ports spanning four decades or old Bordeaux dating from the twenties are sometimes scheduled. Enthusiasts who fill the older Burgundy tastings often can't resist donating special old bottles from their cellars to compare with wines officially in the tasting.

Beginners should watch for discussions and tastings of California white or red varietals and basic-component tastings.

**East Bay**
## VINTAGE WINE CELLAR

*1001 B Street, Hayward 94541. Telephone (415) 886-8525. When: evenings; see monthly calendar.*

Tastings of California varietals. Occasional Saturday afternoon "meet the wine maker" sessions with complimentary tastings. Wine-component tastings are led by Denis Kelly.

# ——WINE CLASSES——

Wine classes help structure your practical wine experience. You can learn the differences between classic types of wine, why a wine tastes the way it tastes, and the effects of grape variety, soil, climate, and vinification on the wine.

Unfortunately there is a surfeit of classes for novices and very few master classes. Check both the teacher and the wine list before enrolling.

**Peninsula**
## ASSU ENOLOGY CLUB

*P.O. Box 8943, Stanford, California 94305. Telephone (415) 328-8247. When: September through June.*

Classes taught by members of the Society of Wine Educators have been offered every quarter for nine years. Eight-session classes in "Basic Tasting," "California Perspectives," and European wine regions are inexpensive and comprehensive. Send for a description.

**San Francisco**
## CALIFORNIA WINE ACADEMY

*311 California Street, Suite 700, San Francisco 94104. Telephone (415) 346-2399.*

The California Wine Academy has classes for beginning and intermediate students who want to learn about wine in an organized classroom environment. The "Wine Basics" class, taught by Denis Kelly, focuses on developing sensory perception of wine, and includes wine vocabulary and component tasting. "Sharpening Your Wine Skills," taught by wine writer Richard Paul Hinkle, emphasizes developing a discriminating palate and building a sound wine memory. There are also one-day seminars in component tasting and a holiday class in champagnes.

**San Francisco**
## CRANE AND KELLEY

*2111 Union Street, San Francisco 94123. Telephone (415) 563-3606.*

Dave Crane periodically gives a class for novices, providing orientation in the world of wine and answers to questions on serving, selecting, and cellaring wine.

**East Bay**
## DENIS KELLY

*4482 Montgomery Street, Oakland 94611. Telephone (415) 658-8615.*

Denis Kelly, a founding director of the Society of Wine Educators, teaches wine appreciation classes in the East Bay. "Wines of the World" presents the great wines of major wine-producing regions of the world in six sessions. "Wine Appreciation" presents California and European wines in four sessions. Six wines are tasted with a variety of dishes in each of four sessions of "Wine and Food."
   Put your name on Denis's mailing list for future classes in German wines, wines of northern Italy, cognac, wine making, etc.

**Napa Valley**
## NAPA VALLEY WINE LIBRARY ASSOCIATION COURSES

*c/o James E. Beard, Wine Course Chairman, P.O. Box 16, St. Helena 94574.*

The Napa Valley Wine Library Association gives weekend courses in the spring and late summer. The "Introduction to Wine Appreciation" is an informal elementary course presented by wine professionals from the Napa Valley wineries. Lectures, field trips, and tastings cover sensory evaluation; grape varieties; wine production; and the selecting, storing, and tasting of wines. The fee includes a year's membership in the Association.

**East Bay**
## JEANNE QUAN CATERING

*Jeanne Quan, 2163 Vine Street, Berkeley, 94709. Telephone (415) 841-6500 ex. 188, or 848-9713.*

Jeanne Quan, a caterer with background in wine retailing, consults and teaches classes in stocking wine cellars.

**San Francisco**
## SAN FRANCISCO STATE UNIVERSITY EXTENSION

*1600 Holloway, San Francisco 94132. Telephone (415) 469-1373.*

For the third year San Francisco State University Extension will offer a wine appreciation course taught by Jean Wolfe Walzer, a wine consultant and founder of Dégustation. "To Taste, But Not To Drink: An Introduction to Wine" meets one evening a week for eight weeks. Learn vocabulary, tasting techniques, and characteristics of major wine varietals through tastings of wines from different countries, with a special emphasis on California wines.

**San Francisco**
## UC BERKELEY EXTENSION

*Extension Center, 55 Laguna Street, San Francisco 94102. Telephone (415) 642-4111.*

Wine consultant Mel Knox and wine maker Jim Olsen of JW Morris teach a four-meeting class on the "Wines of California and Europe," emphasizing comparisons of wine-making techniques and characteristics of California and European wines of similar types.
   Best bet: Mel Knox's course, "Winemakers of California." At each of the four meetings devoted to one grape variety, two wine makers discuss their

philosophy and wine-making techniques. His "Component Tasting" examines sensory components of wine.

## Davis
## UC DAVIS EXTENSION

*UC Davis, Davis 95616. Telephone (916) 752-6021.*

The oenology department at UC Davis offers weekend courses of interest to wine buffs in the greater Bay Area.

Students in the "Intensive Wine Weekend," given each fall at the end of the harvest in either Napa or Sonoma Valley, attend lectures, tastings, and winery tours. The faculty members discuss varietal wines, dessert and aperitif wines, and champagne making. The fee includes wines, dinners, and lunches, but not accommodations.

The "Sensory Evaluation of Wine" weekend, held on the Davis campus, "focuses on enhancing the critical tasting ability of the serious oenophile" and on building a sound wine memory. Lectures and tastings of doctored wines teach you to determine levels of sweetness, tannin, acid, and alcohol as well as wine defects and off-odors. You'll see local wine merchants and tasters honing their palates in this serious class. Because it's given just once a year and limited to fifty students, it fills rapidly. The fee includes two lunches, a handbook, and all wines.

There's also a series of one-day lectures on subjects of interest to home wine makers and owners of small wineries.

Call or write Jim Lapsley, program specialist, for a complete description of all courses.

## San Francisco
## WINE AND FOOD SHOP

*254 West Portal Avenue, San Francisco 94127. Telephone (415) 731-3062.*

The Wine and Food Shop periodically schedules a four-week wine and cheese class taught by wine buyer Kim Baker and Eileen Glickman.

## San Francisco
## THE WINE EDUCATION CENTER
## OF SAN FRANCISCO

*Vintners Building, 655 Sutter Street, Suite 408, San Francisco 94102. Telephone (415) 863-WINE.*

This year the Wine Education Center of San Francisco begins its first series of classes for both the wine professional and the serious wine enthusiast (under the directorship of Scottie McKinney, founder of Charcuterie Cooking School). The Center will offer wine appreciation classes for the consumer, viticulture and oenology courses for the home wine maker, and classes for the restaurateur and wine bar owner, for sommeliers, and for retailers and wholesalers.

Most classes will meet once a week, but there will also be intensive three-day seminars with classes, lectures, and workshops, all focused on one aspect of wine education.

Write for a brochure and schedule.

## Napa Valley
## THE WINE SCHOOL

*1200 Oak Avenue, St. Helena 94574. Telephone (707) 963-7903.*

Owner Lisa Vandewater, a chemist working with small wineries and home wine makers, gives highly technical classes in many phases of small winery and home wine making, including microbiology. But she also offers one-day or weekend classes in the sensory evaluation of wines for interested consumers as well as professionals, where she demonstrates the more sophisticated aspects of organoleptic investigation of wine and the role of analytical tasting in assessing wine development.

Other weekend classes include wine processing at home and tasting wines at home. The school plans to add a wine appreciation course to the curriculum sometime in 1982: a series of once-a-week tastings of selected wines with a lecture and discussion of the wines presented.

# ——WINE DINNERS——

Comparative wine tastings are somewhat abstract—certain wines will perform well when tasted with other wines, but put them in a real-life laboratory, in the middle of a meal, and they behave very differently. Special wine luncheons and dinners demonstrate how wines react with certain foods and explore ways to orchestrate the many wines in a fine meal.

### San Francisco
### CLIFT HOTEL

*Geary at Taylor Street, San Francisco 94108. Telephone (415) 775-4700.*

Every other month the Clift Hotel invites a Napa Valley wine maker to present a one-hour tasting of his wines before serving a six-course dinner with wines in the main dining room. The tasting is at 7:30, with dinner following at 8:30; reserve one week in advance. Dinners are announced in the hotel's bimonthly newsletter, *Seasonings*.

### San Francisco
### CRANE AND KELLEY

*2111 Union Street, San Francisco 94123. Telephone (415) 563-3606.*

Crane and Kelley has a seasonal dinner-lecture series. Spring's theme was Burgundy, with three evenings devoted to

one aspect of the wines from the region. The first dinner, at the Hayes Street Grill, featured 1978 white Burgundies. The second, at Andalou in San Rafael, compared 1969 and 1978 red Burgundies, and the last, at Piedmont's Bay Wolf restaurant, evaluated 1972 red Burgundies.

### San Francisco
### DEGUSTATION

*P.O. Box 77233, San Francisco 94107. Telephone (415) 285-8019.*

Dégustation holds tasting dinners twice a month in the lovely wine-tasting room at the back of Jean Wolfe Walzer's Victorian house. The food is prepared by private caterers; the wines come from Ms. Walzer's eclectic cellar.

On weekends, she sometimes arranges a tour and tasting at a small winery, followed by a lavish catered picnic and more tasting.

### Napa Valley
### D'VINE WINE TOURS

*Susan Benz, P.O. Box 224, St. Helena 94574. Telephone (707) 963-2164.*

Enjoy a relaxed, informal day visiting three premium wineries in a comfortable van driven by Susan Benz, your experienced guide. The charge includes a gourmet picnic lunch and wines from selected wineries. Reserve at least one day ahead, one week ahead for large groups.

### San Francisco
### ROBERT GOODHUE'S
### WINE TASTING

*55 Sutter Street Suite 359, San Francisco 94104. Telephone (415) 956-1271.*

Mr. Goodhue plans a wine dinner once or twice a month for regulars at his tastings. A recent dinner with five

Chardonnays ended with a '78 Long botrytised Johannesberg Riesling and the '71 Château Climens Sauternes.

**San Francisco**
## SHIRLEY SARVIS' WINE AND FOOD TASTINGS

*Fournou's Ovens, Stanford Court Hotel, Powell and California, San Francisco 94108. Telephone (415) 989-355 Ex. 101, or 981-1910. When: Wednesdays, 12 to 2. Reserve ahead.*

On Wednesdays you can join well-known food writer Shirley Sarvis at her ongoing series of wine and food tastings at Fournou's Ovens in the Stanford Court Hotel. Each week Ms. Sarvis matches five wines with a four-course luncheon. Is a soft white wine better with a cream-sauced shrimp dish than a steely Chablis? Discover why certain wines have an affinity for certain foods as Ms. Sarvis discusses the fascinating interaction of food and wine.

**Peninsula**
## THE TASTING ROOM

*Weimax Wines and Spirits, 1178 Broadway, Burlingame 94010. Telephone (415) 343-0182.*

Burlingame's Tasting Room sponsors a "Wine and Dine" dinner series monthly at La Potinière Restaurant in San Mateo. There has been a Stag's Leap wine dinner, a dinner with John Williams from Spring Mountain, and a Zinfandel dinner.

**Contra Costa**
## WALNUT CREEK WINE AND CHEESE CENTER

*1522 North Main Street, Walnut Creek 94596. Telephone (415) 935-7780.*

Every six weeks the Walnut Creek Wine and Cheese Center has a wine dinner. A fish barbecue accompanied with French and California champagnes, and an Italian dinner with aperitifs, Italian wines, and a dessert wine have been recent events.

# —WINE SOCIETIES—

Once wine becomes a passion, the obvious step is to join a wine society where you'll meet other aficionados of the grape. Indulge in wine gossip, trade newly discovered *petits vins*, and attend regular wine tastings and lectures with other committed oenophiles.

**Paris**
## LE CLUB DE L'ACADEMIE DU VIN

*25 Royale (Cité Berryer), Paris 75008. Telephone 265 09 82.*

If you're planning a trip to Paris this year, join Le Club de l'Academie du Vin first. When you get to Paris, you can attend wine tastings and take classes at L'Academie du Vin at preferential prices. And here at home you'll receive their quarterly twenty-page bulletin. Written in both English and French, it's filled with information on French vineyards and vintages, notes from the club's weekly tastings, and market reports region by region.

The annual dues for members from abroad is F 100 or, at last check, just about $20.

**San Francisco**
## LES AMIS DU VIN

c/o *The Wine House, 1535 Bryant Street, San Francisco 94103. Telephone (415) 495-8486.*

Les Amis du Vin is an open-membership club. The annual dues include a subscription to their bimonthly magazine, *Wine.* Nonmembers are welcome to attend monthly tastings at the World Affairs Center on Sutter Street. The tastings are large, seventy-five to a hundred people, with informal ranking of wines by handhold, and discussion afterward.

The club also invites guest speakers, plans visits to local wineries, and sponsors wine and gastronomic tours to France, Italy, Spain, and Portugal.

**Napa Valley**
## NAPA VALLEY WINE LIBRARY ASSOCIATION

*P.O. Box 328, St. Helena 94574. Telephone (707) 963-5244.*

The $10 annual membership fee gives you access to the specialized wine library (within the Saint Helena public library), a subscription to the newsletter listing new wine books in the collection and dates of the spring and summer wine appreciation classes, and an invitation to the gala tasting in August—in itself well worth the price of the membership.

**San Francisco**
## THE VINTNERS CLUB

*Vintners Building, 655 Sutter Street, San Francisco 94102. Telephone (415) 885-5900.*

The Vintners Club is a private club open to anyone with a serious interest in wine. The comprehensive series of wine tastings and the extensive wine library attract many members of the wine trade. Resident memberships are $300 plus monthly dues of $12.50.

Double-blind sit-down tastings are held every Thursday from 4:30 to 6:00 and are open to members and guests. The club also sponsors lectures and seminars, field trips to the wine country, and wine dinners for its members.

**San Francisco**
## THE WINE AND FOOD SOCIETY OF SAN FRANCISCO

*311 California Street, San Francisco 94104. Telephone (415) 397-4393.*

The San Francisco chapter of the Wine and Food Society was the first in this country and, with 170 members, all of them men, is still the most exclusive. New members must have a serious interest in food and wine and must be sponsored by a member and approved by a membership committee. Membership is $300 plus a $125 annual fee.

The Society has its own wine cellar at John Walker's wine store and holds private monthly tastings and dinners.

# —— WINE BOOKS ——

One of the best ways to learn about wine is by independent study. Start by reading about a wine, then drink a good example and compare your impressions with what you've read.

Every good bookstore carries a few classic wine texts alongside the cookbooks, but specialized books are harder to find. Check used-book stores such as Moe's in Berkeley, Holmes Bookstore in San Francisco and Oakland, or Columbus Avenue Books in San Francisco for used copies of the classics. The first edition of Hugh Johnson's useful *World*

*Atlas of Wine* differs little from the current edition. Copies of Leon Adams's historical *The Wines of America* surface occasionally. Request a search for hard-to-find titles that interest you.

When you've read all the currently published and available sources, there are specialized wine libraries to consult: The most accessible is the Napa Valley Wine Library, newly housed in the public library in St. Helena (telephone [707] 963-5244). The large collection includes international books and periodicals, oral histories, and memorabilia. Books can be requested through your local library, too. With your $10 annual membership, you receive a listing of the books in the extensive collection, notices of classes, a subscription to the newsletter, and an invitation to the annual August wine tasting.

Another valuable resource is the Alfred Fromm Rare Wine Books Library inside the Wine Museum at 663 Beach Street, San Francisco (telephone [415] 673-6990). Students, researchers, and writers may consult the large collection, which includes rare books dating from 1550 and titles in seven languages.

Members of the private Vintner s Club (655 Sutter Street, San Francisco 94102, telephone [415] 885-5900) have the use of the club's large wine library with well over a thousand volumes, an extensive file of wine lists, and subscriptions to international wine publications.

**San Francisco**
## THE BOOKSTALL

*708 Sutter Street, San Francisco 94109. Telephone (415) 673-5446. Hours: M–SAT 12–5:30.*

This old-, rare-, and used-book store specializes in cookbooks, among others. Their catalog, *Bon Appetit,* has a beverage section that lists a great many works on cocktails, bars, and mixing drinks,

and also includes wine books such as Renato Dettori's 1953 *Italian Wines and Liquors,* Cyril Ray's *The Complete Imbiber,* a book on port published by Istituto do Vinho do Porto, and a turn-of-the-century book on homemade liqueurs.

**San Francisco**
## CONNOISSEUR WINE IMPORTS

*462 Bryant Street, San Francisco 94107. Telephone (415) 433-0825. Hours: M–F 9–5:30, SAT 9–4.*

Connoisseur Wine Imports carries the hard-to-find Christie's wine publications written by English experts. Michael Broadbent's concise *Winetasting* is one of the most useful basic books you can own. Both Sara Bradford's *Port* and Cyril Ray's monograph on Mouton Rothschild are excellent. While there, check the exceptional German wines and older Sauternes in this warehouse-like store.

**San Francisco**
## COOKBOOK CORNER

*620 Sutter Street, San Francisco 94102. Telephone (415) 673-6281. Hours: M–SAT 11–5:30.*

Just up Sutter Street from the Williams-Sonoma cookware store and across from wine merchants Draper and Esquin, *inside* the YWCA, is a bookstore devoted entirely to cookbooks. Cookbook Corner's wine section is not extensive, but there are unexpected finds studded among the old and new standards: a German wine atlas, a guide to the wine roads of Italy.

*Search service provided. Mail orders welcome.*

## San Francisco
# THE EUROPEAN BOOK COMPANY

*925 Larkin, San Francisco 94109. Telephone (415) 474-0626. Hours: M–F 9:30–6, SAT 9:30–5.*

Books on wine in French; also guides to French vineyards.

## East Bay
# HOUSEHOLD WORDS

*P.O. box 7231, Berkeley 94707. Mail order.*

When librarian Kay Caughran retired after twenty years at the Berkeley library, she started a business dealing in used, out of print, and rare books associated with "cooking, eating, drinking, and kindred subjects," *Household Words* catalogs the books she's gathered in her wide-ranging researches. Wine lovers might be tempted by a 1933 edition of Saintsbury's *Notes on a Cellar Book*; Everett Crosby's *The Vintage Years*, the story of a vineyard only thirty-five miles from mid-town Manhattan; or books on the history of wines and spirits, wine cookery, and guides to the wine country. For wine makers, she has occasional French works on vinification, technical information for vintners, and one irresistible work on how to make wine from cabbages, turnips, or apple peels.
*Catalog $2.*

## San Francisco
# THE INTERNATIONAL CORNER

*500 Sutter Street, San Francisco 94102. Telephone (415) 981-1666. Hours: M–F 9:30–6, SAT 9:30–5.*

This European bookstore has a wide range of books on wine in French, from general-information pocket books and guides to France's wine country to specialized texts on specific wines and regions.

## Michigan
# THE WINE AND FOOD LIBRARY

*1207 West Madison, Ann Arbor, Michigan 48103. Telephone (313) 663-4894. Mail order.*

List the books you'd like to find and write for an updated listing of the books in Jan Longone's collection. An impassioned food and wine scholar, Ms. Longone performed a miracle for one wine student: she turned up two copies of the privately published bible of Bordeaux, Cocks et Feret's *Bordeaux et Ses Vins.*

## San Francisco
# THE WINE APPRECIATION GUILD

*1377 Ninth Avenue, San Francisco 94122. Telephone (415) 566-3532. Hours: M–F 8:30–3:30.*

If you're unable to find a book at any of your usual haunts, call the Wine Appreciation Guild, which distributes English-language wine books to local bookstores. Their stock includes Faber and Faber's fine English series on famous wine regions, usually very difficult to find here; an English sommelier's guide called *Wine Service in the Restaurant*; and the classic *Port* by George Robertson.
     And if they can't suggest a nearby store that stocks your book, they'll sell it to you by mail.

## CHINESE MARKETS

For years, San Francisco's Chinatown was centered along Grant Avenue, but through the years the real shopping area has been moving up the hill to Stockton Street. Now Chinatown is edging its way onto Powell Street and crossing Broadway to North Beach.

You'll do better in Chinatown if you shop where the Chinese do. Prices are lower, too, away from Grant at stores geared toward the Chinese community rather than the tourists. Shop shrewdly, as the Chinese do, stopping in at all the different stores along your way. Buy a handful of flat Chinese chives in one store, a half dozen speckled quail eggs or bags of fleshy *shiitake* mushrooms in another. One produce store might have tender baby hearts of Chinese broccoli at a good price; another, bundles of perfect long beans or fresh ginger root tinged with rose at the edges.

On Stockton Street, stop in at Kwong Jow, the Chinese sausage makers, for sweetish *lop cheong.* Pick up your *won ton* skins around the corner at Ping Yuen Drugstore, then a little roast pig at Sun Sang Market, fresh ground pork and a Dungeness crab somewhere else. You can buy your favorite brand of hot bean sauce in one of the many general Chinese groceries.

But for all kinds of cooking, Chinatown has beautiful produce, the freshest poultry in town, an abundance of fresh seafood, and good meat. Pork is the specialty here, with almost every part of the pig for sale.

After a few hours' absorbing shopping, it's time to set down your heavy bags and rest your weary feet in one of Chinatown's many *dim sum* parlors. At Tung Fong Dim Sum, a cozy shop on Pacific Avenue, they bring out assorted trays of *dim sum* rather than the usual rolling carts, but have just as many kinds as some of the larger establishments like the Hong Kong Tea House across the street. Yank Sing Restaurant on Broadway is good, too, one of the oldest *dim sum* parlors in Chinatown.

The very best time to shop in Chinatown is early on Saturday and Sunday when there are lots of street vendors, too. You'll see trucks parked along Stockton Street selling tiny Delta clams, snails, quail eggs, and game birds. If you notice a crowd gathered around a van, go up and investigate. Its darkened interior might be lined with cages of quail, squab, and pheasant. Someone holds out two 5-dollar bills; the van's owner ties the wings of a gorgeous pheasant and puts the live bird into a brown paper bag. Another woman stacks handmade wooden cages filled with live poultry and game birds right on the roof of her van to advertise her wares. Later in the afternoon you might see some boys arrive with a big plastic trash can full of live fish. Suddenly everyone on the street is waving dollar bills and trying to get close enough to buy some fish. An older Chinese woman elbows her way out of the flailing circle with three or four fish in a plastic bag.

"What kind of fish?"

"One dollar," she answers, smiling and proud.

You'll see people selling Japanese-style persimmons on the street corners for half the price in the stores, or young Vietnamese girls with a few fish spread in front of them on newspapers. Two more are selling packaged dried black mushrooms and foil-wrapped Vietnamese sausages. An old woman holds out gorgeous ivory almonds in the shell.

Go. Enjoy the spirited bustle and the visual delight of San Francisco's unique Chinese market. And Oakland's smaller Chinatown is wonderful, too, much less crowded, not at all touristic, with plenty of parking.

*Note:* See also sections such as Take-Out, Pastry, Charcuterie, and Produce for specific Chinese foods. Many of the stores listed in the General Oriental section carry Chinese foods. See Cookware for Chinese utensils, woks, etc.

## San Francisco
## THE CHINESE GROCER

*209 Post Street, San Francisco 94108. Telephone (415) 391-8764 or 982-0125. Mail order.*

For those intimidated by the confusion and bustle of Chinatown stores, the Chinese Grocer makes it easy to shop for Chinese groceries. You can order everything including cooking equipment and hard-to-find ingredients by mail from a descriptive list of groceries. Everything is clearly labeled in English: dried lotus leaves (soak them briefly in water, wrap around rice and meat mixtures, then steam the tiny bundles); dried oysters for stir-fry dishes and soups; water-chestnut flour to make a light batter for your deep-fried foods; unusual spices such as dried white lotus seeds, star anise, and Szechwan peppercorns.

The Chinese Grocer publishes a newsletter on Chinese cooking, called *Wok Talk*, with informative articles on Chinese ingredients, recipes, Chinese cooking techniques, and food notes from travelers in China. Subscriptions to the bimonthly newsletter are $9.50 per year.

Send for a descriptive list of groceries. Minimum order $15.00.

## San Francisco
## HING LUNG COMPANY

*1261 Stockton Street, San Francisco 94133. Telephone (415) 397-5521. Hours: 9–6 daily.*

Hing Lung Company is a good place to start your Chinatown shopping. Stocked with a wide range of imported Chinese foodstuffs, the store is still not too large or confusing to be overwhelming. You'll find all the basic canned and bottled goods on your shopping list, plus spices and a good selection of dried noodles.

Sometimes you'll find good-quality dried *shiitake* mushrooms on sale. Those with thicker meat, grown in winter, are sold packaged in clear boxes. Chinese often bring a box of these mushrooms, or a fresh duck, or a box of good tea when visiting a relative who lives outside of Chinatown.

The tea selection is good here. The packaged round "pillows" or cylinders called Po Nay tea is the same strong black tea you order in tea houses to cut the heaviness of *dim sum.* Another favorite type comes in a basket, wrapped in paper and tied with a ribbon. Foo Cha Kan Wa tea is the bitter herb tea taken very strong when you're sick. The taste is so terrible, it's usually followed with a salted plum to set your mouth straight.

You can buy ammonium carbonate here, the secret ingredient in the restaurant technique of making "glassy" shrimp—it makes the shrimp firm. They also have curing salt for red pork; it's the only way you can achieve the requisite color.

Like most Chinese groceries, Hing Lung has salted duck eggs in little plastic packets, as well as earthenware crocks of black salted eggs cured in a lime and sulphur solution. You have to wash them off before using. Mix the runny white into a meat patty, leaving the rich yolk for the top. The yolks are also used for the centers of moon cakes or in *dim sum.*

East Bay
## HONG KEE MARKET

*385 Eighth Street, Oakland 94607. Telephone (415) 444-4244. Hours: 9–6 daily.*

Hong Kee is like a remarkable library where all the books are shelved without any discernable order. It may take a long time to find the items on your shopping list, but along the way you're sure to find something intriguing: tied bundles of dried fish skin, packages of shredded rice grain, little flats of speckled quail eggs. Peer into the crates still waiting to be unpacked: jars of salted fish pieces, silver skin side out, glistening through the brine and oil; cans of *proc,* or palm sugar; packages of white jelly fungus from the Egret River in the People's Republic of China.

Hong Kee has plenty of Chinese foodstuffs, including fat spirals of dried conger pike maw, and deep urns of salted and preserved eggs. There are lots of Thai foodstuffs, too: cooked pork skin, fresh tamarind, frozen coconut milk, young coconut, frozen fish balls, jars of pickled mudfish, shrimp paste, chili pastes, and a comprehensive selection of hot and hottest chili sauces.

East Bay
## KWONG FAR COMPANY

*940 Webster Street, Oakland 94607. Telephone (415) 465-7960. Hours: 8–7 daily.*

Kwong Far Company is owned by three brothers who rotate positions at the fish, meat, and deli counters so that they all know the entire business. The delicatessen is at the front, with a sit-down eating area. In back is the neat supermarketlike store with wide aisles. Everything is clearly labeled in both English and Chinese, with prices well marked, too.

As you browse down the wide aisles, you'll see seven-pound cans of tomato catsup sitting next to five-pound tins of plum sauce and thin soy sauce. The array of spices includes Szechwan red peppers, star anise, and dried mandarin orange peel. Gallon cans of peanut oil sit next to bottles of regular or black sesame oil. The tea selection is extensive, and you'll also find packages of dried watercress, cole, and sweet potato for use in soups.

Check the freezer for fish curd, bean curd, bean curd strips, jellyfish, and frozen prepared pot stickers, dumplings, and *dim sum.*

The produce section is stocked with a basic selection of Chinese vegetables. Across from it, you can usually buy live carp, sucker, blackfish, and prawns from a tank. The fish counter is stocked with fresh fish, both filleted and whole. If you need a special whole fish for a banquet dish, let them know a day ahead of time. The shellfish includes clams, oysters, and mussels. Sea urchin and eel are often available.

The store's meat counter carries extensive cuts of pork and beef, plus beef and hog blood as well as several kinds of tripe. The deli oven can turn out 12 golden-brown pigs or 144 ducks at one time. At Chinese New Year, they usually sell over 60 pigs a day.

San Francisco
## KWONG JOW SAUSAGE MANUFACTURING COMPANY

*1157 Grant Avenue, San Francisco 94133. Telephone (415) 397-2562. Hours: M–F 9–5, SAT 9–4:30, SUN 8:30–4:30.*

Great bunches of chewy Chinese sausage called *lop cheong,* made with sweet Cantonese-style pork, duck liver, or beef, are hung across the back of this tiny store. To one side, you'll see garlands of mahogany *cha siew* (barbecued pork), barbecued pork snouts, and curly twists of bacon rind for seasoning Chinese dishes. Cut sausages into rounds and serve steamed with rice or use in stir-fry dishes.

### East Bay
### KWONG ON TEONG

*720 Webster Street, Oakland 94607. Telephone (415) 452-0690. Hours: 10:30–5:30 daily.*

Kwong On Teong seems like a Chinese country store, with its wide planked floor and an open storefront with produce arranged on wooden steps. Dozens of Smithfield hams and smaller pepper-coated country-style picnics hang overhead. Apothecary candy jars hold almonds, preserved plums, candied ginger, brown ginger. The rest of the store is filled with general Chinese foodstuffs. Rice bowls, soupspoons, and spun-steel woks are sold at the back.

Most of the meat is sold wholesale to restaurants, but they do sell ground pork and pork butt to retail customers.

### San Francisco
### LUN WAH GROCERY

*1117 Stockton Street, San Francisco 94133. Telephone (415) 986-0756. Hours: 9–6 daily.*

Lun Wah Grocery has Chinatown's tiniest deli counter, with wonderful Chinese fried chicken and pickled pigs' feet sauced with black vinegar and fresh ginger. But besides this, Lun Wah is a general-Chinese-goods store. Fat spirals of pale pike maw hang from the ceiling like decorations for a street festival. Underneath, there's a profusion of dried squid and fish, dried mushrooms, teas, and canned goods. Don't hesitate to ask what anything is; the clerks here are helpful.

Pick up a half dozen tiny speckled quails' eggs, a bundle of flat Chinese chives, and some fresh green *cilantro*. Buy a flat of thirty eggs; they'll wrap them in Chinese newspaper and tie it neatly with string.

### San Francisco
### MAN FUNG
### CHINA TRADING COMPANY

*1301 Stockton Street, San Francisco 94133. Telephone (415) 433-8678. Hours: M–F 10–6, SAT–SUN 9–6.*

Man Fung China Trading Company has choice goods from mainland China in abundance. Fill your string bag with Fukienese dried sweet potato; dried preserved and pickled vegetables from all over China; teas from Yunnan; hot bean sauce in ceramic jars; Szechwan pickled vegetables; and soft, candied preserved peaches and pears.

### San Francisco
### MANLEY PRODUCE COMPANY

*1101 Grant Avenue, San Francisco 94133. Telephone (415) 982-1490. Hours: 8:30–5:30 daily.*

Manley Produce is one of the oldest Chinese groceries in Chinatown. They have just about everything, but the prices are higher than in the stores on Stockton Street. Listed as a mail-order source for Oriental ingredients in the back of countless Chinese and Oriental cookbooks, Manley Produce has had lots of practice shipping exotic foodstuffs.

### East Bay
### MAN LUNG COMPANY

*383 Eighth Street, Oakland 94607. Telephone (415) 451-9248. Hours: M–SAT 9:30–6:30.*

A young woman hums Chinese tunes behind the counter while you browse through the overstuffed aisles of Man Lung Company: whole dried salted fish from Hong Kong; vermicelli from China, Thailand, and the Philippines; pillow-sized bags of prunella; Korean dried laver (seaweed); packages of dried baby squid and fish; plus sweet preserved fruits like snow plum and plum ginger.

A table at the back holds bouquets of Chinese greens and herbs. And yard-high ceramic tubs are packed with salted eggs, so black they look like lumps of coal, or preserved eggs covered with sawdust. At the front are sectioned fresh lotus roots; cartons of soya drink from Hong Kong; and fresh rice noodles, thick and opaque. Fragrant Chinese sausages from Kwong Jow in San Francisco hang overhead along with Virginia pepper-coated smoked pork shoulder and picnic ham. Out front, there are crates of the most beautiful long beans.

## San Francisco
## METRO FOOD COMPANY

*641 Broadway, San Francisco 94133. Telephone (415) 982-1874. Hours: 9:30–6 daily.*

Metro Food Company is the only Shanghai store in Chinatown. Here you can find many ingredients unavailable elsewhere in San Francisco. The small freezer case just at the entrance holds all manner of fish caught in the South and East China seas, such as yellow croaker or pomfret, a fish with a very small head and lots of sweet flaky flesh. These are all flash frozen right when they're caught, so when you unthaw them, you must be sure to gut them.

Metro Food buys Szechwan vegetables in bulk and then repackages them. They also have jellyfish in bulk, sold from big crocks in three or four

grades and prices. Everywhere else it's sold already packaged and is usually a lower grade, from Southeast Asia. Since jellyfish is salted and dried, to use it you must soak it overnight and parboil it before shredding. Properly prepared, it gives Chinese dishes a wonderful crunchy texture.

Check the back refrigerator cases stocked with noodle dough, dumplings, and fish cakes or rice cakes, as well as a selection of fresh bean curd skin in three or four different sizes. Use it to roll up a savory stuffing, then slice the roll into short lengths and deep-fry. The sweet rice pudding, fermented and strong, is sometimes added at the final stage in making a hot Szechwan sauce. There are fresh packaged fava beans, too, which the Chinese use as much as, if not more than, the Italians.

## East Bay
## THE OAKLAND MARKET

*401 Ninth Street, Oakland 94607. Telephone (415) 835-4919. Hours: 9:30–6 daily.*
*378 Eighth Street, Oakland 94607. Telephone (415) 832-1286. Hours: M–SAT 9:15–6:15.*

Since there are two Oakland Markets, the owners can buy in enough quantity to keep prices in both of these large, well-organized stores low.

In hot weather, the Ninth Street store is the coolest place in Oakland's Chinatown, with its fans moving the air overhead and its refrigerated produce cases. The produce is plentiful and very fresh. Much of it looks unfamiliar: "cow's ears," and big bundles of "swamp cabbage," to be stir-fried and served with a black bean sauce. Other bundles of strange greens and herbs are meant for your Chinese soup pot.

A six-foot-long shelf is packed with dried mushrooms and fungus; *shiitake* mushrooms from tiny buttons up to the most expensive thick-skinned beauties; black fungus and white jelly fungus. You'll find huge bundles of dried fish skin, dried lotus root, and Hunan-style garlic with chili; and a soup mix from Hong Kong with vermicelli, dried shrimp, and dried mushrooms. The refrigerator stocks packages of salted turnips, cabbage, and frozen dried fish stacked like so many sticks.

## Peninsula
## ORIENTAL MARKET

*413 San Antonio Road, Mountain View 94042. Telephone (415) 948-1188. Hours: M-SAT 10-7, SUN 10:30-5.*

General Chinese groceries.

## East Bay
## ORIENT GROCERY

*337 Eighth Street, Oakland 94607. Telephone (415) 465-1140. Hours: 9:30-6:30 daily.*

Recently remodeled, Orient Grocery is more a western-style supermarket of Oriental food than the usual crowded Chinese grocery. On a tour through the store's spacious aisles, you'll see preserved and salted eggs, tins of long-tailed anchovies, canned shark's fin soup, bean curd sheet in fabulous packages from Hong Kong, and many grades of dried mushrooms. Dried chestnuts, black-eyed peas, black beans, almonds, peanuts, pistachios, and cashews are sold in bulk.

The refrigerator holds cartons of soya, mango, and sugar cane drink from Taiwan, as well as fresh rice noodles and *won ton* wrappers.

## San Francisco
## QUONG SANG CHONG AND COMPANY

*32 Wentworth Alley, San Francisco 94108 Telephone (415) 781-2590. Hours: M-SAT 9:30-5.*

Quong Sang Chong and Company is one of the most curious stores in all of Chinatown. Hidden in a tiny alley, the store's windows hold an elegant display of birds' nests ("healthful simmered with ginseng," says a little typed note of explanation). These are rare, made by swallows with fine seaweed. The nutritious nests are also traditionally used to flavor a rich chicken soup called Bird's Nest Soup, of course. They are graded, each having its own virtues— "Old Yellow Mountain," "Golden Thread," or "Thailand Red Bird's Nest,"— and each is exquisitely packaged.

Besides birds' nests, the store sells only a few other items. They have lots of the infamous sea cucumbers, black and ashy. These large and perfect specimens are of a quality hard to find in the rest of Chinatown. Bins of shark skin, fish stomachs, and shark's fin, the last a rare delicacy used in soups, complete the exotic selection. In addition, there are cans of sesame oil and a very few staples.

## East Bay
## WING LUNG COMPANY

*1947 Grove Street, Berkeley 94704. Telephone (415) 843-4488. Hours: M, W, F 10:30-6; T, TH, SAT 10-6.*

Wing Lung Company is another tiny store cram-packed with Chinese goods— sacks of rice, woks, mushrooms, spices,

Chinese sausage, and fresh noodles—plus some Thai foodstuffs, too: packaged chili pastes and hot sauces.

## San Francisco
## WING SING CHONG COMPANY

*1076 Stockton Street, San Francisco 94133. Telephone (415) 982-4171. Hours: 9–5:30 daily.*

Wing Sing Chong Company is a Chinese grocery on the corner of Stockton and Jackson. Since the store also wholesales goods, this is a good place to buy black mushrooms, Chinese and Thai hot sauces, Oriental spices, dried seafood, and vegetables. You can also find sturdy round Chinese chopping blocks here.

## San Francisco
## WING TAT
## TRADING COMPANY

*1601 Powell Street, San Francisco 94133. Telephone (415) 397-8076. Hours: 7–6 daily.*

The entire front of this Powell Street store on the current edge of Chinatown opens onto the street. In warm weather Wing Tat's side wall is lined with wooden crates draped with *bok choy* and Swiss chard set out to dry. Inside, it's a charming store, neat and colorful, well-supplied with every kind of canned, bottled, dried, pickled, and preserved Chinese foodstuff.

## San Jose Area
## THE WOK SHOP

*252 Race Street, San Jose 95126. Telephone (408) 295-5563. Hours: M–SAT 10:30–5:30.*

Chinese groceries and cookware, but no produce.

# GENERAL
# ORIENTAL

The following stores all carry more than one kind of Oriental food, including Chinese, Japanese, Korean, Filipino, Indonesian, Vietnamese, Thai, and Hawaiian.

## East Bay
## ALOTOYA ORIENTAL FOODS

*313 Union Square Mall, Union City 94587. Telephone (415) 471-3135. Hours: M–F 10–7, SAT 10–5, SUN 12–5.*

Alotoya Oriental Foods has Chinese, Japanese, and Philippine groceries, plus frozen fish.

## Stockton
## ASAHI-YA

*229 East Alpine Avenue, Stockton 95204. Telephone (209) 464-9341. Hours: M–F 9–6, SAT 9–4.*

Japanese foods and fresh fish.

## East Bay
## BERKELEY BOWL
## MARKET PLACE

*2777 Shattuck Avenue, Berkeley 94705. Telephone (415) 841-1458. Hours: M–F 9–7, SAT 9–6.*

Oriental produce, fresh fish for *sashimi, sukiyaki* meat, fresh noodles, and Oriental groceries. On Fridays, they have *sushi* to take out.

**Contra Costa**
## DIABLO ORIENTAL FOOD AND DELICACIES

*2590 North Main Street, Walnut Creek 94596. Telephone (415) 933-2590. Hours: M-SAT 10-6.*

Mostly Chinese foodstuffs, but some Filipino, too. Oriental produce.

**San Jose Area**
## DOBASHI MARKET

*240 Jackson Street, San Jose 95116. Telephone (408) 295-7794. Hours: M-T, TH-SAT 9:30-7:30, WED 9:30-7, SUN 9:30-4:30.*

Japanese foods, fresh vegetables, sometimes fresh fish.

**Peninsula**
## EASY FOODS COMPANY

*299 Castro Street, Mountain View 94041. Telephone (415) 969-5595. Hours: M-SAT 10-6, SUN 12-5.*

Easy Foods has imported food from China, Taiwan, Hong Kong, Japan, the Philippines, Korea, Thailand, and Indonesia. Frozen imported fish, fresh Oriental vegetables, and lemon grass are available seasonally.

**East Bay**
## FAR EAST FOOD STORE

*31861 Alvarado Boulevard, Union City 94587. Telephone (415) 487-1900. Hours: 10-7:30 daily.*

Chinese, Japanese, and Filipino foods.

**East Bay**
## FAR EAST ORIENTAL FOODS

*27098 Hesperian Boulevard, Hayward 94545. Telephone (415) 887-1325. Hours: M-F 10-7, SAT 10-6 or 7, SUN 10-6.*

Chinese, Japanese, Philippine foods; some ingredients for all the Oriental cuisines; fresh Oriental produce, too.

**East Bay**
## HAN IL ORIENTAL KOREAN MARKET

*22550 Main Street, Hayward 94541. Telephone (415) 582-8949. Hours: M-SAT 10:30-7:30.*

Korean foodstuffs. Fresh frozen fish.

**Contra Costa**
## KEIKO ORIENTAL FOODS

*3417 Chestnut Avenue, Concord 94519. Telephone (415) 798-3477. Hours: M-SAT 9:30-6, SUN 1-5.*

Mainly Japanese foods, but some Chinese. Fresh fish for *sashimi* when available, and Japanese produce.

**San Jose Area**
## LEE'S FOOD STORE

*1998 Homestead Road, Santa Clara 95051. Telephone (408) 296-2690. Hours: M-F 10-8:30, SAT 9-9, SUN 10-8.*

Mostly Japanese foods, including produce and *sukiyaki* meat.

**East Bay**
## MISSION MARKET

*20848 Mission Boulevard, Hayward 94541. Telephone (415) 276-1234. Hours: M–F 10–6, SAT 10–5.*

Japanese foods, Oriental vegetables, fresh tuna and bonito.

**San Jose Area**
## MUSASHI ORIENTAL FOODS

*962 West El Camino Real, Sunnyvale 94087. Telephone (408) 735-1590. Hours: M–SAT 9:30–6, SUN 1–5.*

Mostly Japanese; some Chinese foodstuffs. Fresh fish.

**Peninsula**
## NAK'S ORIENTAL MARKET

*1151 Chestnut, Menlo Park 94025. Telephone (415) 325-2046. Hours: M–SAT 9:30–6:30.*

Mostly Japanese and Chinese foodstuffs; fresh produce and, sometimes on Fridays, fresh fish for *sashimi.*

**East Bay**
## NOMURA'S MARKET

*29583 Mission Boulevard, Hayward 94544. Telephone (415) 581-1195. Hours: M–SAT 9:30–6, SUN 11–4.*

Nomura's Market specializes in Oriental groceries and fresh fish, too. But they also have Hawaiian foods: *poi,* fish cakes, Hawaiian fish, and king bread, a light sweet bread.

**Contra Costa**
## ORIENTAL FOOD FAIR

*10368 San Pablo Avenue, El Cerrito 94530. Telephone (415) 526-7444. Hours: M–F 9–6, SAT 9–5:30.*

Oriental Food Fair specializes in Japanese and Hawaiian foods. The small fish counter sells fresh fish, including squid and octopus. They also have beef for *teriyaki* and *sukiyaki* and an even thinner cut of beef for making *shabu-shabu,* beef cooked in broth.

The store stocks basic Oriental produce such as bitter melon, Japanese eggplant, *gobo* root, *kabocha* squash, and *renkon* (fresh lotus root).

From Hawaii, there's *malolo* and orange or strawberry drink syrup, Hawaiian *sanbai-zuke* (pickled radish in soy sauce), pickled Maui onions, *takuwan* (pickled radish), macadamia nuts, frozen coconut milk, crackers, guava juice, fresh *poi,* and a Hawaiian sweet bread similar to the Portuguese version. Other Hawaiian foods such as *ti* leaves, and Hawaiian and tropical fish, are available if ordered in advance.

For Indonesian cooking, they have homemade *ketjap* from Otten Indonesian Foods in Richmond. An Indonesian soy-based cooking condiment, it is genuine, thick, and sweet and pours like molasses.

There are Korean-style *kim chee* pickles, Japanese vermicelli, Philippine *lumpia* wrappers, Chinese egg rolls, frozen fish, and other ingredients for these Asian cuisines.

**San Jose Area**
## ORIENTAL GROCERY

*3443 El Camino Real, Santa Clara 95051. Telephone (408) 984-0448. Hours: M–SAT 9:30–8:30, SUN 9:30–6.*

Japanese and Korean foodstuffs. Fresh fish and vegetables.

## Marin County
### PACIFIC FOOD CENTER

*1924 Fourth Street, San Rafael 94901. Telephone (415) 457-8866. Hours: 10-6 daily.*

Marin's center for Oriental foodstuffs, including fresh produce and, when available, fresh fish.

## East Bay
### QUONG WOR FOOD COMPANY

*725 Webster Street, Oakland 94607. Telephone (415) 451-7840. Hours: M-SAT 8:30-6, SUN 8:30-5.*

Quong Wor Food Company is a small friendly store, just across the street from Lock Goon, where you should refuel mid-shopping trip with a steaming bowl of barbecued pork *won ton* soup.

The store does have good basic Chinese foodstuffs, but also lots of Thai and Vietnamese foods. From Thailand, you'll find *margosa* (brown herb), *laos* and dried lemon grass, chili fish sauce, jars of hot *sambal oeluk*, regular and glutinous rice flour, *chantaboon* rice sticks, tapioca, many kinds of vermicelli, and delicate edible rice paper impressed with a basket pattern. From Vietnam, there are the smaller Vietnamese-style rice papers; little jars of freshly prepared *mam tom chua*, or shrimp sauce, made with whole shrimp and grated carrots; and Vietnamese fish and anchovy sauces.

## Stockton
### REDWOOD MARKET

*1319 East Harding Way, Stockton 95205. Telephone (209) 464-0136. Hours: 8-8 daily.*

Fresh fish, Oriental foods.

## San Jose Area
### SALOM ORIENTALS

*1647 North Capitol Avenue, San Jose 95132. Telephone (408) 923-3820. Hours: M-SAT 10-7, SUN 10-6.*

Filipino, Thai, Japanese, Chinese, and Korean foodstuffs.

## East Bay
### SAM YICK COMPANY

*389 Eighth Street, Oakland 94607. Telephone (415) 832-0662. Hours: M-SAT 9:30-6:30, SUN 9:30-6.*

The produce at Sam Yick Company is gorgeously displayed in wooden boxes mounted high off the street, a gridlike still life of bitter melon, Chinese broccoli, Napa cabbage, long beans, and soup greens. When you first look into the dark store, it seems quite small, but go in; there are long narrow aisles behind the front counter, ending with a stack of giant rice sacks.

The right side of the store is filled with Philippine foodstuffs: beautiful dried fish skewered in a herringbone pattern, yellow mung beans, banana catsup, several kinds of salty *bagoong*, sweet jack fruit preserve, papaya pickle, sweet banana, purple *ube* (yam), and coconut jams. Philippine baked goods and pastries are at the front.

The goods from Thailand include tiny dried anchovies, *deli* (another kind of dried fish), pickled whole garlic, tamarind candy, and rice paper.

## Stockton
### STAR FISH MARKET

*320 South El Dorado, Stockton 95203. Telephone (209) 466-7344. Hours: M-SAT 8-6:45, SUN variable hours.*

Fresh fish, Oriental foods.

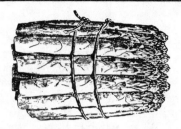

## Peninsula
## TAKAHASHI COMPANY

*221 South Claremont, San Mateo 94402. Telephone (415) 343-0394. Hours: M–SAT 9–6.*

Almost seventy-five years old now, San Mateo's Takahashi Company may be the best source for Oriental foods in the San Mateo area. You'll find bonito and other fish fresh enough for *sashimi;* fresh Oriental produce; *tofu;* and fresh and dried noodles as well as pickled, dried, and canned foods. The store also has ingredients for Chinese, Philippine, Korean, and Hawaiian cuisines, as well as a small selection of Thai, Indonesian, and Vietnamese foods.

## Stockton
## WAKI'S FISH MARKET

*1335 South Lincoln, Stockton 95206. Telephone (209) 465-1567. Hours: 9–6:45 daily.*

Fresh fish and ingredients for Japanese and Chinese cooking.

## San Francisco
## WING HING
## TRADING COMPANY

*1128 Grant Avenue, San Francisco 94133. Telephone (415) 986-4108. Hours: 8–6:30 daily.*

Wing Hing has general Chinese foods, but here you'll find ingredients for Filipino and Vietnamese cuisines, too. The freezer holds fish from Philippine,

Thai, and Vietnamese waters as well as frozen coconut milk, Philippine *longaniza* sausage, guava and other tropical fruits, and "Oriental" spaghetti sauce.

Well provided with the respective fish and anchovy sauces for both cuisines, the store also stocks tropical fruits—sometimes huge green papayas big as coconuts—and fragile *lumpia* wrappers imported from the Philippines. These thin circles of dough are usually filled with a savory pork, shrimp, and vegetable filling. Served with a peanut-based hot sauce, they make a wonderful light summer supper.

Look around. A crate of dazzling orange whole salted shrimp might inspire you to buy them as a substitute for the more traditional *trassi,* or shrimp paste.

## Contra Costa
## WOK MARKET

*1762 Salvio Street, Concord 94520. Telephone (415) 798-0872. Hours: M–SAT 9:30–5:30, SUN 11:30–3:30.*

Chinese, Japanese, and Indonesian foodstuffs.

# GERMAN
# MARKETS

See also Charcuterie, Bread, and Pastry.

## San Jose Area
## INGRID'S DELICATESSEN

*3515 El Camino Real, Santa Clara 95051. Telephone (408) 246-2311. Hours: M–F 9–6, SAT 9–5:30.*

Ingrid's Delicatessen has German-style dark rye breads, mustards, sausages, Westphalian ham, and other German groceries, including baking spices. There's a selection of cheese, as well as candies and cookies imported from Germany.

## San Francisco
## LEHR'S GERMAN SPECIALTIES

*1581 Church Street, San Francisco 94131. Telephone (415) 282-6803. Hours: M–SAT 10–6, SUN 12–6.*

Lehr's German Specialties stocks cosmetics, records, magazines, and foodstuffs—all imported from Germany.

For your winter soups, you can find little packets of dried mushrooms from the Black Forest: *Pfifferlings* (chanterelles) and *Steinpilze* (yellow boletus). There are also concentrated red currant, blackberry, and raspberry syrups for *Berliner Weisse* (a special beer), and spice mixes for either *Sauerbraten* or goulash.

For your holiday baking they have bundt pans, wooden cookie molds, clear sheet gelatin, and mixed spices for *Pfefferkuchen,* or spice cake. Christmas brings imported *Stollen,* cookies, and the traditional marzipan in the shape of little piggies and Santas—even wonderful marzipan *potatoes!* And all year, there's the city's most inspiring selection of Swiss chocolate bars, with every imaginable flavoring.

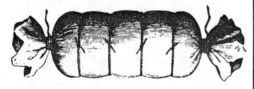

## San Francisco
## HANS SPECKMANN

*1550 Church Street, San Francisco 94131. Telephone (415) 282-6850. Hours: SUN–F 11–6, SAT 11–7.*

Hans Speckmann is the city's best-stocked German delicatessen. The *Wurstwaren* selection alone is formidable, with ten to twenty different kinds of German sausages: bratwurst, bockwurst, knockwurst, kielbasa, frankfurters, and paprika sausages from a variety of producers including Saag's, Evergood, Usinger, and Schaller. The tempting hams come in many different styles: Westphalian (a lightly smoked ham, traditionally made from pigs fed on acorns in Westphalia's huge oak forests), Black Forest, *Bauern, Schinken, Lackschinken,* and *Praeger.* Then there is the Swiss specialty, *Bündnerfleisch,* an air-dried beef; *Leberkäse,* a pork and veal meat loaf usually served with a fried egg on top; head cheese; liverwurst; *Gelbwurst;* and blood pudding.

And, of course, there is an array of *Senf* (mustard) and *Kren* (horseradish), and dark sourdough rye breads, some from the local Münchner Kindl Bakery. Others are flown in from the German community in Toronto; the *Fräulein* behind the counter will cut you a thick slab from a huge five-pound loaf of light country rye or the coarser *Yaegerbrot.* Buy moist, whole-grain pumpernickels in flat square packages.

As for *Bier,* they've got beers and more beers—twenty kinds from Germany, and others from Holland, Czechoslovakia, Austria, and the rest of Europe. A dark little alcove toward the back holds a selection of German wines from Kabinett to Spatlëse, along with California's German-style wines.

Christmas at Speckmann's brings smoked eel, fresh geese, *Bücklinge* (another kind of smoked fish), smoked goose breast, loaves of sugar-dusted Dresdner *Stollen,* and a selection of Christmas cookies for *der bunte Teller.*

No shopping trip to Speckmann's is complete without lunch or *Abrendbrot* (light supper) in the cozy back restaurant. Start with a stein of the very good German draft beer. Then try a sampling of the *Wurstwaren* sold up front, with good dark bread and a delicious pickled-herring-and-beet salad followed by the *Sauerbraten* or the Tartar steak.

# INDIAN MARKETS

## San Francisco/East Bay
### BOMBAY BAZAR

*548 Valencia Street, San Francisco 94110. Telephone (415) 621-1717. Hours T–SAT 10:30–6, SUN 12–5.*
*1034 University Avenue, Berkeley 94710. Telephone (415) 848-1671. Hours: T–F 10–6:30, SAT 10–7, SUN 11–6*

The Parman family are both importers and exporters, wholesalers and retailers of Indian foodstuffs at their two Bombay stores located in San Francisco and Berkeley.

In San Francisco, the store's central area displays rows and rows of white plastic tubs filled with Indian dry goods, some of them unavailable elsewhere: flours, including yellow split pea, *aata* (whole wheat), *sooji* (semolina), *channa* (chick pea), rice, white corn, and yellow corn; fine-grained *basmati* rice in bulk; *roti* flour for bread; and, of course, lots of colorful flat-grained *dals*, both split and whole: the bright orange *masoor dal*; *channa dal* (chick-pea); tiny white *urad dal*; the bigger cream *urad dal*; a type of split *urad* mixed black and white; golden oily *toor dal*; two kinds of yellow *moong dal*; and *val dal* and *lobhia*, or black-eyed peas. Even more unusual flours are prepackaged: gram flour *besan*, white *moong* flour, *urad* (white lentil) flour, and *matbia* flour.

One area of shelves is completely stacked with gallon jars of the innumerable Indian spices. Alongside familiar fenugreek, fragrant green cardamom and the hard-to-find larger black cardamom, turmeric, and coriander and mustard seeds, there is dried *kari* leaf, *zafran* (saffron), *gullah, kanku, isabgul, sindon, kamarkas, gundur, amba urhale, kala namah,* and *ganthode*, plus the large nuts called *sopari*, or betel nut.

They have all kinds of packaged *garam masala* (spice mixes for meat, for fish, for *dal*); some packages look like tea boxes and are intended for particular dishes: *Dhanak masala, vendaloo masala, khuma masala, Kashmiri masala, biriyani masala,* and *kurma masala*. There are curry pastes and row on row of jars of pickles and chutneys. Try the *tikka* paste made with curry and fruit juices, for grilling and barbecue. Chilies include mixed lime mango, sweet mango, lemon, Bombay.

Find just the special canned goods and vegetables—such as *methi*, or fenugreek greens—you'll need for your recipe. There are cans of the commonly used vegetable *ghee* (clarified sweet butter is called *usli ghee*), *pappadams* (crisp bread made from lentil flour), and *sam papar* (dried sheets of mango pulp).

On the back shelves, you'll find Indian tonics, cough syrup for babies, and a collection of oils: coconut, mustard, sweet almond. Also found here is *vark*, gossamer sheets of edible silver or gold foil used to decorate splendid pilafs or other banquet dishes.

You can pick up the essentials for Indian cooking at the front door: fresh coconut, garlic, and ginger, and sometimes fresh tamarind to give a sour taste to your chutneys. On Saturdays, they have fresh produce coming in from Canada and the Fiji Islands: *guwar, karala,* drumsticks, ripe mangoes, and special pickling mangoes with very small seeds so they can be cut easily. Don't forget to pick up some fresh *paan* (betel leaves) to chew as a relaxing finish to a long Indian meal.

## San Francisco
### HAIG'S DELICACIES

*642 Clement Street, San Francisco 94118. Telephone (415) 752-6283. Hours: M–SAT 10–6.*

Haig's Delicacies has a king's ransom of chutneys, pickles, *pappadams*, spices, spice pastes, and other ingredients for Indian cuisine.

**East Bay**
## ORIENTAL LUCKY MART

*Housewives' Market, 818 Jefferson, Oakland 94607. Telephone (415) 465-7807. Hours: M–SAT 9–6.*

Oriental Lucky Mart, a Philippine grocery, has exotic fresh vegetables used in both Filipino and Indian cuisines, including *mahungay*, known as *karala* to Indians, and fresh taro leaves, known as *patra*.

**East Bay**
## G. B. RATTO AND COMPANY

*821 Washington Street, Oakland 94607. Telephone (415) 832-6503. Hours: M–SAT 8–5.*

G. B. Ratto claims to specialize in "Middle Eastern and Greek kitchen essentials," but they have many items for Indian cuisine also: *basmati* rice, *dals*, chutneys, pickles, special flours, mustard oil, and a wonderful selection of individual spices in big glass jars: both green and black cardamom, mustard seed, fenugreek, turmeric, coriander, saffron, and dozens more. Weigh them out yourself.

# INDONESIAN MARKETS

For *tempeh*, see Natural Foods section. Some of the stores listed in the General Oriental section carry Indonesian foods.

**San Francisco**
## HAIG'S DELICACIES

*642 Clement Street, San Francisco 94118. Telephone (415) 752-6283. Hours: M–SAT 10–6.*

Haig's Delicacies has at least as many Indonesian food products as it does Middle Eastern foodstuffs. You'll find a big selection of all the commercially prepared imported condiments and *sambals*, including *oelek, paja, asem badjak, manis, serdadoe, brandal, kemirie,* and *taotjo*. These are used like Indian chutneys—spooned on the side of your rice or curry—and will keep a long time in the refrigerator.

*Boemkoe*, or spice mixes, with a base of ginger, pepper, cumin, coriander, and *galangale* or *laos*, include *osehoseh; godok* and *petjil* for poultry; *lawar* and *toesoek* for meat, *bebotole* for seafood. Use these to make a variety of stewed or curry-like dishes.

*Trassi*, a salty paste of dried, pounded, and fermented shrimp, is a basic flavoring used all over Southeast Asia. Lemon grass and *daoen salam*, Indonesian laurel leaves, are also used extensively. *Laos* is a root used fresh in Southeast Asia, but only available here dried; also sold here are pressed cakes of sour tamarind, and *krupuk*, colorful shrimp crackers.

The sticky *ketjap manis*, or sweet Indonesian soy sauce, made from soy boiled with spices, is the origin of our word *ketchup*. The imported commercial variety sold here cannot compare with a fragrant and strong home preparation. Coconut comes shredded fine, in large flake, or powdered as fine as talcum powder, as well as creamed in jars or pressed into an oil sold in plastic containers. Tamarind lovers should try the preserved tamarind candy.

*Mail order.*

## San Jose Area
## ORI-DELI
## ORIENTAL DELICATESSEN

*5479 Snell Avenue, San Jose 95123. Telephone (408) 578-6262. Hours: T–F 10–8, SAT 12–9, SUN 4–9.*

This San Jose deli specializes in Dutch-Indonesian foods: imported spice pastes, Dutch cheeses, *krupuk* (shrimp chips), *lumpia* wrappers, *sambals*, and Dutch pastries.

The proprietors also prepare *rijsttafel*, *nasi goreng* (a savory rice dish), various *saté* (skewered chicken or pork with a spicy peanut sauce), and *lumpia* to take out.

## Contra Costa
## OTTEN INDONESIAN FOODS

*322 Key Boulevard, Richmond 94802. Telephone (415) 232-9511. Hours: Mornings; call first.*

Mary Otten, born in the formerly Dutch Batavia—Djakarta today—is famous for her cooking in the Bay Area's Dutch-Indonesian community. With her daughter, Irena (also an excellent cook, and a former ballet dancer and circus performer), she makes Dutch-Indonesian specialties from her catering kitchen in Richmond.

Irena explains that her mother "cooked during the war to keep us in food. She cooked for her friends, but for a long time it was just a hobby. But when Father died I told her to sell her house, move closer to me, and we'd start a food business together with a big catering kitchen."

Big wooden crates filled with *krupuk* (shrimp chips) and imported spices sit stacked just outside the door. They import ingredients directly from Indonesia, via Holland. "We are not substituting anything. Everything is authentic."

The women make their own *tempeh* (Indonesian fermented soybean cake), *sambals* (fiery chili pastes eaten as a condiment like chutney), and *gado-gado* peanut sauce for the famous salad of *tofu* and lightly poached and fresh vegetables.

Mary and Irena's Dutch side comes forward at Christmas when they make dozens and dozens of Dutch *banquit-letters*, all on special order: letters made of delicate puff pastry and almond paste—you can choose your own initial—that celebrate the arrival of Sinterklaas on December 5. Traditionally he arrives on horseback and is met by crowds of cheering children all over Holland. It is customary to present your friends with cookies in the shape of their initials on this day.

The Ottens' *kerstaven* (Christmas staffs) and *kerstkransen* (Christmas wreaths) are made with the same flaky pastry as the letters.

At the same season they make a marvelous cake called *spekkoek*, or "bacon" cake, from a recipe handed down from Mary Otten's grandmother. The cake takes over three hours to bake and is made by special order only. Two buttery batters, one light and one dark, both warmed with fresh-ground spices, are poured alternately into a cake pan in the thinnest possible layers. Each layer is cooked till done under a broiler, and then another fine layer is added. When the tall cake is cut, the dozens of fine layers are striated dark and light, resembling bacon.

For a description of Otten's prepared foods, see the Take-Out section.

Some of their products are also available at the Wok Store in Concord and Spice Islanders in Mountain View.

**Peninsula**
## SPICE ISLANDERS

*1350 Grant Road, Mountain View 94042. Telephone (415) 961-0427. Hours: T–SAT 10–6.*

Spice Islanders specializes in Dutch-Indonesian foods: spices and spice pastes from Indonesia, lemon grass, peanut sauces, sweet rice, *lumpia* wrappers, *krupuk, ketjap,* and their own *sambals* as well as those of Mary Otten. They have flour and cake mixes from Holland, special imported baking pans, rice steamers, and mortars and pestles. Take-out foods include Dutch sausage rolls, *lumpia,* and croquettes.

To make the feast of Sinterklaas on December 5 into a special event for your children, get chocolate letters and marzipan animals from Spice Islanders to stuff their shoes. Directly from Holland there are almond cookies, filled *speculaas* (honey gingerbread), and charming *speculaas* dolls. *Spekkoek* ("bacon" cake) and *kerstkransen* (Christmas wreaths) are baked by Mary Otten in Richmond. Take out your best Delft Blue and have a *prettige Sinterklaas.*

# ITALIAN MARKETS

See also Pastry, Bread, Take-Out, Pasta and Dough, Gourmet Markets, Coffee, Cookware, Ice Cream.

**San Francisco**
## ARMANINO'S DELICATESSEN

*2599 San Bruno Avenue, San Francisco 94134. Telephone (415) 468-2624. Hours: M–F 9–6, SAT 8–6.*

You won't find Armanino inside anymore—he's developed a factory nearby to package chives and his own brand of *pesto.* The store, owned by a Lucchese family now, is stranded on San Bruno Avenue in a neighborhood once largely Italian. Many of the older Italians have moved away—to Santa Rosa, near the wine country, where there is a beautiful climate for growing vegetables.

Sadly, the bulk of Armanino's business is sandwiches now, but because of that, there's a good selection of cold meats: *toscana* salami, *coppa, galantina, cotechino* sausage (a fine-textured pork sausage, originally made in Modena), *pancetta.*

The store sells Italian pasta, but also a very good pasta from Canada, where they have good-quality durum wheat; staples like *baccalà,* tins of anchovies, and olives; and some good imported cheeses such as *pecorino fresco, provolone auricchio,* and *romano italiano.* There is a mountain of jars of antipasto in front of the counter, and above it hang kitchen necessities like *agnolini* and ravioli cutters, a wooden polenta board with the traditional wooden knife, and a set of tubes for making *cannoli.*

**East Bay**
## BRAIDA'S ITALIAN DELICATESSEN

*7081 Village Parkway, Dublin 94566. Telephone (415) 828-1883. Hours: M–F 10–5:30, SAT 10–5.*

Salami, *coppa,* imported cheeses, homemade salads, olives, but no fresh pasta.

**San Francisco**
## FLORENCE ITALIAN DELI AND RAVIOLI FACTORY

*1412 Stockton Street, San Francisco 94133. Telephone (415) 421-6170. Hours: M–SAT 8–5:30.*

Across the steet from Panelli Brothers, Florence Italian Deli and Ravioli's windows are stacked tall with tins of olive oil and imported *pomodori* packed with basil and bearing beautiful red and yellow labels. The store is frequented by older Italian women dressed in traditional black and speaking in rapid dialect. Like a neighborhood store in Italy, it carries all the necessities: little packets of *lievito*, or vanilla-suffused baking powder (on its packet, little angels float heavenward bearing a cake as light as yours will be if you use this brand of *lievito*); packets of soothing camomile tea drunk as a *digestivo* after a big meal; *china bisteri*, a bitter aperitif to stimulate the appetite; and big jars of Brioschi, an effervescent antacid.

Big open sacks of golden polenta, mottled cranberry beans, plump *ceci* beans (garbanzo), lentils, dried fava beans, small cloth bags of Arborio rice crowd the entrance. And on the shelves, you'll find the latest in Italian gastronomy aids: instant polenta, instant *gnocchi*, and bouillon cubes for making *zuppa*.

They have the same brand of imported Italian spices, Bertolini brand, sold in tiny neighborhood stores all over Italy: *cannella regina* (cinnamon), *spiedarrosto* (ginger, rosemary, parsley, sage, oregano, bay leaf), and basil, oregano, parsley, nutmeg, the most common spices for cooking. (But where are the familiar Italian cellophane packets with miniature graters and two whole nutmegs?)

The front counter is invaded by a sea of canned *antipasti*, three-pound tins of salted anchovies and sardines. The cheeses are a real Italian-American selection: ricotta, *asiago, caciocavallo*, provolone, Gorgonzola and domestic blues, Jacks, Swiss, romano, and *grana padano*. ("Grana" refers to the grainlike texture, similar to that of Parmesan).

The favorite of the salami lineup is southern-style *soppressata* and hot *coppa* by the East Coast firm Citterio. Florence also has homemade meat-stuffed ravioli, *tortellini*, frozen potato *gnocchi*, and fresh pasta: *tagliarini, tagliatelle*, and *fettuccine* in both egg and spinach doughs.

## Marin County
## GARATTI GROCERY

*926 B Street, San Rafael 94901. Telephone (415) 453-2849. Hours: M–SAT 8–6.*

A lovely Italian delicatessen with fresh pasta, *baccalà*, olives, cold cuts, etc.

## East Bay/Contra Costa
## GENOVA DELICATESSEN AND RAVIOLI FACTORY

*4937 Telegraph Avenue, Oakland 94609. Telephone (415) 652-7401. Hours: M–F 9–6, SAT 8–6, SUN 8–5.*
*1105 North California Boulevard, Walnut Creek 94596. Telephone (415) 939-3838. Hours: 9–6 daily.*

Back in the twenties, the stretch of Telegraph Avenue in Oakland near Fiftieth used to be the center of an Italian neighborhood as lively as North Beach. There's not much left now—just two Italian delis on one block and, across the street, an Italian pastry shop. But business is still brisk, and you can get the feel of the old neighborhood. People crowd into Genova; you can hear the loud Italian greetings from the corner, and, even across the street, you can smell tomatoes, garlic, and *frittata* cooking.

Genova's tiny corner location is marked with a green awning and a blue and white sign. The ample windows are stuffed with pasta machines; old-fashioned wooden box cheese graters; ravioli pins; imported pasta in all the inventive shapes (*fusilli, creste di gallo, rigatoni*, and the requisite *perciatelli* for a true *pasta amatriciana*); tins of imported olive oil ornate with lions, olive branches, and beautiful virgins; dried *ceci* (garbanzo) beans and *lupini* beans.

The cheerful clerks bustle behind the counter and joke with old customers as they dish out marinated olives, slabs of Genova's excellent homemade zucchini or artichoke *frittata*, or weigh out a piece of ripe Gorgonzola or the tender fresh ricotta made in Danville. They have fine homemade sausages, *pancetta* (unsmoked Italian bacon), and a stupendous stock of Italian cold cuts.

You can buy their fresh spinach and egg *fettuccine* uncut, too, for *lasagne verdi* or *cannelloni*. In back, check the bags of chestnut flour (available just in winter, for Tuscan *castagnaccio*, a flat chestnut-flour cake), fragrant *porcini* mushrooms, polenta flour both fine and coarse (a mix is recommended), dried chestnuts, inexpensive Chilean mushrooms, small sacks of *superfino* Arborio rice for Venetian *risotto*.

Behind the counter there are tins of anchovies, imported plum tomatoes, *peperonata*, artichoke hearts, *caponata* (Sicilian eggplant relish). Sometimes you can find big loaves of thick-crusted *pane casarecchio*.

---

**San Francisco**
## LUCCA DELICATESSEN

*2120 Chestnut Street, San Francisco 94123. Telephone (415) 921-7873. Hours: M-F 9-6:30, SAT 7:30-6:30, SUN 8-6.*

The tiny deli on Chestnut Street celebrated its fifty-first anniversary last August; it is still the most authentic Italian deli in the city. It classifies as *rosticceria*, too; the small windows are daily stuffed with fragrant chickens roasted with herbs and vegetables; salads; high *frittate* green with zucchini; sandwiches made on big rounds of sourdough and sold whole, in halves, or in quarters; and bowls of flour and grains.

Ed Bosco's grandfather came from Lucca where he used to make "cheese, sausages, everything. He even grew his own vegetables." He continued to do the same when the family moved to America.

Mornings start at 6 am for Ed Bosco. First he puts a turkey in to roast and then he and his assistant Louie begin to make ravioli by hand. They take a yard-wide slab of fresh pasta rolled very thin, place it carefully on the long table, spread it with a savory stuffing of finely chopped meat, Swiss chard, and cheese, and then carefully drape another sheet of pasta on top. Rolling an old-fashioned ravioli pin over the top, Ed marks and presses down the pasta to make small pillows of dough and stuffing. Then they cut the ravioli apart with pastry wheels and box them.

Ed asks, "Louie, don't you wish you had a dollar for every ravioli you've made?" Louie has been making ravioli every day for forty-three years. Ed himself is no greenhorn at it. He started helping his dad cut it thirty-two years ago, and the senior Mr. Bosco made it every day himself until two years ago.

At the back of the store, there are large aging racks for cheese. The top rungs are for dry Monterey Jack, popular with the Italian community, then several huge wheels of *parmigiano reggiano* sit in majestic calm below. Ed sells Rocca brand when it is 2-1/2 years old, as well as the delicious nutty domestic *asiago*.

Old Italian ladies squeeze past the crowd at the front to buy whole anchovies under salt from a big open tin; these have a sweeter flesh and better flavor than the fillets in oil.

It's a rare thing to find an Italian deli in this country with good salads; Lucca's salads haven't been overly Americanized: home-cooked pigs' feet salad, lovely mixed vegetable salad, and marinated kidney bean and garbanzo bean salads, too, all dressed with homemade mayonnaise.

Up front there are fat *grissini* from Cuneo bakery in North Beach, good salami and cold cuts, plus sausages, fresh pasta, and, on Friday, spinach pasta.

## San Francisco
## LUCCA RAVIOLI COMPANY

*1100 Valencia at Twenty-second, San Francisco 94110. Telephone (415) 647-5581. Hours: M–SAT 9–6.*

For over fifty years Lucca Ravioli has been supplying the Mission with homemade sausages (sweet and regular), fresh pasta, *pesto* sauce, *focaccia* (from Liguria Bakery in North Beach), homemade pizza (made in big square pans every day—cheese, mushroom, or sausage), and ravioli (sold boxed, either cheese and spinach or beef and pork with Swiss chard and eggs). Lucca, along with Dianda Italian-American Pastries, is an isolated remnant of the Mission's once substantial Italian neighborhood. Lucca sells lots of wine, sandwiches, and pizza, but they've got all the Italian basics, too, including *baccalà*, stockfish, salami, anchovies, and capers. The big bargain here is the cheese—try the imported Brie and Camembert, big bricks of Jack and Cheddar cheeses, wheels of romano and Parmesan.

## San Francisco
## MOLINARI DELICATESSEN

*373 Columbus Avenue, San Francisco 94133. Telephone (415) 421-2337. Hours: M–SAT 8–5.*

Molinari Delicatessen has been around since well before the earthquake: it was started in 1896. Bob Mastrelli directs the business now. Molinari is incredibly jammed with everything to do with Italian food. Crates of the north's noble Barolo rub shoulders with southern Campania's Lacrima Christi, big bottles of Soave, and soft fruity Bardolinos and Barberas. Festive cartons of imported *panettone* vie with boxes of Italian candy and *biscotti.*

Near the door, a big open sack of *alba funghi* (dried *porcini* mushrooms) with their earthy autumn fragrance of damp forests sits next to whole dried stockfish—stiff as boards—which Italians have obtained for centuries from the Scandinavian countries, little wooden boxes packed with boneless fillets of stockfish, and two kinds of hard grayish *baccalà* (dried salt cod). The drier *crispello* type (with skin) has more flavor, while the whiter type without skin is softer, having had a wetter cure. Use it to make *baccalà alla vicentina* (a characteristic dish of the Veneto, now the Friday dish in *trattorie* all over Italy). Don't miss the sacks of imported semolina for southern-style pasta and certain pastries, or the cloth sacks of pearly rice for a velvety *risotto.*

At the back stretches the counter, well-supplied with salami (Molinari salami is an outgrowth of the original business), pink *mortadella*, rolls of *pancetta* (unsmoked bacon cured in salt and spices), *prosciutto cotto, coppa*, and a whole array of Italian cold cuts. Years ago the store used to make its own cured meats; they still make fresh sausages in three styles—Italian, sweet Italian with fennel, or hot southern-style *calabrese* (also with fennel)—plus fresh breakfast pork links.

The countermen weigh out powdery strands of fresh pasta, green and pale gold. Four or five thousand pounds of it goes out the door every week, much of it to restaurants. Molinari makes two kinds of ravioli in the workshop in back—either stuffed with ricotta, Parmesan, and eggs, or with beef and veal, Parmesan, and eggs. The handmade *tortellini* (familiarly called "Venus's navel" in Bologna) are stuffed with prosciutto, egg, Parmesan, and butter. A box serves four as a first course, two as an entrée.

Unfortunately, the salads have lost their Italian roots and cater to the most assimilated "Italian-American" tastes. But the olives are lovely, and in front of the counter are *condimenti* like *zafferano puro* (saffron) from Milan, balsamic vinegar, and bottles of golden-green *extra-virgine* olive oil from Tuscany.

---

**San Francisco**
## PANELLI BROTHERS DELICATESSEN

*1419 Stockton Street, San Francisco 94133. Telephone (415) 421-2541. Hours: M–SAT 8–5:30.*

Here you'll find all the basics for Italian meals from start to finish: Cynar, the bitter artichoke-based aperitif or *digestivo*; Italian vermouths; bottles of imported *acqua minerale* to cut dark country wine; imported *grissini* (bread sticks) from Turin, where they are the specialty; big five-pound boxes of dried pasta, including the beautiful rococo shape called *creste di gallo*, or cock's comb; six-pound cans of California pear tomatoes in purée for sweet savory tomato sauces; and even packets of imported *pasta integrale* (whole-wheat spaghetti).

Behind the counter are big glass jars filled with garbanzos, dried chestnuts,

anise, pine nuts, whole nutmeg, whole peppercorns. And, of course, there's a bag of whole hot red peppers for dishes from Calabria and Puglia, where they like things *piccante.*

For a savory *salsa* or sumptuous *risotto*, Panelli Brothers carries dried mushrooms: rich *porcini*, delicate California dried mushrooms from the Sierra Nevada, and inexpensive dried South American mushrooms. These last are good to mix with the more expensive and stronger-flavored *porcini*, but they must be soaked or boiled and the first water thrown out to get rid of their harshness, saltiness, and grit.

At the front counter, there is an array of the most popular Italian and domestic cheeses, spicy salami in every size and length, delicious *coppa*, and other cold cuts. The East Coast prosciutto disappears so fast, Panelli sells the coveted prosciutto bones for making a hearty minestrone. They also carry Panama Ravioli Factory pasta and ravioli.

---

**Contra Costa**
## RAPALLO DELICATESSEN

*1922 Oak Park Boulevard, Pleasant Hill 94523. Telephone (415) 937-5477. Hours: M–SAT 9–6, SUN 9–5.*

An Italian delicatessen with salami, cold cuts and sausages, fresh spinach and egg pasta, Roman-style potato *gnocchi*, and fresh meat- and cheese-stuffed ravioli.

---

**Peninsula**
## RIVIERA DELICATESSEN

*2053 Broadway, Redwood City 94063. Telephone (415) 365-4785. Hours: M–SAT 9:30–6.*

Homemade Italian sausages both hot and mild, Italian meats and cheeses, imported dried pasta, but no fresh pasta.

## San Francisco
## ROSSI'S MARKET

*627 Vallejo Street, San Francisco 94133. Butcher: telephone (415) 421-3230; grocery: 986-1068. Hours: M–SAT 7–7.*

Shouldered between Molinari on the corner and Gloria Deli just up the street, Rossi's Market needs to be wily to attract attention. Along the sidewalk out front, the produce man puts out bargain boxes of fat fava beans, baby artichokes for stews, and in winter, long white cardoon stalks for braising with cream and Parmesan. Inside, it's a small supermarket with a decidedly Italian bias: five kinds of olive oil in gallons and smaller sizes, anchovies, plum tomatoes, imported pasta, semolina, Arborio rice. Rossi's doesn't go as far as to sell fist-sized balls of blanched spinach, as they do in Florence's marble market, or trays of tender young salad greens, but they do sell big bunches of perfect deep-green spinach for your *gnocchi* and ravioli and the slightly bitter *radicetta* lettuce for your salads, as well as fresh herbs. Summertime brings golden-cupped zucchini blossoms for deep frying, tender fat asparagus tips, satiny white and yellow zucchini, and sweet ripe peaches to poach in wine.

The meat counter has meaty bones for your minestrone, stewing cuts for your Roman-style *stufato*, thick pork chops or veal cutlets to sauté in olive oil with rosemary, and, in winter, rounds of oxtail for your simmered *coda di bue*.

# JAPANESE MARKETS

For *miso* and seaweed, *mochi*, and *tofu*, see Specialty Foods in the Natural Foods section. See also Pastry, Take-Out, and Cookware sections. Many of the stores listed in the General Oriental section also carry Japanese foods.

## San Francisco
## AMERICAN FISH MARKET

*1790 Sutter Street, San Francisco 94115. Telephone (415) 921-5154. Hours: M–F 8:30–6, SAT 8:30–5:30.*

This market has a wide selection of fresh fish and shellfish, plus frozen fish specialties, fried and steamed fish cakes, fish balls, and *sushi* to take out.

Along with green soybeans and delicious horseradish prepared with sake lees, the American Fish Market has a whole wall of refrigerator cases supplied with Japanese pickles: radish, ginger, lotus root, seaweed, eggplant, cucumber, plum. Clear plastic "sausages" are filled with a tangle of fine yam noodles and other vegetables, or with prepared vegetables and soy beans. There's every kind of *tofu*, plus yam cakes and Day-Glo-colored steamed fish cakes.

The shelves are packed with Japanese condiments: *shoyu*, light Japanese soy sauce, *su* (vinegar made from rice wine), spice mixes, dried flaked seaweed, imported canned goods, teas, and an overwhelming selection of candies, cookies, crackers, and snacks. Try the Japanese snow cone syrup in lemon or lime. Sour *umeboshi*, or pickled plums, will snap an inattentive palate awake in the morning.

You'll also find dried seaweeds and *shimakiki*, dried gourd strips that look like strips of rawhide.

The large produce section includes familiar vegetables and fruits plus some things you'll find only in Japantown:

*kabocha,* the lovely gray-green Oriental pumpkin; white *kabocha; sato imo,* or taro root; Hawaiian yams; and *nagaimo,* a foot-long hairy brown tuber.

## East Bay
## A-1 FISH MARKET

*517 Eighth Street, Oakland 94607. Telephone (415) 832-0731. Hours: M-F, 9-5:30, SAT 9-5.*

A few blocks from Chinatown, just around the corner from Ratto's International Grocers, flanked by Spanish *botánicos* and junk shops, A-1 Fish Market is a surprise: a Japanese food market. The neighborhood is a mix of worn Victorian buildings and newly restored ones. This section of downtown Oakland is slated for a massive restoration program. Meanwhile, before it becomes uptown chic, enjoy the comfortable lived-in feeling of this historic part of Oakland.

A-1's fish counter has the day's finest catches, all at good prices—and with the vagaries of our fishing weather, that sometimes means very few kinds—fresh mackerel, prawns, albacore, bonito, squid. They also have salted salmon and paper-thin beef for *sukiyaki.* To accompany your fish dishes, they have a rainbow of bright Oriental pickled ginger *(beni-shoga)* and vegetables, crocks of orange caviar, and fat tubs of *takuwan* (yellowish or brownish pickled radish), some mixed with kelp.

You'll find all the dried seaweeds *(nori, kombu, wakame),* plus molded fish cakes for appetizers, *tofu* in all its diversity, noodles, crackers, *shoyu, goma-abura* (sesame seed oil), *su* (rice wine vinegar), rice bowls, teapots, and bright *origami* papers.

## East Bay
## BERKELEY NATURAL GROCERY COMPANY

*1334 Gilman Street, Berkeley 94706. Telephone (415) 526-2456. Hours: M-SAT 10-7.*

This health food-gourmet store has one of the best selections of imported *miso,* the Japanese fermented soybean paste used as a base for soups called *misoshiru.* They have *aka miso,* or red *miso; gen mia chia,* brown rice *miso; mugi,* a barley *miso* aged two years; *natto miso,* made with barley and flavored with *kombu* (kelp) and ginger; plus a *miso* made in this country, Cold Mountain, a mellow, pale-golden *miso.*

They also have seaweed: *wakame, arame,* and *hijiki,* and sea vegetables to be used in soup and in briny salads.

## San Francisco
## K. SAKAI COMPANY

*1656 Post Street, San Francisco 94115. Telephone (415) 921-0514. Hours: M-SAT 9-6.*

This big Japantown market always seems to be as crowded as downtown Tokyo. Watch where you're going with your shopping cart. Intersections can be quite a traffic jam. Though it seems at first as if all transactions are conducted in Japanese, the clerks do speak English and will help you locate the items on your shopping list.

Check the produce department first for beautifully groomed Oriental vegetables. The bundled fresh herbs include sweet broad chives and *mitsuba* (Japanese parsley). There's plenty of *horenso* (Japanese spinach); *moyashi* (bean sprouts); Tokyo *kabocha* (a pumpkin used in simmered dishes); hairy brown *nagaimo;* yams from Hawaii; and *sato imo,* or taro root. The delicate fresh snow-puff mushrooms or the *enokitake* mushrooms are a wonderful addition to vegetable dishes. Occasionally, you can find exquisite fresh *matsutake*, or pine mushrooms, grown in pine forests near Seattle. For pickling, they have big bunches of chalky *daikon* with their top leaves, enormous heads of Chinese cabbage, and piles of knobbly fresh ginger.

The fish counter, of course, is plentifully supplied with fresh tuna and albacore, tasty octopus, small local Monterey squid—on occasion, some as long as ten inches. Seasonally, there are piles of firmly close-mouthed clams and small tender abalone in the shell.

The strips of glazed barbecued pork served up from the meat counter are delicious in your noodle dishes. *Sukiyaki* meat is sliced paper thin and layered between paper.

Not far from the fish, you can scoop up hot yellow *daikon* radish pickles called *takuwan* from plastic tubs. An essential part of Japanese meals, vegetables such as *daikon*, Chinese cabbage, turnip radish, and radish greens are pickled either in a heavy brine or a yeasty mash.

Pick up your egg roll wrapper skins and fresh *sukiyaki* or yam noodles from the refrigerator case, where frozen chunks of *kabocha* (Japanese pumpkin) sit alongside American TV dinners. You'll find grayish yam balls, yam cakes, tangled skeins of angel-hair seaweed, and a splendid collection of the colored, steamed, or fried fish cakes called *kamaboko*. Made from a fine purée of whitefish, *kamaboko* originated in the fourteenth century. Poach and serve as appetizers or use slices in soup and noodle dishes.

K. Sakai has just about everything: *miso*; seaseed; rice flour; dried sheaves of *nori* laver for wrapping your *sushi*; dried *udon* and *somen* noodles; *shoyu*, or natural Japanese soy sauce, lighter and less salty than the Chinese version; *dashi-no-moto*, instant *dashi* soup stock made from dried kelp and dried bonito;

*matcha*, the bitter powdered green tea used in the tea ceremony; *wasabi*, horseradish in powdered form; *kanpyo*, dried gourd shavings used as a garnish.

K. Sakai also sells rice; they have six kinds in bags up to one-hundred-pound size: Cal Rose, Kokuh, Kura-Blue Rose, New Rose, Patna, and Tsuru Mai.

**East Bay**
## MISSION MARKET

*20848 Mission Boulevard, Hayward 94540. Telephone (415) 276-1234. Hours: M–F 10–6, SAT 10–5.*

Mission Market is one of the largest distributors of Japanese foodstuffs in the Hayward area. They have fresh Japanese vegetables, canned goods, and fresh fish including bonito and tuna for *sashimi.*

**East Bay**
## NUMANO SAKE

*Fourth and Addison streets, Berkeley 94710. Telephone (415) 540-8250. Hours: 12–6 daily.*

Sake, Japan's distinctive rice wine, has origins far back in Japan's history. Originally available only to priests and the wealthier classes, in this century and the last sake has become a popular drink in every kind of home. In Japan each year now, however, more and more of the small regional breweries making quality sake close down as status-conscious Japanese switch allegiance to western whiskey, beer, and wines.

Sake is a clear, fragrant wine made from pure water and rice innoculated with the mold *aspergillus oryzae*. The subsequent mash is then fermented and later refined to make a wine with 16 percent alcohol.

In Japan, sake is made in several grades according to the quality of the rice and the degree of polishing. The more the rice is polished down to the heart of the kernel, the more expensive and the more fragrant the resulting sake is. Unlike wines made from grapes, sake is not usually aged; it is drunk the same year it is made.

Traditionally sake is warmed before it is served by placing the small serving bottle, or *tokorri,* in a pan of very hot water. The host then serves each guest in thimble-sized porcelain cups called *sakazuki.*

Numano Sake Company in Berkeley is North America's first sake brewery, producing sake from a special strain of rice grown in California's hot Sacramento Valley.

Curiously, at the same time as Americans are discovering the subtleties of *sushi, sashimi,* and other traditional Japanese foods, Numano doesn't want to emphasize the traditional use of sake in a Japanese meal. They have introduced the idea of drinking sake western style, in mixed drinks. To this end, they make two types of sake: *kosho masamune,* intended to be drunk warm in the traditional manner, and Numano Sake California, recommended for drinking iced or in mixed cocktails. They also make *mirin,* a sweet rice wine for cooking.

All of Numano Sake's wines can be tasted daily in their Berkeley tasting room from 10 to 8 daily.

---

**San Francisco**
# TOKYO FISH MARKET

*1908 Fillmore Street, San Francisco 94115. Telephone (415) 931-4561. Hours: W–SUN 9–6:30.*

This relaxed market has a good selection of fresh-looking seafood: octopus, bonito, tuna. In front there are small plastic containers of Japanese pickled ginger and vegetables in a confusion of bright yellow and hot pink. Big colored tubs hold more *tsukemono,* or cucumber pickles; *takuwan, daikon* radish; and *nara zuke,* Japanese melon pickled in sake lees.

The refrigerator has fresh *udon* noodles, several kinds of *tofu,* yam cakes, *sukiyaki* noodles, *kim chee,* pickled Chinese cabbages, fish cakes, etc.

The shelves of this Japanese grocery store are stocked with little tubs of *miso,* bags of roasted soybean flour, unhusked dark-brown pearl barley, chocolate-colored *shabu* seeds, refreshing green tea both loose and in bags, enormous dried *shiitake* mushrooms, as well as cans of meaty *matsutake* mushrooms from Japan's pine forests.

Here as in other Japanese markets, there are dried *soba,* the beautiful grayish noodles of Tokyo and northern Japan. Made from buckwheat, these are used in hearty winter noodle dishes. The finer *udon,* or wheat noodles, come from southern Japan, where they're used to make refreshing cold noodle dishes in summer. The *tomoshiraga soba* is made of white wheat and cut fine as thread. The store also has lovely *somen,* Japanese vermicelli made from hard-wheat flour, in celadon green—flavored with green tea—or fungus color, flavored with pine tree mushrooms. The pale raspberry *shiso-somen* is colored with beefsteak leaves.

Boxes of little rolled bundles of seaweed, each neatly tied, are for *tempura.* The boxes of basic produce spill out onto the street: generous bundles of beautiful green scallions, sleek purple-black Japanese eggplants, fleshy spinach, fresh white *daikon,* Chinese cabbage, and fresh bean sprouts. Long brown *gobo,* or burdock roots, used to strengthen the ill since the tenth century, sit next to single boxes of onions, garlic, lemons, bananas, and yams.

# KOREAN MARKETS

Several of the stores in the General Oriental section carry Korean foodstuffs.

## East Bay
## HAN IL ORIENTAL KOREAN MARKET

*22550 Main Street, Hayward 94540. Telephone (415) 582-8949. Hours: M-SAT 10:30–7:30.*

This Korean grocery has no fresh fish, but it stocks imported frozen fish as well as all the dried varieties.

## San Francisco
## KUKJEA MARKET

*2805 Taraval Street, San Francisco 94116. Telephone (415) 681-0333. Hours: 10:30–8 daily.*

You can find all kinds of things for Korean cuisine at Kukjea, a Korean market on Taraval Street. A lack of fluent Korean is a distinct disadvantage here: signs for everything are scribbled in Korean on broad white paper plates. The only English you'll find is on the packages themselves, when they have it. But you can sniff and investigate, and theorize on the possible use of all these truly exotic and unfamiliar things. You'll find big bundles of grayish-green bean threads, Korean-style vermicelli, imported canned goods from Korea, sardine-shaped cans of *perilla* leaves, dried Japanese eggplant, and dark-brown dried bracken and platycodon.

Korean cuisine is not known for its sublety: bags of chili spices, hot pepper powder, whole chili, and chili sliced in fine threads abound. (It gets awfully cold in winter there, as any fans of "M*A*S*H" should know.)

It looks as if they took all the strangest creatures of the seas, dried them and packaged them in cellophane; long squiggly fish, Alaska pollack, fish with withered elongated bodies, shrimp, cuttlefish, anchovies, plates of filefish, and small elongated silver fish curled like horseshoes. And what they didn't dry, they froze. Check the freezerful of mysterious fish and squid and things.

To cook and serve it all, there are piles of brassy gold containers, pots, and individual serving bowls as well as inexpensive big earthenware soup bowls.

## East Bay
## PUSAN MARKET

*1125 Webster Street, Oakland 94607. Telephone (415) 832-3731. Hours: M-SAT 9-7, SUN 11-6.*

The sign in front advertises "Korean red ginseng." Pusan Market, just a short walk away from Oakland Chinatown, is a very tiny store, crammed with Korean foodstuffs floor to ceiling. It's so unobtrusive from the street, you'd never notice the store unless you already knew it was there. And, in fact, you're likely to see only Koreans shopping in this little market.

Walk gingerly through the short narrow aisle precariously stacked with foodstuffs. Though the clerk might not be warmly friendly, it's still all right to poke and sniff and pull out discoveries: tubs of dried beans; jars filled with spices and the necessary chilies for putting up your own *kim chee*; translucent circles of rice paper made from green bean paste; vermicelli imported from Korea; Korean-style soy sauce; and *soo boc,* or bean paste. You'll see bags of Indian millet, millet flour, roasted corn, malted barley, malt flour, and even fermented soybean flour.

The refrigerator holds fermented soybean *tofu,* salted yellow crocker fish, and all kinds of *kim chee*—radish, radish with top, *mat na ni* (mixed), Chinese cabbage—as well as jars of salted shrimp, anchovies, kingfish, clams, and a pink paste made from seasoned pollock entrails.

The stock of dried salty things beloved by Koreans gives up a mysterious musty smell: salted sea mustard, dried peppers, sweet potato stem, filefish and other creatures of the sea.

How and where to use all these discoveries? Consult the huge *Home Encyclopedia of Cooking with Practical Korean Recipes,* or take home the small illustrated recipe card book, *Korean Home Cooking,* by J. Wang.

# LATINO MARKETS

The Franciscan fathers knew the best place to build their mission: the sun shines brighter and the air feels warmer in the Mission District than in most other parts of the city. The old Victorian houses are painted the bright colors of undisguised joy, and some of the streets are so narrow that people can reach across and almost touch each other from the windows. Young, graceful mothers walk their children in the afternoon sun. Schoolchildren crowd *panaderías* for the last batch of hot *semitas* or warm spiced *churros* rolled in sugar. And cooks of all kinds wander happily down the streets bearing huge bags of groceries.

The stores are intimate, crammed high with produce, dry goods, shelves of bottles, and columns of tins. So much is packed into so little space that shoppers have to search hard to find everything they want. Many treasures are half-hidden: the tiniest corner of *bacalao* (salt cod) might peep out of a cardboard box betraying its presence. But what *is* visible is often unrecognizable to the uninitiated. Don't worry—questions are welcomed. The curious are rewarded with smiles, instructions, and, above all, recipes.

There are real seasons in the Mission stores, and the colors of the produce change accordingly. Winter brings bright bitter oranges. In the spring there are green papery-husked *tomatillos* and fresh *nopalitos,* or cactus leaves. The tropical fruits such as *guayaba* and *nisperos* come and go throughout the year, perfuming the air. And year round there are fresh warm tortillas, interesting cheeses, spicy homemade sausages, and a whole world of tastes and smells to inspire the adventurous cook.

An afternoon's shopping expedition to the Mission will give you a heady dose of the Latino experience. But even if you don't live in the neighborhood, there are Mexican and Latino-style bakeries and delicatessens scattered all over the Bay Area where you can find many of the items described in the Mission area entries.

*Note:* For fresh *masa* see Pasta and Dough. For tortillas see Bread.

---

**San Francisco**
# RAUL BARRAZA "B" PRODUCTOS MEXICANOS

*2840 Mission Street, San Francisco 94110. Telephone (415) 824-4474. Hours: M–SAT 8:30–5.*

Raul comes from Durango "where," he says, "all the men are beautiful"—adding wistfully, "but I was born near the Sinaloa border." A songwriter, his musical creations include "Amor Hippy," "Durango Heroes," and "La Flor de Chilicote." He is also the author of "Y

Por Que Somos Pobres Los Pobres?" (Why Are We Poor Folk Poor?), a discourse on the causes of poverty, written in the style of the seventeenth-century Spanish moralists: "We all make mistakes in life, it is well known, but when we give up and decide to join the ranks of poverty, we make a life-long mistake."

You might go in on a day when he is wearing his *norteño* outfit: a *guayabera* shirt, a *paliacate* (bandana), and a cowboy hat. He may be chatting with one of his girlfriends, but she will wait patiently while he concentrates on helping you.

"I sell twenty-five kinds of *chile*," he boasts. Among them are *pasilla*, sometimes called *chile negro*, thin, dark and pungent; *ancho*, the most used of the dried red chilies, large, broad, full-flavored and mild; *mulato*, a dark red-brown, slim and tapered. The smoky *chipotle*, small, very hot, and brick red, is available pickled as well as fresh.

But Barraza's chief glory is an assortment of cheeses: *chontaleño*, used for *quesadillas* and beans; *capulín*, which is somewhat like *feta* and delicious inside *pupusas* (fried Salvadoran *masa* rounds); *patacón*, a cousin of *capulín*, named after *patacónes*, or Spanish gold coins.

He also sells *piloncillo* (or *panocha*), solid brown sugar; tamarind, fresh and dried; and Café Bustelo, a favorite among Latin Americans because of its flavorful dark roast. He has another morning treat—*jícaro* or *morro* seeds for *horchata*, a grain-flavored drink made with milk.

"Three kinds of chocolate," he points out proudly, showing off the well-known Iberra brand as well as Abuelita and Tikal. And for a rich, nostalgic dessert, he has Dulce de Brevas, authentic Colombian figs in heavy syrup, to be eaten with fresh cream cheese.

## San Francisco
## CASA LUCAS MARKET

*2934 Twenty-fourth Street, San Francisco 94110. Telephone (415) 826-4334. Hours: 8-7 daily.*

Don Xavier is an elegant man who used to be in the wine importing business. His well-organized store specializes in West Indian, Caribbean, and Central American foods not found elsewhere. Hundreds of specialty items are tucked neatly into rows of shelves: canned breadfruit, dried pigeon peas, Jamaican curry powder, *adobo* seasoning, and cans of prepared *sofrito*.

Don Xavier sells La Bodega, an excellent sherry wine vinegar; and Baturro chorizo, imported from Spain in tins, as well as a locally made Spanish-style chorizo. The Spanish *turrón*, an egg, almond, and sugar confection similar to Italian *torrone*, comes in two classic versions: soft *jijona*, made with egg yolks, and hard *alicante*, made with egg whites and wafers.

He has real Brazilian *dendê* oil, the yellow-orange palm oil used in the cuisine of the Bahia region of Brazil; cans of *cayuma* (sea turtle); stuffed *nopalitos* (cactus pieces); *papas criollas* (small Colombian potatoes for *ajiaco*); and *ollueos*, a potato-like vegetable from the Andes. There is hominy (dried whole white corn); manioc flour for cakes and breads and to thicken *feijoida*; Brazilian black beans. Of course he has *bacalao* (salt cod), but he also has the dense dried beef necessary for a *feijoida completa*. Lard is sold in big red plastic tubs.

The back refrigerator case stocks frozen and peeled yucca, to save your hands and your time, and frozen pulp of *mamey* and *guanábana* for the traditional puréed fruit drinks, or *aguas*.

The guava products take up a whole shelf: canned whole guavas, guava cream,

guava paste, and *bocadillos beleños*
(Colombian guava paste squares covered
with sugar granules).

Don Xavier's produce is excellent.
Sometimes he brings in green coconuts
still in the husk, called *pipas*, and in the
winter he has fresh bitter oranges for
making real marmalade. The juice is
used as a marinade for meat and poultry
dishes, too. Next to the cash register is
an ever-changing selection of unusual
tropical fruits that are good, but lack
the sweetness that comes from a full
tropical sun.

### San Francisco
### CASA SANCHEZ

*2778 Twenty-fourth Street, San Francisco
94110. Telephone (415) 282-2400. Hours:
M–SAT 9–6:30, SUN 9–5.*

In the front of the Sanchez family store
is a small counter with basic staples
and canned goods. Behind that is a
take-out section with sausages and
dark green *chiles poblanos* stuffed with
thick slices of cheese.

But the store's main works are in the
back, dominated by a vast tortilla-
making factory. There are vats for
cooking the corn and huge dough-
rolling machines that turn out tortillas
for the Mission's Latino community.
The Sanchez's regular corn tortillas are
the best in the area.

### San Francisco
### EL PESCADOR

*3150 Twenty-fourth Street, San Francisco
94110. Telephone (415) 647-2440. Hours:
8–7 daily.*

El Pescador has fresh fish and shellfish
and Latino meat cuts, plus *bacalao*, tins
of sardines, boxes of lard, and bags of
cornhusks.

### Peninsula
### LA AZTECA MARKET

*1531 Main Street, Redwood City 94063.
Telephone (415) 368-3486. Hours: 9–
8:30 daily.*

A complete market with all the ingredients for Mexican cuisine. The small
kitchen in back makes *burritos*, enchiladas, tacos, and *flautas*.

### San Francisco
### LA BORINQUEÑA

*3000 Twenty-fourth Street, San Fran-
cisco. Telephone (415) 282-2556. Hours:
8–7:30 daily; summer closing hours 8 or
8:30.*

Euripedes Quiles, the owner, is an old
*borinqueño* (Puerto Rican). His store is
well stocked, but the most exciting
items here are a number of seldom-
seen homemade pork specialties: *patas
de cerdo* (pigs' feet) and *cuchiflito* (similar to a tripe stew, but made with pork
stomach simmered with spices), *mor-
cillas* (blood sausages), and several kinds
of chunky smoked chorizo. His window
advertises *las tamales cubanas*.

Recently, Señor Quiles's brother Pablo
came up from Los Angeles to teach
him how to make a proper Portuguese-
style *longaniza*, a *linguiça*-type sausage.
The gregarious Pablo Quiles claims to
make the best *paella* this side of the
Rockies. Emphasizing that *paella* is a
*plato internacional*, he proceeded to
give a detailed explanation, complete
with diagram, of his proudest creation:
"You take a big plate of *paella*. You put
a chicken leg in the middle. That's the
stem, and then you put some *camarones*
(shrimp) in a circle to make a rose. You
get some pimiento-stuffed green olives
for the rose buds and cut some strips of
green pepper to make the leaves. Beautiful, eh?"

## San Francisco
## LA CABAÑA

*2919 Sixteenth Street, near Mission, San Francisco 94103. Telephone (415) 861-0434. Hours: M–SAT 8–7:30.*

An unexpected pleasure, this small store has the best selection of home-made Latin American candy in the Mission. Handmade *melcocha* (taffy), *alfajores* (coconut candy), *rosquillas* (a milk candy with coconut), *jamoncillo* (fried milk), and *calabaza enmelada* (honeyed pumpkin). Very sweet, very satisfying, these candies are a traditional Latino way to end a meal. La Cabaña also sells big slabs of *membrillo* (quince) jelly. A slice with a small piece of white cheese is another typical dessert. The *panes dulces* also sold here are seldom eaten for dessert: they are served at breakfast with hot bowls of *café con leche*, or as an afternoon treat, or *merienda*.

La Cabaña also sells tamales, tasty *chicharrón* (fried pork rind), Mexican chorizo, and *queso blanco*, a salty cheese with the imprint of the basket in which it has been pressed. Here, as in other stores, you find *piloncillo*, the small brown sugar cones that serve a variety of purposes throughout tropical America: as a sweetener for beverages; as a dessert, grated and eaten with cheese; or, dissolved in hot water, as a drink to stave off hunger when food is scarce.

## San Francisco
## LA MORENA FACTORY, TORTILLERIA

*3391 Mission Street, San Francisco 94110. Telephone (415) 648-0114. Hours: M–SAT 8–8.*

Aurelio Villareal's store has a warehouselike atmosphere, unlike the cozy crowded spaces of most other Mission District stores. More than anything else it resembles a tropical grocery store, with crates and crates of big green plantains just inside the door. Behind the counter sit big barrels filled with rice, *masa harina* (the maize flour used to make tortillas), yucca flour, dried beans, and packages of sweet Mexican chocolate arranged like brickwork.

The packaged La Morena tortillas are not made on the premises, but they are made nearby, and the handmade ones are delicious.

## San Francisco
## LA PALMA MEXICATESSEN

*2884 Twenty-fourth Street, San Francisco 94110. Telephone (415) 648-5500. Hours: 8–6 daily.*

Owned by Hermanos Haro, this store stocks all the staples and little delicacies required for the many varied cuisines of Mexico.

There's a huge array of cellophane-packaged Michoacán spices with their names stamped in Spanish. The shelves are filled with every variety of canned chili and all kinds of bottled hot sauces with a *caliente* thermometer on the side of the label. There is a big selection of whole dried chilies as well as quantities of dried ground chilies stacked on the shelf like so many sacks of shaded henna. Dried corn husks for steaming tamales fill a bin to overflowing.

When fresh *nopalitos* (fleshy pieces of prickly pear cactus) are in season, they are cut in pieces and sold by the bag. Cook them in salted water until tender, rinse them well in cold water to remove the slime, and use them in salads and in egg or cheese dishes.

The refrigerator case holds homemade chorizo, both pork and beef; individual cinnamon-flavored rice puddings; small packages of fresh basket-drained cheeses; Mexican-style cream cheese; and fresh herbs.

The deli at the back of the store dishes up a variety of tasty snacks: *gorditas* (thick tortillas) spread with beans, cheese, and sauce; *tostadas*, tamales, and tacos; delicious versions of *chile verde* and *chile colorado*. You can also buy fresh *salsa* by the pint.

But La Palma is especially renowned as a *tortillería*. Freshly made tortillas are tender, delicate, and delicious, a completely different experience from the sad leathery rounds sold in most supermarkets. The ones here are baked on big griddles in the back of the store several times a day. Tall stacks of still-steaming tortillas completely cover the counter. They're wonderful, but the real delicacies here are the thicker hand-patted tortillas made by some of the skilled women in the back. The flavor of the corn is sweet and irresistible; the smell is golden, fresh, and comforting.

La Palma will also make four-inch cocktail-size tortillas if you order them one day in advance.

**San Francisco**
## LATIN AMERICAN IMPORT COMPANY NO. 1 AND NO. 2

*3403 Mission Street, San Francisco 94110. Telephone (415) 648-0844. Hours: 8:30–6 daily.*
*3064 Twenty-fourth Street, San Francisco 94110. Telephone (415) 282-4277. Hours: M-F 9-6, SAT 9-5:30, SUN 9-5.*

Don't be deceived by the bare appearance of the shelves of Latin American Imports No. 2 on Twenty-fourth Street. Look carefully, because owner Napoleón Guerrero, a Nicaraguan, stocks things that other stores do not carry: pure essence of vanilla; rose and strawberry syrup in corked bottles from Guatemala; tins of *almibar natural de icaco* (tropical fruit preserves); tamarind concentrate; and *frijoles volteados* (Guatemalan refried beans) both black and red.

At the counter you will find small bricks of *socarro guerrero* (Guatemalan

raw sugar) with the smell and taste of fresh sugar cane juice, *galletas* (hardtack crackers), whisks for frothy almond-scented Mexican chocolate, and carved gourds for your *yerba maté*. You might try the Salvadoran pineapple coffee cake, some of the Central American cheeses and *cremas*, or the Nicaraguan-style chorizo kept on the refrigerator shelves. When you leave, maybe carrying a *paste*, or whole loofa, for your bath, watch out for the fishing nets on the floor—you might trip on their unusual catch of green coconuts.

**East Bay**
## MI RANCHO MARKET

*464 Seventh Street, Oakland 94607. Telephone (415) 451-2393. Hours: M-SAT 8-6.*

Robert Berber, Jr., whose family is from Michoacán, has owned Mi Rancho for twenty-seven years. In the back of the store, the tortilla factory turns out countless corn and flour tortillas, some of them the delicious hand-patted kind. But if you want to make your own, Mi Rancho has tortilla presses and *masa* flour, both coarse ground for tamales and fine ground for tortillas. And to save you effort, they'll even sell you their own prepared dough.

They have Mexican-style cheeses (*queso ranchero, queso Jalisco,* and *panella*) and fat, stubby chorizo made specially for them in Los Angeles. A truck loaded down with Mi Rancho's ever-changing selection of fresh chilies comes up from central Mexico once a week. They have impressive amounts of dried chilies, too, loose or prepackaged, plus bags of all the powdered chilies (New Mexico, California, *ancho,* etc.), wonderful for making Yucatán-style barbecue sauce.

There are neat rows of cellophane-packaged spices: *jinjiba, saladitos,* red grains of *achiote* for staining Caribbean and African dishes, *alcabar, tamarindo, tomillo* (thyme), *chia* (sage), and *yerba buena* (spearmint).

For parties, you can buy giant cans of white hominy, a No. 8 jar of *mole* paste, and No. 6 cans of *chiles jalapeños, chiles serranos,* refried beans, or *tomatillos.* Don't forget a fifty-pound bag of pinto beans and a carton of corn chips.

### San Francisco
### MI RANCHO MARKET

*3365 Twentieth Street, San Francisco 94110. Telephone (415) 647-0580. Hours: M–SAT 9–9, SUN 9–7.*

This source of imported and local Latin American food supplies has a produce section, a butcher shop, a bakery, and an extensive canned goods section. Because of its supermarketlike atmosphere however, it is not as appealing as the smaller stores.

# MIDDLE EASTERN MARKETS

In the Middle East, shopping is an all-day adventure for the senses. People wend their way through crowded streets loud with the sound of lively bargaining and the tinny wail of Middle Eastern music. Shoppers go from one intriguing stall to another in search of spices or vegetables and fruits ripened under the full Mediterranean sun.

While we have no bustling bazaars in the Bay Area, we do have a wealth of Middle Eastern food stores hidden away in unlikely neighborhoods where you can find everything you'll need to cook an exotic banquet. Once inside any of these shops, you'll think you're in the heart of Athens, Alexandria, or Ankara. In fact, with a little store-hopping, you can turn up spices and exotica that would have made the fortune of any ambitious merchant on the ancient spice route.

*Note:* See also Cookware and Pastry. For *filo* dough, see Pasta and Dough.

### Peninsula
### ARMEN'S DELI

*54 West Thirty-seventh Avenue, San Mateo 90731. Telephone (415) 572-8871. Hours: M–SAT 10–6.*

This store's many Middle Eastern customers have found it through Armen's Deli's only advertisement: on the Armenian radio hour.

You'll find staples for all the Levantine cuisines here—spices, olives, bulgur, *tahini*—but the emphasis is Armenian. The *basturma, soujouk,* and *lavash* are all made in Fresno, a center of California's large Armenian community.

Armenian women are justly famous for their cooking. Mrs. Arahi Soghomonian shows her skill with classic *hummus, tabbouleh,* and grape leaves stuffed with rice and vegetables. But her specialty is *lahmejun,* a homemade round flat bread covered with a savory spiced lamb mixture made with meat she grinds herself. She'll also make trays of a number of Armenian pastries for parties on special order.

### San Francisco
### GREEK AMERICAN FOOD IMPORTS

*223 Valencia Street, San Francisco 94103. Telephone (415) 864-0978. Hours: M–F 9–6, SAT 9–5:30, SUN 9–1.*

With its blue and white storefront, Grecian pillars, statue of Venus de Milo, and Cyrillic-lettered sign, Greek American Food Imports seems out of place on Valencia Street. Inside, the light feels blue and white, as in Greece, and the fresh scent of olive oil soap pervades. In the back, a group of dark-suited men are having a lively discussion in Greek.

Owners Mr. and Mrs. Apostopoulos stock seven kinds of Greek olive oil by the gallon and a truly Mediterranean array of sweet preserves: rose petal, quince, grape, bitter orange, and skin orange. For the sweet tooth, there is *mastic* in heavy syrup, the hard resin used throughout the eastern Mediterranean to flavor puddings and desserts. The eggplant preserves and the plump Doric-brand capers are tempting.

The cheeses alone are worth the trip to the store. The selection includes imported and domestic *kasseri; kefalograviera*, a table cheese; and soft and hard *mizithra*, a kind of Greek ricotta. Imported *kefalotiri*, made with sheep's milk, is hard and salty; it's good grated in *pastitsio* (the Greek pasta casserole flavored with cinnamon), or cubed, then grilled or fried and served with a squeeze of lemon. To make *tiropites*, the cheese-filled *filo* triangles, use the Greek sheep's milk *feta* in brine, inexpensive in six-pound jars. There are also Bulgarian and Epiros *fetas* from the barrel. The Apostopouloses also carry *reggas* (smoked herring) and *bakaliaros* (dried codfish).

Watching customers come and go, I remark how beautiful Greek men's eyes are. "Beautiful eyes, beautiful everything," says Mrs. Apostopoulos and smiles at her husband, who is from Pyrgos, in the Peloponnesus.

### San Francisco
### HAIG'S DELICACIES

*642 Clement Street, San Francisco 94118. Telephone (415) 752-6283. Hours: M-SAT 10-6.*

You hear a Babel of languages spoken in Haig's Delicacies—Armenian, Farsi,

Thai, British-accented English of the East Indies—spoken by customers all buying from the selection of curries, spice pastes, and Indonesian condiments. But Haig's is best known as a Middle Eastern food store.

There are shelves of Middle Eastern staples: imported canned goods, bottled olives, beans and spices in four-ounce envelopes. The lavish pastry counter will cater to the whims of any harem: *lokum* (Turkish delight), apricot delight, birds' nests (made with shredded *filo* dough called *kataifa*), and apricot paste from Syria. As for *mezze* (appetizers), he has olives, *fetas* in brine, *dolmas* and *hummus* (a garbanzo bean purée with sesame seed paste). He sells three kinds of *filo* dough for making your own sweet pastries and savories: the familiar Apollo brand, Indo-European from Los Angeles, and Sheherazade, freshly made right in the neighborhood.

For the large Armenian community in the area, there is *basturma* (a mahogany-colored dried beef coated with a reddish spice paste), *soujouk* ( a spicy beef sausage), *lahmejun* (Armenian-style pizza made with ground lamb), Armenian string cheese, and stacks of packaged *lavash* (big rounds of crisp flat bread) baked daily in Fresno.

You can ask for green coffee beans to roast fresh yourself Bedouin-style, and enameled Turkish coffee pots to make it in. And you'll find tiny tea glasses for serving glass after glass of the sticky sweet beverage as they do in Istanbul.

## San Francisco
## HOUSE OF COFFEE

*1618 Noriega Street, San Francisco 94122. Telephone (415) 681-9363. Hours: T–SAT 9:30–6:30.*

Coffee is the main item here, and the aroma clings to the air. The Armenian proprietor, Mr. Davletian, is very knowledgeable; his entire family was in the coffee business in Romania. Mr. Davletian's coffee comes from all over the world, and he roasts it to order right in the store. But Middle Eastern staples line the shelves. You'll find fava beans, cheeses, okra pickles, and a delicious *lokum* made by a gentleman from the island of Ciros. These days Iranian pistachios are difficult to find, but when available Mr. Davletian sends them to Germack's in Detroit for roasting. Lately, California-grown nuts are being sent there, too, for the same high-quality roasting.

## San Jose Area
## INTERNATIONAL DELICATESSEN AND BAKERY

*795 The Alameda, San Jose 95126. Telephone (408) 286-2036. Hours: M–F 9–5, SAT 11–3.*

Don't become so mesmerized by the pastries sold at the International Delicatessen that you miss the rest of the goods crowded into this narrow, long store: Greek wines, oil-cured olives from Egypt, sacks of grains and flours, even *smeed,* the semolina used in Arabian pastries. The delicious "sweetmeats" are made at the Greek bakery next door (Hun-i-nut), where they stretch their own *filo* dough by hand. It's sold in one-pound packages of plain large sheets or prebuttered in four-layer strips ready to use in elaborate layered pastries.

Their own *filo* pastries show a Byzantine elaboration of form. Drenched in honey and rich with nuts, they're made only with sweet butter, clarified to remove the liquid and milk solids. The crisp, buttery pastry is evidence of this extra care and expense. The round Greek wedding cookies, *kourabiethes*, with a walnut filling, will charm you with their sweetness and delicacy.

## San Francisco
## ISTANBUL

*Woolen Mill Building, Ghirardelli Square, 900 North Point, San Francisco 94109. Telephone (415) 441-7740. Hours: SUN–TH 10–6, F–SAT 10–9.*

Istanbul has the kind of pastry case that transfixes passersby in the old part of that fabulous Turkish city. There are trays and trays of Teta Panagiotides's perfect Greek pastries, and on special order owner Mr. St. Jacques can have round tins of her *baklava* made for mailing as gifts, or in smaller cuts for parties. Serve them with an iced drink made from natural Bulgarian rose oil.

At Istanbul you can find bags of *zahter* (a hybrid of oregano) and the sour spice *sumac* for sprinkling Persian style over shish kebab. *Zahter* mixed with *sumac* and sesame seed is used as a dipping spice for *pita* bread drenched in olive oil. For an authentic Greek *avgolemono* soup, you can buy the real *minestra*, or rice-shaped pasta, called birds' tongues in Arabic. Cook it in rich chicken stock, then thicken the soup with egg yolk and season with lemon. Bags of *stragalia* (roasted white chickpeas) and *macabraes* (slightly salted chick-peas), along with salted roasted pumpkin, watermelon, squash, and melon seeds, are eaten as snacks or pounded with spices and nuts to make dipping mixtures for Arabic bread or hard-cooked eggs.

**San Jose Area**
## MIDDLE EAST FOODS

*26 Washington, Santa Clara 95050. Telephone (408) 248-5112. Hours: M–SAT 10–8, SUN 12–4.*

George Kachakji's Middle East Foods serves the large Arab community in the San Jose area. In addition to food-stuffs, he sells Arabic magazines and newspapers and traditional musical instruments such as the *oud.*

The serious Middle Eastern cook can find the makings for regional dishes from Persia, Saudi Arabia, Syria, Egypt, Greece, and Turkey here. If you need a *feta* cheese, he has five kinds, each in its milky brine, plus a milder Syrian white cheese not often seen. Mr. Kachakji will even tell you how to make a tray of Assyrian *feta* cheese pastries with one of the four brands of *filo* dough he sells. All of his *filo* dough sweets are tempting—compare an elegant *baklava* with pistachios with the more usual walnut-filled version. For your own pastry fillings and garnishes, he has both domestic and Iranian pistachios.

**East Bay**
## MIDDLE EAST MARKET

*2054 San Pablo Avenue, Berkeley 94702. Telephone (415) 548-2213. Hours: M–F 10–6, SAT 10:30–5:30.*

Down the center aisle of this treasury of Middle Eastern goods runs a double line of buckets filled with mouthwatering fat brown Persian raisins, Turkish apricots, sliced and slivered almonds, watermelon seeds, and sugar-coated chick-peas. The wide range of low-priced legumes, grains, and flours includes yellow and brown fava beans, Egyptian *ful*, and high-quality Pakistani *basmati* rice. If you like pistachios, try the imported Iranian nuts in five-pound bags or small cans.

Here you will find meaty walnuts and bottled pomegranate juice, the makings for the delicious Iranian chicken dish, *faisinjin.* The extensive spice section includes classic rosemary and tarragon, plus exotics such as *mahlub* and *zahter*, jujube, and sweet basil seeds for Persian-style sour pickling. Mr. Mizrai also carries valerian and dried blue borage flowers, used by dervishes to make a medicinal tea. Hard whitish chips called *katyra* are ground and mixed with henna and lotus, a kind of shampoo, to make a potion for split ends.

Try the homemade *torshi*, sour vegetables aged with spices and vinegar. The best is garlic, aged three years, and even better at ten. Frozen smoked shad and smoked fish from the Caspian sea are sold here for cooking with rice or for simply frying. Pour *pekmez* (grape-juice molasses) over shaved ice to make Persian-style snow cones. With a few days' notice, you can order Iranian pastries made with rice flour, roasted chick-pea flour, honey, and walnuts.

**Contra Costa**
## NARSAI'S MARKET

*389 Colusa Avenue, Kensington 94707. Telephone (415) 527-3737. Hours: M–SAT 10–7, SUN 10–4.*

Restaurateur and food personality Narsai David has created two sausages with a Middle Eastern flavor for his Narsai's Market: a Moroccan lamb sausage faintly sweet with curry, spices, and currants, and an Assyrian lamb sausage flavored with pomegranate juice, wine, and basil. The sausages are lean, delicious grilled, and just as good prepared slightly rare as well cooked.

The store's homemade *tabbouleh* and *hummus* are both excellent, and the *dolmas* are fresh and lemony. Occasionally the pastry chef will make an extravagant *filo*-dough pastry with flavored honey and pistachio nuts.

Each day the deli features a different take-out entrée, often a Middle Eastern dish such as *moussaka*. Many excellent dishes from the Levant also appear on Narsai's catering lists.

## East Bay
# G. B. RATTO AND COMPANY

*821 Washington, Oakland 94607. Telephone (415) 832-6503. Hours: M–SAT 8–5.*

This Victorian storefront with its wide-open doorway rimmed with bins of beans, rice, and grains almost spilling out into the street is the closest thing around to a Mediterranean market. Head for the spices first. All are in gallon jars clearly labeled with name and price by the ounce. You can sniff out the grade of paprika you want to buy and measure out just how much you want on the scale. (It's best to buy small quantities of spices often to ensure freshness.) There's fenugreek, *takmeria falooda* (seed of sherbet), whole dried ginger, *habat el baraka* (black caraway seeds), dried dates, and sumac. They even have angelica root and *kishk*, a Persian dried milk product sold in chalky white lumps. There's a big sack of dried *mouloukia* leaves, used with a meaty stock to prepare an Egyptian soup eaten since the time of the pharoahs. The scent of the Greek hills pulls at you from bundles of fragrant wild oregano and sage.

Ratto imports its own high-quality *couscous* in bulk, and there are six kinds of bulgur in big bins: whole natural, whole pearled, extra-fine, fine, medium, and coarse. Top lamb and vegetable *couscous* with *harissa* sauce, an extremely hot red pepper sauce from Tunisia sold in tubes, made with garlic, cumin, and caraway. Further exploring turns up dried brown Egyptian fava beans and the very small ones called *ful medames*, used to make the

Egyptian national dish of the same name, served with olive oil, a squeeze of lemon, and hard-boiled eggs. The orangey-red lentils make a thick soup with lamb bones and cumin. Canned *dolmas* from Greece, pomegranate juice, cans of Greek cooking fat, jars of preserves, grape leaves, olives, six brands of Greek olive oil fill shelf after shelf.

Ratto imports its own very good Bulgarian sheep's milk *feta* and Greek olives. The Athens brand *filo* dough handles beautifully because it's never been frozen. Jars of *tarama* (a deep salmon-colored carp roe caviar) sit next to jars of *lakerda* (bonito chunks packed in olive oil, Greek style) and Fresno-made *basturma* and *soujouk*.

The liquor department is formidable, with lots of Greek wine (retsina, *mavro-daphne, rodytys*), Metaxa (Greek brandy), and several kinds of anise-flavored *arak* and *ouzo* from all over the Levant.

## San Francisco
# SAMIRAMIS IMPORTS

*2990 Mission Street, San Francisco 94110. Telephone (415) 824-6555. Hours: M–SAT 10–6.*

Behind the display of Arabic records, eight-tracks, and cassettes are bin upon bin of spices and dry goods, tins of *tahini, hummus* from Lebanon, five brands of imported *couscous*. There's also *maftoul*, a pasta-like *couscous* substitute said to be lighter on the stomach, and the different kinds of whole-wheat grains (green, roasted, peeled, or unpeeled) used for making soup. Check the refrigerator case: Mr. Koury carries some interesting white cheeses such as *shaheera*, tart drained yogurt balls in olive oil; Danish and Bulgarian *feta*; *halloumi*, a salty sharp processed goat cheese from Cyprus; and Latin American *queso fresco*, a good substitute in Middle Eastern dishes that require a milder cheese. You will find Armenian string cheese and a packaged dry yogurt used as a soup starter mixed with hot water.

By the time you reach the salt cod, the *basturma*, and the *soujouk*, you might be dancing in time to the Bagdhad fiddle. Make sure you don't trip over the cartons of carved-wood cookie molds for making *mamool*, the delicious semolina pastries filled with dates and nuts that are also sold here.

Mr. Kouri will grind your own Arab-style coffee: two-thirds Arabian to one-third dark French for best flavor, he says, plus a dash of cardamom.

### San Francisco
### SHEHERAZADE BAKERY

*1935 Lawton Street, San Francisco 94122. Telephone (415) 681-8439. Hours: T–F 9–6, M and SAT 9–5.*

This may be the last of the small bakeries to make its own *filo* dough without preservatives, since San Francisco's Ballas and Delphi both closed in the last few years. Sheherazade's *filo* dough is supple and handles like silk, a pale wheat color flecked with dark.

They also make a line of *filo* dough pastries including plump *baklava, kadaiff, bourma,* and birds' nests, all delicious, freshly made, and dripping with honey. The *lokum* is superb, not too sweet, studded with pistachios and walnuts.

### San Jose Area
### TARVER'S DELICACIES

*1338 South Mary Avenue in De Anza Shopping Center, Sunnyvale 94087. Telephone (408) 732-1892. Hours: M–F 9:30–7, SAT 9:30–6.*

It's not quite the narrow dark streets of an old bazaar. In fact, it's the most American of shopping centers, but once inside Tarver's Delicacies, it's hard to remember you're in Sunnyvale. You'll see the East's crowded shelves of exotic jams and syrups, decorative tins of olive oils, cans and jars of Middle Eastern foodstuffs bright with gaudy labels. When someone opens one of the big jars of spices to weigh out an ounce of yellow turmeric, its pungent aroma fills the store. There are teas and coffees in the Oriental fashion, green beans for your roasting, and coffee mills for your grinding. Among the display of cooking utensils, you will catch the warm gleam of long-handled copper Turkish coffee pots nipped in at the waist. There are new copper goods and some antique ones, marked with long usage.

The board game called *taflu* sold here is the same the Crusaders brought back from the East and called backgammon.

### San Francisco
### TOTAH'S FOODS
### FROM THE MIDDLE EAST

*624 Irving Street, San Francisco 94122. Telephone (415) 681-5858. Hours: M–F 10–9, SAT 10–8, SUN 10–6.*

Totah's *falafel* is delicious. The outside is crisp, the inside delicate and green with parsley. The *tabbouleh* is very green too, made with fine bulgur, lots of lemon, small bits of cucumber, and a touch of mint. The *baba ghanoush,* freshly baked eggplant creamed with *tahini,* has more lemon than garlic, as does the *hummus* purée. Everything is made in the kitchen at the back of the store and is sold both retail and wholesale. You can also buy Totah's *falafel* as dry mix or frozen, ready for frying.

If you're tempted by one of the Egyptian jams (date, figs, orange, apricot) don't forget to take home a bottle of the *arak* from Ramallah. The tradition is to offer a spoonful of jam to your guests, followed by a sip of iced water and then a small glass of *arak* or cup of strong Turkish coffee.

# PHILIPPINE MARKETS

Many of the stores listed in the General Oriental section carry Philippine foods.

## San Francisco
## LUISA G. EVANGELISTA

*1201 Howard Street, San Francisco 94103. Telephone (415) 626-5070. Hours: M–SAT 9–5:30, SUN 10–5.*

The Evangelista family imports, wholesales, and retails Philippine foods. From Howard Street in the South of Market area, you walk under a palm-thatched entranceway to enter a large store, light and well-organized. Filipino familes shop for jars of mauve *bagoong alamong* (salted shrimp fry), *bagoong monamon delis* (salted anchovies), *bagoong sisi* (salted oyster), and *bagoong tahong* (salted clams). The most common type of *bagoong* is anchovy based, but there are lots of varieties, all fermented fish or shellfish pastes, used to season and salt dishes. Also found here are *taba ng talangka* (crab paste with citrus juice, ginger, and spices), and *balao* (cooked fermented shrimp fry with garlic and rice). You could spend hours wondering how they stacked the tiniest silver fish so perfectly in the jar of *bagoong padas.*

There are dried fish, dozens of kinds, and frozen fish including *tangigi,* Spanish mackerel, and salted mullet.

The freezer holds coconut milk; *buko* (young coconut); tropical guava; quick-frozen banana leaves (still green, rather than dried, for making steamed packages); grated cassava; black grains of toasted sweet rice; *tocino* (a sweetened soy-cured pork eaten with rice); Philippine sausage and mild *longaniza* sausage; plus *lumpia* wrappers and large egg roll wrappers. *Lumpia* are usually filled with pork, shrimp, and *ubod,* or heart of palm.

Grab a few boxes of Knorr-brand soups. Here, it's *sinigang* broth. Just add your favorite *sangkap,* or dried fish. For starch, you'll find rice, rice stick noodles, *pancit* (Philippine-style noodles), and tapioca pearls in bags.

Many Philippine dishes have a sweet-sour taste achieved with the liberal use of special vinegars such as *sukang paombong* (a white vinegar made from nipa sap) and *sukang iloco* (a vinegar made from sugar cane sap). The ubiquitous *patis,* a strained and quite strong fermented fish sauce, is used both in cooking and as a seasoning set on the table along with a jar of some kind of *bagoong.*

The small produce area features Japanese eggplant, bitter melon, long beans, *taro* root, distinctive leaves and herbs for soups, and sweet cooking bananas.

For your sweet tooth, there's a coconut jam, a jam made from sticky purple *ube* yams, and popular jack fruit preserves. They also have *pastillas,* cream-colored candies from the Philippines, and *buko* balls made with young coconut. You'll find all the makings for another favorite: *suman,* glutinous rice mixed with coconut milk and palm sugar steamed in a green banana leaf, and *puto,* a light cake made with the same ingredients.

**San Jose Area**
## GIGI'S ORIENTAL MART

*1807 El Camino Real, Santa Clara 95051. Telephone (408) 243-1591. Hours: 10–7 daily.*

This store emphasizes Philippine foods.

**Stockton**
## GO ORIENT IMPORTS

*502 South San Joaquin, Stockton 95203. Telephone (209) 463-4845. Hours: M–F 9:30–5:30; sometimes open on Saturday.*

A full line of Philippine foodstuffs.

**Peninsula**
## MAHARLIKA FOOD MARKET

*87 Oriente, Daly City 94104. Telephone (415) 467-3933. Hours: T–SUN 10–7.*

A full line of Philippine foods.

**Peninsula**
## NIPA HUT TRADING COMPANY

*19 San Pedro Road, Daly City 94014. Telephone (415) 755-7845. Hours: M–SAT 9–7, SUN 9–5.*

A full line of Philippine foodstuffs.

**East Bay**
## ORIENTAL LUCKY MART

*818 Jefferson Street, Housewives' Market, Oakland 94607. Telephone (415) 465-7807. Hours: M–SAT 9–6.*

Adeling Castro has owned this store for almost four years. Just a low wall separates Oriental Lucky Mart from the rest of the busy Housewives' Market in Oakland.

Her exotic vegetable section catches the eye immediately. Ms. Castro will gladly tell you what all these mysterious green things are and how to cook them:

*saluyat,* used by both the Egyptians and the Vietnamese, is a green that gets slippery like okra when cooked; *malungay* resembles an elongated okra, straight as a stick (Filipinos eat the leaves, too, whereas Indians eat only the sticks, called *karala*). Taro leaves are used to prepare some Hawaiian dishes and are called *patra* by the Indians. Fresh bamboo shoots are sold just like bean sprouts. You'll find *upo,* or gourd; taro root and *gabe,* or bitter melon. The fleshy green seaweed from Hawaii is used to make a salad with onion, tomato, and salted shrimp. Green papayas can be cooked in stews or grated and pickled with vegetables.

Beware of the *balut,* though, a favorite and rather grisly Manila street food. They take duck eggs with the embryo inside exactly eighteen days old (just before the feathers) and cook it. The eye-catching salted eggs are dyed bright fuschia to distinguish them from regular eggs, and are eaten as a side dish.

You'll find Oriental noodles; rice papers and *lumpia* wrappers; Philippine condiments and snacks; *panucha,* or unrefined brown sugar; saltpeter for chorizo-like sausages. The many kinds of dried fish are delicious roasted over live coals, as in the Philippines. They can be fried, too, but if you do so inside, be prepared for a strong odor.

Don't forget the banana ketchup, made with cane sugar and vinegar.

A freezer holds schools of frozen fish peculiar to native waters, plus frozen coconut cream and grated young coconut for desserts, and a local commercial ice cream made in tropical flavors: *langka* (jack fruit), *macapaino* (glutinous coconut), fresh *buko* (young coconut), *kaymito* (star apple), *atis* (sugar apple), mango, and avocado. The flavors sound wonderful, but, unfortunately, the base is a foamy, overly sweet product.

Castro also has inexpensive marble mortars and pestles and an efficient little coconut grater.

You can taste a wonderful purply yam pudding with coconut, which she sells right at the counter. Adeling Castro also caters Philippine desserts and appetizers.

And for an authentic Philippine *longaniza* sausage, stop in at Taylor's sausage stand, also in Housewives' Market, where one of the sausage makers makes this spicy pork sausage from his grandmother's recipe.

## San Francisco
## PHILIPPINE GROCERY

*3293 Twenty-second Street, San Francisco 94110. Telephone (415) 285-4998. Hours: 10–6 daily.*
*156 Eighteenth Street, San Francisco 94107. Telephone (415) 626-3734. Hours: 10:30–6:30 daily.*
*4929 Mission Street, San Francisco 94112. Telephone (415) 584-4465. Hours: M–F 10–7:30, SAT–SUN 10–7.*

Philippine Grocery is another small neighborhood grocery on Twenty-second Street. Everything is so pristine and neat, it seems like someone is playing store. There are no empty spaces; everything is geometrically arranged. One wall has a complete selection of vermicelli and noodles, all stacked high and each neatly labeled, in shades of white to yellow: curly, squiggled, straight, opaque, translucent. The small, neat

packages of spices—all with their Philippine names—include bay, *aniz*, and golden *casubia* (saffron), plus saltpeter for making your own *longaniza* sausage. Then there's a wonderful soldierly array of tropical jams made from yam or coconut sport or jack fruit.

A plus: all the frozen fish are labeled in English, including, of course, whole *bangus* fish and all the considerable varieties of smoked fish. There is *tapa* (seasoned beef), beef tripe, and pints of beef blood for thickening stews.

The produce section is a crowd of boxes of most-used ingredients: garlic, yams, Japanese eggplants, long beans, coconut, ginger, tamarind, cones of dark-brown *panocha* sugar, and dried banana flowers. All the makings except the chicken for *puchero*, the Philippines' Sunday stew.

Behind the produce, bright fuschia salted eggs and *tapa* (beef marinated in brown sugar, burgundy wine, and soy) compete for your attention.

A wall of cookies and snacks includes tins of Filipino *turrones di casay*, a nougat made with cashews, honey, coconut milk, and flour.

## San Jose Area
## SALOM ORIENTALS

*1647 North Capitol Avenue, San Jose 95111. Telephone (408) 923-3820. Hours: 10–7 daily.*

Ingredients for Philippine cuisine.

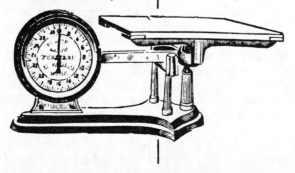

# SCANDINAVIAN MARKETS

## San Francisco
## AFFOLTER BROTHERS MEATS

*2283 Market Street, San Francisco 94114. Telephone (415) 621-4100. Hours: M-SAT 9-6.*

Market Street's Affolter Brothers Meats makes homemade *medisterpolse* (a Danish pork sausage), *potatis korv* (potato sausage), liver paste, and *morbrad* (pork tenderloin).

They also supply smoked eels, salt cod, *roget torak* (kippered cod), finnan haddie, frozen Norwegian *lutefisk*, *inlagd sill* (marinated herring), and Iceland herring to the neighborhood's Scandinavian community.

Their stock of basic ingredients for Scandinavian cuisine includes imported lingonberries scooped by the pint from a big bucket, dried green peas, yellow peas, and brown beans for hearty winter soups.

## San Jose Area
## THE DELI FACTORY

*1343 South Winchester Boulevard, San Jose 95128. Telephone (408) 379-8740. Hours: M-F 10-6, SAT 9-6.*

Patti Vjorst makes Danish pork sausage, Swedish potato sausage, and homemade pâté for the Danish Deli in San Jose. Christmas brings homemade veal or pork head cheese, rolled pork, and rolled ham.

The year around they have lingonberries by the pint; Icelandic herring, whole or filleted; Danish beers; dried cod; beans; jams; and other imported ingredients for Scandinavian cuisines. Danish pastries and cakes are baked every day.

## East Bay
## THE NORDIC HOUSE

*3421 Telegraph Avenue, Oakland 94609. Telephone (415) 653-3882. Hours: M-SAT 9-5.*

Visit the Nordic House some cold rainy day just before noon, when the store is filled with smells of good home cooking prepared for the modest lunchtime smorgasbord. Breathe in those comforting aromas while you browse through the store's stock of Scandinavian foodstuffs.

In the morning, Peter Carde is at the store early, making yards and yards of the Scandinavian sausages his customers come long distances to buy (see Charcuterie section).

At Christmas, you will find *uleskinka*, a flavorful Swedish Christmas ham; Danish *flaeskestege*, pork roast with the rind intact; or *fenalaar*, smoked and cured leg of lamb from Norway. Pop them into the oven for a hearty Christmas dinner.

The cheeses are stacked high at the front, pale yellows punctuated with the bright red wrapping of Tybo, descendants of cheeses made since Viking times: Jarlsberg, a delicate Norwegian version of Swiss Emmentaler; mild Danish Samsoe; semi-soft Havarti; and Danablu, Denmark's rich blue cheese made from cow's milk.

There is lots of seafood: frozen *lutefisk* fillets, Icelandic cod fillets, fresh and smoked eel and herring, and slightly salted *matjes* herring fillets. There are buckets of herring, sold by the pint, the quart, and even the gallon: Nordic pickled, fillets in brine, headless in brine, and *matjes* fillets, plus dozens of kinds of bottled herring from Sweden and tins of Swedish anchovies.

Winter staples include big packaged rounds of Swedish flat bread; a Scandinavian-style vinegar made from spirits; and a hoard of dried yellow peas, brown beans, and green peas.

For a northern sweet tooth, there are dozens of Danish—black currant, raspberry, cherry, lingonberry—tins of buttery cookies, candies, northern European chocolate bars, and, at Christmas, fat marzipan piggies.

### San Francisco
### SCANDINAVIAN DELICATESSEN

*2251 Market Street, San Francisco 94114. Telephone (415) 861-9913. Hours: M-F 9-6.*

Scandinavian Delicatessen is a real cafeteria with hearty home-cooked foods. Cold, foggy days bring a crowd of the cold and hungry carrying big plates of steaming hot food to the simple tables. Try the homemade *potatis korv,* or Swedish potato sausage. French wines here are stacked over rows of blue and black Swedish clogs. The refrigerator is stocked with Swedish and Danish beers.

You can also take home Scandinavian-style meats, like the salted leg of lamb; imported Havarti, Lappi, or Jarlsberg cheeses; herring of different kinds by the pint; plus an array of fish from northern countries: smoked salmon from Alaska; fish cakes from Norway; smoked eel, flounder, and codfish from Denmark; finnan haddie and salt cod from Canada; and herring from Iceland. Call a day ahead and you can buy prepared *lutefisk,* already soaked.

Behind the counter, you'll find groceries like Swedish mustards, potato starch flour, vinegars, brown beans, and canned fish balls.

## —THAI MARKETS—

Most of the stores in the Vietnamese section also carry some Thai foodstuffs, as do a few of the stores in the General Oriental section.

### Contra Costa
### MAHANAKORN MARKET

*10557 San Pablo Avenue, El Cerrito 94530. Telephone (415) 525-2777. Hours: 12-5:30 daily.*

The lovely woman at the front counter is Burin Kochaphum, who, with her sister Vaiunee, owns the Mahanakorn Market, an East Bay store specializing in Thai foodstuffs. Both the sisters work for airlines and so can easily go to and from Thailand to bring back special items.

Burin likes to cook and is anxious to explain the use of everything in the store. She'll give you informal recipes or let you copy out recipes from Thai cookbooks she has in English. If you ask what to do with, say, a jar of mudfish, she'll tell you how to make a dip for sticky rice using the fish and chili paste, fish sauce, lime juice, and red peppers.

The sisters have an enormous selection of packaged, premixed curry pastes (Southeast Asian shortcuts that give delicious results). Burin knows exactly what each of them is used for: a green curry paste for a mix of green vegetables; another for crispy fish frying; this one to make a dish of pork and bamboo shoots with coconut milk. Some are for boiling; others for stews with meat, vegetables, or fish.

The array of packaged individual spices is intriguing; among them are *kamin,* whole dried turmeric root; *horapa,* whole dried sweet basil leaves; dried *katurai* flowers (reconstitute by soaking in water); chewy *pru* leaves for old people; leafy *bay ya nag*.

The tiny dried and smoked fish are delicious accompaniments to curries and drinks.

But, above all, the Mahanakorn is the place to stock up on marvelous Thai hot sauces: sweet chili sauce (dip fried squid in it); yellow bean sauce (fry chicken in it with fresh garlic, ginger, and onion); tall bottles of bright yellow or orange chili sauces. Then there are little jars of chili pastes with tamarind or shrimp or fish, meant to be used in fried dishes. Drier canned chili pastes are a stimulating topping for bread, while other pastes are mixed with a little fish sauce to make dipping sauces.

As a cool contrast to all this culinary heat, get some of the packaged Thai tea or coffee. Serve these fragrant spiced drinks over ice, and, if you like, swirled with cream.

The refrigerator holds bags of fresh red bird's-eye chili, or *lombok;* small round green eggplants, limes, pumpkins, and onions; bundles of fresh lemon grass; and plenty of beer.

And for an elegant Thai picnic, the sisters have brought back ornate silver metal food carriers that stack on top of each other for transporting many dishes at once.

As you leave, try one of the pastel sticky-rice confections. They're very sweet and perfumed with jasmine, but delicious.

# VIETNAMESE MARKETS

Some of the stores listed in the General Oriental section also carry Vietnamese foods.

## Contra Costa
### BINH DUONG THUC PAM VIETNAM

*11265B San Pablo Avenue, El Cerrito 94530. Telephone (415) 233-0649. Hours: 10–6 daily.*

This is a small family-run Vietnamese grocery just around the corner from the larger Vina Market. The young couple who run the store are ready to help you with your questions. Ask. They have Vietnamese condiments, rice papers, noodles, and frozen mudfish and catfish from Thailand, as well as homemade Vietnamese sausage. Specialized produce includes fresh tamarind, fresh turmeric root, okra, and sweet finger bananas.

The store is big on sweets: Chinese moon cakes; another pastry of sweet rice with a yellow bean filling; ginger and melon candies; and, at new year's, a special homemade new year candy. The *banh tranc* are discs of dough embedded with coconut and sesame. Fry and eat like potato chips. Saturdays and Sundays they have lots of homemade Vietnamese-style baked goods.

## San Francisco
### MAY WAH TRADING COMPANY

*1265 Stockton Street, San Francisco 94133. Telephone (415) 397-1527. Hours: 7–6 daily.*

This tiny corner store with Vietnamese signs in the window is very different from the usually cluttered Chinese stores. Outside, the neat rows of produce crates hold Chinese herbs for soup, baby Japanese eggplants, delicate hearts of both *bok choy* and Chinese broccoli, Chinese long beans for stir-fry dishes, and a pile of fresh coconuts.

Just inside the door, you'll find bundles of fresh herbs and soup greens. Inside, everything is absolutely neat and very clean. Vietnamese and Thai ingredients are clearly labeled: small cellophane packages of orange peel and ginger root; fish, anchovy, and shrimp sauces; sweet chili sauces; chili pastes; imported rice papers; wet tamarind from Thailand.

The refrigerator case holds fat fresh red chilies; tiny pointed chilies red and green; fresh tamarind and lemon grass; the round lime-green eggplant with its twig still attached; two kinds of Vietnamese sausages, square or oblong and wrapped in foil; and packages of handmade *lumpia* skins.

floor bagging long, red, and very pointed chili peppers from a basketry tray.

Though the store is small, you can find here about just every ingredient—excluding meat, fish, poultry, and some vegetables—for preparing savory Vietnamese dishes, and there's even an English-Vietnamese dictionary to translate your recipes.

Start with the basics: Vietnamese soy sauce and the notorious *nuoc mam*, Vietnam's strong, fermented fish sauce used to salt almost every dish (the Filipino *patis* sauce is similar). The Vietnamese mix it with chili, vinegar, sugar, garlic, and lime juice to make *nuoc cham*, a fiery dipping sauce. Shrimp sauce and anchovy cream are also used to season some dishes. Then choose some tiny green eggplants no bigger than limes; salted radish slices; fresh tamarind; dried *galingale* and lemon grass; fresh ginger, limes, and garlic. The Thai rice paper is used to wrap *cha gio*, little rolls of rice paper fried with a stuffing of pork, crab, and vegetables.

Near the door fresh lemon grass and big bundles of Vietnamese herbs and greens sit next to a bag of long French baguettes.

## San Jose Area
## MEKONG MARKET

*52 South Fourth, San Jose 95112. Telephone (408) 293-0846. Hours: 10–6 daily.*

Vietnamese sausage and produce; Thai foodstuffs.

## East Bay
## SAIGON MARKET

*441 Ninth Street, Oakland 94607. Telephone (415) 465-2223. Hours: 9–6:30 daily.*

Saigon Market is scrunched in a tiny storefront on Ninth Street in Oakland's Chinatown. With goods and produce attractively arranged in baskets and in various containers on the floor, it seems very much like a stall in a Southeast Asian street market.

An older Vietnamese woman, perhaps the mother of the two beautiful women in their twenties, may be seated on the

## Peninsula
## VIETNAM THUC PHAM

*1010 Doyle, Menlo Park 94025. Telephone (415) 326-2501. Hours: M–T, TH–SUN 10–9.*

Vietnamese and Thai foodstuffs.

**Contra Costa**
## VINA MARKET

*Del Norte Plaza, 11299C San Pablo Ave-*
*nue, El Cerrito 94530. Telephone (415)*
*232-0480. Hours: 9–7 daily.*

Vina Market is situated in the middle
of a small all-American shopping center
in El Cerrito. Since the Vietnamese
proprietors themselves import many
of the things they carry, the prices are
very reasonable. Along with strictly
Vietnamese products, you'll find many
Chinese and Indonesian items.

The vast array of imported bottles,
cans, and jars includes Thai and Vietnamese fish sauces; shrimp and crab
pastes; *tuong cu-da,* or Vietnamese soy
sauce; and Indonesian *sambals,* or chili
pastes.

The vermicelli section is a celebration
of noodles of every shape and texture.
The Thai rice flakes are irregular
triangles of transparent rice dough
used in soup. *Thinh,* golden nests of
fried bean thread, obviously homemade,
are used as a garnish. Another shelf
holds the tiniest of tapioca pearls from
Thailand; tapioca flour; tapioca starch;

several kinds of rice flours; and *bot cu
nang,* water chestnut powder. They
also sell sweet black rice for making an
Indonesian fermented rice dish said to
strengthen your blood. The extensive
inventory of rice and beans comes in
sacks as large as fifty and one hundred
pounds.

The freezer holds jellyfish, shrimp,
fish, and egg roll wrappers, while the
refrigerator has fat rolls of foil-wrapped
Vietnamese sausage.

On Fridays, they have fresh Southeast
Asian vegetables: lemon grass, mint,
lily flowers, Chinese spinach, and the
small round eggplants grown by Vietnamese people in Stockton.

And, a familiar sight in Vietnamese
food stores, there's a sack of French
baguettes by the door.

**San Francisco**
## WEE WAH TRADING COMPANY

*1248 Stockton Street, San Francisco*
*94133. Telephone (415) 982-0128. Hours:*
*7:30–6 daily.*

The selection of foodstuffs in the baskets in front of Wee Wah Trading
Company is always changing. One day
you'll see a box of gummy dried baby
oysters (used in soups along with the
packaged dried *bok choy* or cole, they
give a quite different flavor than fresh
oysters). Another time you'll find fresh
lotus root, lengths of fresh sugar cane,
enormous taro roots, or gingko nuts in
the shell. Sometimes they have bundles
of true scallions from a small truck
farmer. They're wonderful looking,
with the tops all curved and green in a
tangle, some of the bulbs double.

Inside, along with bags of salted fish
heads or tiny dried minnows, they
stock small packets of Vietnamese spices;
condiments including *nuoc mam,* the
strong fermented fish sauce; rice papers;
and fiery Thai hot sauces and spice pastes.

# *Index*

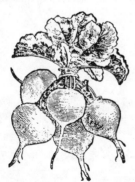

# SHERRY VIRBILA

There's almost nothing to do with food in the Bay Area that Sherry Virbila hasn't done. She has cooked it: while she was still in college she and a group of friends ran the Swallow Café in the University Art Museum; later she went on to become the chef in a number of other restaurants. She has catered it, taught about it, photographed it and written about it in magazines like *New West* (now *California*), *San Francisco*, *California Living*, and *Focus*. But it was while living in Paris, where she was training as a sommelier, that Sherry realized what extraordinarily varied culinary resources the Bay Area possessed, and was inspired to write this book.